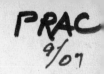

THE SUPERMAN CHRONICLES

VOLUME THREE

SUPERMAN CREATED BY JERRY SIEGEL & JOE SHUSTER

All stories written by Jerry Siegel and illustrated by Joe Shuster and the Superman Studio, unless otherwise noted.

*These stories were originally untitled and are titled here for reader convenience.

Dan DiDio SENIOR VP- EXECUTIVE EDITOR ☆ Bob Joy EDITOR-COLLECTED EDITION
Robbin Brosterman SENIOR ART DIRECTOR ☆ Paul Levitz PRESIDENT & PUBLISHER ☆ Georg Brewer VP-DESIGN & DC DIRECT CREATIVE
Richard Bruning SENIOR VP-CREATIVE DIRECTOR ☆ Patrick Caldon EXECUTIVE VP-FINANCE & OPERATIONS ☆ Chris Caramalis VP-FINANCE
John Cunningham VP-MARKETING ☆ Terri Cunningham VP-MANAGING EDITOR
Alison Gill VP-MANUFACTURING ☆ Hank Kanalz VP-GENERAL MANAGER, WILDSTORM ☆ Jim Lee EDITORIAL DIRECTOR-WILDSTORM
Paula Lowitt SENIOR VP-BUSINESS & LEGAL AFFAIRS ☆ MARYELLEN MCLAUGHLIN VP-ADVERTISING & CUSTOM PUBLISHING
John Nee VP-BUSINESS DEVELOPMENT ☆ Gregory Noveck SENIOR VP-CREATIVE AFFAIRS ☆ Sue Pohja SENIOR VP-BOOK TRADE SALES
Cheryl Rubin SENIOR VP-BRAND MANAGEMENT ☆ Jeff Trojan VP-BUSINESS DEVELOPMENT, DC DIRECT ☆ Bob Wayne VP-SALES

Black and white reconstruction by Rick Keene and Pure Imagination.
Color reconstruction by Bob Le Rose and Daniel Vozzo.

DC Comics, 1700 Broadway, New York, NY 10019
A Warner Bros. Entertainment Company
Printed in Canada. First Printing.
ISBN: 1-4012-1374-X
ISBN 13: 978-1-4012-1374-9
Cover art by Joe Shuster

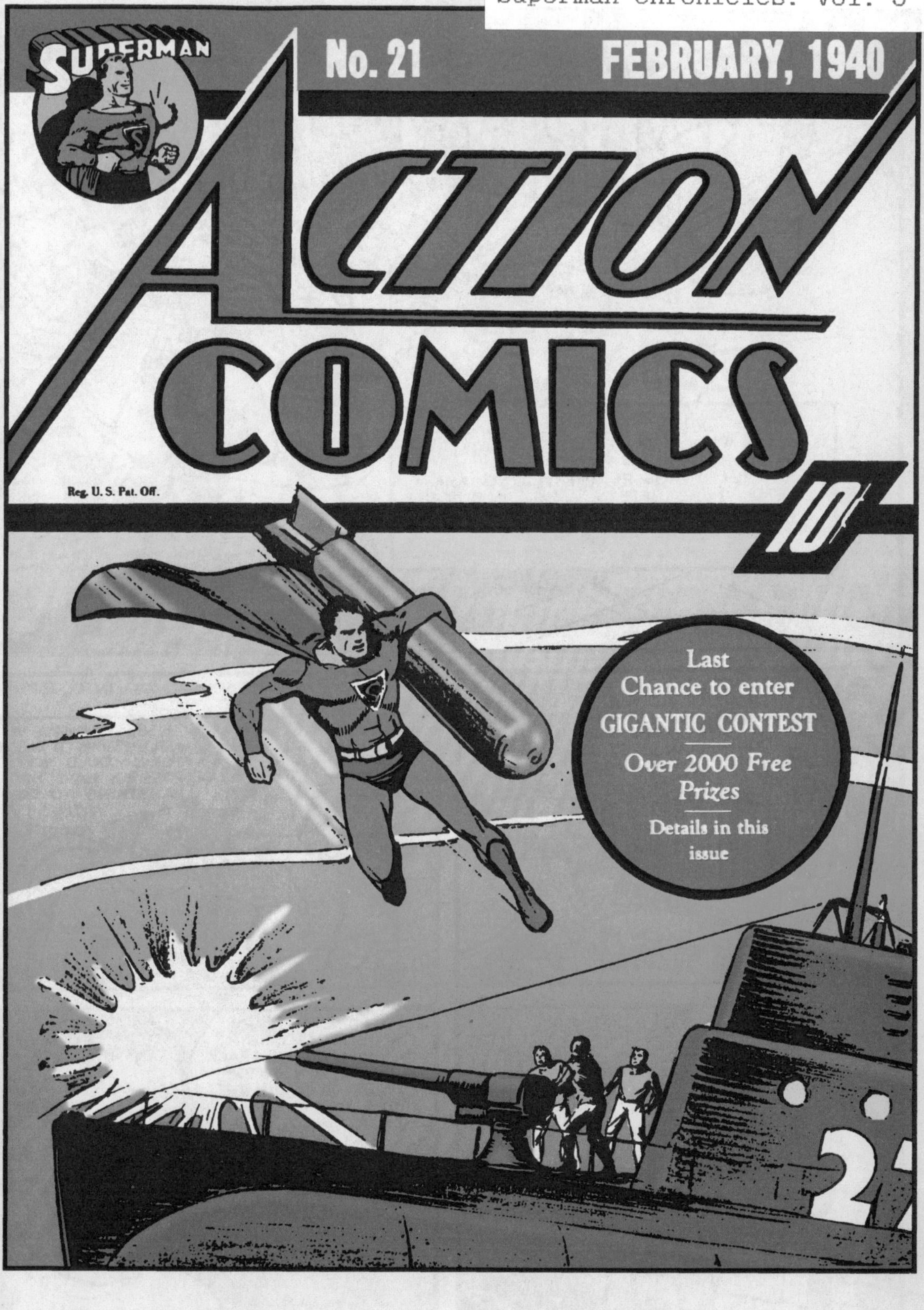
SUPERMAN
No. 21
FEBRUARY, 1940
ACTION COMICS
Reg. U.S. Pat. Off.
10¢
Last Chance to enter GIGANTIC CONTEST
Over 2000 Free Prizes
Details in this issue

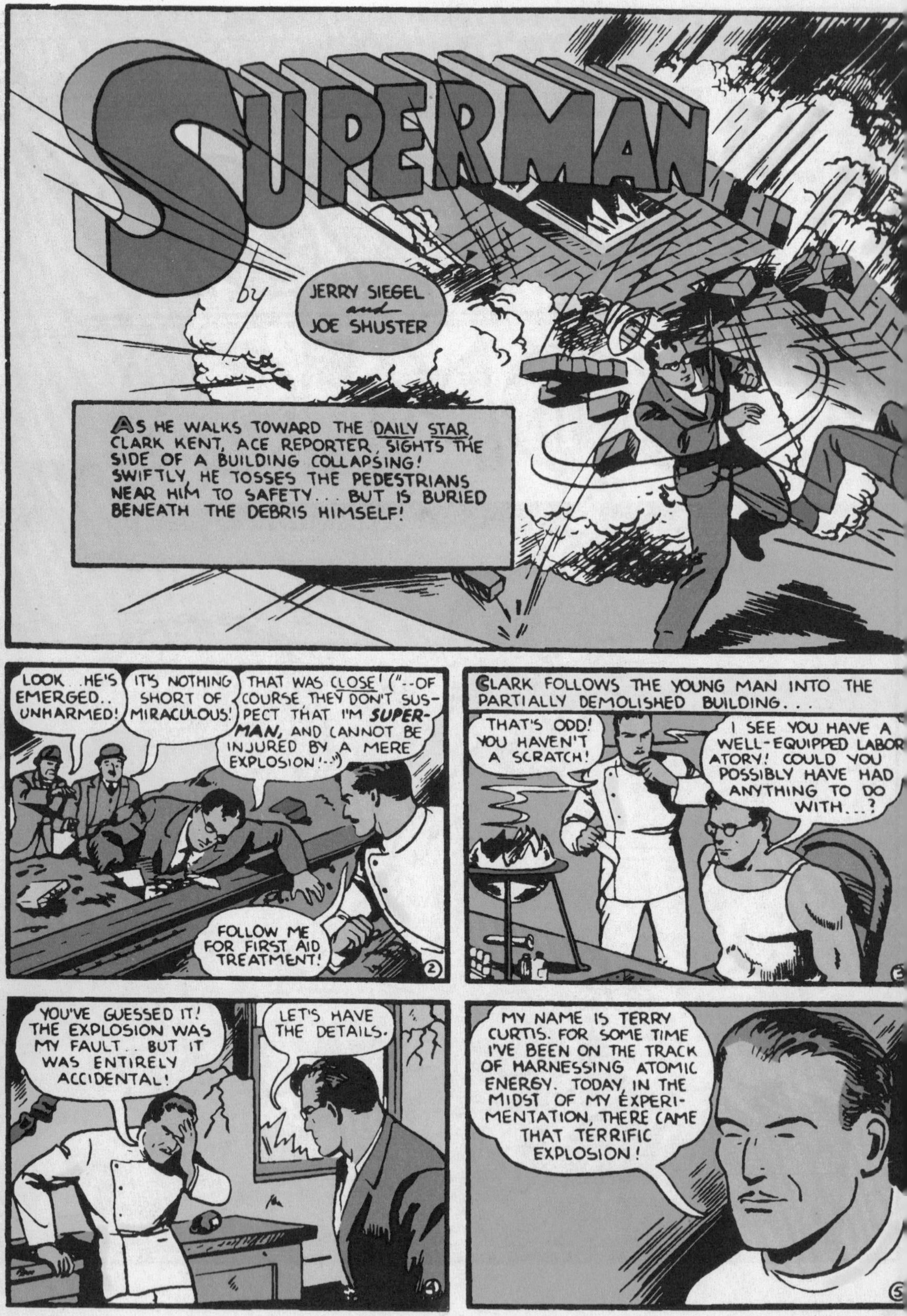
SUPERMAN
by
JERRY SIEGEL and JOE SHUSTER
AS HE WALKS TOWARD THE DAILY STAR, CLARK KENT, ACE REPORTER, SIGHTS THE SIDE OF A BUILDING COLLAPSING! SWIFTLY, HE TOSSES THE PEDESTRIANS NEAR HIM TO SAFETY... BUT IS BURIED BENEATH THE DEBRIS HIMSELF!
LOOK. HE'S EMERGED.. UNHARMED!
IT'S NOTHING SHORT OF MIRACULOUS!
THAT WAS CLOSE! ("--OF COURSE, THEY DON'T SUSPECT THAT I'M SUPERMAN, AND CANNOT BE INJURED BY A MERE EXPLOSION!--")
FOLLOW ME FOR FIRST AID TREATMENT!
2
CLARK FOLLOWS THE YOUNG MAN INTO THE PARTIALLY DEMOLISHED BUILDING...
THAT'S ODD! YOU HAVEN'T A SCRATCH!
I SEE YOU HAVE A WELL-EQUIPPED LABORATORY! COULD YOU POSSIBLY HAVE HAD ANYTHING TO DO WITH...?
3
YOU'VE GUESSED IT! THE EXPLOSION WAS MY FAULT.. BUT IT WAS ENTIRELY ACCIDENTAL!
LET'S HAVE THE DETAILS.
4
MY NAME IS TERRY CURTIS. FOR SOME TIME I'VE BEEN ON THE TRACK OF HARNESSING ATOMIC ENERGY. TODAY, IN THE MIDST OF MY EXPERIMENTATION, THERE CAME THAT TERRIFIC EXPLOSION!
5

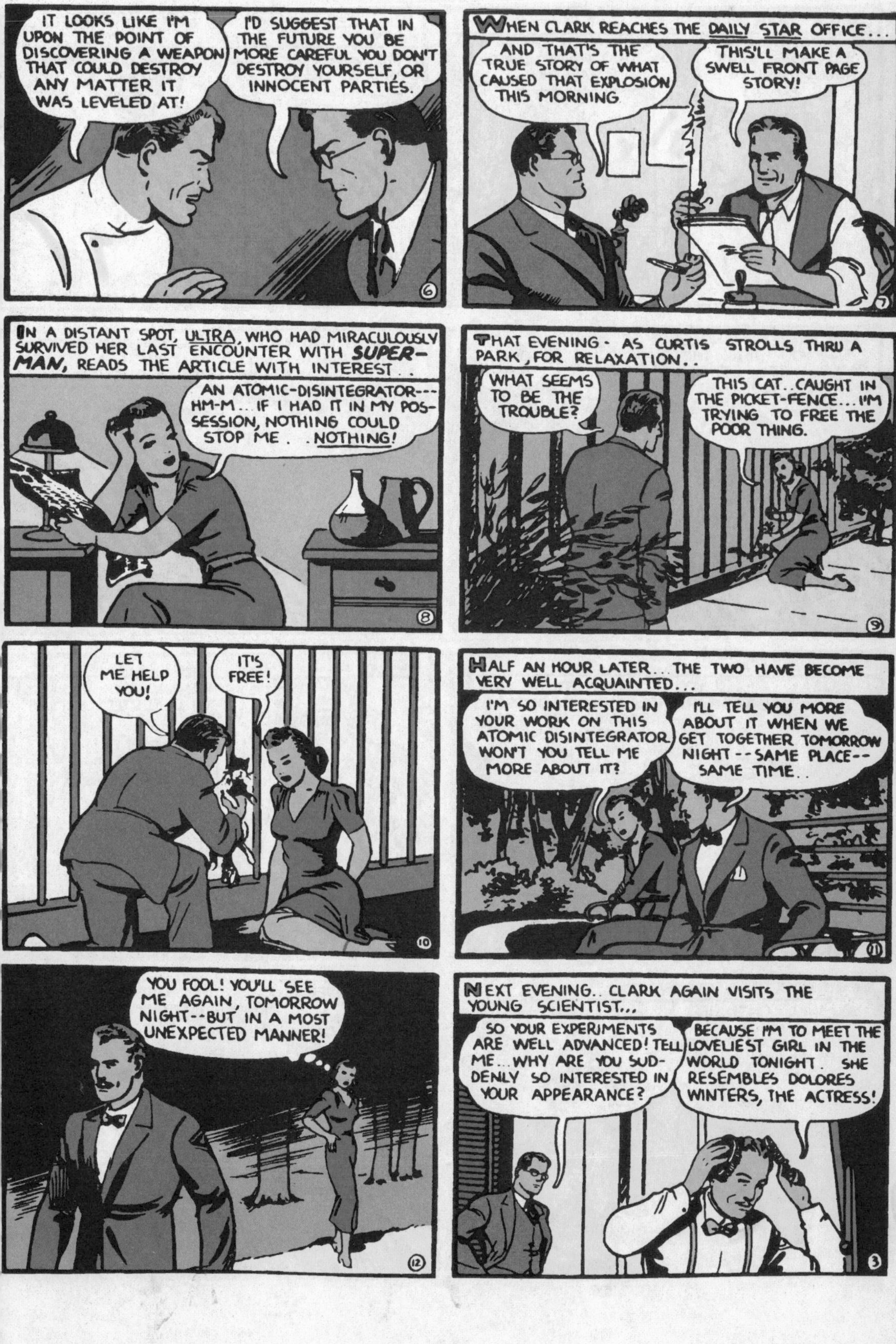
IT LOOKS LIKE I'M UPON THE POINT OF DISCOVERING A WEAPON THAT COULD DESTROY ANY MATTER IT WAS LEVELED AT!
I'D SUGGEST THAT IN THE FUTURE YOU BE MORE CAREFUL YOU DON'T DESTROY YOURSELF, OR INNOCENT PARTIES.
6
WHEN CLARK REACHES THE DAILY STAR OFFICE...
AND THAT'S THE TRUE STORY OF WHAT CAUSED THAT EXPLOSION THIS MORNING
THIS'LL MAKE A SWELL FRONT PAGE STORY!
7
IN A DISTANT SPOT, ULTRA, WHO HAD MIRACULOUSLY SURVIVED HER LAST ENCOUNTER WITH SUPERMAN, READS THE ARTICLE WITH INTEREST..
AN ATOMIC-DISINTEGRATOR--- HM-M... IF I HAD IT IN MY POSSESSION, NOTHING COULD STOP ME . .NOTHING!
8
THAT EVENING - AS CURTIS STROLLS THRU A PARK, FOR RELAXATION..
WHAT SEEMS TO BE THE TROUBLE?
THIS CAT..CAUGHT IN THE PICKET-FENCE... I'M TRYING TO FREE THE POOR THING.
9
LET ME HELP YOU!
IT'S FREE!
10
HALF AN HOUR LATER...THE TWO HAVE BECOME VERY WELL ACQUAINTED...
I'M SO INTERESTED IN YOUR WORK ON THIS ATOMIC DISINTEGRATOR. WON'T YOU TELL ME MORE ABOUT IT?
I'LL TELL YOU MORE ABOUT IT WHEN WE GET TOGETHER TOMORROW NIGHT--SAME PLACE--SAME TIME..
11
YOU FOOL! YOU'LL SEE ME AGAIN, TOMORROW NIGHT--BUT IN A MOST UNEXPECTED MANNER!
12
NEXT EVENING.. CLARK AGAIN VISITS THE YOUNG SCIENTIST...
SO YOUR EXPERIMENTS ARE WELL ADVANCED! TELL ME...WHY ARE YOU SUDDENLY SO INTERESTED IN YOUR APPEARANCE?
BECAUSE I'M TO MEET THE LOVELIEST GIRL IN THE WORLD TONIGHT. SHE RESEMBLES DOLORES WINTERS, THE ACTRESS!
13

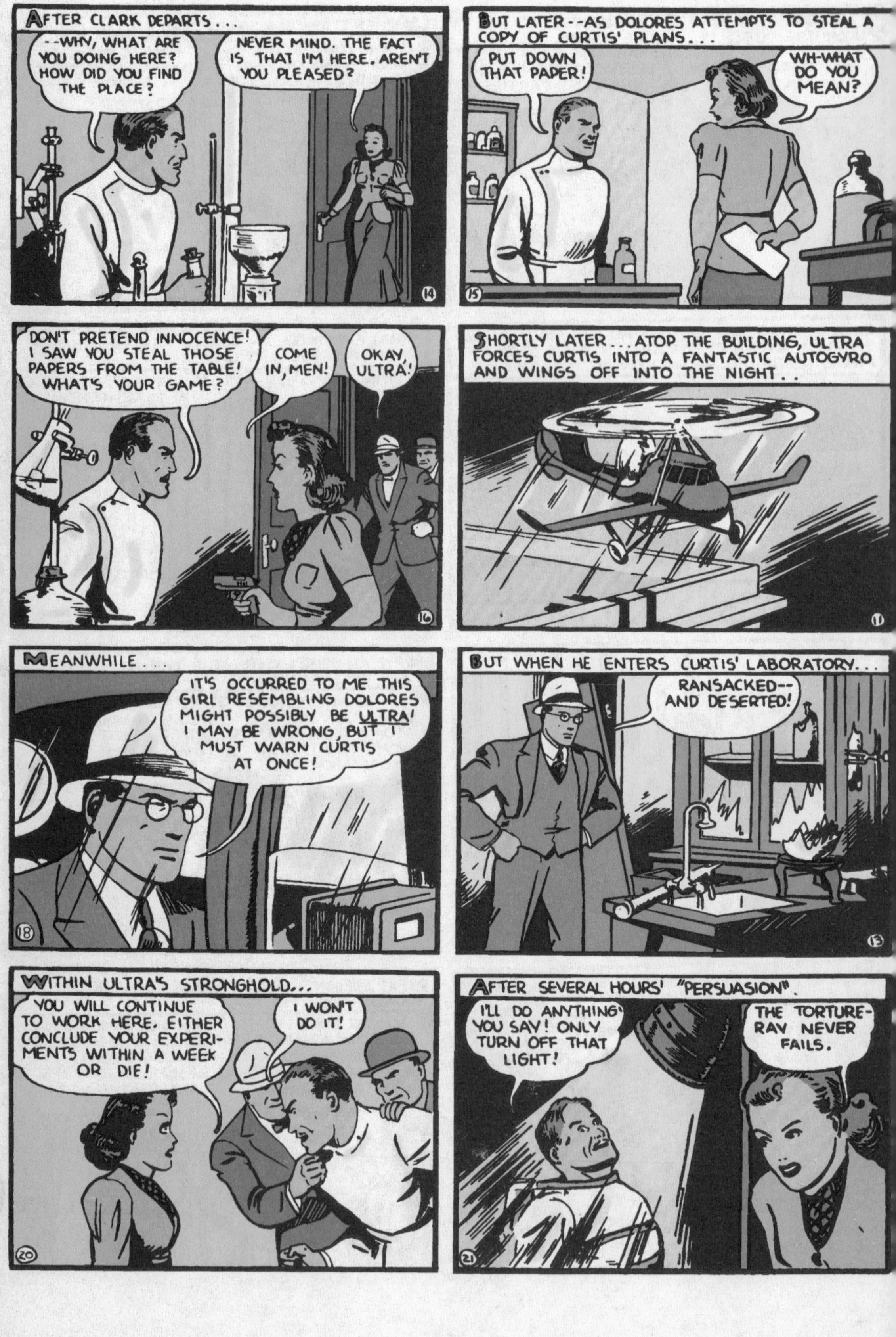
AFTER CLARK DEPARTS...
--WHY, WHAT ARE YOU DOING HERE? HOW DID YOU FIND THE PLACE?
NEVER MIND. THE FACT IS THAT I'M HERE. AREN'T YOU PLEASED?
BUT LATER--AS DOLORES ATTEMPTS TO STEAL A COPY OF CURTIS' PLANS...
PUT DOWN THAT PAPER!
WH-WHAT DO YOU MEAN?
DON'T PRETEND INNOCENCE! I SAW YOU STEAL THOSE PAPERS FROM THE TABLE! WHAT'S YOUR GAME?
COME IN, MEN!
OKAY, ULTRA!
SHORTLY LATER... ATOP THE BUILDING, ULTRA FORCES CURTIS INTO A FANTASTIC AUTOGYRO AND WINGS OFF INTO THE NIGHT..
MEANWHILE...
IT'S OCCURRED TO ME THIS GIRL RESEMBLING DOLORES MIGHT POSSIBLY BE ULTRA! I MAY BE WRONG, BUT I MUST WARN CURTIS AT ONCE!
BUT WHEN HE ENTERS CURTIS' LABORATORY...
RANSACKED--AND DESERTED!
WITHIN ULTRA'S STRONGHOLD...
YOU WILL CONTINUE TO WORK HERE. EITHER CONCLUDE YOUR EXPERIMENTS WITHIN A WEEK OR DIE!
I WON'T DO IT!
AFTER SEVERAL HOURS' "PERSUASION".
I'LL DO ANYTHING YOU SAY! ONLY TURN OFF THAT LIGHT!
THE TORTURE-RAY NEVER FAILS.

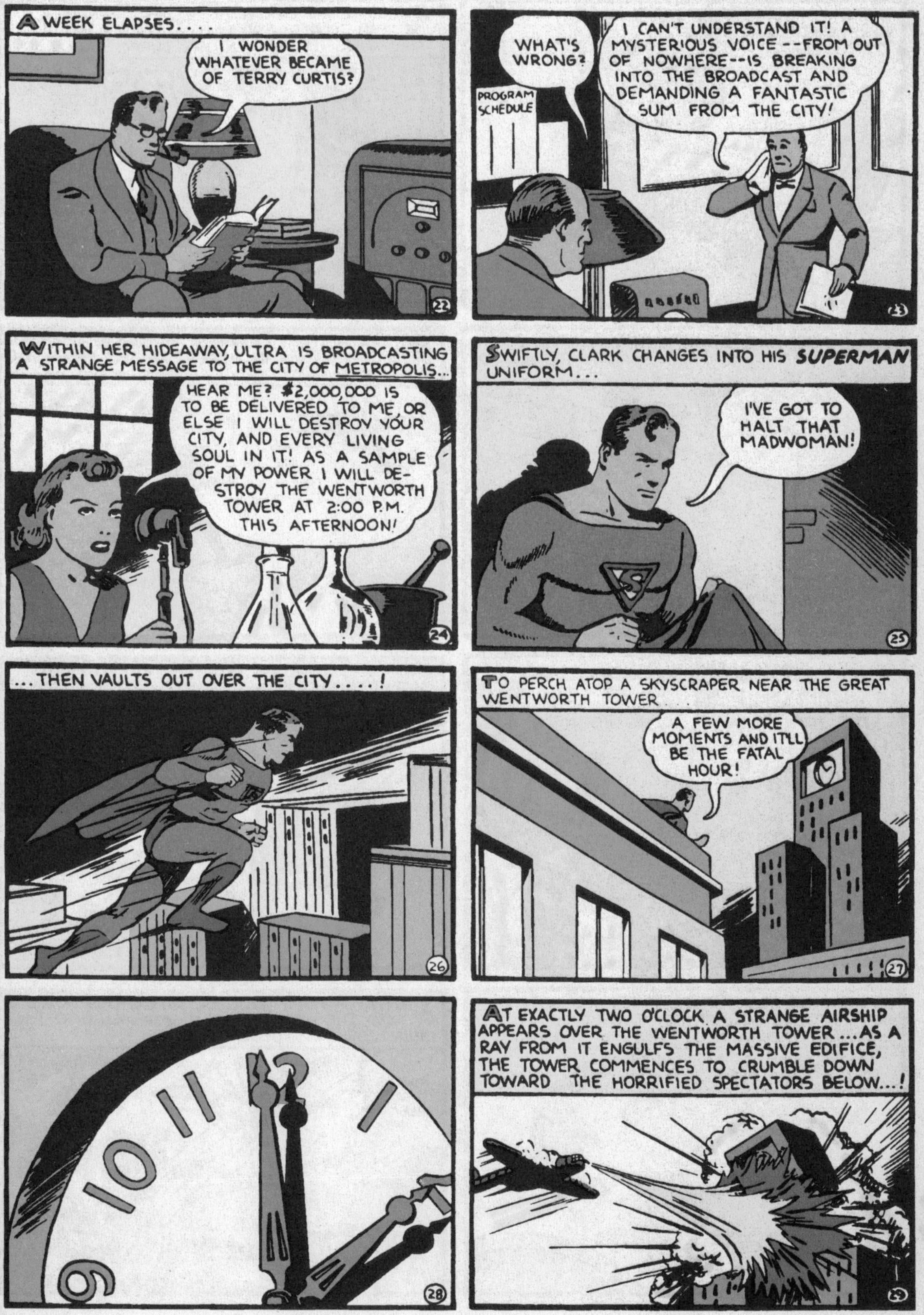
A WEEK ELAPSES....
I WONDER WHATEVER BECAME OF TERRY CURTIS?
PROGRAM SCHEDULE
WHAT'S WRONG?
I CAN'T UNDERSTAND IT! A MYSTERIOUS VOICE--FROM OUT OF NOWHERE--IS BREAKING INTO THE BROADCAST AND DEMANDING A FANTASTIC SUM FROM THE CITY!
WITHIN HER HIDEAWAY, ULTRA IS BROADCASTING A STRANGE MESSAGE TO THE CITY OF METROPOLIS...
HEAR ME? $2,000,000 IS TO BE DELIVERED TO ME, OR ELSE I WILL DESTROY YOUR CITY, AND EVERY LIVING SOUL IN IT! AS A SAMPLE OF MY POWER I WILL DESTROY THE WENTWORTH TOWER AT 2:00 P.M. THIS AFTERNOON!
SWIFTLY, CLARK CHANGES INTO HIS SUPERMAN UNIFORM...
I'VE GOT TO HALT THAT MADWOMAN!
...THEN VAULTS OUT OVER THE CITY....!
TO PERCH ATOP A SKYSCRAPER NEAR THE GREAT WENTWORTH TOWER...
A FEW MORE MOMENTS AND IT'LL BE THE FATAL HOUR!
AT EXACTLY TWO O'CLOCK A STRANGE AIRSHIP APPEARS OVER THE WENTWORTH TOWER...AS A RAY FROM IT ENGULFS THE MASSIVE EDIFICE, THE TOWER COMMENCES TO CRUMBLE DOWN TOWARD THE HORRIFIED SPECTATORS BELOW...!

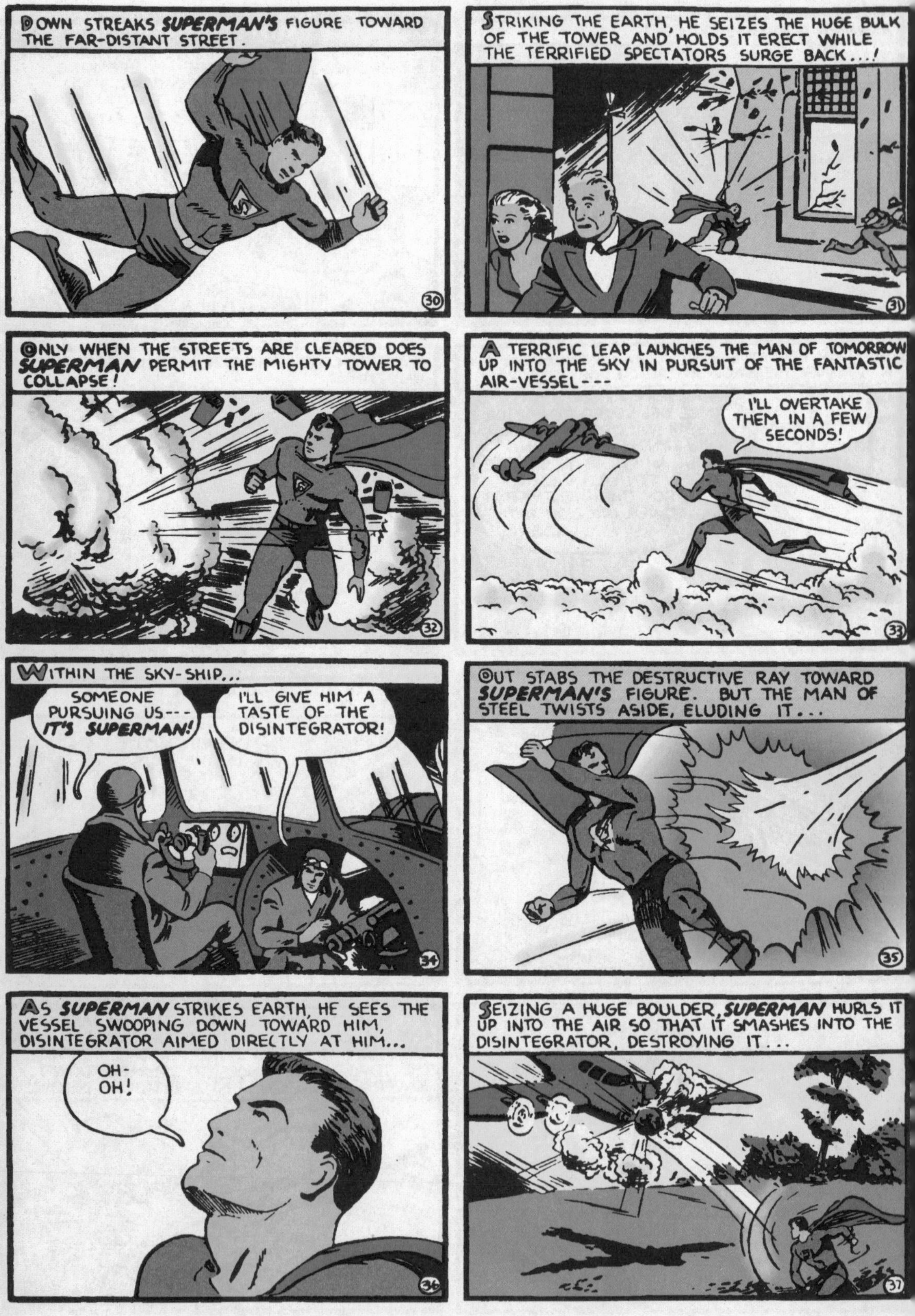
DOWN STREAKS SUPERMAN'S FIGURE TOWARD THE FAR-DISTANT STREET.
30
STRIKING THE EARTH, HE SEIZES THE HUGE BULK OF THE TOWER AND HOLDS IT ERECT WHILE THE TERRIFIED SPECTATORS SURGE BACK...!
31
ONLY WHEN THE STREETS ARE CLEARED DOES SUPERMAN PERMIT THE MIGHTY TOWER TO COLLAPSE!
32
A TERRIFIC LEAP LAUNCHES THE MAN OF TOMORROW UP INTO THE SKY IN PURSUIT OF THE FANTASTIC AIR-VESSEL---
I'LL OVERTAKE THEM IN A FEW SECONDS!
33
WITHIN THE SKY-SHIP...
SOMEONE PURSUING US--- IT'S SUPERMAN!
I'LL GIVE HIM A TASTE OF THE DISINTEGRATOR!
34
OUT STABS THE DESTRUCTIVE RAY TOWARD SUPERMAN'S FIGURE. BUT THE MAN OF STEEL TWISTS ASIDE, ELUDING IT...
35
AS SUPERMAN STRIKES EARTH, HE SEES THE VESSEL SWOOPING DOWN TOWARD HIM, DISINTEGRATOR AIMED DIRECTLY AT HIM...
OH-OH!
36
SEIZING A HUGE BOULDER, SUPERMAN HURLS IT UP INTO THE AIR SO THAT IT SMASHES INTO THE DISINTEGRATOR, DESTROYING IT...
37

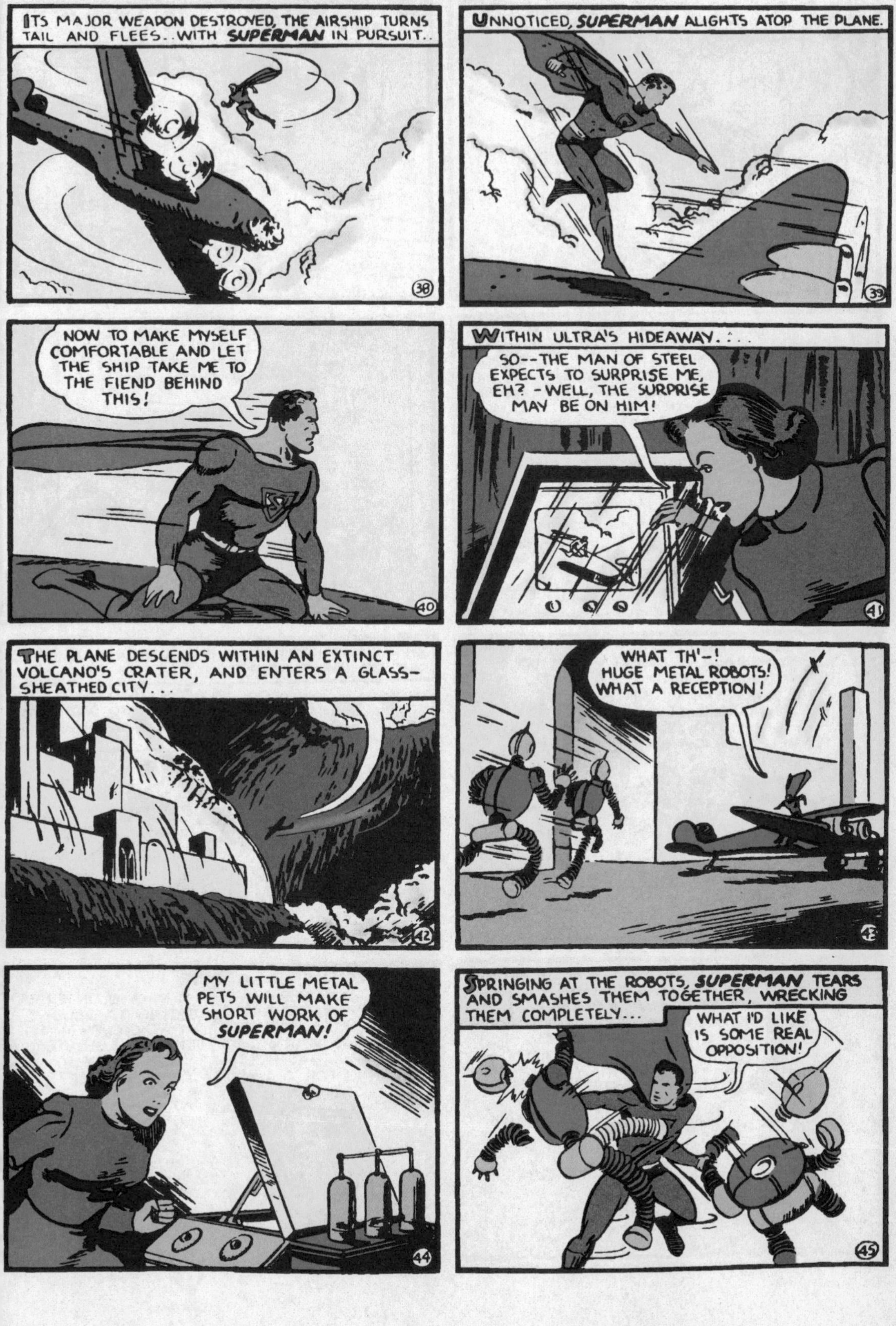

ITS MAJOR WEAPON DESTROYED, THE AIRSHIP TURNS TAIL AND FLEES.. WITH SUPERMAN IN PURSUIT..
38
UNNOTICED, SUPERMAN ALIGHTS ATOP THE PLANE.
39
NOW TO MAKE MYSELF COMFORTABLE AND LET THE SHIP TAKE ME TO THE FIEND BEHIND THIS!
40
WITHIN ULTRA'S HIDEAWAY...
SO--THE MAN OF STEEL EXPECTS TO SURPRISE ME, EH? -WELL, THE SURPRISE MAY BE ON HIM!
41
THE PLANE DESCENDS WITHIN AN EXTINCT VOLCANO'S CRATER, AND ENTERS A GLASS-SHEATHED CITY...
42
WHAT TH'-! HUGE METAL ROBOTS! WHAT A RECEPTION!
43
MY LITTLE METAL PETS WILL MAKE SHORT WORK OF SUPERMAN!
44
SPRINGING AT THE ROBOTS, SUPERMAN TEARS AND SMASHES THEM TOGETHER, WRECKING THEM COMPLETELY...
WHAT I'D LIKE IS SOME REAL OPPOSITION!
45

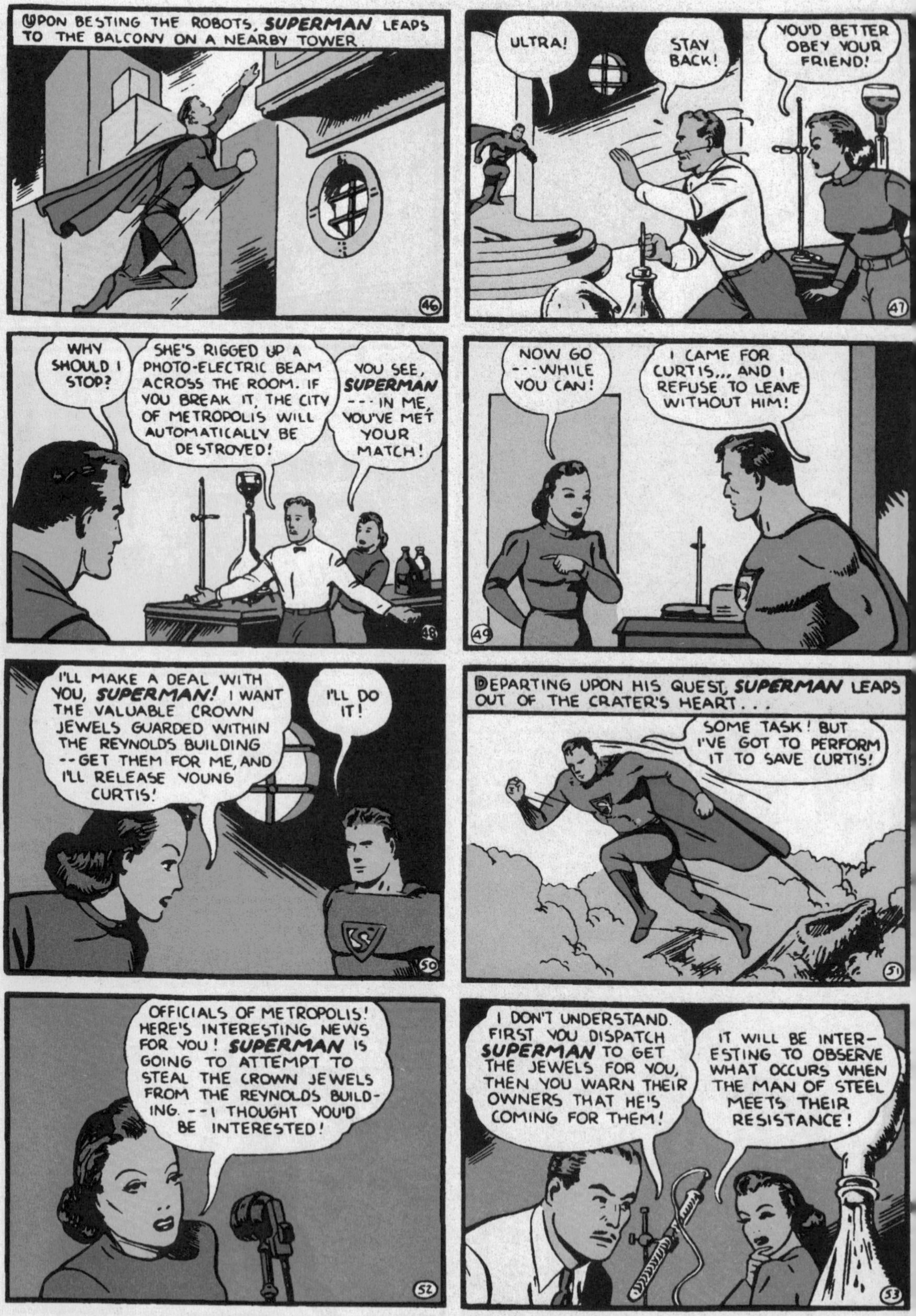
UPON BESTING THE ROBOTS, SUPERMAN LEAPS TO THE BALCONY ON A NEARBY TOWER.
46
ULTRA!
STAY BACK!
YOU'D BETTER OBEY YOUR FRIEND!
47
WHY SHOULD I STOP?
SHE'S RIGGED UP A PHOTO-ELECTRIC BEAM ACROSS THE ROOM. IF YOU BREAK IT, THE CITY OF METROPOLIS WILL AUTOMATICALLY BE DESTROYED!
YOU SEE, SUPERMAN --- IN ME, YOU'VE MET YOUR MATCH!
48
NOW GO --- WHILE YOU CAN!
I CAME FOR CURTIS,,, AND I REFUSE TO LEAVE WITHOUT HIM!
49
I'LL MAKE A DEAL WITH YOU, SUPERMAN! I WANT THE VALUABLE CROWN JEWELS GUARDED WITHIN THE REYNOLDS BUILDING --GET THEM FOR ME, AND I'LL RELEASE YOUNG CURTIS!
I'LL DO IT!
50
DEPARTING UPON HIS QUEST, SUPERMAN LEAPS OUT OF THE CRATER'S HEART...
SOME TASK! BUT I'VE GOT TO PERFORM IT TO SAVE CURTIS!
51
OFFICIALS OF METROPOLIS! HERE'S INTERESTING NEWS FOR YOU! SUPERMAN IS GOING TO ATTEMPT TO STEAL THE CROWN JEWELS FROM THE REYNOLDS BUILDING. --I THOUGHT YOU'D BE INTERESTED!
52
I DON'T UNDERSTAND. FIRST YOU DISPATCH SUPERMAN TO GET THE JEWELS FOR YOU, THEN YOU WARN THEIR OWNERS THAT HE'S COMING FOR THEM!
IT WILL BE INTERESTING TO OBSERVE WHAT OCCURS WHEN THE MAN OF STEEL MEETS THEIR RESISTANCE!
53

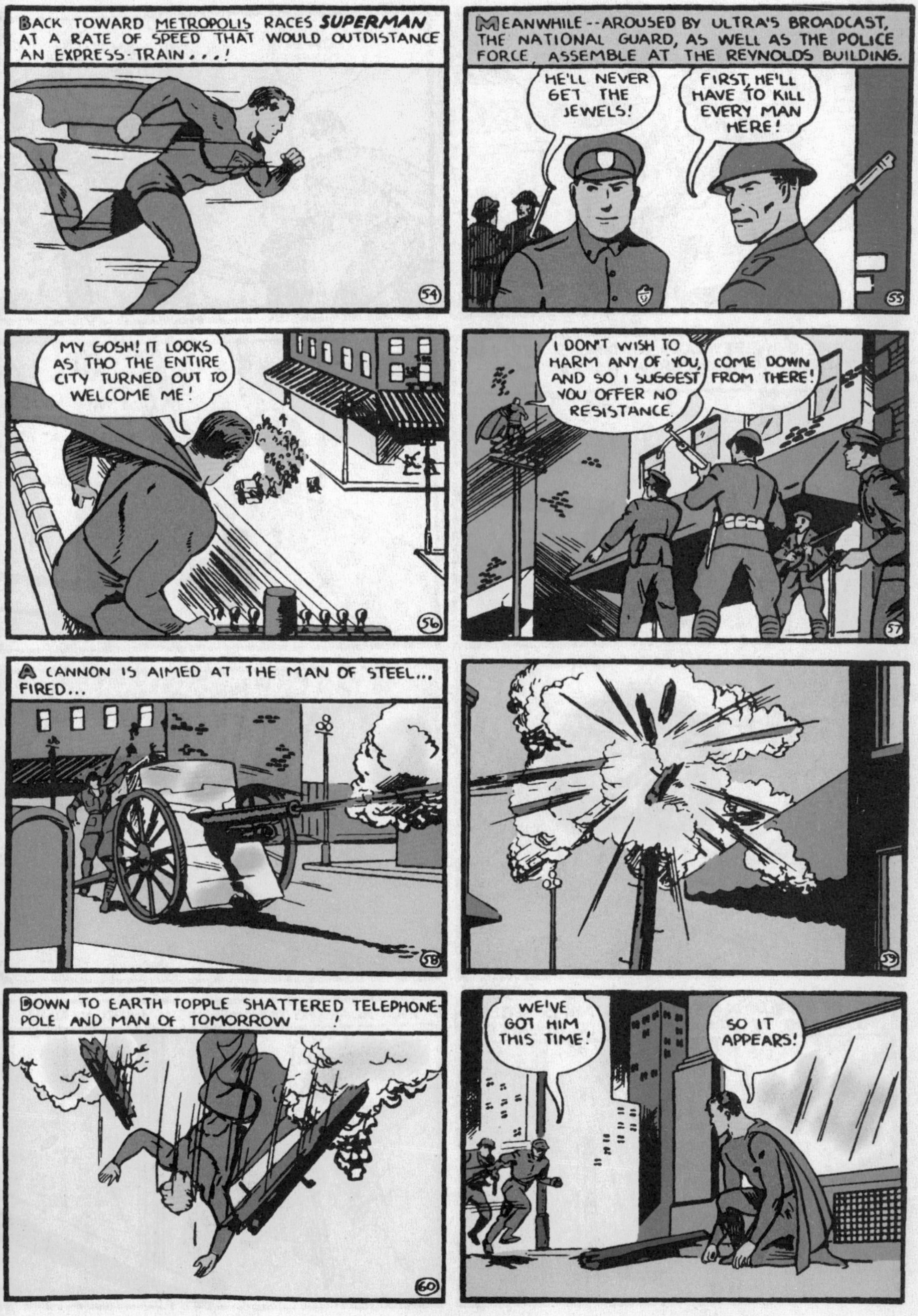
BACK TOWARD METROPOLIS RACES SUPERMAN AT A RATE OF SPEED THAT WOULD OUTDISTANCE AN EXPRESS-TRAIN...!
54
MEANWHILE--AROUSED BY ULTRA'S BROADCAST, THE NATIONAL GUARD, AS WELL AS THE POLICE FORCE, ASSEMBLE AT THE REYNOLDS BUILDING.
HE'LL NEVER GET THE JEWELS!
FIRST, HE'LL HAVE TO KILL EVERY MAN HERE!
55
MY GOSH! IT LOOKS AS THO THE ENTIRE CITY TURNED OUT TO WELCOME ME!
56
I DON'T WISH TO HARM ANY OF YOU, AND SO I SUGGEST YOU OFFER NO RESISTANCE.
COME DOWN FROM THERE!
57
A CANNON IS AIMED AT THE MAN OF STEEL... FIRED...
58
59
DOWN TO EARTH TOPPLE SHATTERED TELEPHONE-POLE AND MAN OF TOMORROW!
60
WE'VE GOT HIM THIS TIME!
SO IT APPEARS!

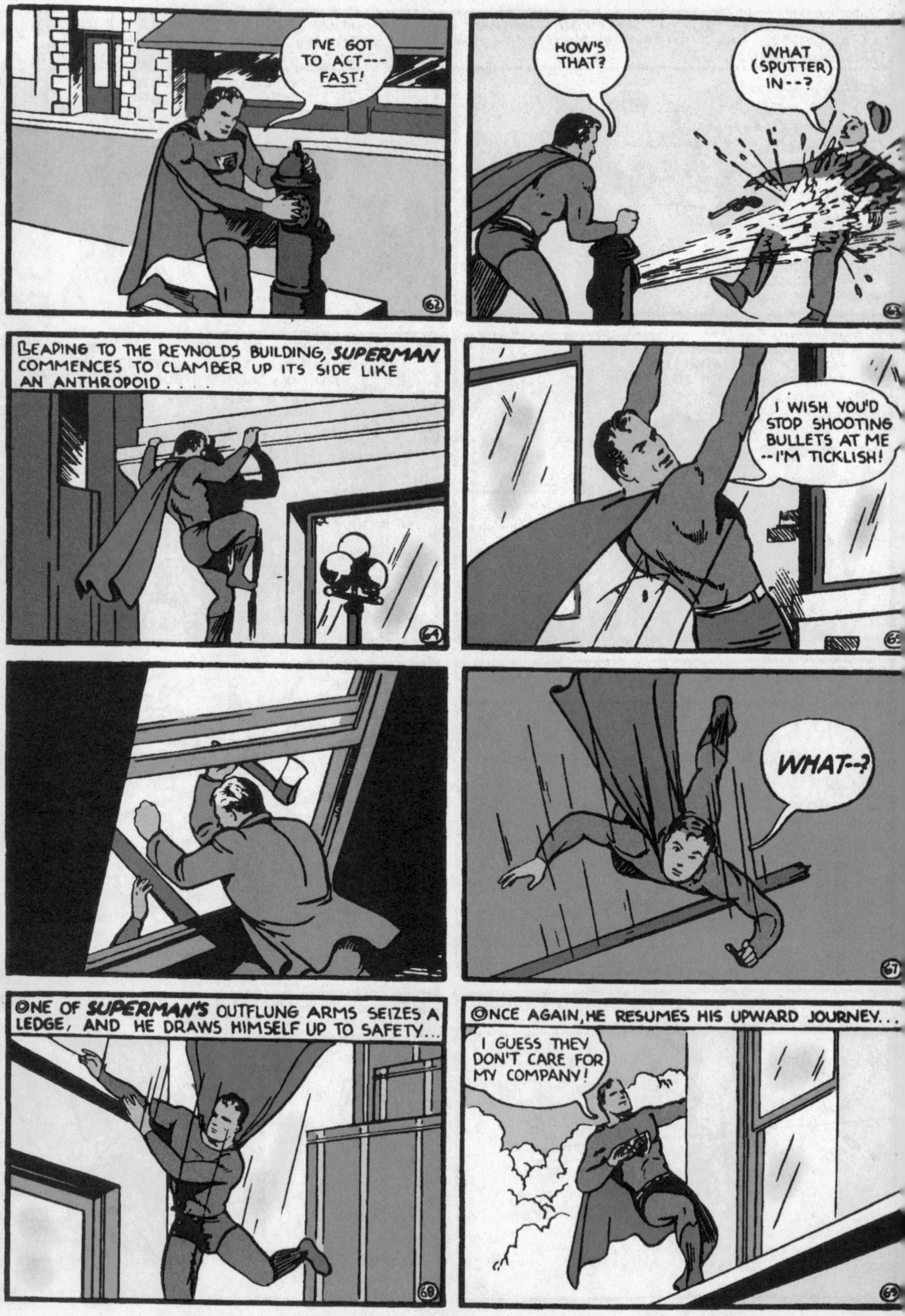
I'VE GOT TO ACT--- FAST!
HOW'S THAT?
WHAT (SPUTTER) IN--?
LEAPING TO THE REYNOLDS BUILDING, SUPERMAN COMMENCES TO CLAMBER UP ITS SIDE LIKE AN ANTHROPOID....
I WISH YOU'D STOP SHOOTING BULLETS AT ME --I'M TICKLISH!
WHAT--?
ONE OF SUPERMAN'S OUTFLUNG ARMS SEIZES A LEDGE, AND HE DRAWS HIMSELF UP TO SAFETY...
ONCE AGAIN, HE RESUMES HIS UPWARD JOURNEY...
I GUESS THEY DON'T CARE FOR MY COMPANY!

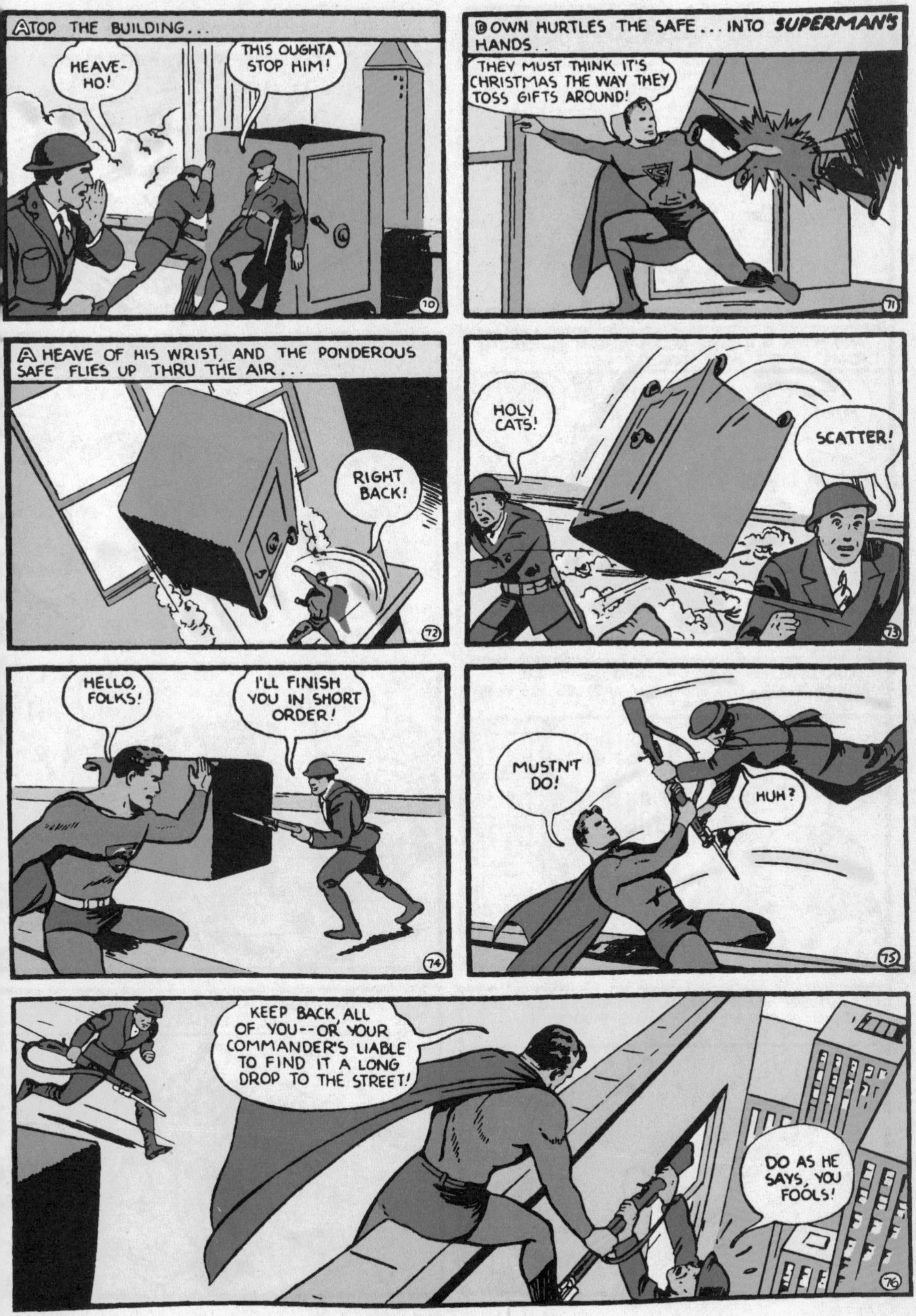
ATOP THE BUILDING...
HEAVE-HO!
THIS OUGHTA STOP HIM!
DOWN HURTLES THE SAFE... INTO SUPERMAN'S HANDS..
THEY MUST THINK IT'S CHRISTMAS THE WAY THEY TOSS GIFTS AROUND!
A HEAVE OF HIS WRIST, AND THE PONDEROUS SAFE FLIES UP THRU THE AIR...
RIGHT BACK!
HOLY CATS!
SCATTER!
HELLO, FOLKS!
I'LL FINISH YOU IN SHORT ORDER!
MUSTN'T DO!
HUH?
KEEP BACK ALL OF YOU--OR YOUR COMMANDER'S LIABLE TO FIND IT A LONG DROP TO THE STREET!
DO AS HE SAYS, YOU FOOLS!

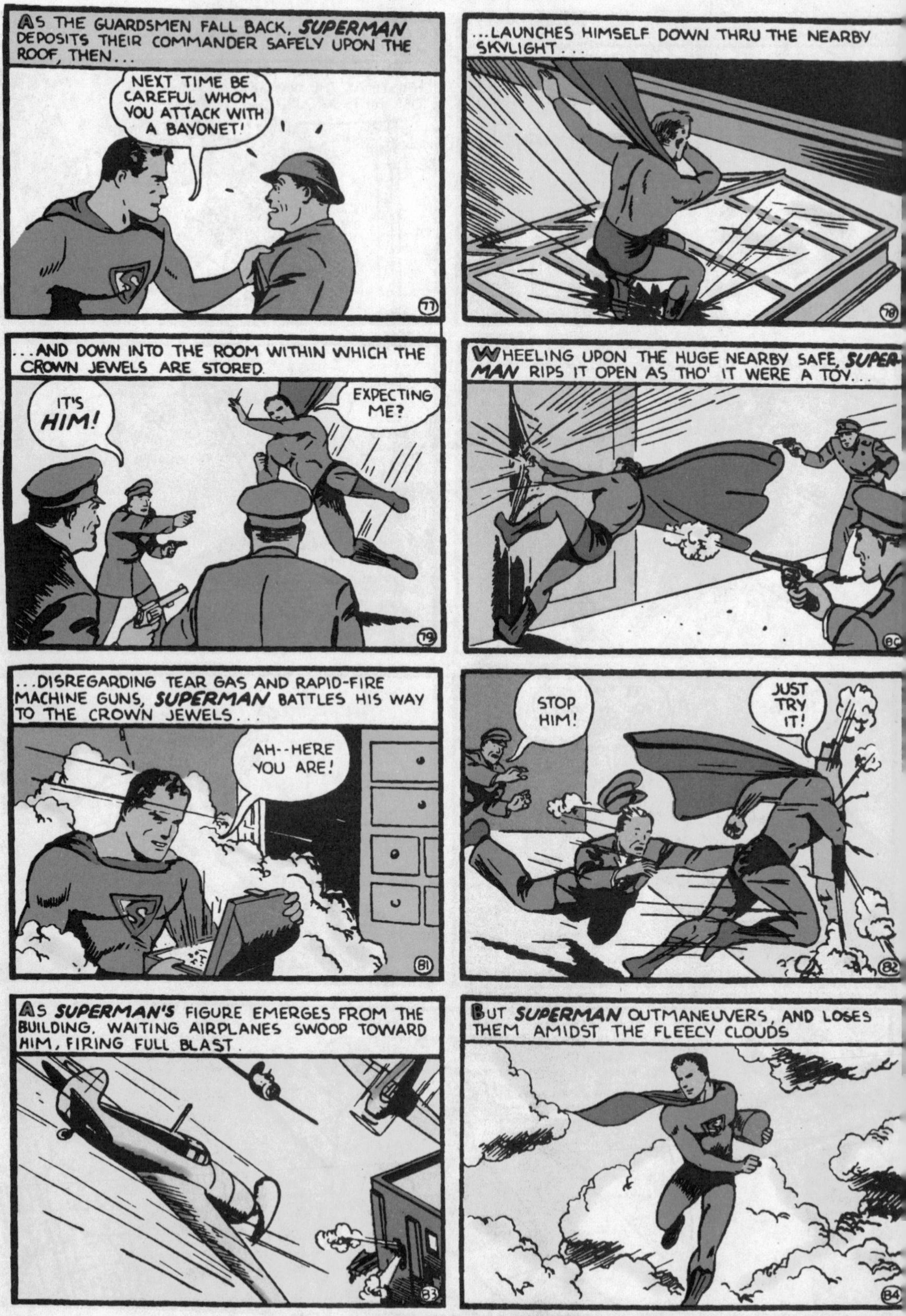
AS THE GUARDSMEN FALL BACK, SUPERMAN DEPOSITS THEIR COMMANDER SAFELY UPON THE ROOF, THEN...
NEXT TIME BE CAREFUL WHOM YOU ATTACK WITH A BAYONET!
77
...LAUNCHES HIMSELF DOWN THRU THE NEARBY SKYLIGHT...
78
...AND DOWN INTO THE ROOM WITHIN WHICH THE CROWN JEWELS ARE STORED.
IT'S HIM!
EXPECTING ME?
79
WHEELING UPON THE HUGE NEARBY SAFE, SUPERMAN RIPS IT OPEN AS THO' IT WERE A TOY...
80
...DISREGARDING TEAR GAS AND RAPID-FIRE MACHINE GUNS, SUPERMAN BATTLES HIS WAY TO THE CROWN JEWELS...
AH--HERE YOU ARE!
81
STOP HIM!
JUST TRY IT!
82
AS SUPERMAN'S FIGURE EMERGES FROM THE BUILDING, WAITING AIRPLANES SWOOP TOWARD HIM, FIRING FULL BLAST.
83
BUT SUPERMAN OUTMANEUVERS, AND LOSES THEM AMIDST THE FLEECY CLOUDS
84

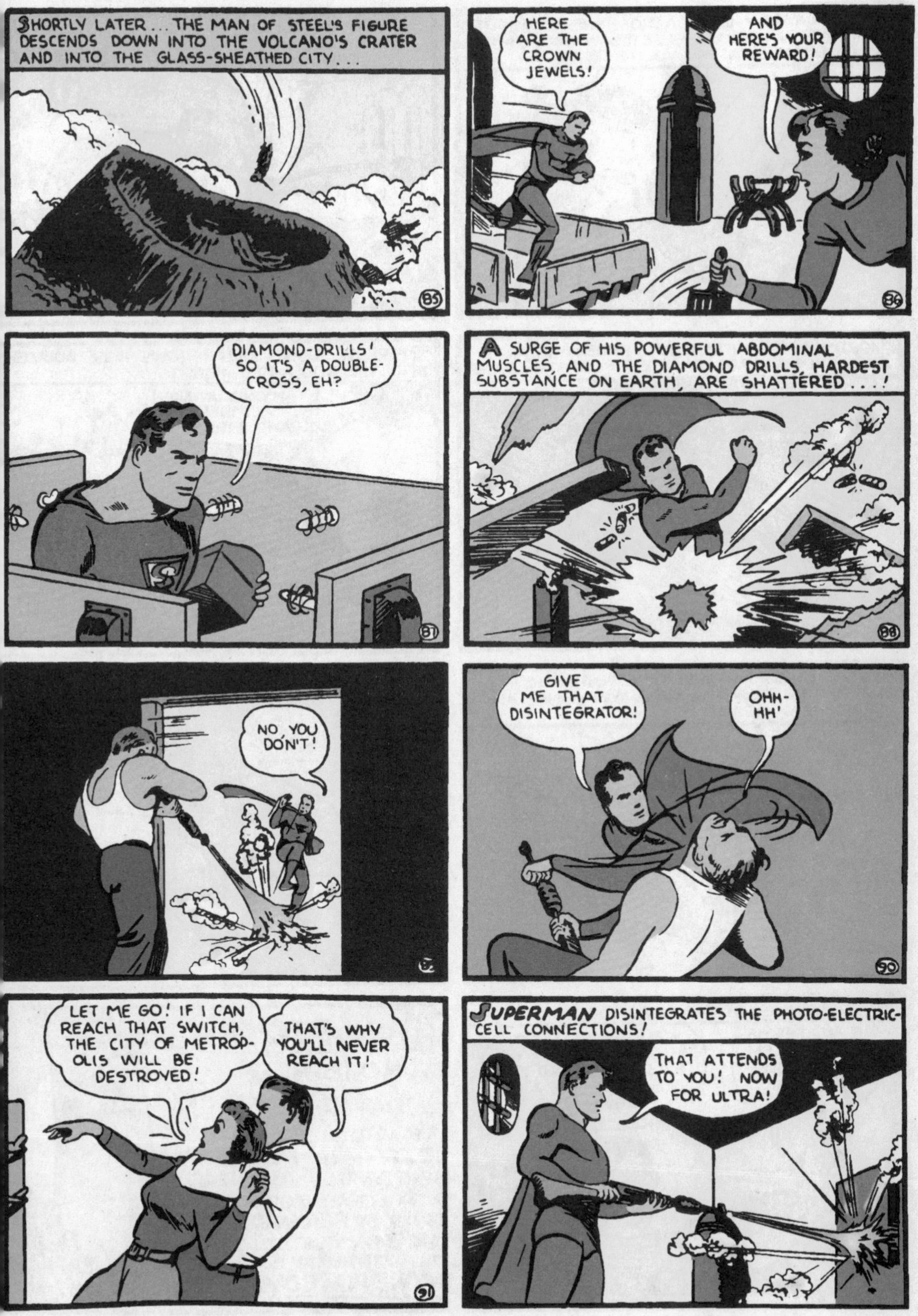
SHORTLY LATER... THE MAN OF STEEL'S FIGURE DESCENDS DOWN INTO THE VOLCANO'S CRATER AND INTO THE GLASS-SHEATHED CITY...
HERE ARE THE CROWN JEWELS!
AND HERE'S YOUR REWARD!
DIAMOND-DRILLS! SO IT'S A DOUBLE-CROSS, EH?
A SURGE OF HIS POWERFUL ABDOMINAL MUSCLES, AND THE DIAMOND DRILLS, HARDEST SUBSTANCE ON EARTH, ARE SHATTERED...!
NO, YOU DON'T!
GIVE ME THAT DISINTEGRATOR!
OHH-HH'
LET ME GO! IF I CAN REACH THAT SWITCH, THE CITY OF METROPOLIS WILL BE DESTROYED!
THAT'S WHY YOU'LL NEVER REACH IT!
SUPERMAN DISINTEGRATES THE PHOTO-ELECTRIC-CELL CONNECTIONS!
THAT ATTENDS TO YOU! NOW FOR ULTRA!

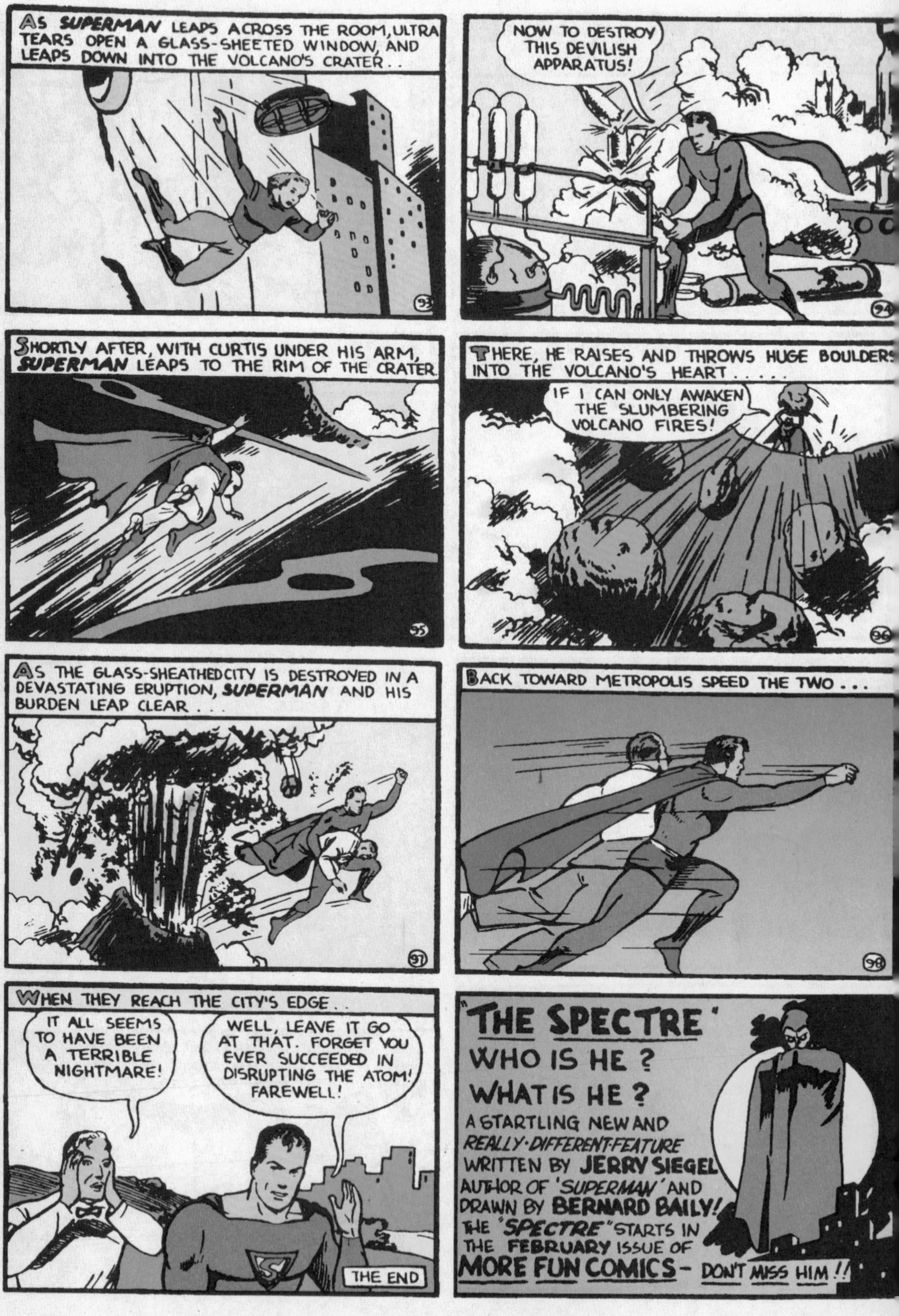
AS SUPERMAN LEAPS ACROSS THE ROOM, ULTRA TEARS OPEN A GLASS-SHEETED WINDOW, AND LEAPS DOWN INTO THE VOLCANO'S CRATER . .
93
NOW TO DESTROY THIS DEVILISH APPARATUS!
94
SHORTLY AFTER, WITH CURTIS UNDER HIS ARM, SUPERMAN LEAPS TO THE RIM OF THE CRATER
95
THERE, HE RAISES AND THROWS HUGE BOULDERS INTO THE VOLCANO'S HEART . . . .
IF I CAN ONLY AWAKEN THE SLUMBERING VOLCANO FIRES!
96
AS THE GLASS-SHEATHED CITY IS DESTROYED IN A DEVASTATING ERUPTION, SUPERMAN AND HIS BURDEN LEAP CLEAR . . .
97
BACK TOWARD METROPOLIS SPEED THE TWO . . .
98
WHEN THEY REACH THE CITY'S EDGE . .
IT ALL SEEMS TO HAVE BEEN A TERRIBLE NIGHTMARE!
WELL, LEAVE IT GO AT THAT. FORGET YOU EVER SUCCEEDED IN DISRUPTING THE ATOM! FAREWELL!
THE END
"THE SPECTRE"
WHO IS HE ?
WHAT IS HE ?
A STARTLING NEW AND REALLY-DIFFERENT-FEATURE WRITTEN BY JERRY SIEGEL AUTHOR OF 'SUPERMAN' AND DRAWN BY BERNARD BAILY! THE "SPECTRE" STARTS IN THE FEBRUARY ISSUE OF MORE FUN COMICS - DON'T MISS HIM!!

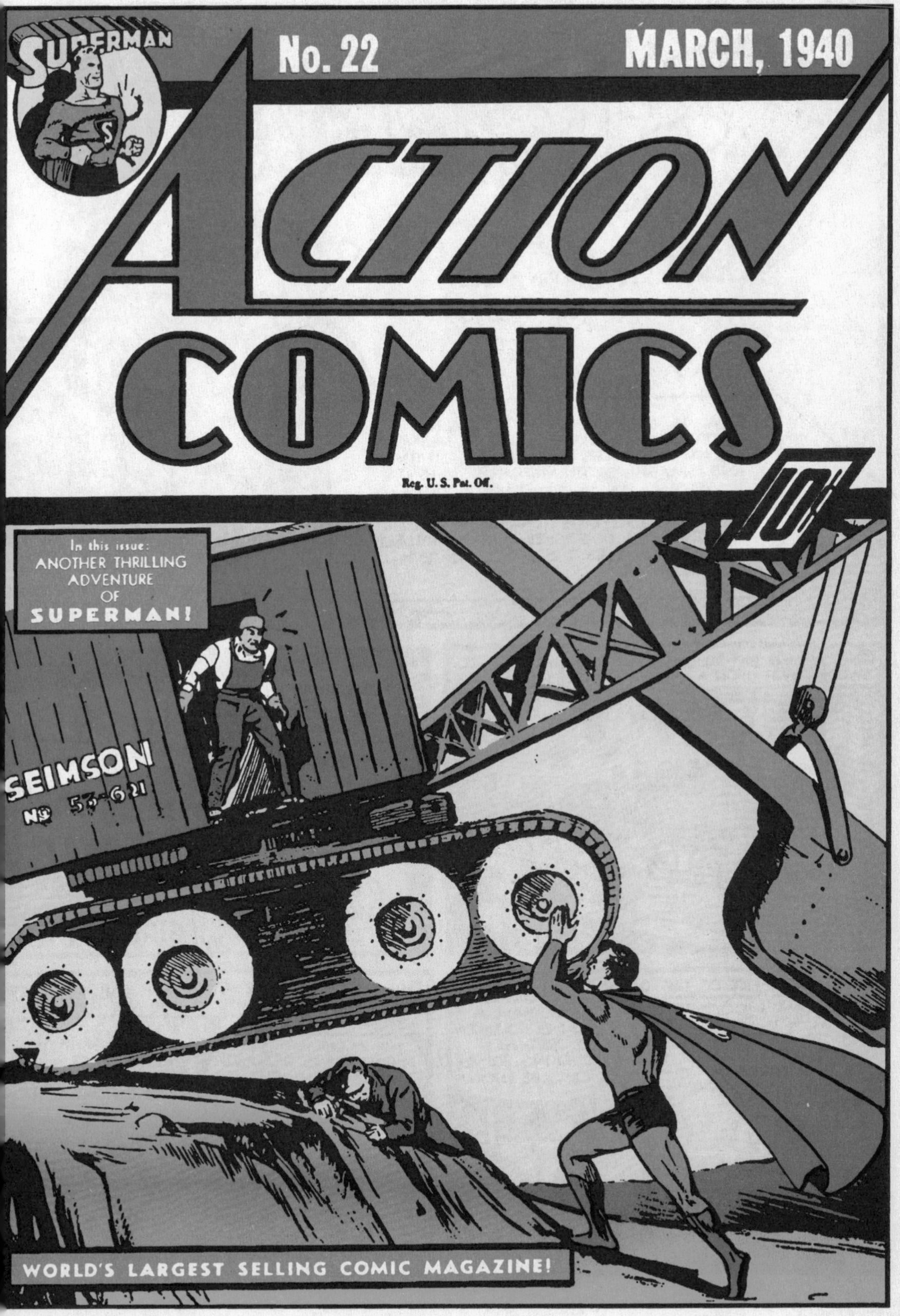
SUPERMAN
No. 22
MARCH, 1940
ACTION COMICS
Reg. U. S. Pat. Off.
10¢
In this issue:
ANOTHER THRILLING
ADVENTURE
OF
SUPERMAN!
SEIMSON
WORLD'S LARGEST SELLING COMIC MAGAZINE!

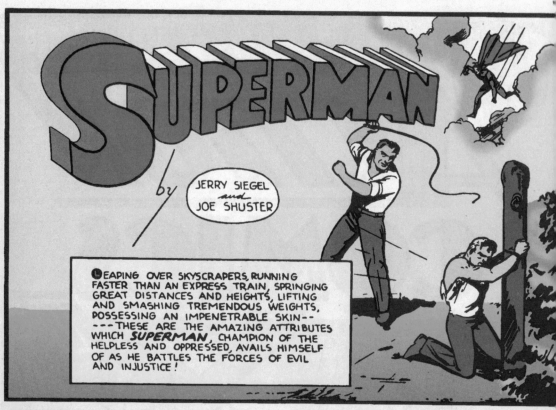

SUPERMAN

by JERRY SIEGEL and JOE SHUSTER

Leaping over skyscrapers, running faster than an express train, springing great distances and heights, lifting and smashing tremendous weights, possessing an impenetrable skin----these are the amazing attributes which SUPERMAN, champion of the helpless and oppressed, avails himself of as he battles the forces of evil and injustice!

The armed battalions of TORAN unexpectedly swoop down upon a lesser nation, GALONIA.

★ Daily Star

EUROPE ★AT WAR!!

DAWN ATTACK SWEEPS OVER ALL OPPOSITION

WARRING POWE GIRD FOR LON

Editorial office of the Daily Star...

CLARK AND LOIS. I WANT BOTH OF YOU TO GO TO LUXOR AT ONCE AS WAR CORRESPONDENTS!

SWELL! I'VE HOPED FOR A VACATION FOR A LONG TIME!

IF YOU HAVE A CHANCE TO ENJOY IT, BETWEEN DUCKING BOMBS, YOU'LL BE LUCKY!

And so when the steamer, BARONTA, sets out to sea, Lois and Clark are passengers aboard..

I-I WONDER IF WE SHOULD HAVE REFUSED THIS ASSIGNMENT. IT'S LIABLE TO PROVE--ER--DANGEROUS.

("-WHY DID THEY HAVE TO SEND THIS WET BLANKET ALONG TO RUIN MY PERFECT ADVENTURE? -")

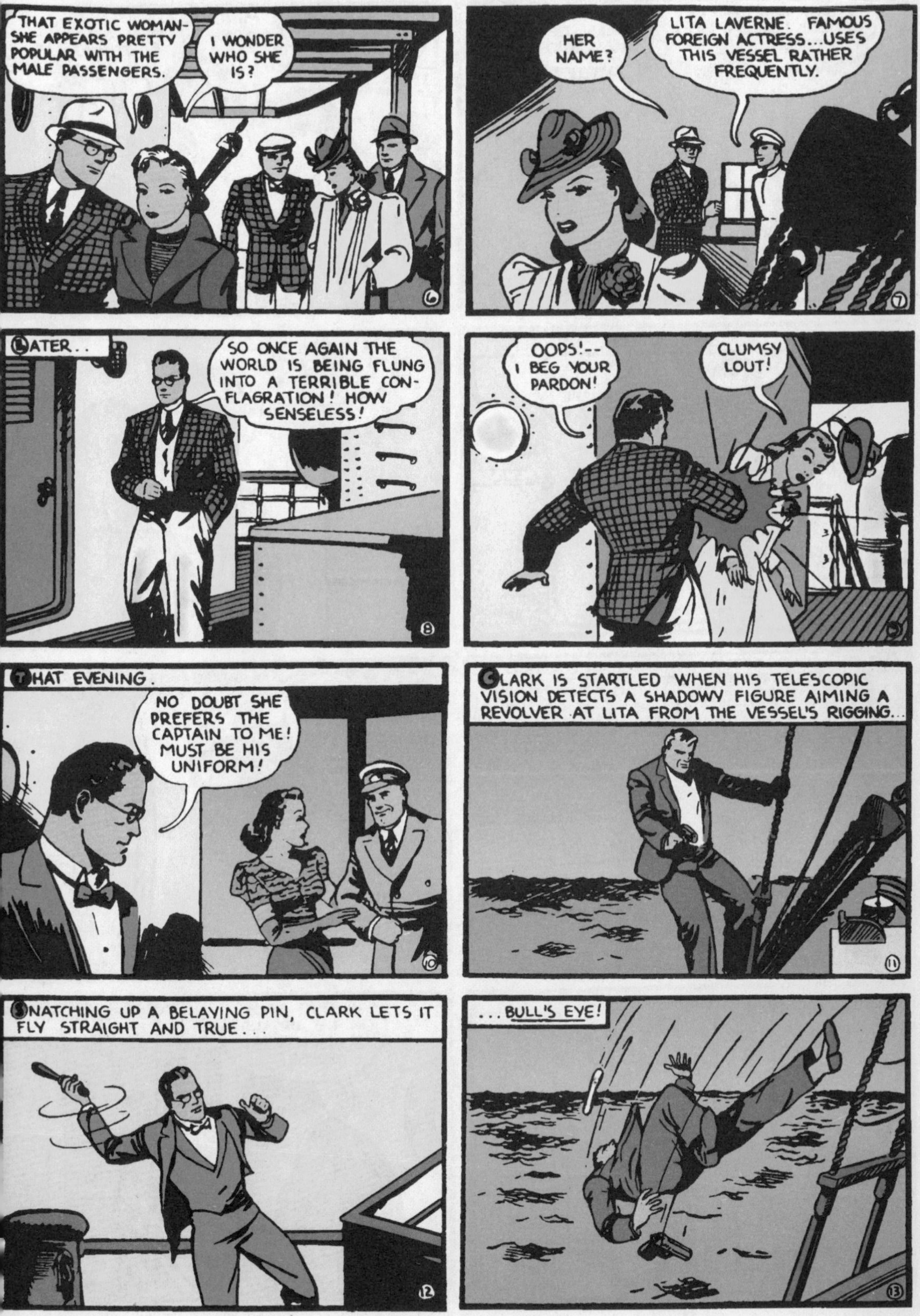
THAT EXOTIC WOMAN- SHE APPEARS PRETTY POPULAR WITH THE MALE PASSENGERS.
I WONDER WHO SHE IS?
HER NAME?
LITA LAVERNE. FAMOUS FOREIGN ACTRESS...USES THIS VESSEL RATHER FREQUENTLY.
LATER..
SO ONCE AGAIN THE WORLD IS BEING FLUNG INTO A TERRIBLE CON-FLAGRATION! HOW SENSELESS!
OOPS!-- I BEG YOUR PARDON!
CLUMSY LOUT!
THAT EVENING.
NO DOUBT SHE PREFERS THE CAPTAIN TO ME! MUST BE HIS UNIFORM!
CLARK IS STARTLED WHEN HIS TELESCOPIC VISION DETECTS A SHADOWY FIGURE AIMING A REVOLVER AT LITA FROM THE VESSEL'S RIGGING...
SNATCHING UP A BELAYING PIN, CLARK LETS IT FLY STRAIGHT AND TRUE...
...BULL'S EYE!

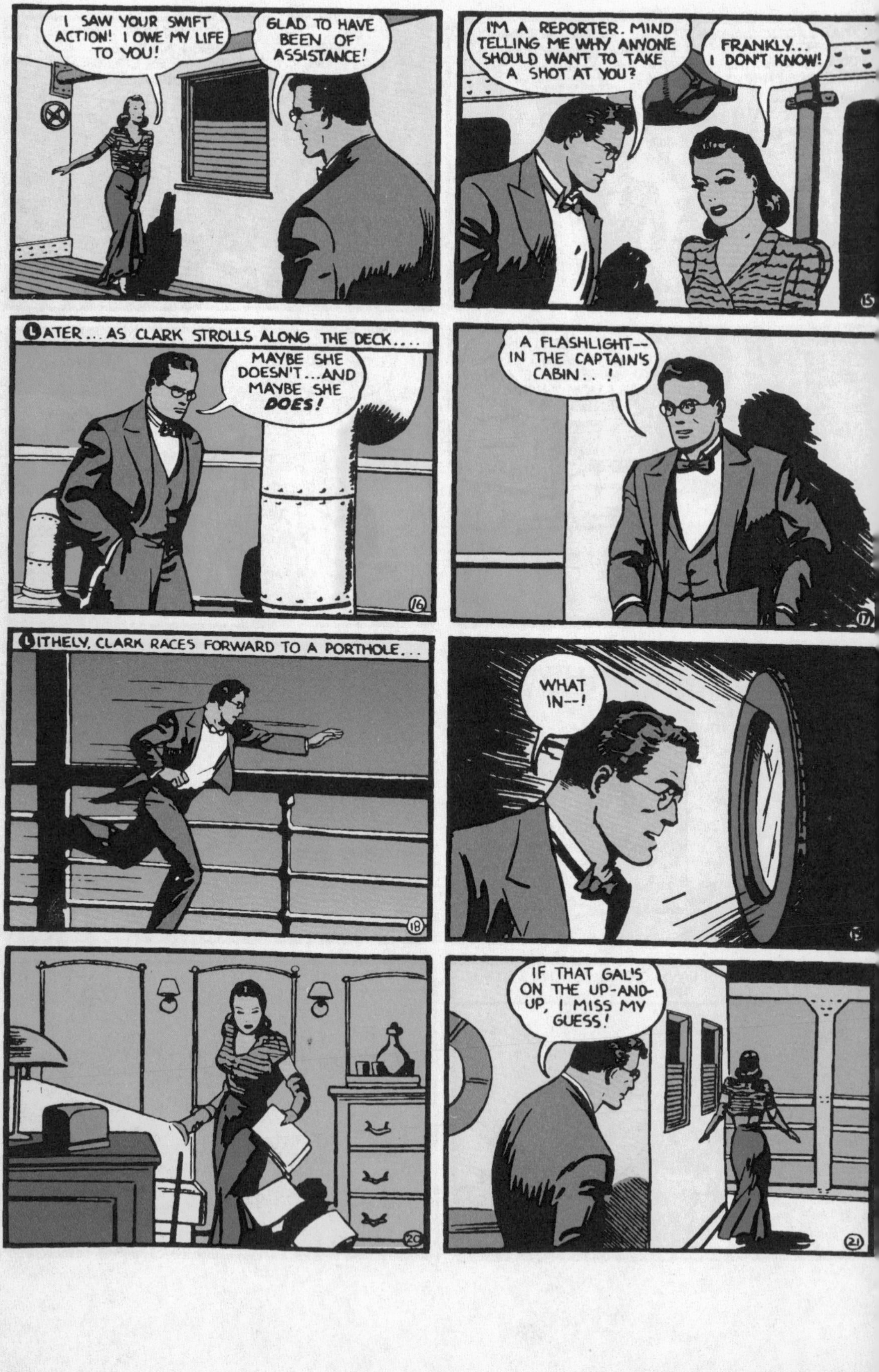
I SAW YOUR SWIFT ACTION! I OWE MY LIFE TO YOU!
GLAD TO HAVE BEEN OF ASSISTANCE!
I'M A REPORTER. MIND TELLING ME WHY ANYONE SHOULD WANT TO TAKE A SHOT AT YOU?
FRANKLY... I DON'T KNOW!
LATER... AS CLARK STROLLS ALONG THE DECK....
MAYBE SHE DOESN'T...AND MAYBE SHE **DOES!**
A FLASHLIGHT-- IN THE CAPTAIN'S CABIN.. !
LITHELY, CLARK RACES FORWARD TO A PORTHOLE...
WHAT IN--!
IF THAT GAL'S ON THE UP-AND-UP, I MISS MY GUESS!

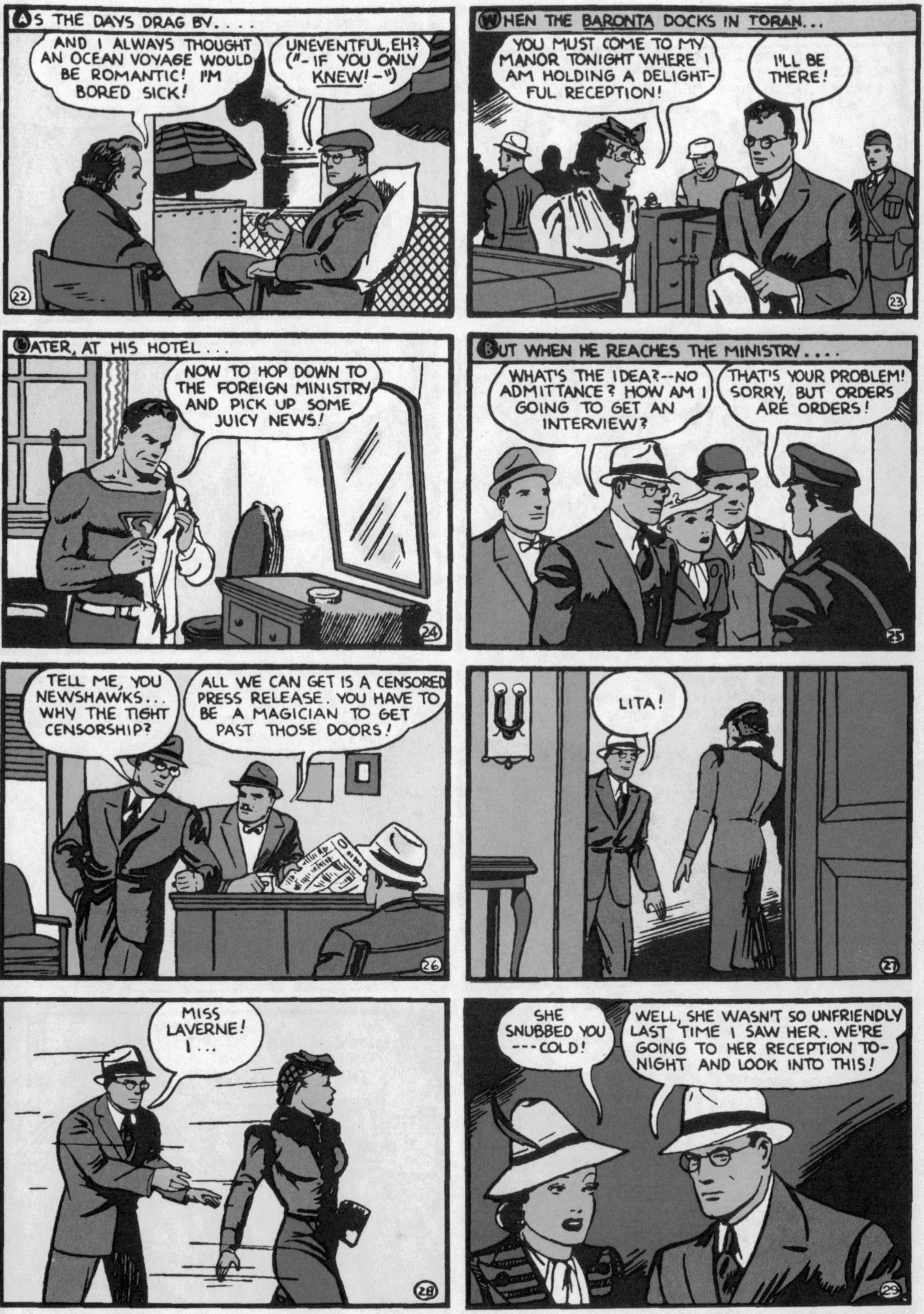
AS THE DAYS DRAG BY....
AND I ALWAYS THOUGHT AN OCEAN VOYAGE WOULD BE ROMANTIC! I'M BORED SICK!
UNEVENTFUL, EH? ("-IF YOU ONLY KNEW!-")
22
WHEN THE BARONTA DOCKS IN TORAN...
YOU MUST COME TO MY MANOR TONIGHT WHERE I AM HOLDING A DELIGHTFUL RECEPTION!
I'LL BE THERE!
23
LATER, AT HIS HOTEL...
NOW TO HOP DOWN TO THE FOREIGN MINISTRY AND PICK UP SOME JUICY NEWS!
24
BUT WHEN HE REACHES THE MINISTRY....
WHAT'S THE IDEA?--NO ADMITTANCE? HOW AM I GOING TO GET AN INTERVIEW?
THAT'S YOUR PROBLEM! SORRY, BUT ORDERS ARE ORDERS!
25
TELL ME, YOU NEWSHAWKS... WHY THE TIGHT CENSORSHIP?
ALL WE CAN GET IS A CENSORED PRESS RELEASE. YOU HAVE TO BE A MAGICIAN TO GET PAST THOSE DOORS!
26
LITA!
27
MISS LAVERNE! I...
28
SHE SNUBBED YOU ---COLD!
WELL, SHE WASN'T SO UNFRIENDLY LAST TIME I SAW HER. WE'RE GOING TO HER RECEPTION TONIGHT AND LOOK INTO THIS!
29

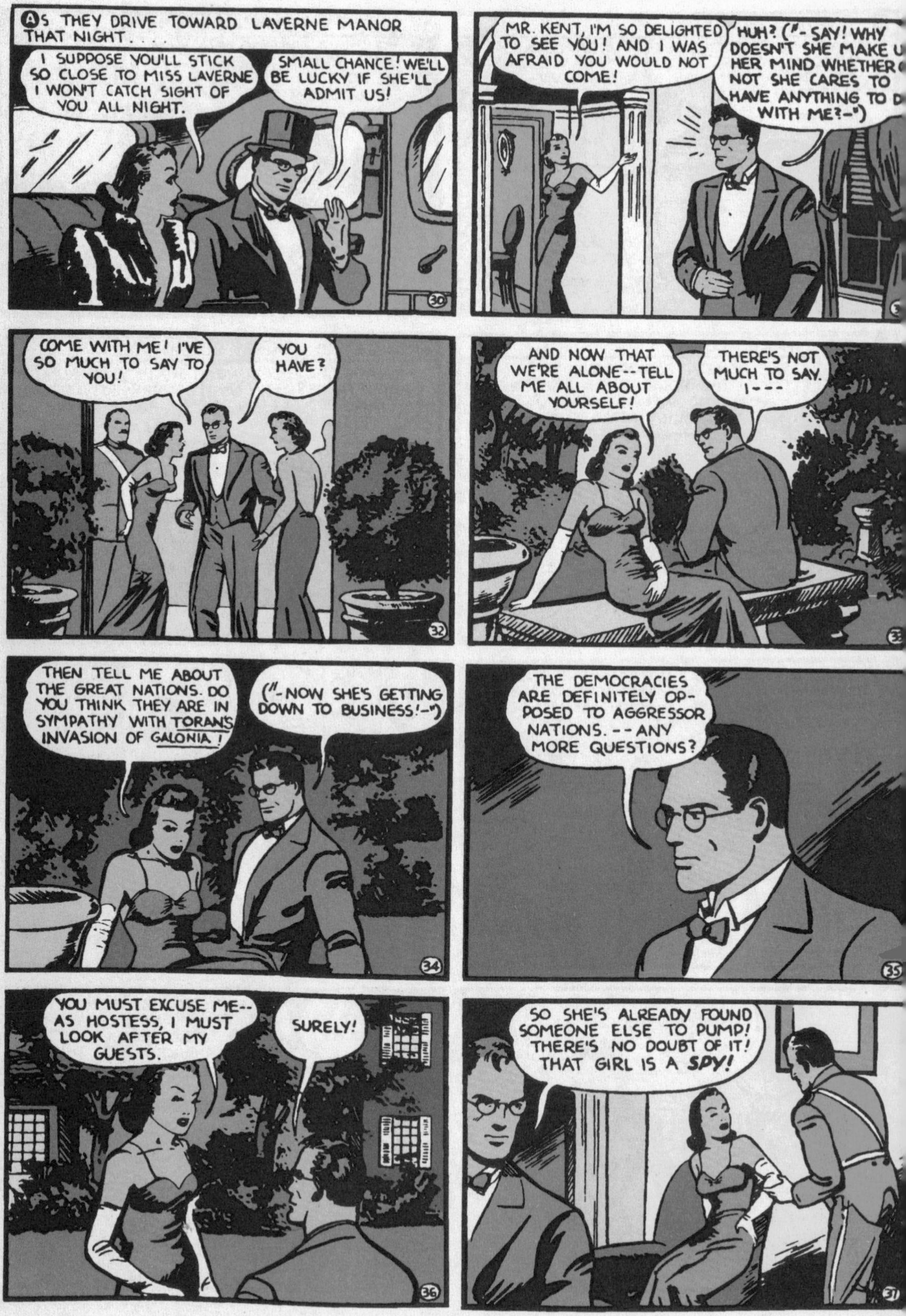
AS THEY DRIVE TOWARD LAVERNE MANOR THAT NIGHT. . . .
I SUPPOSE YOU'LL STICK SO CLOSE TO MISS LAVERNE I WON'T CATCH SIGHT OF YOU ALL NIGHT.
SMALL CHANCE! WE'LL BE LUCKY IF SHE'LL ADMIT US!
30
MR. KENT, I'M SO DELIGHTED TO SEE YOU! AND I WAS AFRAID YOU WOULD NOT COME!
HUH? ("- SAY! WHY DOESN'T SHE MAKE U HER MIND WHETHER NOT SHE CARES TO HAVE ANYTHING TO D WITH ME?-")
COME WITH ME! I'VE SO MUCH TO SAY TO YOU!
YOU HAVE?
32
AND NOW THAT WE'RE ALONE--TELL ME ALL ABOUT YOURSELF!
THERE'S NOT MUCH TO SAY. I---
THEN TELL ME ABOUT THE GREAT NATIONS. DO YOU THINK THEY ARE IN SYMPATHY WITH TORAN'S INVASION OF GALONIA!
("-NOW SHE'S GETTING DOWN TO BUSINESS!-")
34
THE DEMOCRACIES ARE DEFINITELY OPPOSED TO AGGRESSOR NATIONS. --ANY MORE QUESTIONS?
35
YOU MUST EXCUSE ME--AS HOSTESS, I MUST LOOK AFTER MY GUESTS.
SURELY!
36
SO SHE'S ALREADY FOUND SOMEONE ELSE TO PUMP! THERE'S NO DOUBT OF IT! THAT GIRL IS A SPY!
37

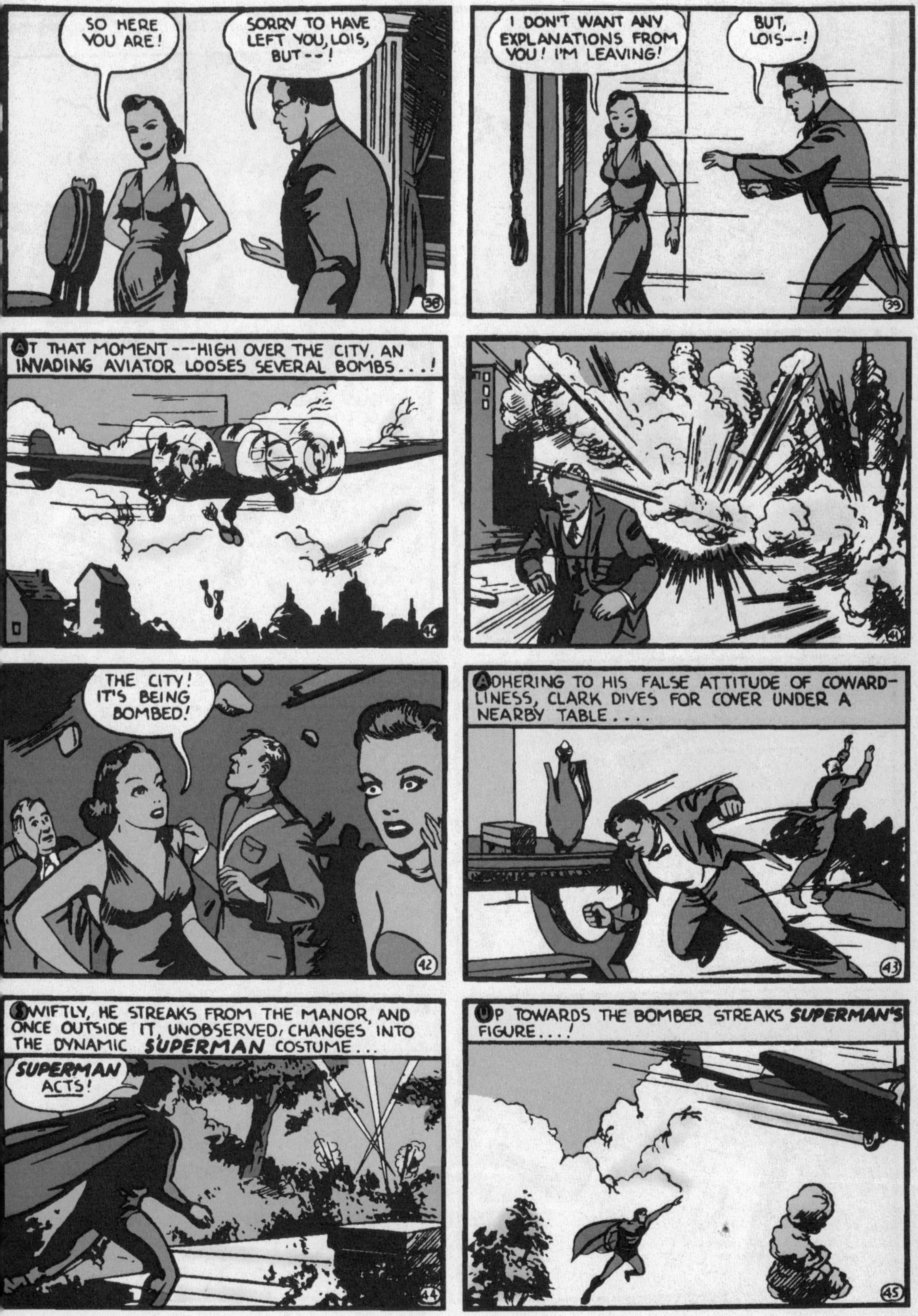
SO HERE YOU ARE!
SORRY TO HAVE LEFT YOU, LOIS, BUT--!
38
I DON'T WANT ANY EXPLANATIONS FROM YOU! I'M LEAVING!
BUT, LOIS--!
39
AT THAT MOMENT---HIGH OVER THE CITY, AN INVADING AVIATOR LOOSES SEVERAL BOMBS...!
40
41
THE CITY! IT'S BEING BOMBED!
42
ADHERING TO HIS FALSE ATTITUDE OF COWARDLINESS, CLARK DIVES FOR COVER UNDER A NEARBY TABLE....
43
SWIFTLY, HE STREAKS FROM THE MANOR, AND ONCE OUTSIDE IT, UNOBSERVED, CHANGES INTO THE DYNAMIC SUPERMAN COSTUME...
SUPERMAN ACTS!
44
UP TOWARDS THE BOMBER STREAKS SUPERMAN'S FIGURE...!
45

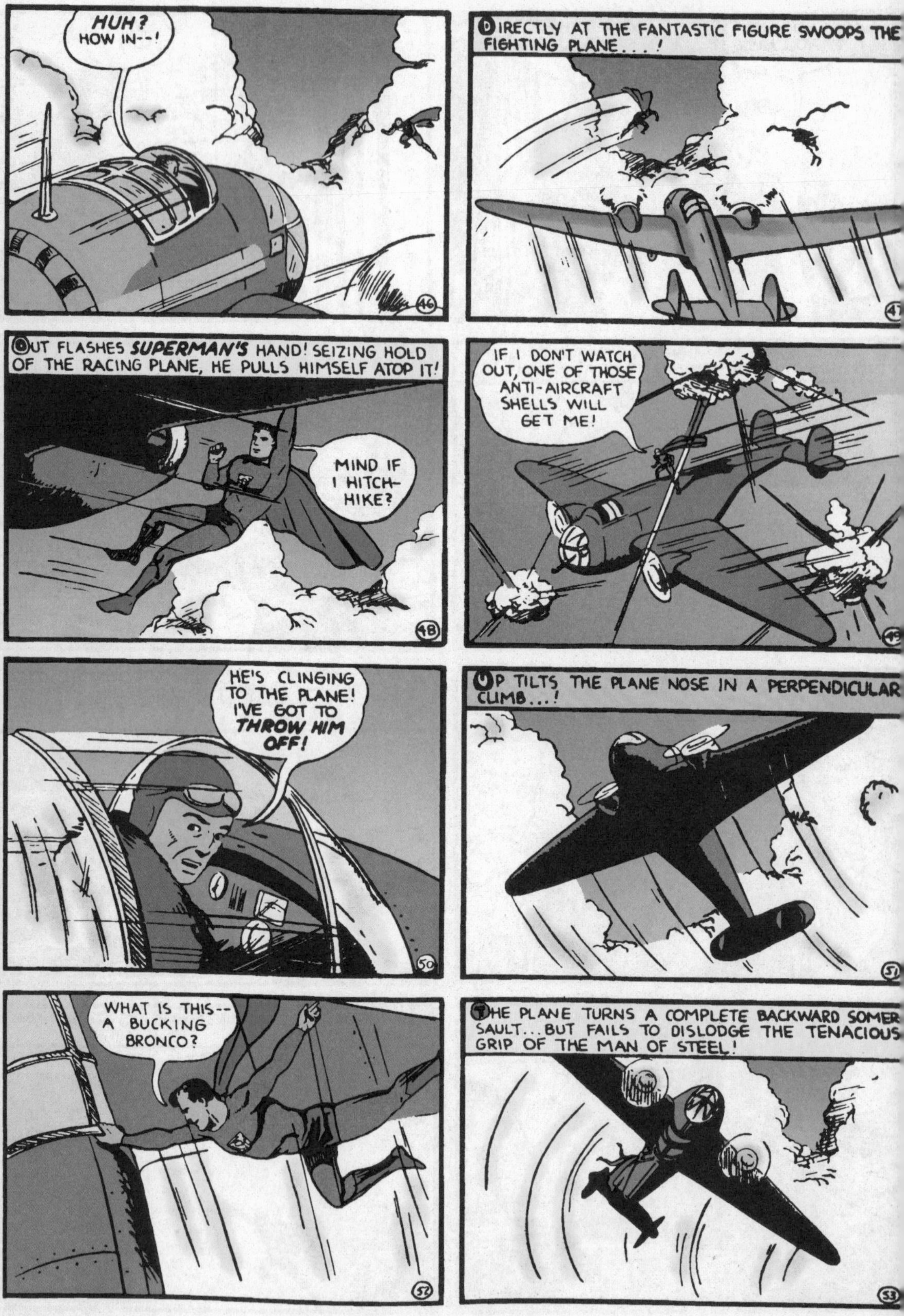
HUH? HOW IN--!
46
DIRECTLY AT THE FANTASTIC FIGURE SWOOPS THE FIGHTING PLANE...!
OUT FLASHES SUPERMAN'S HAND! SEIZING HOLD OF THE RACING PLANE, HE PULLS HIMSELF ATOP IT!
MIND IF I HITCH-HIKE?
48
IF I DON'T WATCH OUT, ONE OF THOSE ANTI-AIRCRAFT SHELLS WILL GET ME!
HE'S CLINGING TO THE PLANE! I'VE GOT TO THROW HIM OFF!
50
UP TILTS THE PLANE NOSE IN A PERPENDICULAR CLIMB...!
WHAT IS THIS-- A BUCKING BRONCO?
52
THE PLANE TURNS A COMPLETE BACKWARD SOMER SAULT...BUT FAILS TO DISLODGE THE TENACIOUS GRIP OF THE MAN OF STEEL!
53

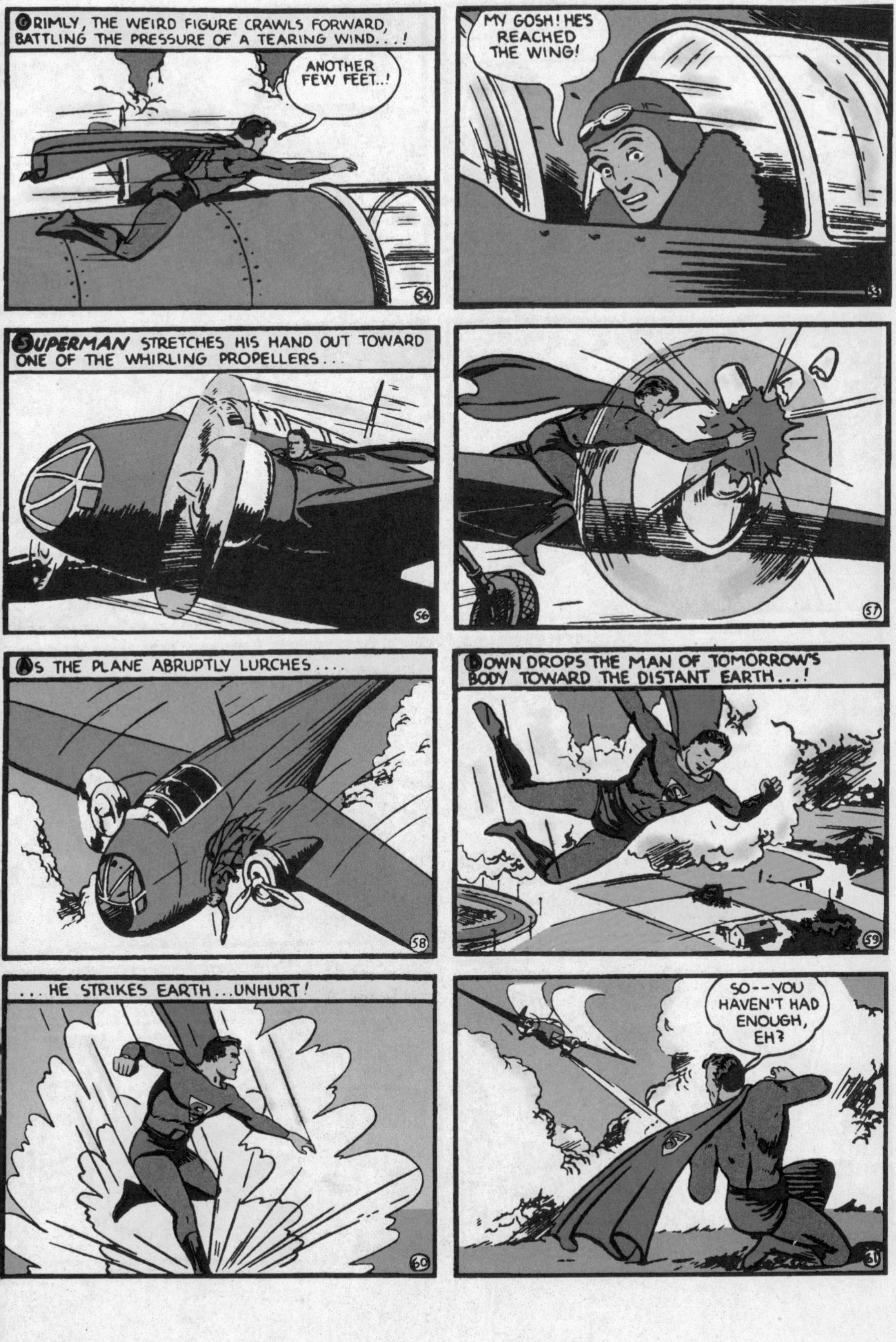
GRIMLY, THE WEIRD FIGURE CRAWLS FORWARD, BATTLING THE PRESSURE OF A TEARING WIND...!
ANOTHER FEW FEET..!
MY GOSH! HE'S REACHED THE WING!
SUPERMAN STRETCHES HIS HAND OUT TOWARD ONE OF THE WHIRLING PROPELLERS...
AS THE PLANE ABRUPTLY LURCHES....
DOWN DROPS THE MAN OF TOMORROW'S BODY TOWARD THE DISTANT EARTH...!
...HE STRIKES EARTH...UNHURT!
SO--YOU HAVEN'T HAD ENOUGH, EH?

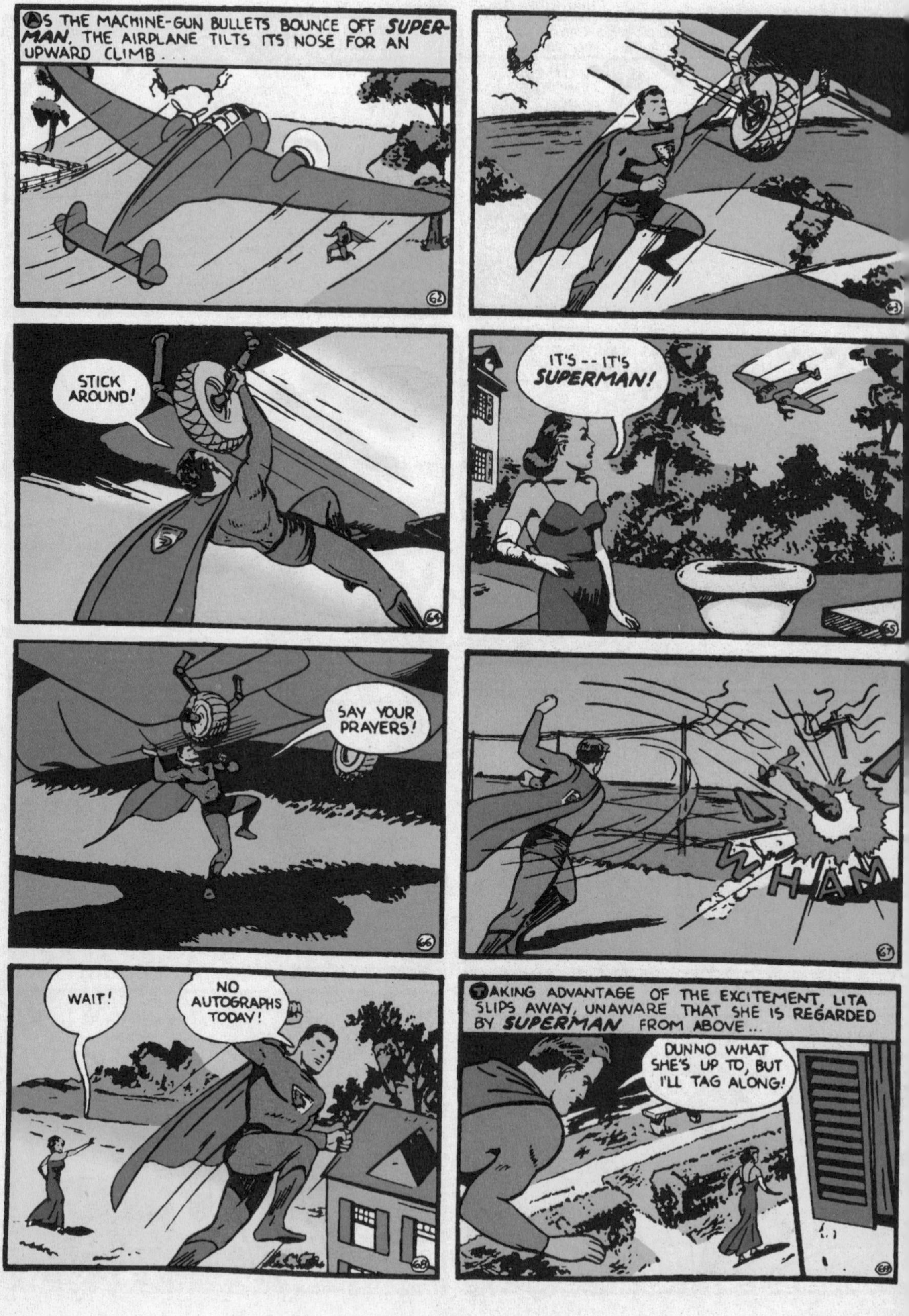

AS THE MACHINE-GUN BULLETS BOUNCE OFF SUPERMAN, THE AIRPLANE TILTS ITS NOSE FOR AN UPWARD CLIMB . . .
STICK AROUND!
IT'S -- IT'S SUPERMAN!
SAY YOUR PRAYERS!
WHAM
WAIT!
NO AUTOGRAPHS TODAY!
TAKING ADVANTAGE OF THE EXCITEMENT, LITA SLIPS AWAY, UNAWARE THAT SHE IS REGARDED BY SUPERMAN FROM ABOVE...
DUNNO WHAT SHE'S UP TO, BUT I'LL TAG ALONG!

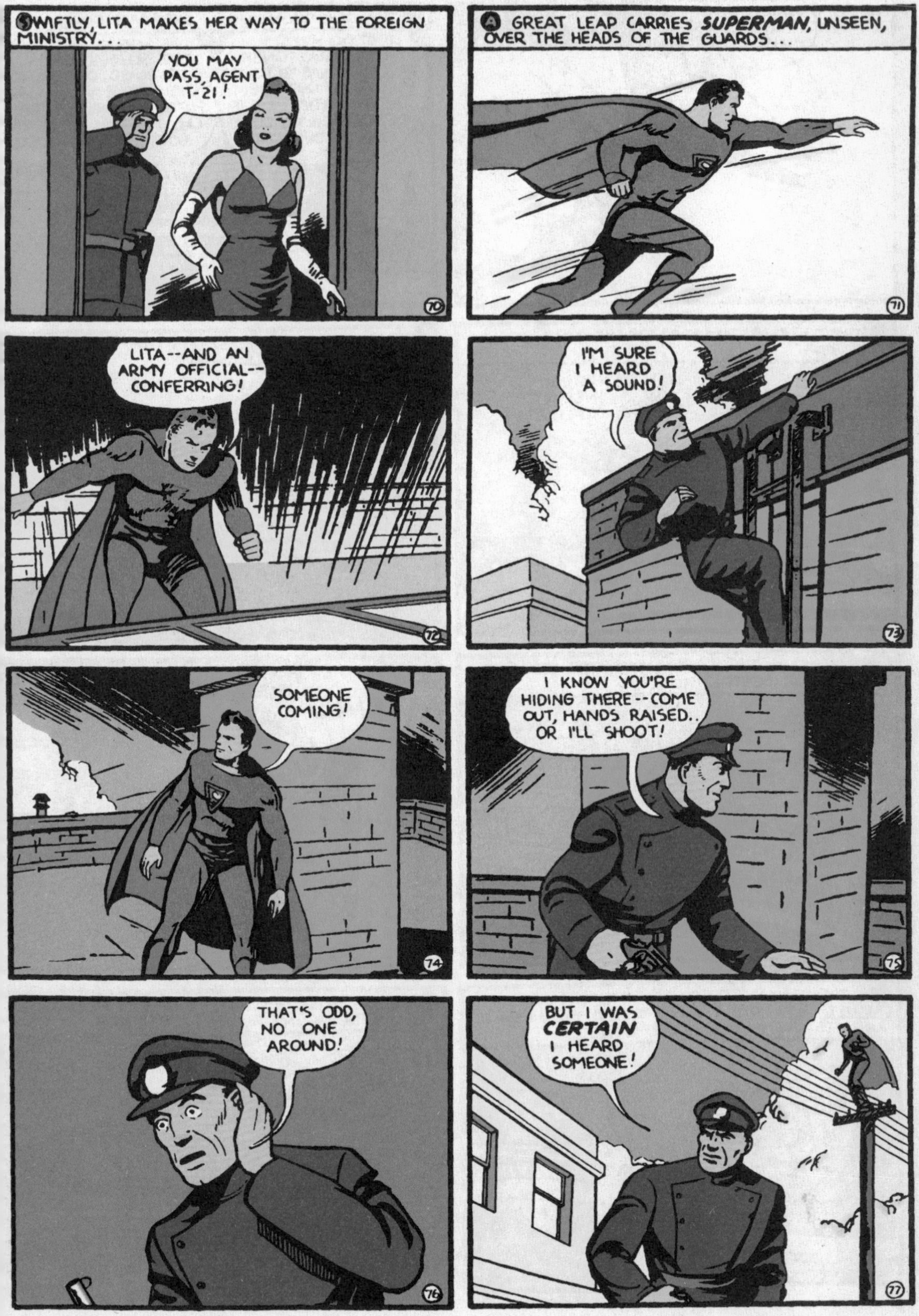
SWIFTLY, LITA MAKES HER WAY TO THE FOREIGN MINISTRY...
YOU MAY PASS, AGENT T-21!
70
A GREAT LEAP CARRIES SUPERMAN, UNSEEN, OVER THE HEADS OF THE GUARDS...
71
LITA--AND AN ARMY OFFICIAL--CONFERRING!
72
I'M SURE I HEARD A SOUND!
73
SOMEONE COMING!
74
I KNOW YOU'RE HIDING THERE--COME OUT, HANDS RAISED.. OR I'LL SHOOT!
75
THAT'S ODD, NO ONE AROUND!
76
BUT I WAS CERTAIN I HEARD SOMEONE!
77

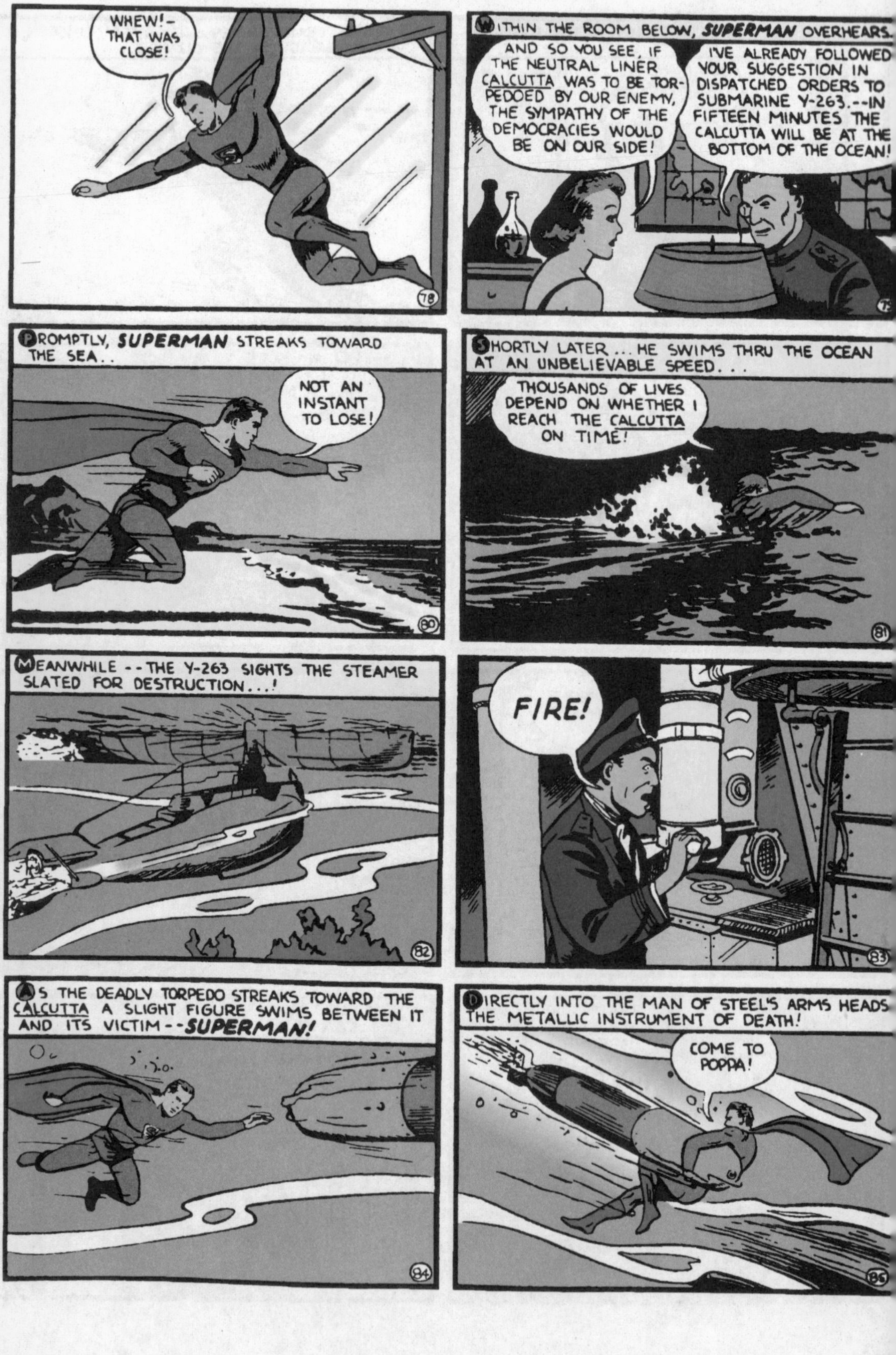

WHEW!- THAT WAS CLOSE!
WITHIN THE ROOM BELOW, SUPERMAN OVERHEARS.
AND SO YOU SEE, IF THE NEUTRAL LINER CALCUTTA WAS TO BE TORPEDOED BY OUR ENEMY, THE SYMPATHY OF THE DEMOCRACIES WOULD BE ON OUR SIDE!
I'VE ALREADY FOLLOWED YOUR SUGGESTION IN DISPATCHED ORDERS TO SUBMARINE Y-263.--IN FIFTEEN MINUTES THE CALCUTTA WILL BE AT THE BOTTOM OF THE OCEAN!
PROMPTLY, SUPERMAN STREAKS TOWARD THE SEA..
NOT AN INSTANT TO LOSE!
SHORTLY LATER... HE SWIMS THRU THE OCEAN AT AN UNBELIEVABLE SPEED...
THOUSANDS OF LIVES DEPEND ON WHETHER I REACH THE CALCUTTA ON TIME!
MEANWHILE --THE Y-263 SIGHTS THE STEAMER SLATED FOR DESTRUCTION...!
FIRE!
AS THE DEADLY TORPEDO STREAKS TOWARD THE CALCUTTA A SLIGHT FIGURE SWIMS BETWEEN IT AND ITS VICTIM--SUPERMAN!
DIRECTLY INTO THE MAN OF STEEL'S ARMS HEADS THE METALLIC INSTRUMENT OF DEATH!
COME TO POPPA!

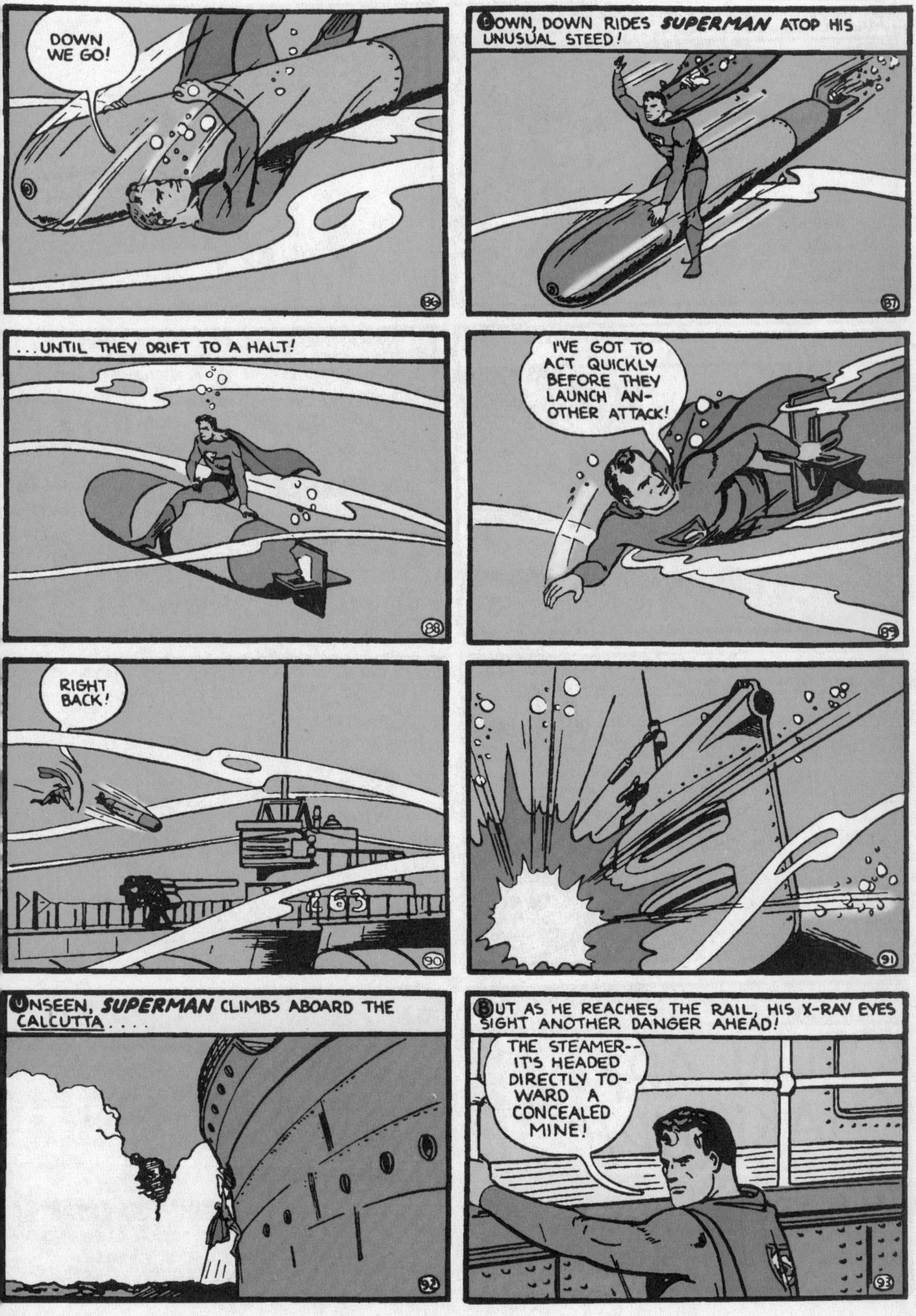
DOWN WE GO!
DOWN, DOWN RIDES SUPERMAN ATOP HIS UNUSUAL STEED!
...UNTIL THEY DRIFT TO A HALT!
I'VE GOT TO ACT QUICKLY BEFORE THEY LAUNCH AN-OTHER ATTACK!
RIGHT BACK!
UNSEEN, SUPERMAN CLIMBS ABOARD THE CALCUTTA....
BUT AS HE REACHES THE RAIL, HIS X-RAY EYES SIGHT ANOTHER DANGER AHEAD!
THE STEAMER-- IT'S HEADED DIRECTLY TO-WARD A CONCEALED MINE!

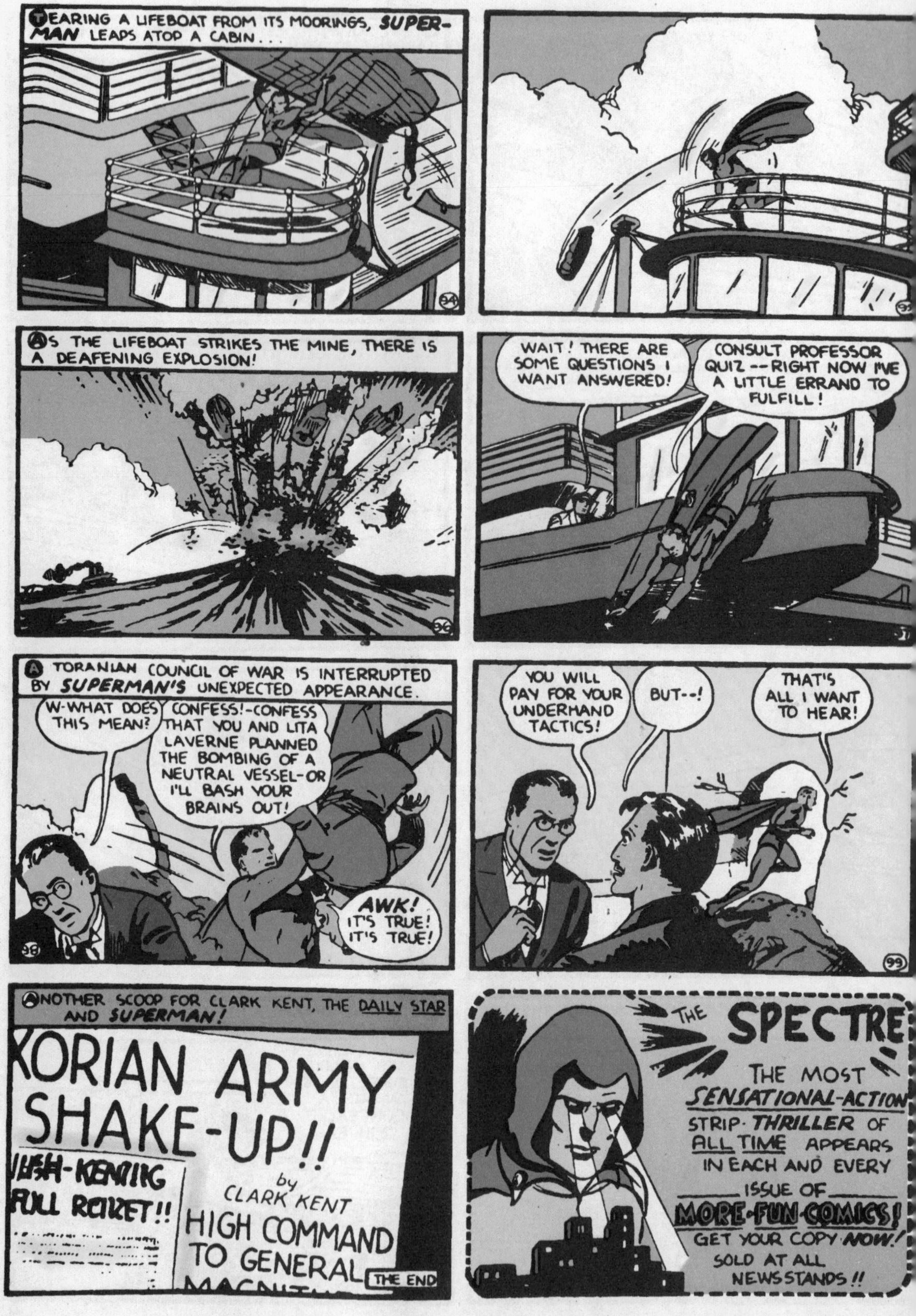
TEARING A LIFEBOAT FROM ITS MOORINGS, SUPERMAN LEAPS ATOP A CABIN . . .
AS THE LIFEBOAT STRIKES THE MINE, THERE IS A DEAFENING EXPLOSION!
WAIT! THERE ARE SOME QUESTIONS I WANT ANSWERED!
CONSULT PROFESSOR QUIZ --RIGHT NOW I'VE A LITTLE ERRAND TO FULFILL!
A TORANIAN COUNCIL OF WAR IS INTERRUPTED BY SUPERMAN'S UNEXPECTED APPEARANCE.
W-WHAT DOES THIS MEAN?
CONFESS!-CONFESS THAT YOU AND LITA LAVERNE PLANNED THE BOMBING OF A NEUTRAL VESSEL-OR I'LL BASH YOUR BRAINS OUT!
AWK! IT'S TRUE! IT'S TRUE!
YOU WILL PAY FOR YOUR UNDERHAND TACTICS!
BUT--!
THAT'S ALL I WANT TO HEAR!
ANOTHER SCOOP FOR CLARK KENT, THE DAILY STAR AND SUPERMAN!
ORIAN ARMY SHAKE-UP!!
by CLARK KENT
HIGH COMMAND TO GENERAL
THE END
THE SPECTRE
THE MOST SENSATIONAL-ACTION STRIP-THRILLER OF ALL TIME APPEARS IN EACH AND EVERY ISSUE OF MORE FUN COMICS! GET YOUR COPY NOW! SOLD AT ALL NEWSSTANDS!!

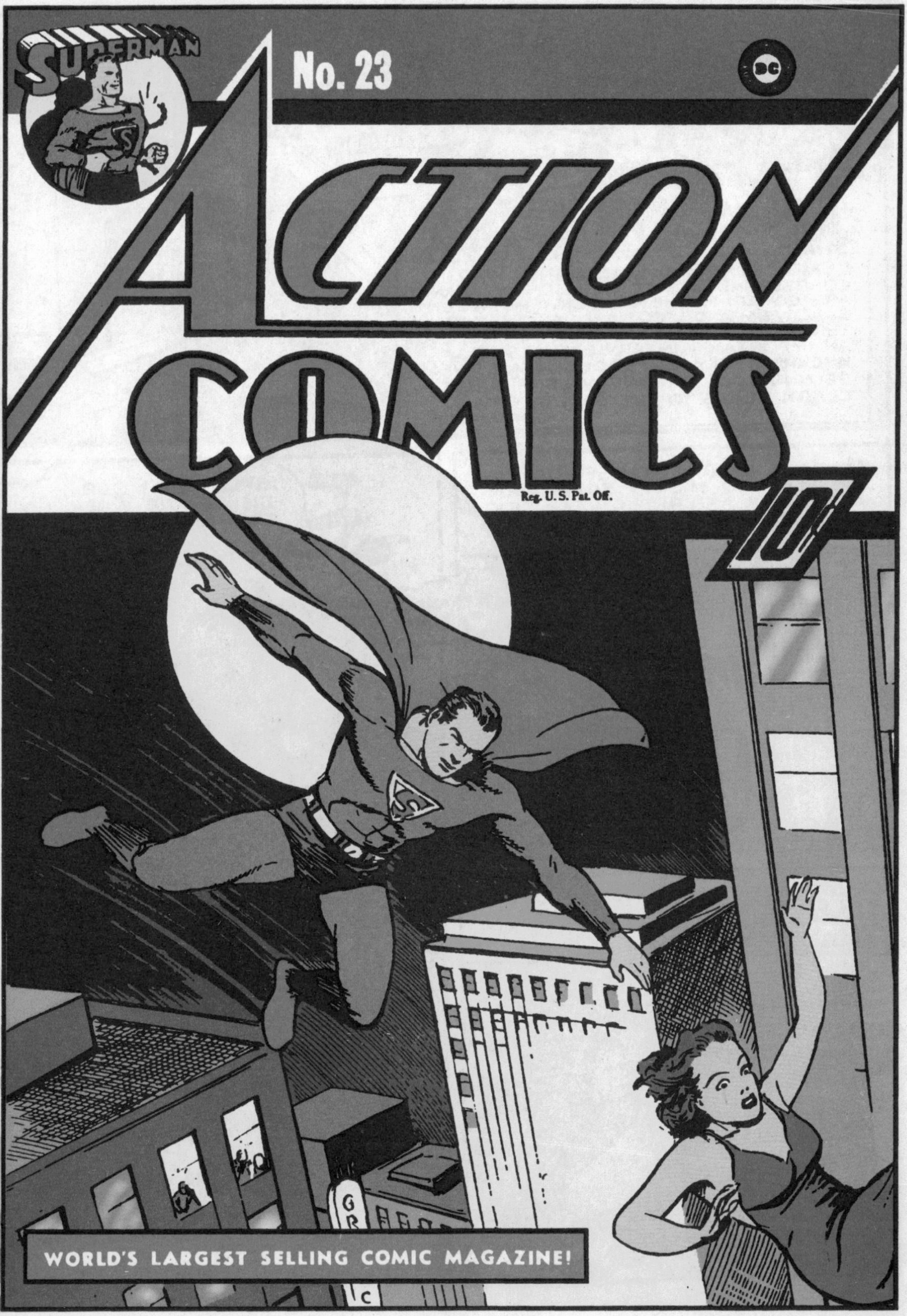
SUPERMAN
No. 23
DC
ACTION COMICS
Reg. U.S. Pat. Off.
10¢
WORLD'S LARGEST SELLING COMIC MAGAZINE!

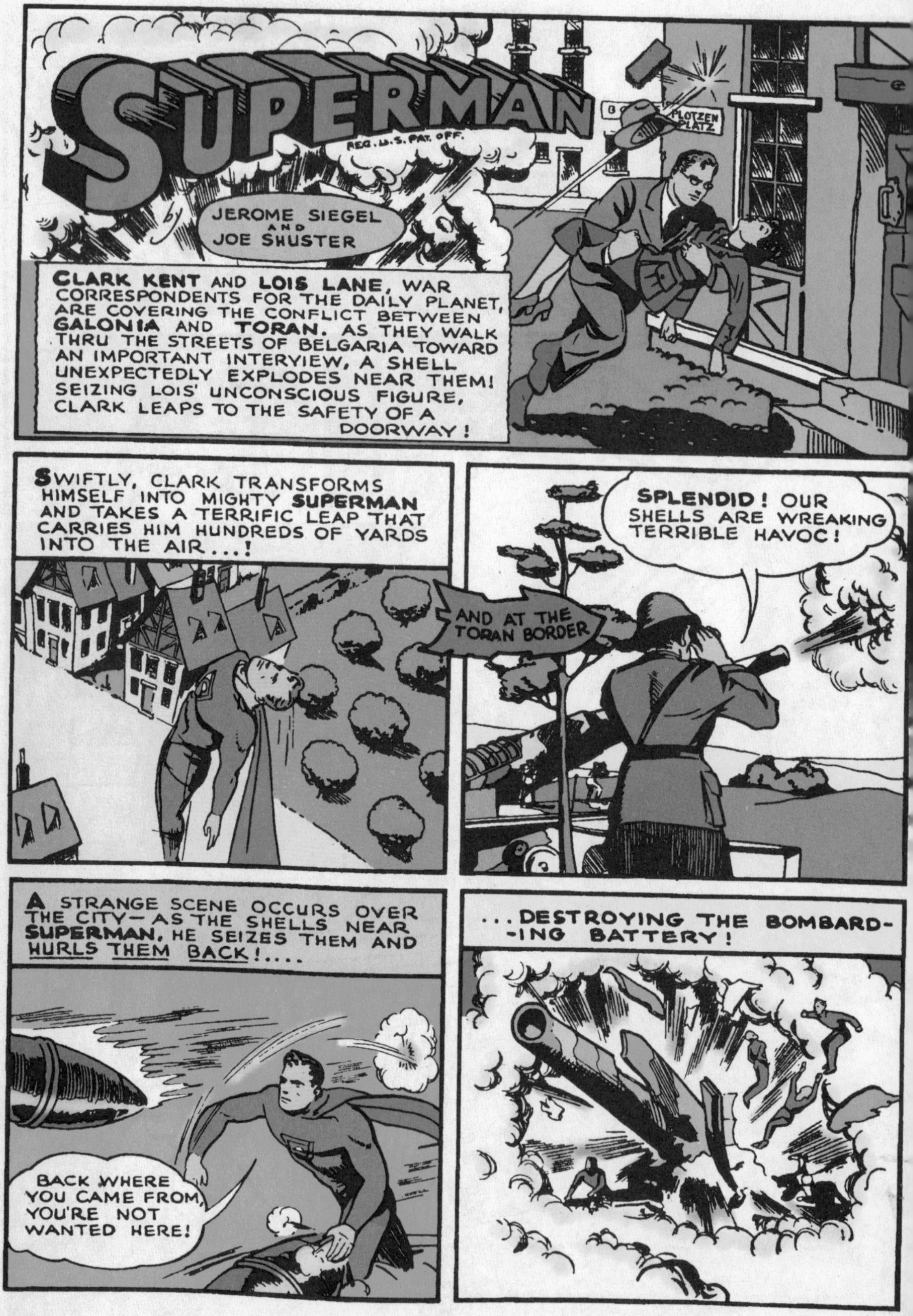
SUPERMAN
REG. U.S. PAT. OFF.
by JEROME SIEGEL AND JOE SHUSTER
PLOTZEN PLATZ
CLARK KENT AND LOIS LANE, WAR CORRESPONDENTS FOR THE DAILY PLANET, ARE COVERING THE CONFLICT BETWEEN GALONIA AND TORAN. AS THEY WALK THRU THE STREETS OF BELGARIA TOWARD AN IMPORTANT INTERVIEW, A SHELL UNEXPECTEDLY EXPLODES NEAR THEM! SEIZING LOIS' UNCONSCIOUS FIGURE, CLARK LEAPS TO THE SAFETY OF A DOORWAY!
SWIFTLY, CLARK TRANSFORMS HIMSELF INTO MIGHTY SUPERMAN AND TAKES A TERRIFIC LEAP THAT CARRIES HIM HUNDREDS OF YARDS INTO THE AIR...!
AND AT THE TORAN BORDER
SPLENDID! OUR SHELLS ARE WREAKING TERRIBLE HAVOC!
A STRANGE SCENE OCCURS OVER THE CITY—AS THE SHELLS NEAR SUPERMAN, HE SEIZES THEM AND HURLS THEM BACK!....
BACK WHERE YOU CAME FROM, YOU'RE NOT WANTED HERE!
...DESTROYING THE BOMBARD--ING BATTERY!

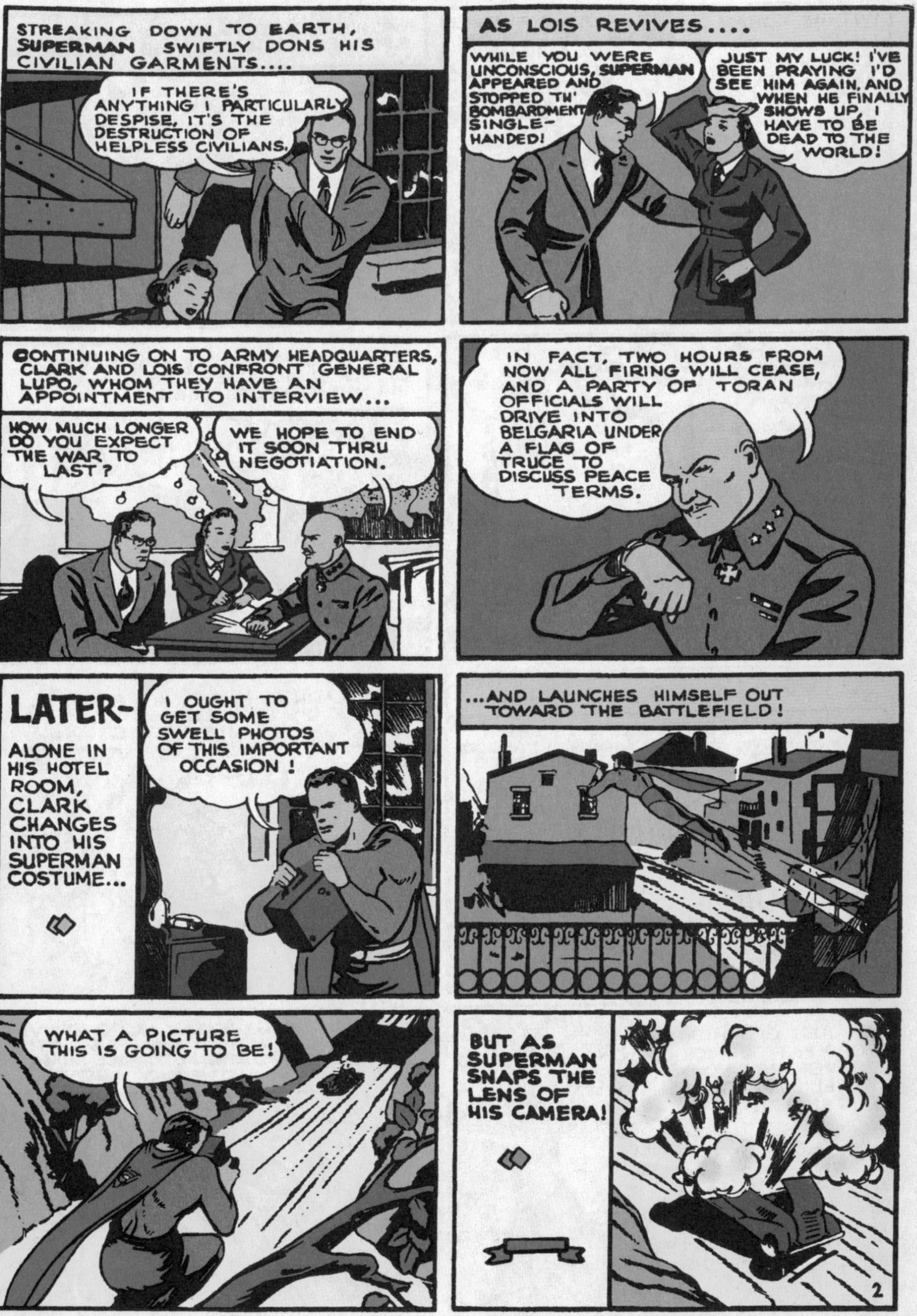
STREAKING DOWN TO EARTH, SUPERMAN SWIFTLY DONS HIS CIVILIAN GARMENTS....
IF THERE'S ANYTHING I PARTICULARLY DESPISE, IT'S THE DESTRUCTION OF HELPLESS CIVILIANS.
AS LOIS REVIVES....
WHILE YOU WERE UNCONSCIOUS, SUPERMAN APPEARED AND STOPPED TH' BOMBARDMENT SINGLE-HANDED!
JUST MY LUCK! I'VE BEEN PRAYING I'D SEE HIM AGAIN, AND WHEN HE FINALLY SHOWS UP, I HAVE TO BE DEAD TO THE WORLD!
CONTINUING ON TO ARMY HEADQUARTERS, CLARK AND LOIS CONFRONT GENERAL LUPO, WHOM THEY HAVE AN APPOINTMENT TO INTERVIEW...
HOW MUCH LONGER DO YOU EXPECT THE WAR TO LAST?
WE HOPE TO END IT SOON THRU NEGOTIATION.
IN FACT, TWO HOURS FROM NOW ALL FIRING WILL CEASE, AND A PARTY OF TORAN OFFICIALS WILL DRIVE INTO BELGARIA UNDER A FLAG OF TRUCE TO DISCUSS PEACE TERMS.
LATER-
ALONE IN HIS HOTEL ROOM, CLARK CHANGES INTO HIS SUPERMAN COSTUME...
I OUGHT TO GET SOME SWELL PHOTOS OF THIS IMPORTANT OCCASION!
...AND LAUNCHES HIMSELF OUT TOWARD THE BATTLEFIELD!
WHAT A PICTURE THIS IS GOING TO BE!
BUT AS SUPERMAN SNAPS THE LENS OF HIS CAMERA!
2

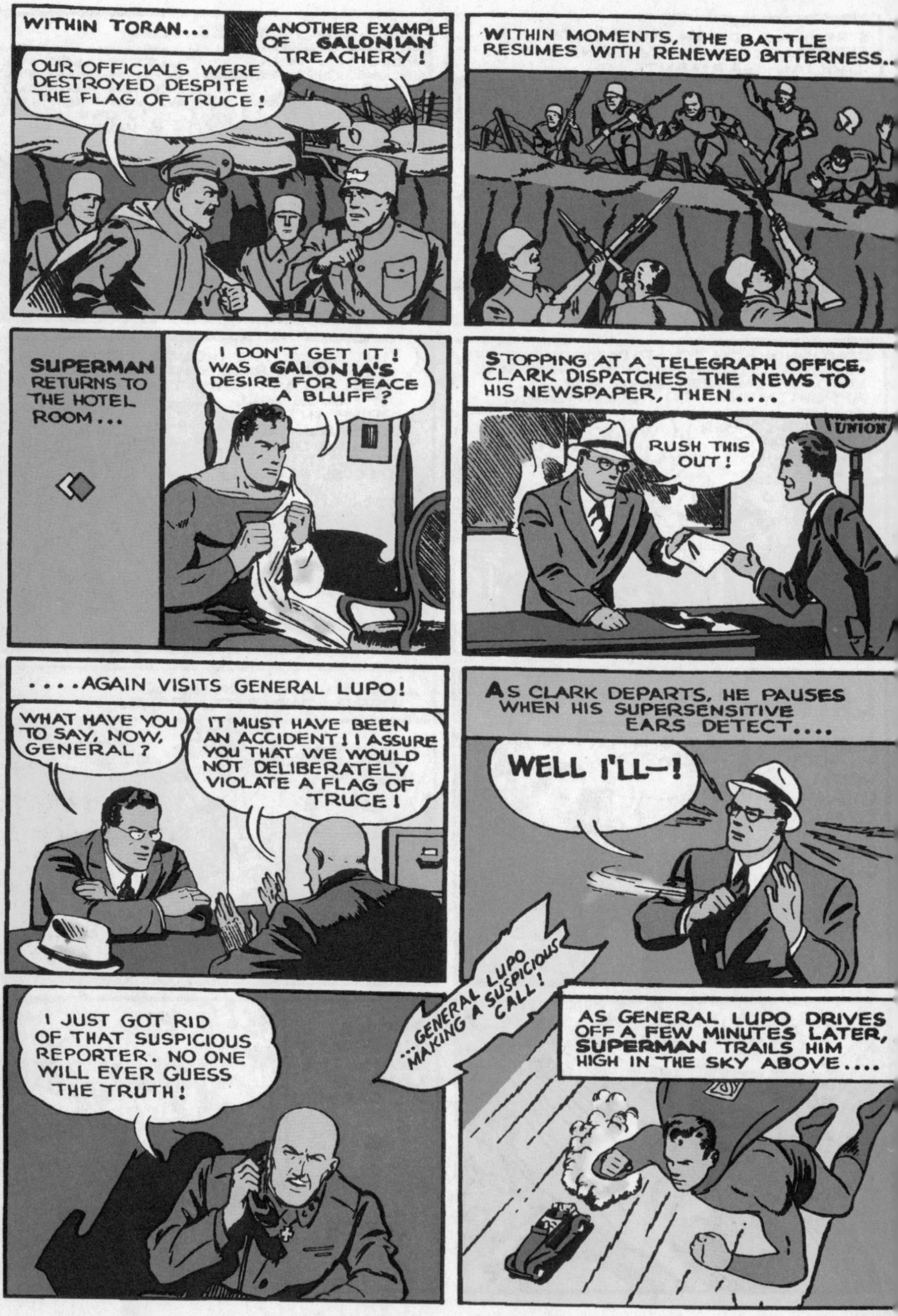
WITHIN TORAN...
OUR OFFICIALS WERE DESTROYED DESPITE THE FLAG OF TRUCE!
ANOTHER EXAMPLE OF GALONIAN TREACHERY!
WITHIN MOMENTS, THE BATTLE RESUMES WITH RENEWED BITTERNESS..
SUPERMAN RETURNS TO THE HOTEL ROOM...
I DON'T GET IT! WAS GALONIA'S DESIRE FOR PEACE A BLUFF?
STOPPING AT A TELEGRAPH OFFICE, CLARK DISPATCHES THE NEWS TO HIS NEWSPAPER, THEN....
RUSH THIS OUT!
UNION
....AGAIN VISITS GENERAL LUPO!
WHAT HAVE YOU TO SAY, NOW, GENERAL?
IT MUST HAVE BEEN AN ACCIDENT! I ASSURE YOU THAT WE WOULD NOT DELIBERATELY VIOLATE A FLAG OF TRUCE!
AS CLARK DEPARTS, HE PAUSES WHEN HIS SUPERSENSITIVE EARS DETECT....
WELL I'LL—!
...GENERAL LUPO MAKING A SUSPICIOUS CALL!
I JUST GOT RID OF THAT SUSPICIOUS REPORTER. NO ONE WILL EVER GUESS THE TRUTH!
AS GENERAL LUPO DRIVES OFF A FEW MINUTES LATER, SUPERMAN TRAILS HIM HIGH IN THE SKY ABOVE....

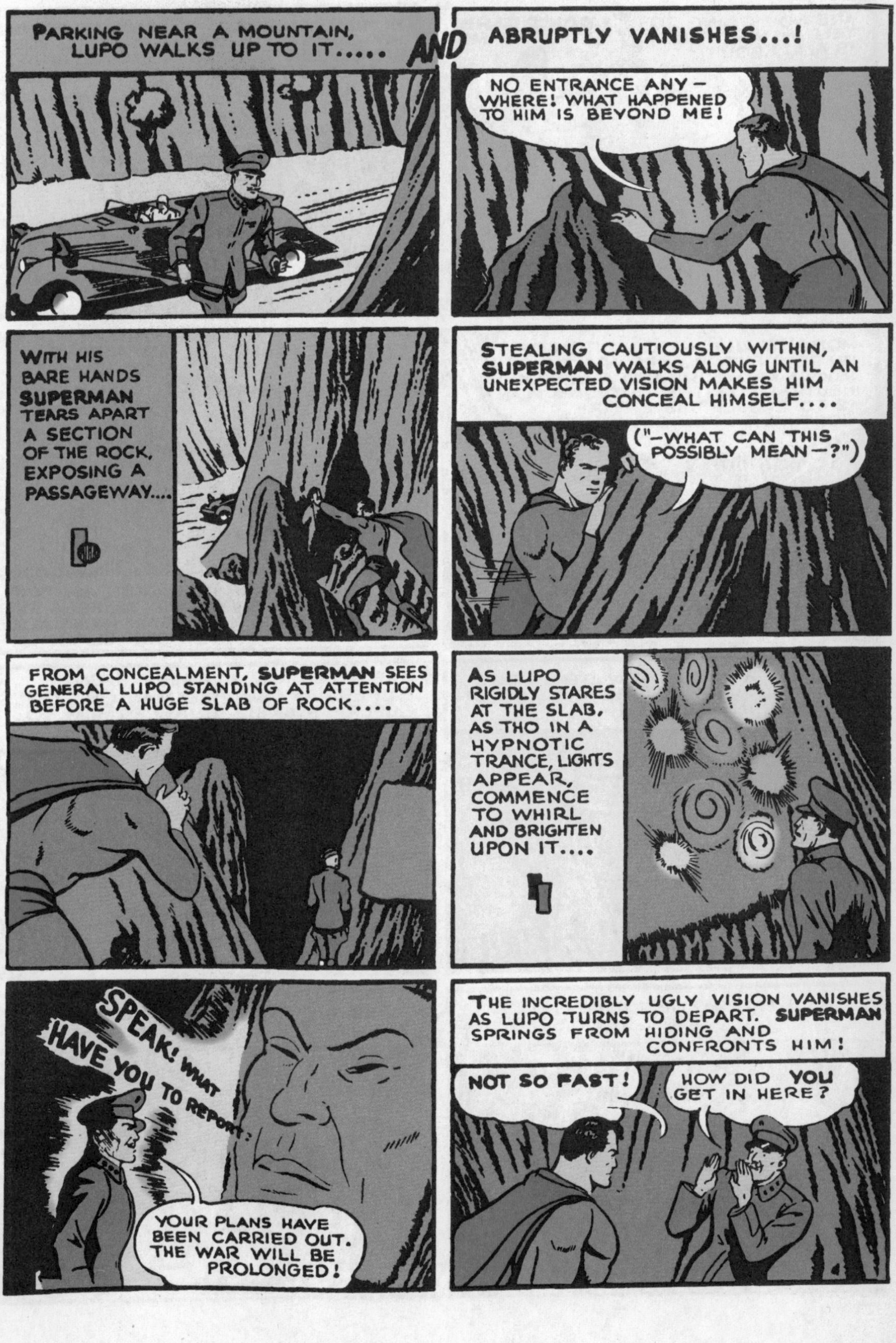
PARKING NEAR A MOUNTAIN, LUPO WALKS UP TO IT.....
AND
ABRUPTLY VANISHES...!
NO ENTRANCE ANY-WHERE! WHAT HAPPENED TO HIM IS BEYOND ME!
WITH HIS BARE HANDS SUPERMAN TEARS APART A SECTION OF THE ROCK, EXPOSING A PASSAGEWAY....
STEALING CAUTIOUSLY WITHIN, SUPERMAN WALKS ALONG UNTIL AN UNEXPECTED VISION MAKES HIM CONCEAL HIMSELF....
("-WHAT CAN THIS POSSIBLY MEAN-?")
FROM CONCEALMENT, SUPERMAN SEES GENERAL LUPO STANDING AT ATTENTION BEFORE A HUGE SLAB OF ROCK....
AS LUPO RIGIDLY STARES AT THE SLAB, AS THO IN A HYPNOTIC TRANCE, LIGHTS APPEAR, COMMENCE TO WHIRL AND BRIGHTEN UPON IT....
SPEAK! WHAT HAVE YOU TO REPORT?
YOUR PLANS HAVE BEEN CARRIED OUT. THE WAR WILL BE PROLONGED!
THE INCREDIBLY UGLY VISION VANISHES AS LUPO TURNS TO DEPART. SUPERMAN SPRINGS FROM HIDING AND CONFRONTS HIM!
NOT SO FAST!
HOW DID YOU GET IN HERE?

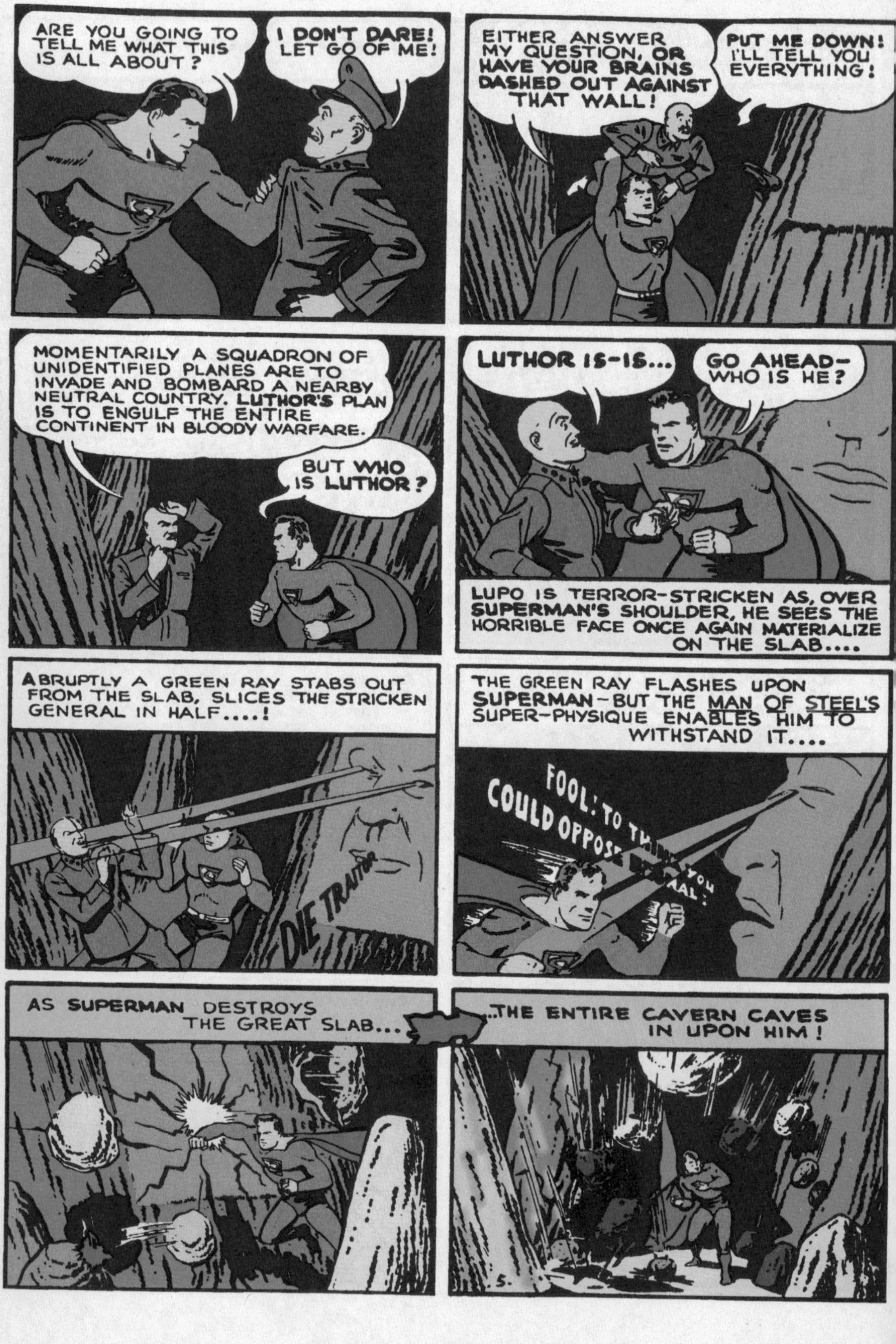
ARE YOU GOING TO TELL ME WHAT THIS IS ALL ABOUT?
I DON'T DARE! LET GO OF ME!
EITHER ANSWER MY QUESTION, OR HAVE YOUR BRAINS DASHED OUT AGAINST THAT WALL!
PUT ME DOWN! I'LL TELL YOU EVERYTHING!
MOMENTARILY A SQUADRON OF UNIDENTIFIED PLANES ARE TO INVADE AND BOMBARD A NEARBY NEUTRAL COUNTRY. LUTHOR'S PLAN IS TO ENGULF THE ENTIRE CONTINENT IN BLOODY WARFARE.
BUT WHO IS LUTHOR?
LUTHOR IS-IS...
GO AHEAD- WHO IS HE?
LUPO IS TERROR-STRICKEN AS, OVER SUPERMAN'S SHOULDER, HE SEES THE HORRIBLE FACE ONCE AGAIN MATERIALIZE ON THE SLAB....
ABRUPTLY A GREEN RAY STABS OUT FROM THE SLAB, SLICES THE STRICKEN GENERAL IN HALF....!
DIE TRAITOR
THE GREEN RAY FLASHES UPON SUPERMAN—BUT THE MAN OF STEEL'S SUPER-PHYSIQUE ENABLES HIM TO WITHSTAND IT....
FOOL! TO
COULD OPPOSE
YOU
AS SUPERMAN DESTROYS THE GREAT SLAB...
...THE ENTIRE CAVERN CAVES IN UPON HIM!
5.

AVAILING HIMSELF OF HIS INCREDIBLE STRENGTH, SUPERMAN FLAILS ABOUT....

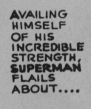

...AND SUCCEEDS IN BURROWING HIS WAY OUT INTO THE SUNLIGHT!

A SQUADRON OF UNIDENTIFIED BOMBERS — HEADED TOWARD THE NEUTRAL NATION!

AS THE HINDMOST BOMBER SIGHTS SUPERMAN'S FIGURE SUSPENDED IN THE EMPTY AIR BEFORE HIM, THE GUNNER FRANTICALLY ATTEMPTS TO SHOOT HIM DOWN...

A MAN — IN THE SKY — IMPOSSIBLE!

OUT YOU GO! ODD — YOUR UNIFORM IS ENTIRELY UNFAMILIAR!

AS THE REMAINDER OF THE SQUADRON SWOOPS AT HIM, SUPERMAN SHOOTS DOWN TWO OF THEM....

OUT OF AMMUNITION! NOW TO SET THE CONTROLS...

CLIMBING OUT UPON THE PLANE'S WING, SUPERMAN PLUCKS TWO OF THE PLANES OUT OF THE AIR AND SMASHES THEM TOGETHER...!

JUST ONE MORE ENEMY PLANE TO GO!

CRASH!

6.

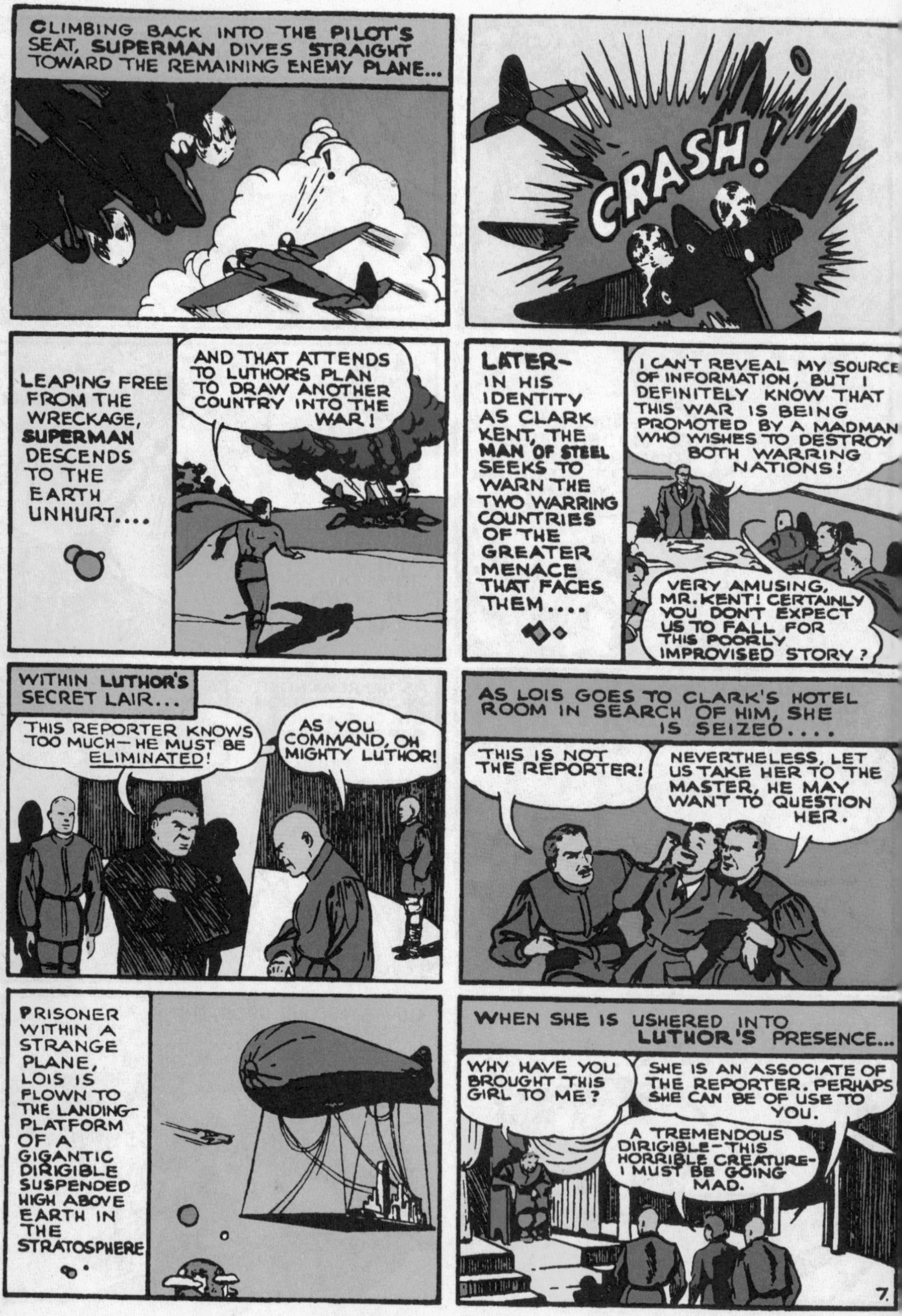

CLIMBING BACK INTO THE PILOT'S SEAT, SUPERMAN DIVES STRAIGHT TOWARD THE REMAINING ENEMY PLANE...
CRASH!
LEAPING FREE FROM THE WRECKAGE, SUPERMAN DESCENDS TO THE EARTH UNHURT....
AND THAT ATTENDS TO LUTHOR'S PLAN TO DRAW ANOTHER COUNTRY INTO THE WAR!
LATER- IN HIS IDENTITY AS CLARK KENT, THE MAN OF STEEL SEEKS TO WARN THE TWO WARRING COUNTRIES OF THE GREATER MENACE THAT FACES THEM....
I CAN'T REVEAL MY SOURCE OF INFORMATION, BUT I DEFINITELY KNOW THAT THIS WAR IS BEING PROMOTED BY A MADMAN WHO WISHES TO DESTROY BOTH WARRING NATIONS!
VERY AMUSING, MR. KENT! CERTAINLY YOU DON'T EXPECT US TO FALL FOR THIS POORLY IMPROVISED STORY?
WITHIN LUTHOR'S SECRET LAIR...
THIS REPORTER KNOWS TOO MUCH— HE MUST BE ELIMINATED!
AS YOU COMMAND, OH MIGHTY LUTHOR!
AS LOIS GOES TO CLARK'S HOTEL ROOM IN SEARCH OF HIM, SHE IS SEIZED....
THIS IS NOT THE REPORTER!
NEVERTHELESS, LET US TAKE HER TO THE MASTER, HE MAY WANT TO QUESTION HER.
PRISONER WITHIN A STRANGE PLANE, LOIS IS FLOWN TO THE LANDING-PLATFORM OF A GIGANTIC DIRIGIBLE SUSPENDED HIGH ABOVE EARTH IN THE STRATOSPHERE
WHEN SHE IS USHERED INTO LUTHOR'S PRESENCE...
WHY HAVE YOU BROUGHT THIS GIRL TO ME?
SHE IS AN ASSOCIATE OF THE REPORTER. PERHAPS SHE CAN BE OF USE TO YOU.
A TREMENDOUS DIRIGIBLE—THIS HORRIBLE CREATURE— I MUST BE GOING MAD.
7.

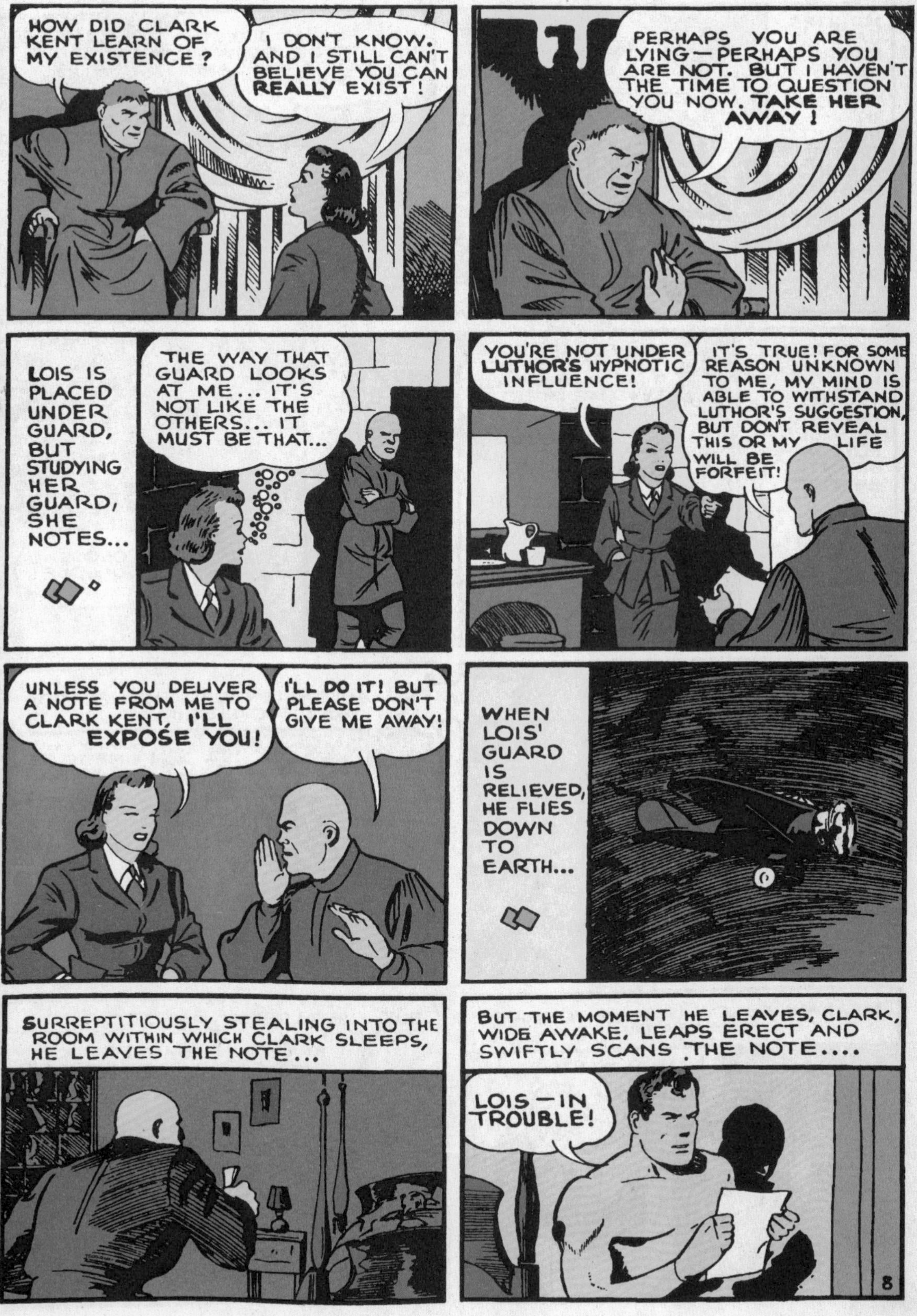

HOW DID CLARK KENT LEARN OF MY EXISTENCE?
I DON'T KNOW. AND I STILL CAN'T BELIEVE YOU CAN REALLY EXIST!
PERHAPS YOU ARE LYING—PERHAPS YOU ARE NOT. BUT I HAVEN'T THE TIME TO QUESTION YOU NOW. TAKE HER AWAY!
LOIS IS PLACED UNDER GUARD, BUT STUDYING HER GUARD, SHE NOTES...
THE WAY THAT GUARD LOOKS AT ME... IT'S NOT LIKE THE OTHERS... IT MUST BE THAT...
YOU'RE NOT UNDER LUTHOR'S HYPNOTIC INFLUENCE!
IT'S TRUE! FOR SOME REASON UNKNOWN TO ME, MY MIND IS ABLE TO WITHSTAND LUTHOR'S SUGGESTION, BUT DON'T REVEAL THIS OR MY LIFE WILL BE FORFEIT!
UNLESS YOU DELIVER A NOTE FROM ME TO CLARK KENT, I'LL EXPOSE YOU!
I'LL DO IT! BUT PLEASE DON'T GIVE ME AWAY!
WHEN LOIS' GUARD IS RELIEVED, HE FLIES DOWN TO EARTH...
SURREPTITIOUSLY STEALING INTO THE ROOM WITHIN WHICH CLARK SLEEPS, HE LEAVES THE NOTE...
BUT THE MOMENT HE LEAVES, CLARK, WIDE AWAKE, LEAPS ERECT AND SWIFTLY SCANS THE NOTE....
LOIS—IN TROUBLE!
8

MINUTES LATER, **SUPERMAN** LEAPS FROM THE HOTEL IN PURSUIT OF THE FLEEING GUARD...

HE'S FLYING DIRECTLY UP INTO THE SKY AT A STRAIGHT ANGLE, AND OUT OF VIEW!

SUPERMAN CROUCHES AND TENSES HIS MUSCLES FOR A GIGANTIC EFFORT...

MY GUESS IS THAT FOLLOWING THAT PLANE WILL LEAD ME DIRECTLY TO LOIS!

...STEELY MUSCLES PROPEL **SUPERMAN** UP—UP—INTO THE STRATO-SPHERE...

A COLOSSAL DIRIGIBLE!

CATCHING ONTO THE LANDING PLATFORM'S EDGE WITH ONE HAND, **SUPERMAN** DRAWS HIMSELF UP...

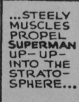
...AND ATTENDS TO TWO GUARDS WHO DISCOVER HIM!

RACK!

SORRY— NO TIME TO BE GENTLE!

MEANWHILE—LOIS IS BEING TORTURED BY HER GUARD....

LUTHOR WANTS THE TRUTH FROM YOU!

BUT I'VE ALREADY TOLD YOU ALL I KNOW!

C'MON! TALK FAST!

9

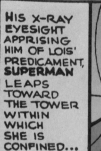

HIS X-RAY EYESIGHT APPRISING HIM OF LOIS' PREDICAMENT, **SUPERMAN** LEAPS TOWARD THE TOWER WITHIN WHICH SHE IS CONFINED...

I'LL ATTEND TO THAT BRUTE IN SHORT ORDER.

SUPERMAN!

HOW'S THAT!

QUICK! TAKE MY ARM—WE'VE GOT TO GET OUT OF HERE!

I'D ADVISE YOU NOT TO LEAVE!

I DON'T FEAR YOU—YOU CAN'T HARM ME!

BUT THE GIRL—SHE IS NOT INVULNERABLE! EITHER SUBMIT OR SHE DIES!

FOR LOIS' SAKE, **SUPERMAN** PERMITS THE GIRL AND HIMSELF TO BE ESCORTED BY GUARDS INTO LUTHOR'S PRESENCE...

KEEP YOUR CHIN UP!

WITH YOU NEARBY, I'VE NOTHING TO FEAR!

WHAT SORT OF CREATURE ARE YOU?

JUST AN ORDINARY MAN—BUT WITH TH' BRAIN OF A SUPER-GENIUS! WITH SCIENTIFIC MIRACLES AT MY FINGERTIPS, I'M PREPARING TO MAKE MYSELF SUPREME MASTER OF TH' WORLD!

MY PLAN? TO SEND THE NATIONS OF THE EARTH AT EACH OTHER'S THROATS, SO THAT WHEN THEY ARE SUFFICIENTLY WEAKENED, I CAN STEP IN AND ASSUME CHARGE!

THE ONLY THING YOU SHOULD STEP INTO IS A STRAIGHT-JACKET!

ACCEDING TO LUTHOR'S DEMANDS, **SUPERMAN** PERMITS HIMSELF TO BE CHAINED TO THE WALL WHILE FOUR GREEN RAYS BORE STEADILY AT HIM....

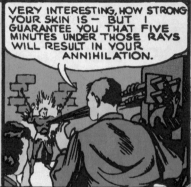

VERY INTERESTING, HOW STRONG YOUR SKIN IS — BUT I GUARANTEE YOU THAT FIVE MINUTES UNDER THOSE RAYS WILL RESULT IN YOUR ANNIHILATION.

10

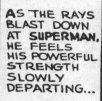

AS THE RAYS BLAST DOWN AT SUPERMAN, HE FEELS HIS POWERFUL STRENGTH SLOWLY DEPARTING...

SEE HOW I DESTROY MIGHTY SUPERMAN! NO ONE CAN STAND IN LUTHOR'S PATH—NO ONE!

BAH! I TIRE AT THE SLOW RATE OF DESTRUCTION! WITH THIS POWERFUL RAY, I'LL BLAST OUT CITIES IN MOMENTS!

BUT, BEFORE LUTHOR CAN PUT HIS GREAT RAY INTO OPERATION, SUPERMAN ACTS....

DUCK, LOIS!

CURSING, LUTHOR WHIRLS ANOTHER GREAT RAY UPON SUPERMAN, BLASTS IT FULL AT HIM....

NOW, DIE!

THAT RAY— IT'S SAPPING ALL MY STRENGTH!

SUMMONING UP HIS LAST BIT OF ENERGY, SUPERMAN CATAPULTS ACROSS THE ROOM AT THE RAY MACHINE, DESTROYING IT!

WHAM!

11.

42

DON'T HARM ME, AND I'LL GIVE YOU UNLIMITED RICHES!
I THOUGHT YOU'D PROVE YELLOW IF THE SITUATION WERE REVERSED!
WITH LOIS AND LUTHOR UNDER EACH ARM, SUPERMAN RACES THRU A CORRIDOR....
WHERE ARE YOU GOING?
TO THE DIRIGIBLE'S CONTROL ROOM!
WHEN THEY REACH THE CONTROL ROOM....
DESTROY HIM! BLOT HIM OUT!
YOU'RE WELCOME TO TRY!
THE GUARDS REACT AS THO THEY HAD ENCOUNTERED AN INDESTRUCTIBLE FORCE! EASILY, SUPERMAN SENDS THEM FLYING IN ALL DIRECTIONS....
LOOK— I'M JUGGLING!
TURNING FROM THE COWED GUARDS, SUPERMAN TURNS TO THE GREAT MECHANISM THAT KEEPS THE DIRIGIBLE AFLOAT...
...AND TEARS IT APART WITH HIS BARE HANDS!
AS THE GREAT DIRIGIBLE TOPPLES DOWN TOWARD THE DISTANT EARTH, TWO FIGURES SPRING FREE FROM IT.... SUPERMAN BEARING LOIS....
CA RASH!
12

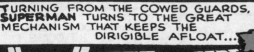

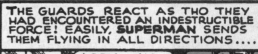

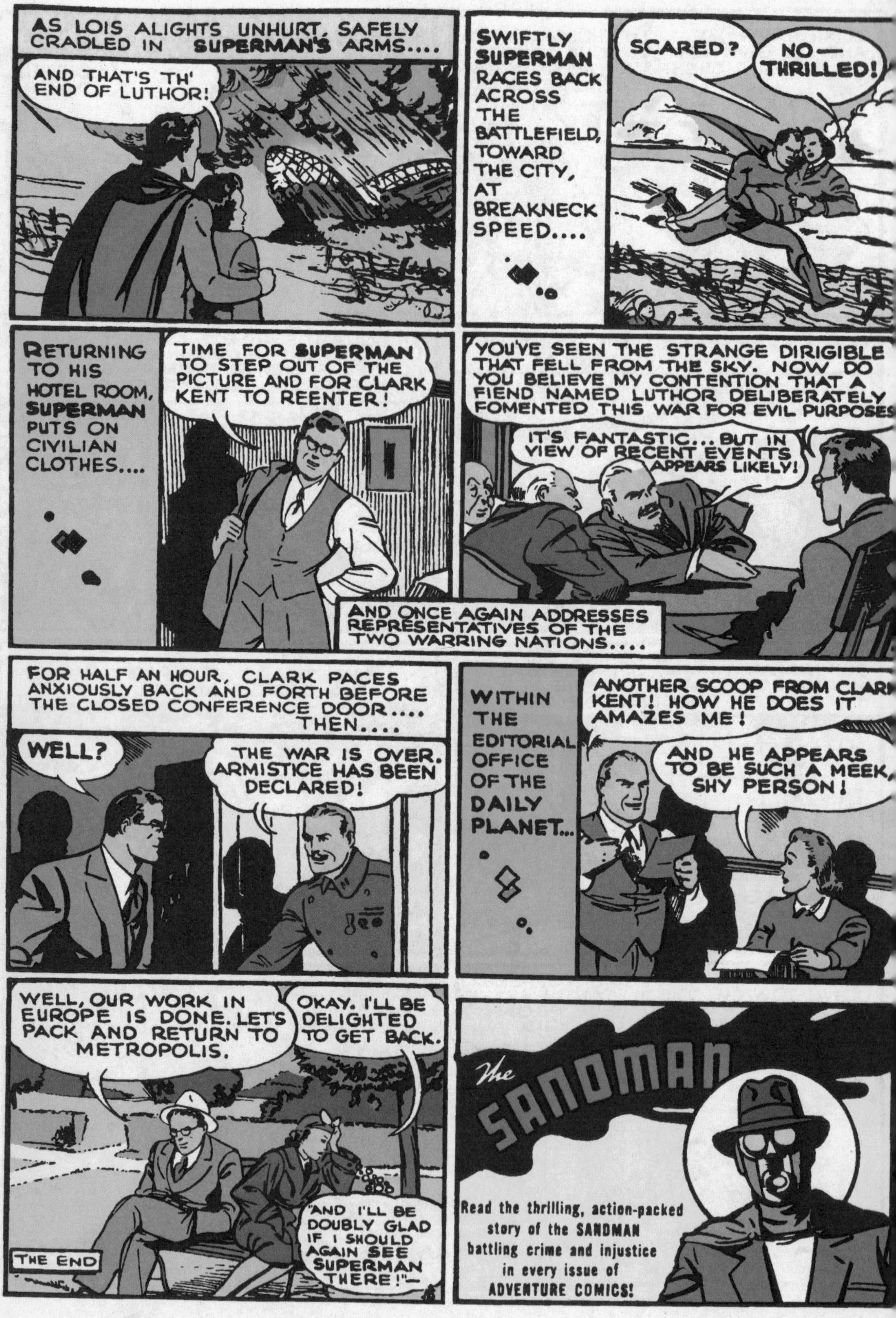
AS LOIS ALIGHTS UNHURT, SAFELY CRADLED IN SUPERMAN'S ARMS....
AND THAT'S TH' END OF LUTHOR!
SWIFTLY SUPERMAN RACES BACK ACROSS THE BATTLEFIELD, TOWARD THE CITY, AT BREAKNECK SPEED....
SCARED?
NO— THRILLED!
RETURNING TO HIS HOTEL ROOM, SUPERMAN PUTS ON CIVILIAN CLOTHES....
TIME FOR SUPERMAN TO STEP OUT OF THE PICTURE AND FOR CLARK KENT TO REENTER!
YOU'VE SEEN THE STRANGE DIRIGIBLE THAT FELL FROM THE SKY. NOW DO YOU BELIEVE MY CONTENTION THAT A FIEND NAMED LUTHOR DELIBERATELY FOMENTED THIS WAR FOR EVIL PURPOSES
IT'S FANTASTIC... BUT IN VIEW OF RECENT EVENTS APPEARS LIKELY!
AND ONCE AGAIN ADDRESSES REPRESENTATIVES OF THE TWO WARRING NATIONS....
FOR HALF AN HOUR, CLARK PACES ANXIOUSLY BACK AND FORTH BEFORE THE CLOSED CONFERENCE DOOR.... THEN....
WELL?
THE WAR IS OVER. ARMISTICE HAS BEEN DECLARED!
WITHIN THE EDITORIAL OFFICE OF THE DAILY PLANET...
ANOTHER SCOOP FROM CLARK KENT! HOW HE DOES IT AMAZES ME!
AND HE APPEARS TO BE SUCH A MEEK, SHY PERSON!
WELL, OUR WORK IN EUROPE IS DONE. LET'S PACK AND RETURN TO METROPOLIS.
OKAY. I'LL BE DELIGHTED TO GET BACK.
"AND I'LL BE DOUBLY GLAD IF I SHOULD AGAIN SEE SUPERMAN THERE!"—
THE END
The SANDMAN
Read the thrilling, action-packed story of the SANDMAN battling crime and injustice in every issue of ADVENTURE COMICS!

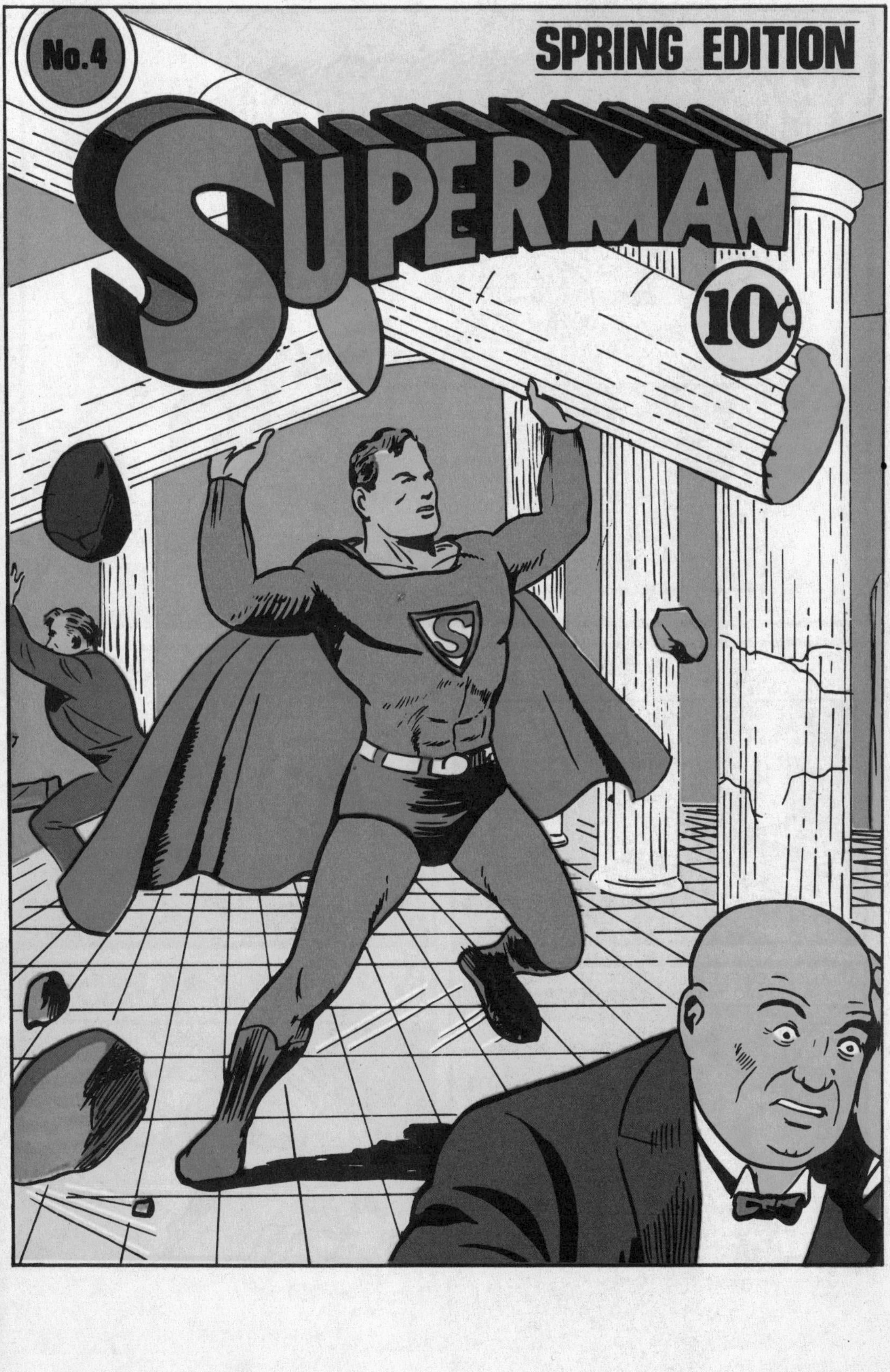
No. 4
SPRING EDITION
SUPERMAN
10¢

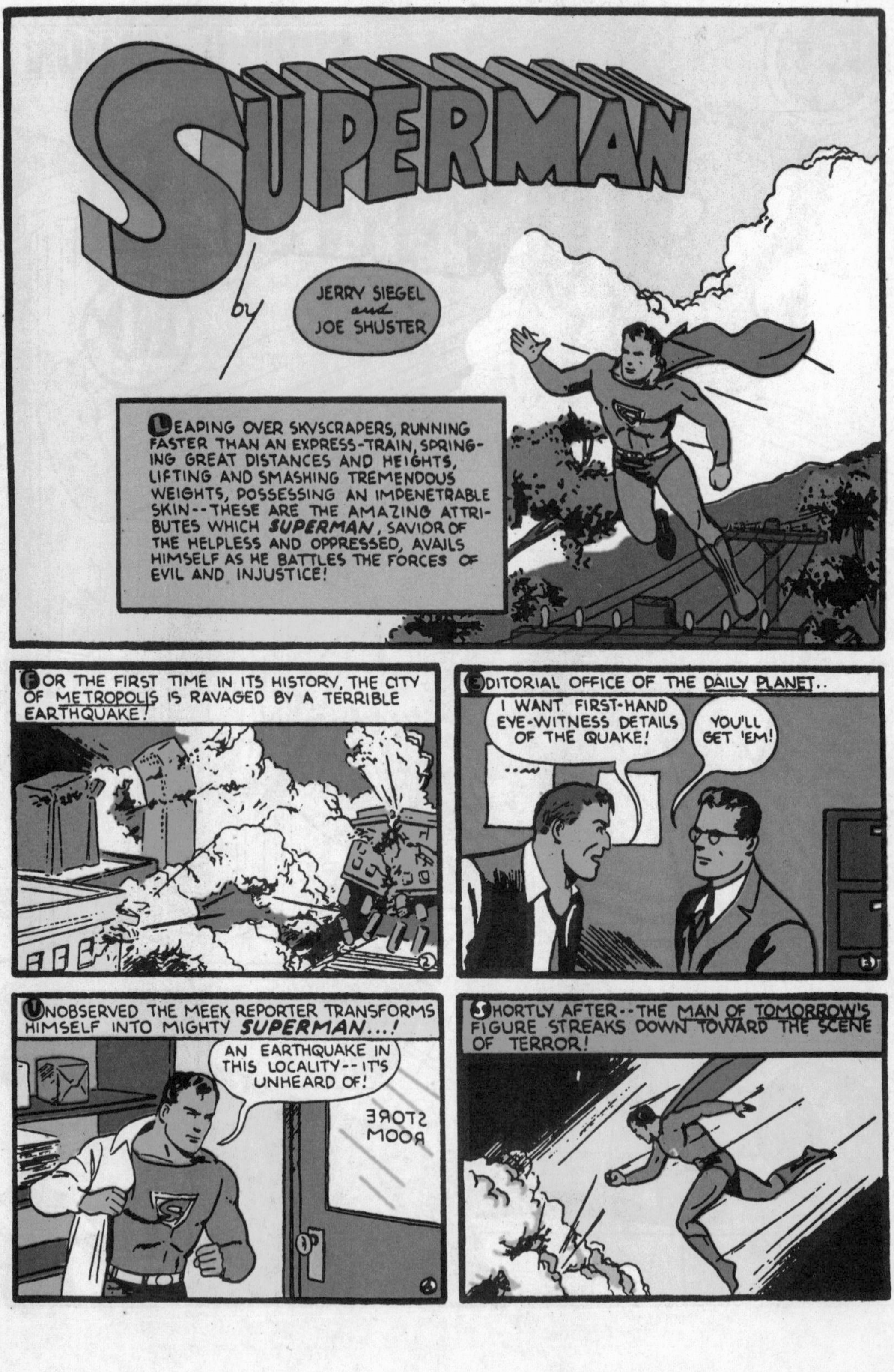
SUPERMAN
by
JERRY SIEGEL and JOE SHUSTER
LEAPING OVER SKYSCRAPERS, RUNNING FASTER THAN AN EXPRESS-TRAIN, SPRINGING GREAT DISTANCES AND HEIGHTS, LIFTING AND SMASHING TREMENDOUS WEIGHTS, POSSESSING AN IMPENETRABLE SKIN--THESE ARE THE AMAZING ATTRIBUTES WHICH SUPERMAN, SAVIOR OF THE HELPLESS AND OPPRESSED, AVAILS HIMSELF AS HE BATTLES THE FORCES OF EVIL AND INJUSTICE!
FOR THE FIRST TIME IN ITS HISTORY, THE CITY OF METROPOLIS IS RAVAGED BY A TERRIBLE EARTHQUAKE!
EDITORIAL OFFICE OF THE DAILY PLANET..
I WANT FIRST-HAND EYE-WITNESS DETAILS OF THE QUAKE!
YOU'LL GET 'EM!
UNOBSERVED THE MEEK REPORTER TRANSFORMS HIMSELF INTO MIGHTY SUPERMAN...!
AN EARTHQUAKE IN THIS LOCALITY--IT'S UNHEARD OF!
STORE ROOM
SHORTLY AFTER--THE MAN OF TOMORROW'S FIGURE STREAKS DOWN TOWARD THE SCENE OF TERROR!

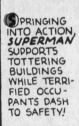SPRINGING INTO ACTION, *SUPERMAN* SUPPORTS TOTTERING BUILDINGS WHILE TERRIFIED OCCUPANTS DASH TO SAFETY!

HURRY! IT'LL GIVE WAY IN A FEW SECONDS!

HIS AMAZING STRENGTH AND SPEED BRINGING HIM TO WHEREVER THERE IS NEED OF HIS ASSISTANCE!

MY BOY-- PINNED UNDER THAT WRECKAGE!

HE'LL BE FREE IN A MOMENT!

WHEN THE EARTHQUAKE SUBSIDES, *SUPERMAN* LEAPS AWAY WITH THE GRATEFUL CHEER OF THOUSANDS RINGING IN HIS WAKE...!

LATER NICE ARTICLE YOU HANDED IN-- PARTICULARLY THE *SUPERMAN* ANGLE!

I'VE LEARNED THAT THE DISTURBANCE WAS CAUSED BY A NEW WEAPON THE ARMY IS TESTING WHICH ARTIFICIALLY CAUSES EARTHQUAKES. THE MACHINE RAN WILD DURING THE TEST. - I'LL VISIT ITS INVENTOR FOR AN INTERVIEW.

PROFESSOR MARTINSON? I'M CLARK KENT OF THE DAILY PLANET. HOW ABOUT A STORY CONCERNING YOUR NEW DISCOVERY!

I'D BE DELIGHTED!

CLARK SEATS HIMSELF. WHILE HIS BACK IS TURNED--

MEDDLER!

NOT A TICK! HE'S DONE FOR!

WHAT CLARK'S ASSAILANT DOES NOT REALIZE IS THAT KENT POSSESSES THE ABILITY TO TEMPORARILY HALT THE BEATING OF HIS HEART. CLARK IS PLAYING POSSUM TO LEARN WHAT THE SITUATION IS!

OUT YOU GO--TO A MANGLED DEATH!

Ⓓ OWN HURTLES THE REPORTER'S FIGURE--!

Ⓐ BRUPTLY--OUT FLASHES ONE OF HIS HANDS, CLUTCHING THE SIDE OF THE SKYSCRAPER IN A STEELY GRIP, HALTING HIS PLUNGE!

TIME OUT!

Ⓘ T TAKES BUT A FEW SECONDS TO REMOVE HIS OUTER GARMENTS.... THEN HE COMMENCES TO CLIMB SWIFTLY BACK TOWARD THE LABORATORY ---- AS *SUPERMAN!*

NOW IT'S *MY* TURN!

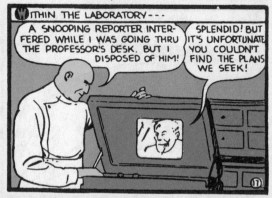

Ⓦ ITHIN THE LABORATORY ---

A SNOOPING REPORTER INTERFERED WHILE I WAS GOING THRU THE PROFESSOR'S DESK. BUT I DISPOSED OF HIM!

SPLENDID! BUT IT'S UNFORTUNATE YOU COULDN'T FIND THE PLANS WE SEEK!

Ⓐ T A DISTANT SPOT...

("-*SUPERMAN* EAVESDROPPING! I'LL ATTEND TO HIM!-")

Ⓢ HORTLY AFTER--A WEIRD PLANE APPEARS IN THE SKY AND RELEASES A DEADLY BOMB DOWN TOWARD THE MAN OF STEEL'S FIGURE...

THIS HAS GOT TO STOP BEFORE BOMBS FALL ON INNOCENT PEOPLE IN THE STREET!

Ⓐ FLIP OF *SUPERMAN'S* WRIST, AND THE BOMB HURTLES BACK TO ITS SOURCE, DESTROYING THE PLANE!

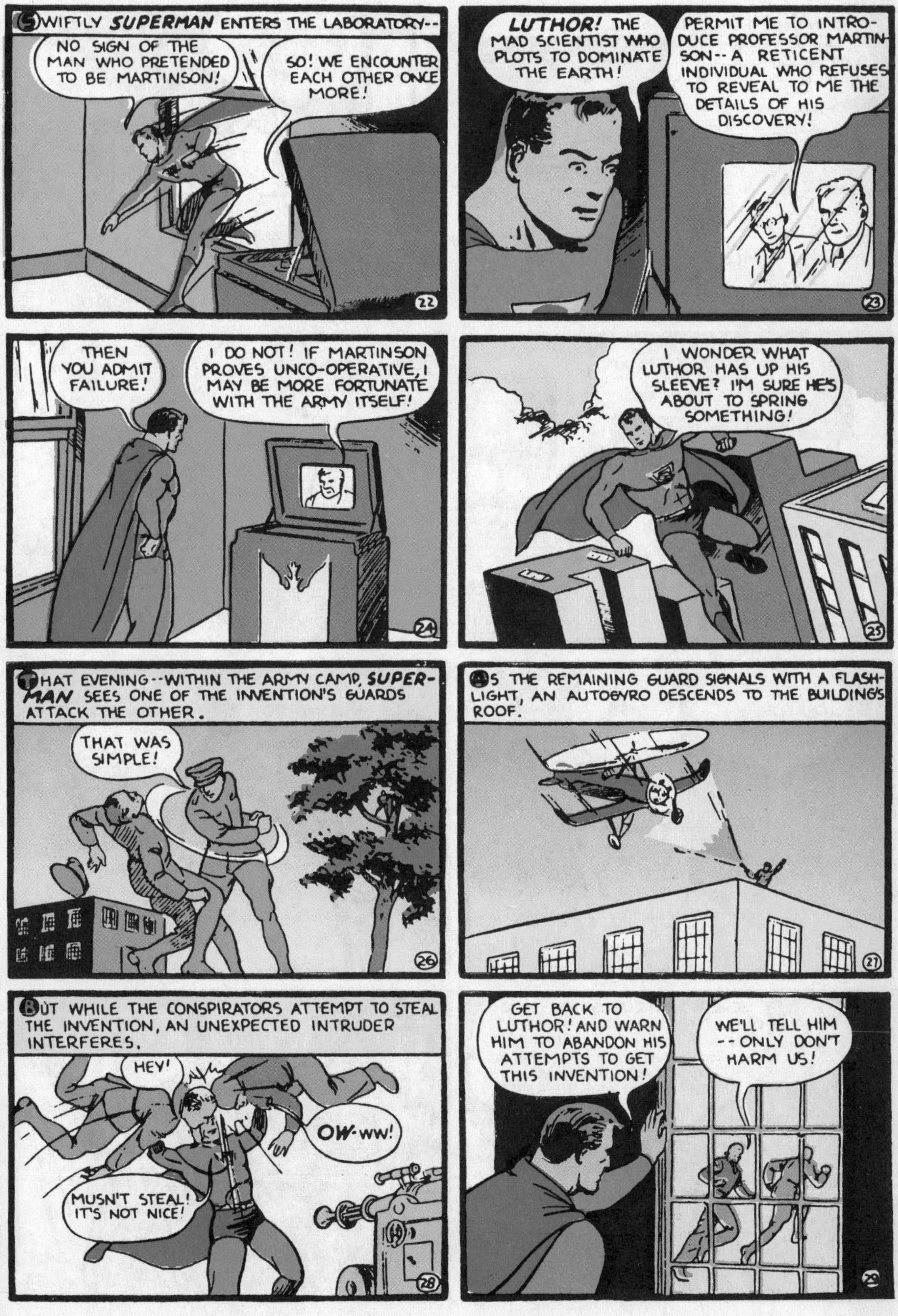
SWIFTLY SUPERMAN ENTERS THE LABORATORY--
NO SIGN OF THE MAN WHO PRETENDED TO BE MARTINSON!
SO! WE ENCOUNTER EACH OTHER ONCE MORE!
22
LUTHOR! THE MAD SCIENTIST WHO PLOTS TO DOMINATE THE EARTH!
PERMIT ME TO INTRODUCE PROFESSOR MARTINSON-- A RETICENT INDIVIDUAL WHO REFUSES TO REVEAL TO ME THE DETAILS OF HIS DISCOVERY!
23
THEN YOU ADMIT FAILURE!
I DO NOT! IF MARTINSON PROVES UNCO-OPERATIVE, I MAY BE MORE FORTUNATE WITH THE ARMY ITSELF!
24
I WONDER WHAT LUTHOR HAS UP HIS SLEEVE? I'M SURE HE'S ABOUT TO SPRING SOMETHING!
25
THAT EVENING--WITHIN THE ARMY CAMP, SUPERMAN SEES ONE OF THE INVENTION'S GUARDS ATTACK THE OTHER.
THAT WAS SIMPLE!
26
AS THE REMAINING GUARD SIGNALS WITH A FLASHLIGHT, AN AUTOGYRO DESCENDS TO THE BUILDING'S ROOF.
27
BUT WHILE THE CONSPIRATORS ATTEMPT TO STEAL THE INVENTION, AN UNEXPECTED INTRUDER INTERFERES.
HEY!
OW-WW!
MUSN'T STEAL! IT'S NOT NICE!
28
GET BACK TO LUTHOR! AND WARN HIM TO ABANDON HIS ATTEMPTS TO GET THIS INVENTION!
WE'LL TELL HIM -- ONLY DON'T HARM US!
29

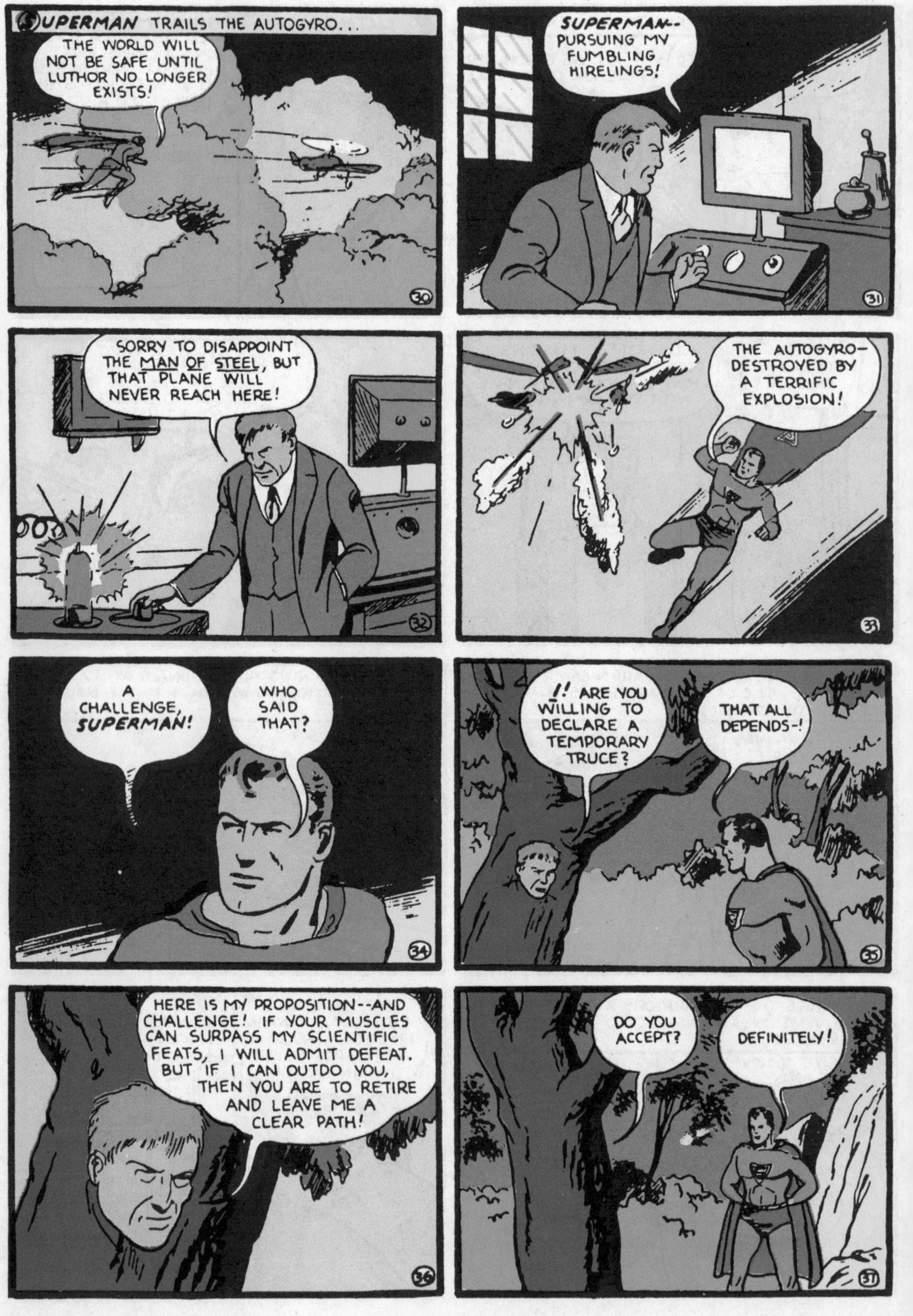
SUPERMAN TRAILS THE AUTOGYRO...
THE WORLD WILL NOT BE SAFE UNTIL LUTHOR NO LONGER EXISTS!
30
SUPERMAN-- PURSUING MY FUMBLING HIRELINGS!
31
SORRY TO DISAPPOINT THE MAN OF STEEL, BUT THAT PLANE WILL NEVER REACH HERE!
32
THE AUTOGYRO-DESTROYED BY A TERRIFIC EXPLOSION!
33
A CHALLENGE, SUPERMAN!
WHO SAID THAT?
34
!! ARE YOU WILLING TO DECLARE A TEMPORARY TRUCE?
THAT ALL DEPENDS-!
35
HERE IS MY PROPOSITION--AND CHALLENGE! IF YOUR MUSCLES CAN SURPASS MY SCIENTIFIC FEATS, I WILL ADMIT DEFEAT. BUT IF I CAN OUTDO YOU, THEN YOU ARE TO RETIRE AND LEAVE ME A CLEAR PATH!
36
DO YOU ACCEPT?
DEFINITELY!
37

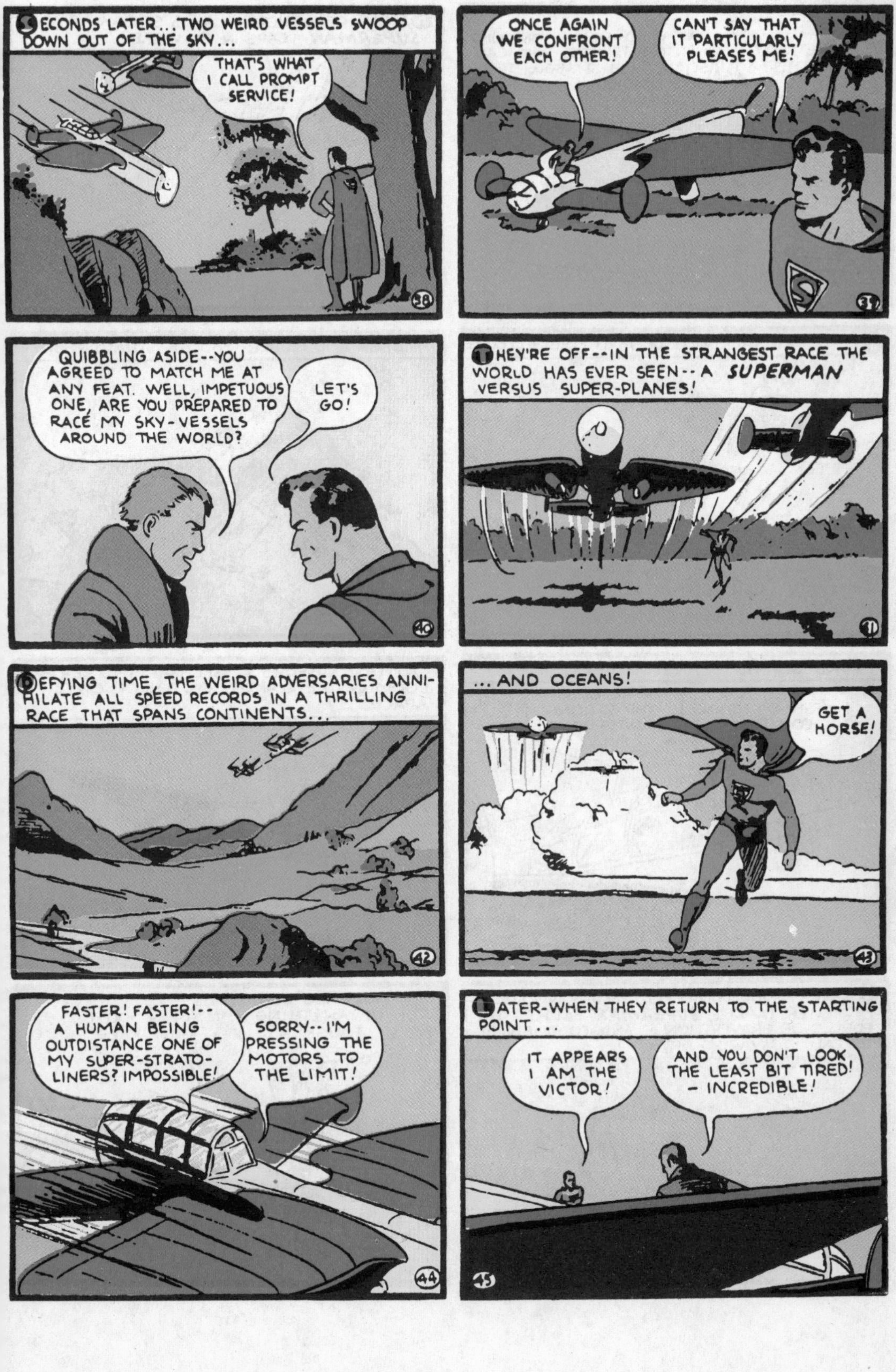
SECONDS LATER...TWO WEIRD VESSELS SWOOP DOWN OUT OF THE SKY...
THAT'S WHAT I CALL PROMPT SERVICE!
38
ONCE AGAIN WE CONFRONT EACH OTHER!
CAN'T SAY THAT IT PARTICULARLY PLEASES ME!
39
QUIBBLING ASIDE--YOU AGREED TO MATCH ME AT ANY FEAT. WELL, IMPETUOUS ONE, ARE YOU PREPARED TO RACE MY SKY-VESSELS AROUND THE WORLD?
LET'S GO!
40
THEY'RE OFF--IN THE STRANGEST RACE THE WORLD HAS EVER SEEN--A SUPERMAN VERSUS SUPER-PLANES!
41
DEFYING TIME, THE WEIRD ADVERSARIES ANNIHILATE ALL SPEED RECORDS IN A THRILLING RACE THAT SPANS CONTINENTS...
42
...AND OCEANS!
GET A HORSE!
43
FASTER! FASTER!--A HUMAN BEING OUTDISTANCE ONE OF MY SUPER-STRATO-LINERS? IMPOSSIBLE!
SORRY--I'M PRESSING THE MOTORS TO THE LIMIT!
44
LATER-WHEN THEY RETURN TO THE STARTING POINT...
IT APPEARS I AM THE VICTOR!
AND YOU DON'T LOOK THE LEAST BIT TIRED! - INCREDIBLE!
45

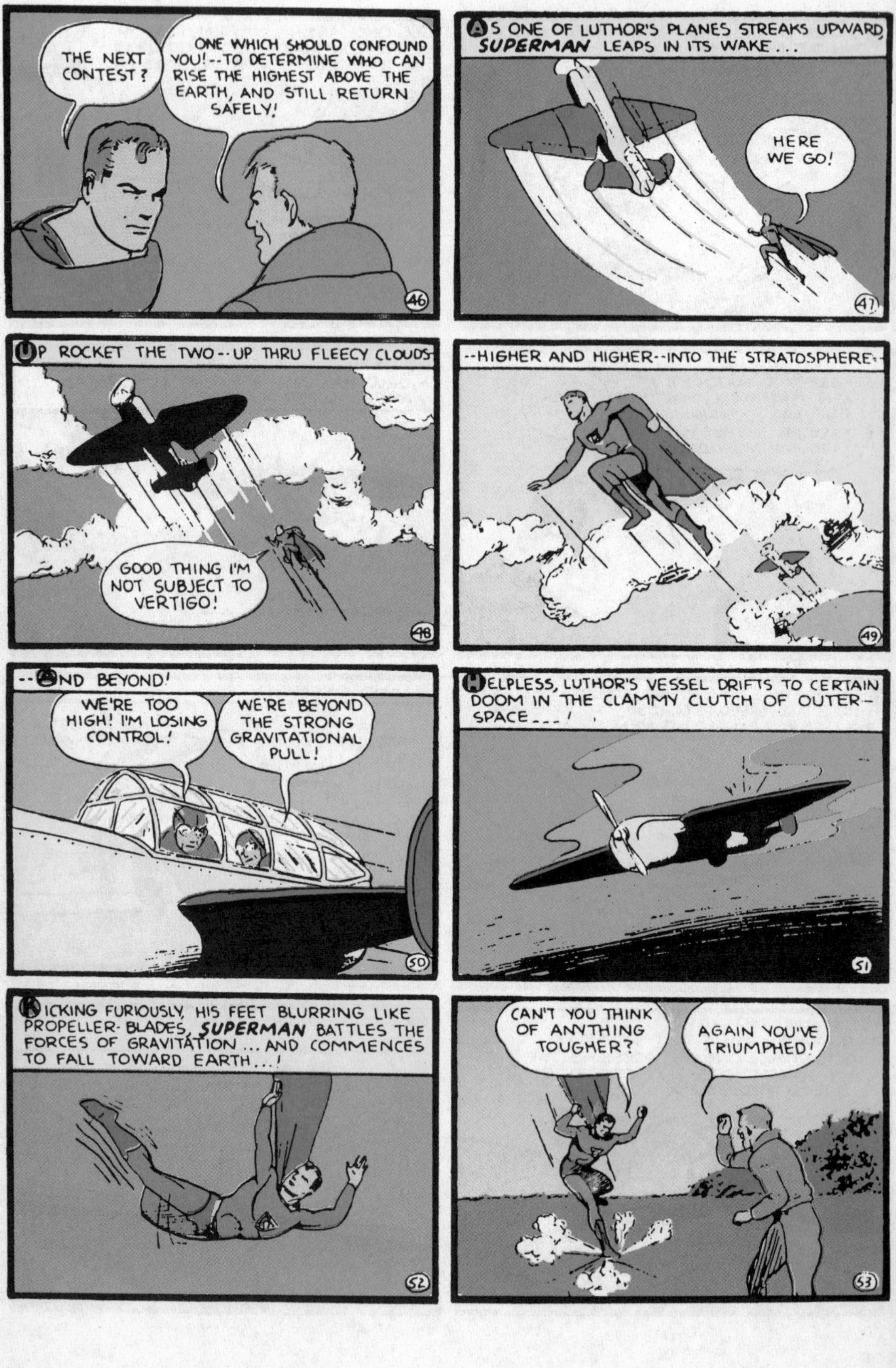
THE NEXT CONTEST?
ONE WHICH SHOULD CONFOUND YOU!--TO DETERMINE WHO CAN RISE THE HIGHEST ABOVE THE EARTH, AND STILL RETURN SAFELY!
46
AS ONE OF LUTHOR'S PLANES STREAKS UPWARD, SUPERMAN LEAPS IN ITS WAKE...
HERE WE GO!
47
UP ROCKET THE TWO--UP THRU FLEECY CLOUDS-
GOOD THING I'M NOT SUBJECT TO VERTIGO!
48
--HIGHER AND HIGHER--INTO THE STRATOSPHERE--
49
--AND BEYOND!
WE'RE TOO HIGH! I'M LOSING CONTROL!
WE'RE BEYOND THE STRONG GRAVITATIONAL PULL!
50
HELPLESS, LUTHOR'S VESSEL DRIFTS TO CERTAIN DOOM IN THE CLAMMY CLUTCH OF OUTER-SPACE...!
51
KICKING FURIOUSLY, HIS FEET BLURRING LIKE PROPELLER-BLADES, SUPERMAN BATTLES THE FORCES OF GRAVITATION... AND COMMENCES TO FALL TOWARD EARTH...!
52
CAN'T YOU THINK OF ANYTHING TOUGHER?
AGAIN YOU'VE TRIUMPHED!
53

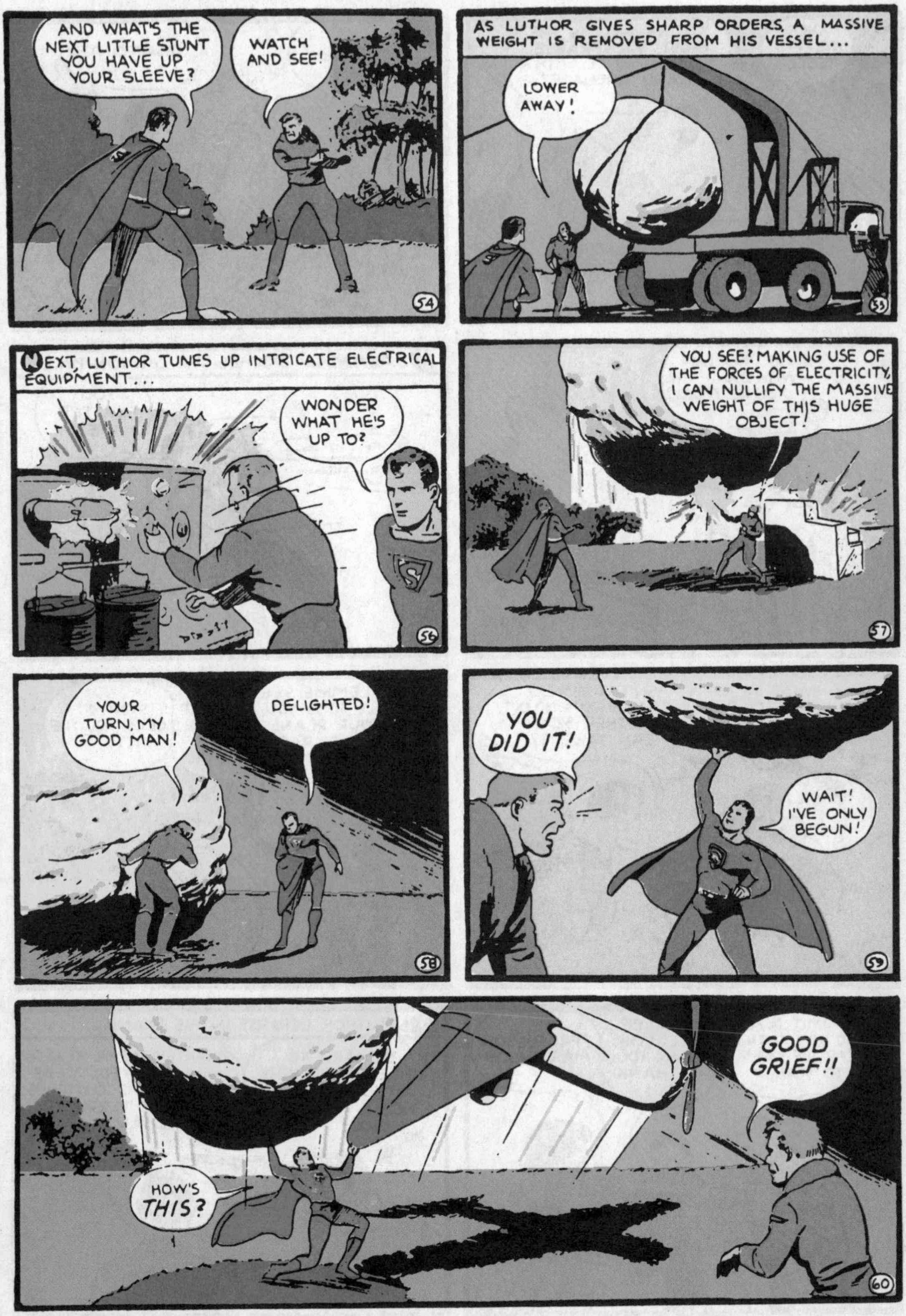
AND WHAT'S THE NEXT LITTLE STUNT YOU HAVE UP YOUR SLEEVE?
WATCH AND SEE!
54
AS LUTHOR GIVES SHARP ORDERS, A MASSIVE WEIGHT IS REMOVED FROM HIS VESSEL...
LOWER AWAY!
55
NEXT, LUTHOR TUNES UP INTRICATE ELECTRICAL EQUIPMENT...
WONDER WHAT HE'S UP TO?
56
YOU SEE? MAKING USE OF THE FORCES OF ELECTRICITY, I CAN NULLIFY THE MASSIVE WEIGHT OF THIS HUGE OBJECT!
57
YOUR TURN, MY GOOD MAN!
DELIGHTED!
58
YOU DID IT!
WAIT! I'VE ONLY BEGUN!
59
GOOD GRIEF!!
HOW'S THIS?
60

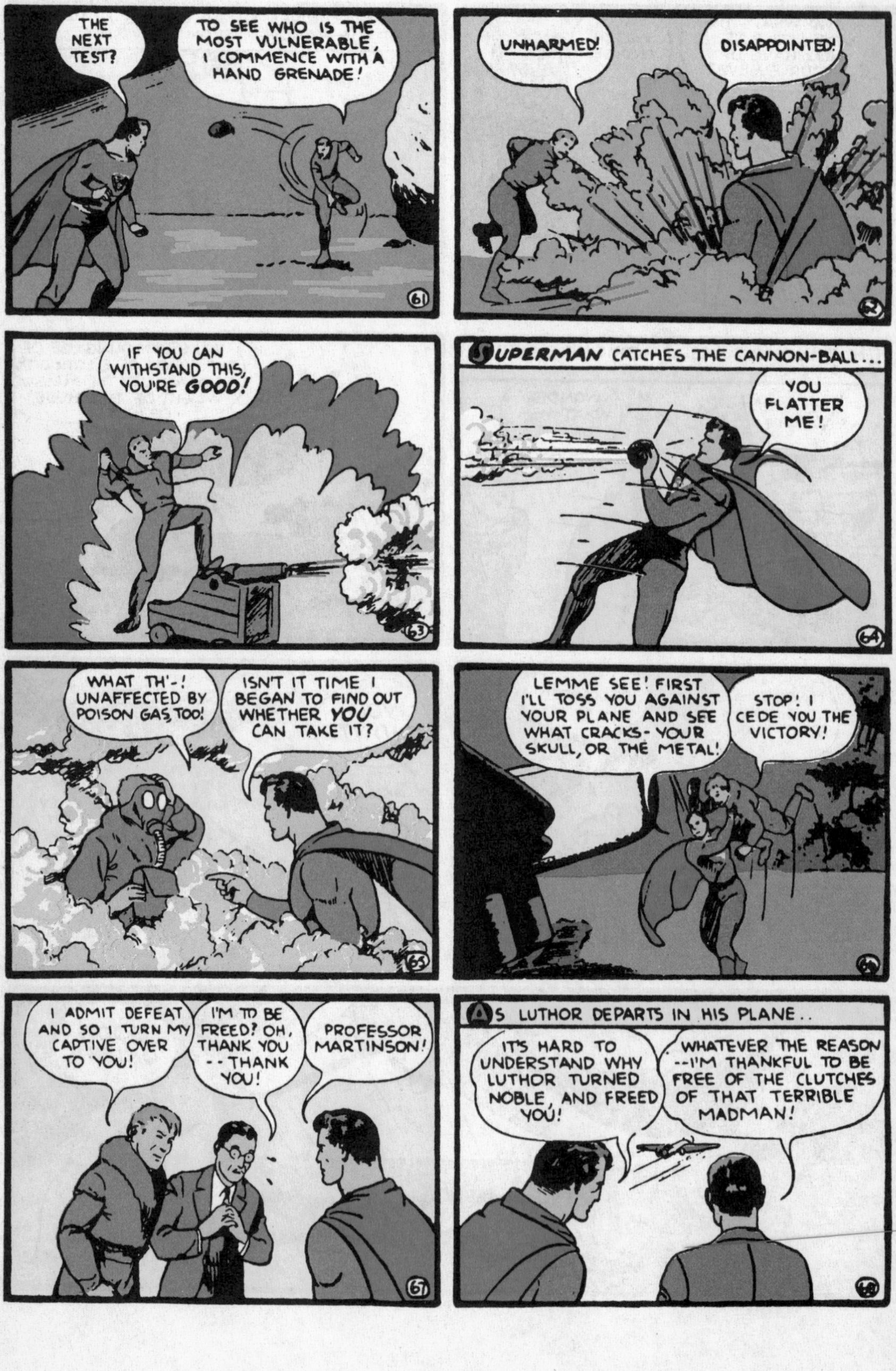
THE NEXT TEST?
TO SEE WHO IS THE MOST VULNERABLE, I COMMENCE WITH A HAND GRENADE!
61
UNHARMED!
DISAPPOINTED!
62
IF YOU CAN WITHSTAND THIS, YOU'RE GOOD!
63
SUPERMAN CATCHES THE CANNON-BALL...
YOU FLATTER ME!
64
WHAT TH'-! UNAFFECTED BY POISON GAS, TOO!
ISN'T IT TIME I BEGAN TO FIND OUT WHETHER YOU CAN TAKE IT?
65
LEMME SEE! FIRST I'LL TOSS YOU AGAINST YOUR PLANE AND SEE WHAT CRACKS- YOUR SKULL, OR THE METAL!
STOP! I CEDE YOU THE VICTORY!
66
I ADMIT DEFEAT AND SO I TURN MY CAPTIVE OVER TO YOU!
I'M TO BE FREED? OH, THANK YOU --THANK YOU!
PROFESSOR MARTINSON!
67
AS LUTHOR DEPARTS IN HIS PLANE..
IT'S HARD TO UNDERSTAND WHY LUTHOR TURNED NOBLE, AND FREED YOU!
WHATEVER THE REASON --I'M THANKFUL TO BE FREE OF THE CLUTCHES OF THAT TERRIBLE MADMAN!
68

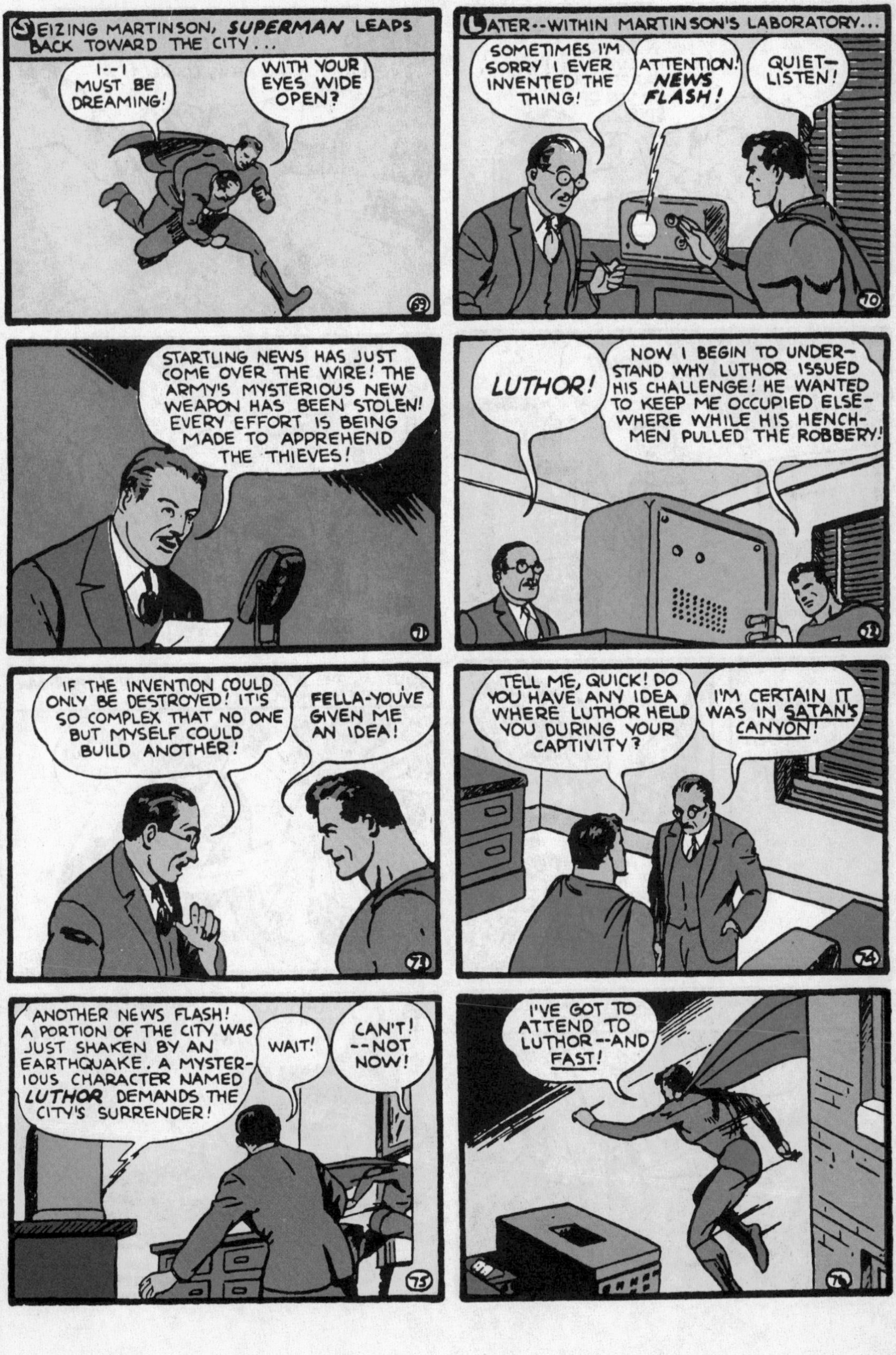
SEIZING MARTINSON, SUPERMAN LEAPS BACK TOWARD THE CITY...
I--I MUST BE DREAMING!
WITH YOUR EYES WIDE OPEN?
LATER--WITHIN MARTINSON'S LABORATORY...
SOMETIMES I'M SORRY I EVER INVENTED THE THING!
ATTENTION! NEWS FLASH!
QUIET-LISTEN!
STARTLING NEWS HAS JUST COME OVER THE WIRE! THE ARMY'S MYSTERIOUS NEW WEAPON HAS BEEN STOLEN! EVERY EFFORT IS BEING MADE TO APPREHEND THE THIEVES!
LUTHOR!
NOW I BEGIN TO UNDERSTAND WHY LUTHOR ISSUED HIS CHALLENGE! HE WANTED TO KEEP ME OCCUPIED ELSEWHERE WHILE HIS HENCHMEN PULLED THE ROBBERY!
IF THE INVENTION COULD ONLY BE DESTROYED! IT'S SO COMPLEX THAT NO ONE BUT MYSELF COULD BUILD ANOTHER!
FELLA-YOU'VE GIVEN ME AN IDEA!
TELL ME, QUICK! DO YOU HAVE ANY IDEA WHERE LUTHOR HELD YOU DURING YOUR CAPTIVITY?
I'M CERTAIN IT WAS IN SATAN'S CANYON!
ANOTHER NEWS FLASH! A PORTION OF THE CITY WAS JUST SHAKEN BY AN EARTHQUAKE. A MYSTERIOUS CHARACTER NAMED LUTHOR DEMANDS THE CITY'S SURRENDER!
WAIT!
CAN'T! --NOT NOW!
I'VE GOT TO ATTEND TO LUTHOR--AND FAST!

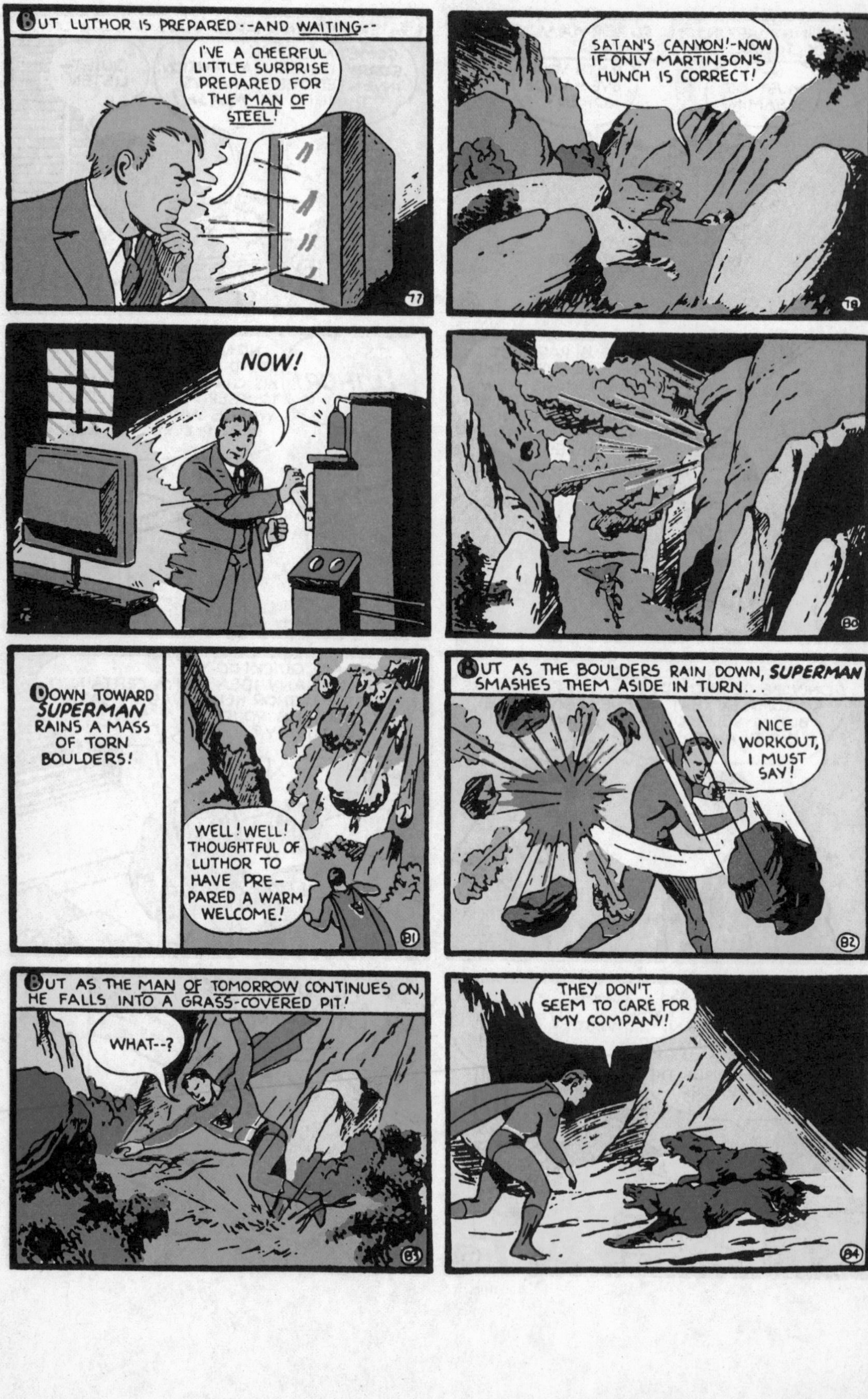
BUT LUTHOR IS PREPARED--AND WAITING--
I'VE A CHEERFUL LITTLE SURPRISE PREPARED FOR THE MAN OF STEEL!
SATAN'S CANYON!-NOW IF ONLY MARTINSON'S HUNCH IS CORRECT!
NOW!
DOWN TOWARD SUPERMAN RAINS A MASS OF TORN BOULDERS!
WELL! WELL! THOUGHTFUL OF LUTHOR TO HAVE PRE-PARED A WARM WELCOME!
BUT AS THE BOULDERS RAIN DOWN, SUPERMAN SMASHES THEM ASIDE IN TURN...
NICE WORKOUT, I MUST SAY!
BUT AS THE MAN OF TOMORROW CONTINUES ON, HE FALLS INTO A GRASS-COVERED PIT!
WHAT--?
THEY DON'T SEEM TO CARE FOR MY COMPANY!

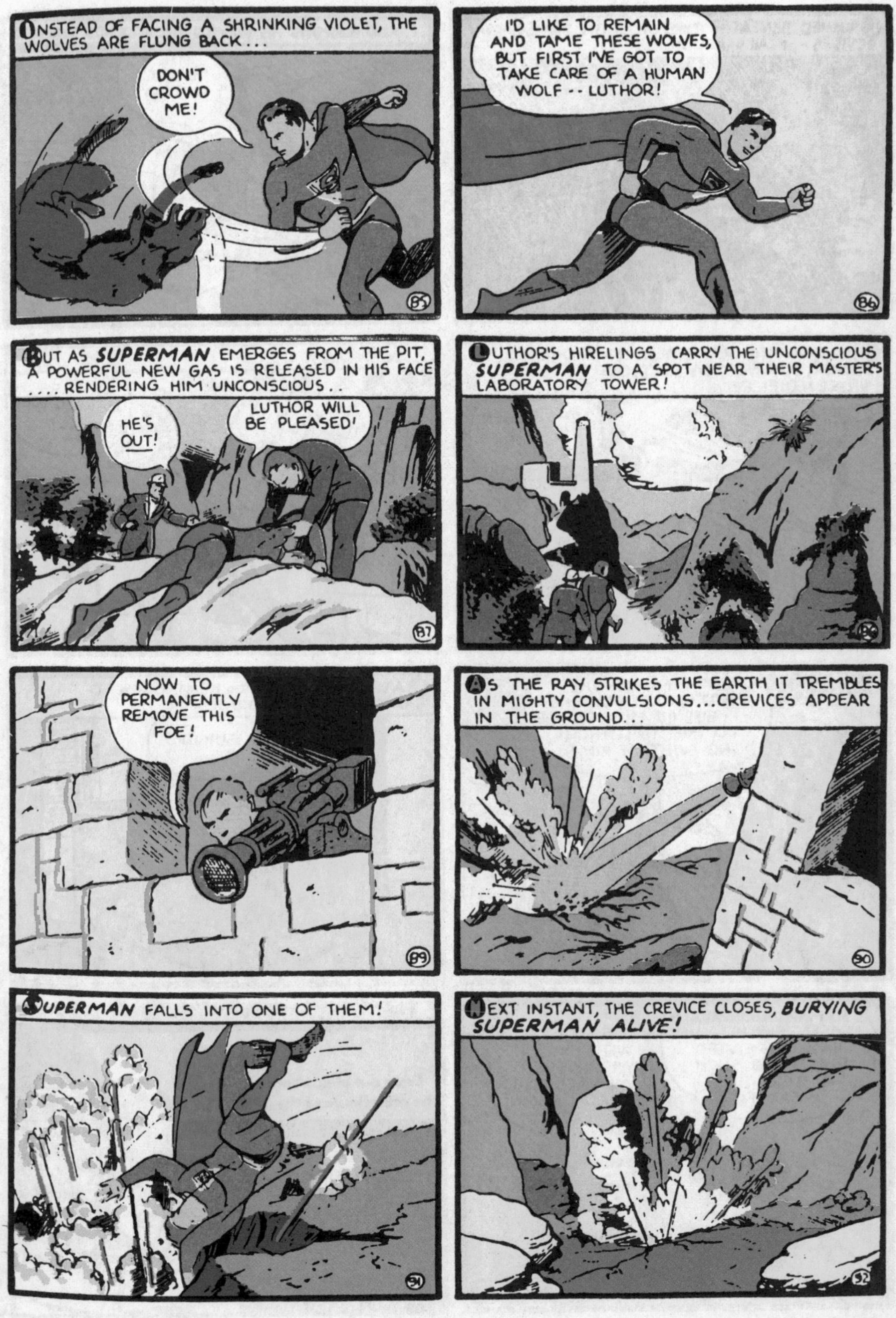
ONSTEAD OF FACING A SHRINKING VIOLET, THE WOLVES ARE FLUNG BACK...
DON'T CROWD ME!
I'D LIKE TO REMAIN AND TAME THESE WOLVES, BUT FIRST I'VE GOT TO TAKE CARE OF A HUMAN WOLF -- LUTHOR!
BUT AS SUPERMAN EMERGES FROM THE PIT, A POWERFUL NEW GAS IS RELEASED IN HIS FACE .... RENDERING HIM UNCONSCIOUS..
HE'S OUT!
LUTHOR WILL BE PLEASED!
LUTHOR'S HIRELINGS CARRY THE UNCONSCIOUS SUPERMAN TO A SPOT NEAR THEIR MASTER'S LABORATORY TOWER!
NOW TO PERMANENTLY REMOVE THIS FOE!
AS THE RAY STRIKES THE EARTH IT TREMBLES IN MIGHTY CONVULSIONS...CREVICES APPEAR IN THE GROUND...
SUPERMAN FALLS INTO ONE OF THEM!
NEXT INSTANT, THE CREVICE CLOSES, BURYING SUPERMAN ALIVE!

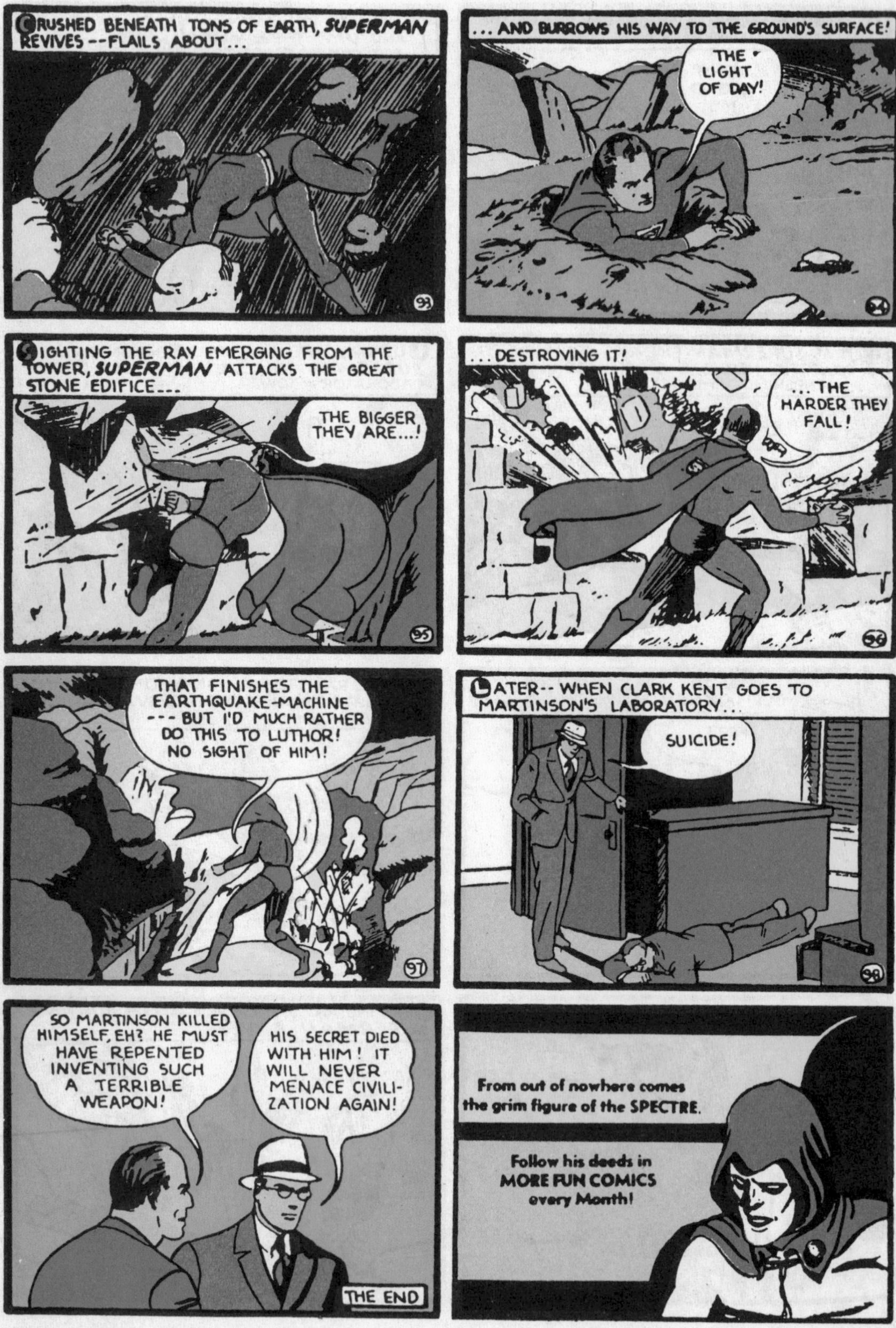
CRUSHED BENEATH TONS OF EARTH, SUPERMAN REVIVES --FLAILS ABOUT...
93
... AND BURROWS HIS WAY TO THE GROUND'S SURFACE!
THE LIGHT OF DAY!
94
SIGHTING THE RAY EMERGING FROM THE TOWER, SUPERMAN ATTACKS THE GREAT STONE EDIFICE...
THE BIGGER THEY ARE...!
95
... DESTROYING IT!
... THE HARDER THEY FALL!
96
THAT FINISHES THE EARTHQUAKE-MACHINE --- BUT I'D MUCH RATHER DO THIS TO LUTHOR! NO SIGHT OF HIM!
97
LATER-- WHEN CLARK KENT GOES TO MARTINSON'S LABORATORY...
SUICIDE!
98
SO MARTINSON KILLED HIMSELF, EH? HE MUST HAVE REPENTED INVENTING SUCH A TERRIBLE WEAPON!
HIS SECRET DIED WITH HIM! IT WILL NEVER MENACE CIVILIZATION AGAIN!
THE END
From out of nowhere comes the grim figure of the SPECTRE.
Follow his deeds in MORE FUN COMICS every Month!

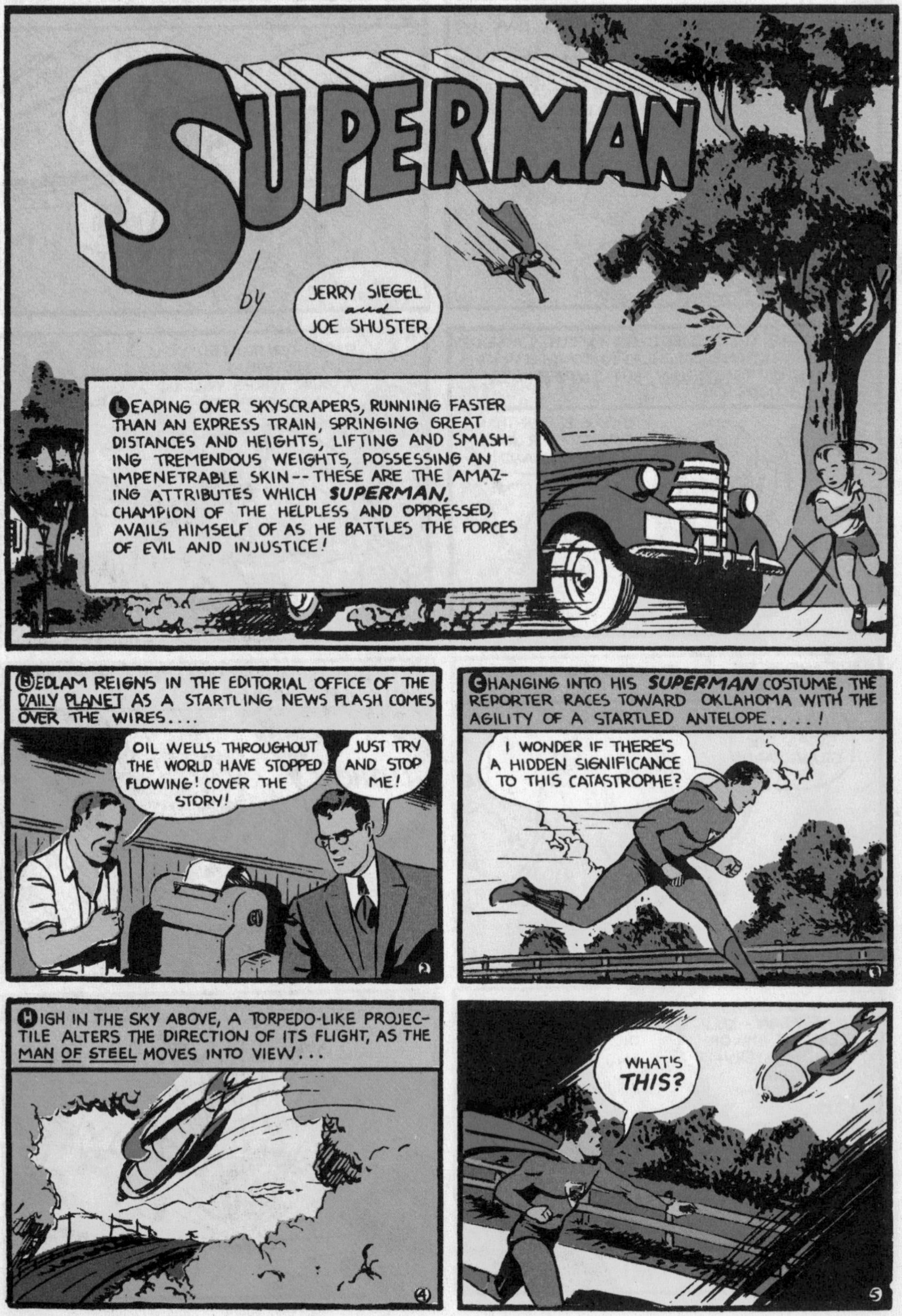
SUPERMAN
by
JERRY SIEGEL and JOE SHUSTER
LEAPING OVER SKYSCRAPERS, RUNNING FASTER THAN AN EXPRESS TRAIN, SPRINGING GREAT DISTANCES AND HEIGHTS, LIFTING AND SMASHING TREMENDOUS WEIGHTS, POSSESSING AN IMPENETRABLE SKIN--THESE ARE THE AMAZING ATTRIBUTES WHICH SUPERMAN, CHAMPION OF THE HELPLESS AND OPPRESSED, AVAILS HIMSELF OF AS HE BATTLES THE FORCES OF EVIL AND INJUSTICE!
BEDLAM REIGNS IN THE EDITORIAL OFFICE OF THE DAILY PLANET AS A STARTLING NEWS FLASH COMES OVER THE WIRES....
OIL WELLS THROUGHOUT THE WORLD HAVE STOPPED FLOWING! COVER THE STORY!
JUST TRY AND STOP ME!
CHANGING INTO HIS SUPERMAN COSTUME, THE REPORTER RACES TOWARD OKLAHOMA WITH THE AGILITY OF A STARTLED ANTELOPE....!
I WONDER IF THERE'S A HIDDEN SIGNIFICANCE TO THIS CATASTROPHE?
HIGH IN THE SKY ABOVE, A TORPEDO-LIKE PROJECTILE ALTERS THE DIRECTION OF ITS FLIGHT, AS THE MAN OF STEEL MOVES INTO VIEW...
WHAT'S THIS?

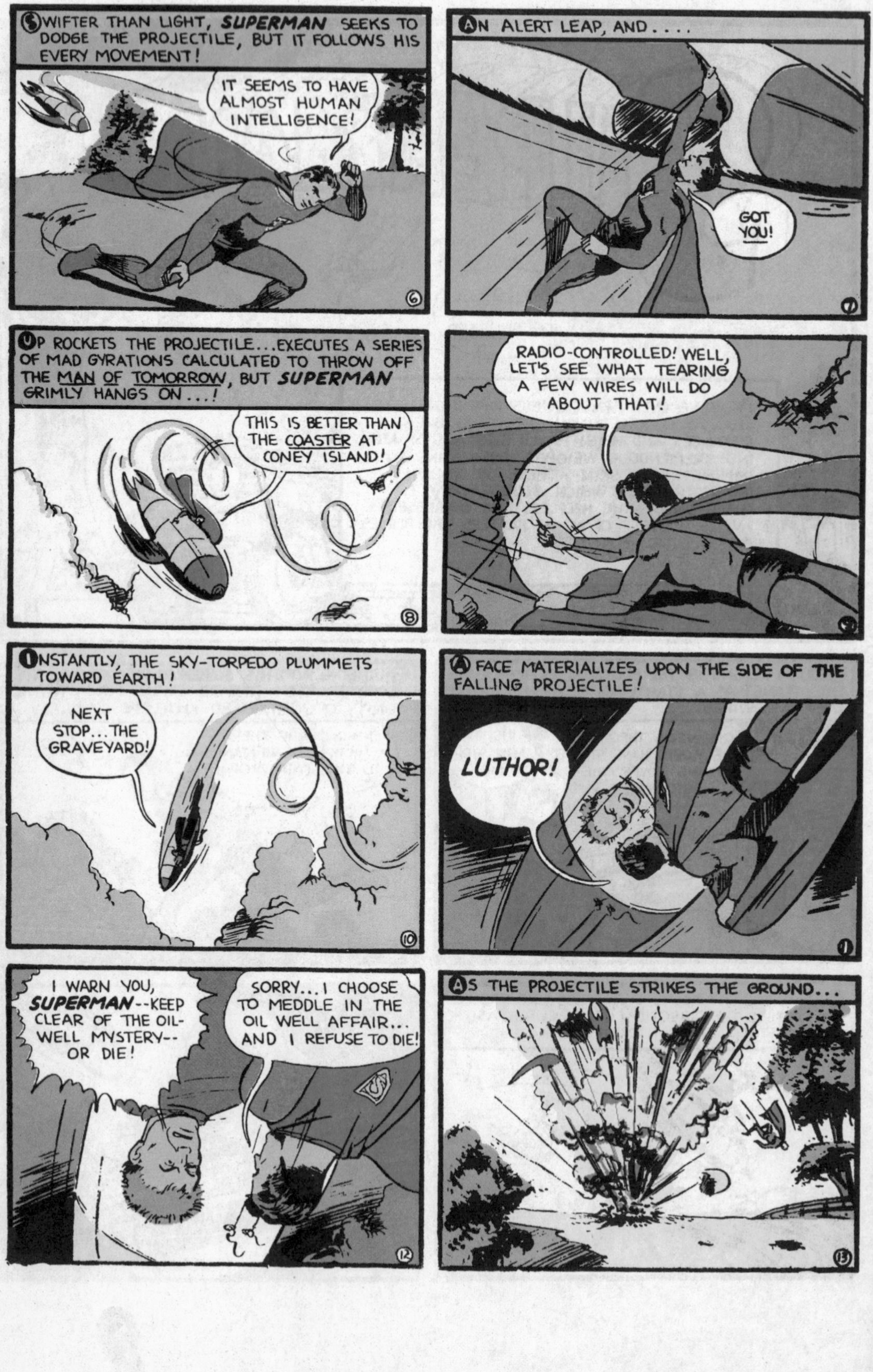
SWIFTER THAN LIGHT, SUPERMAN SEEKS TO DODGE THE PROJECTILE, BUT IT FOLLOWS HIS EVERY MOVEMENT!
IT SEEMS TO HAVE ALMOST HUMAN INTELLIGENCE!
AN ALERT LEAP, AND....
GOT YOU!
UP ROCKETS THE PROJECTILE...EXECUTES A SERIES OF MAD GYRATIONS CALCULATED TO THROW OFF THE MAN OF TOMORROW, BUT SUPERMAN GRIMLY HANGS ON...!
THIS IS BETTER THAN THE COASTER AT CONEY ISLAND!
RADIO-CONTROLLED! WELL, LET'S SEE WHAT TEARING A FEW WIRES WILL DO ABOUT THAT!
INSTANTLY, THE SKY-TORPEDO PLUMMETS TOWARD EARTH!
NEXT STOP...THE GRAVEYARD!
A FACE MATERIALIZES UPON THE SIDE OF THE FALLING PROJECTILE!
LUTHOR!
I WARN YOU, SUPERMAN--KEEP CLEAR OF THE OIL-WELL MYSTERY--OR DIE!
SORRY...I CHOOSE TO MEDDLE IN THE OIL WELL AFFAIR...AND I REFUSE TO DIE!
AS THE PROJECTILE STRIKES THE GROUND...

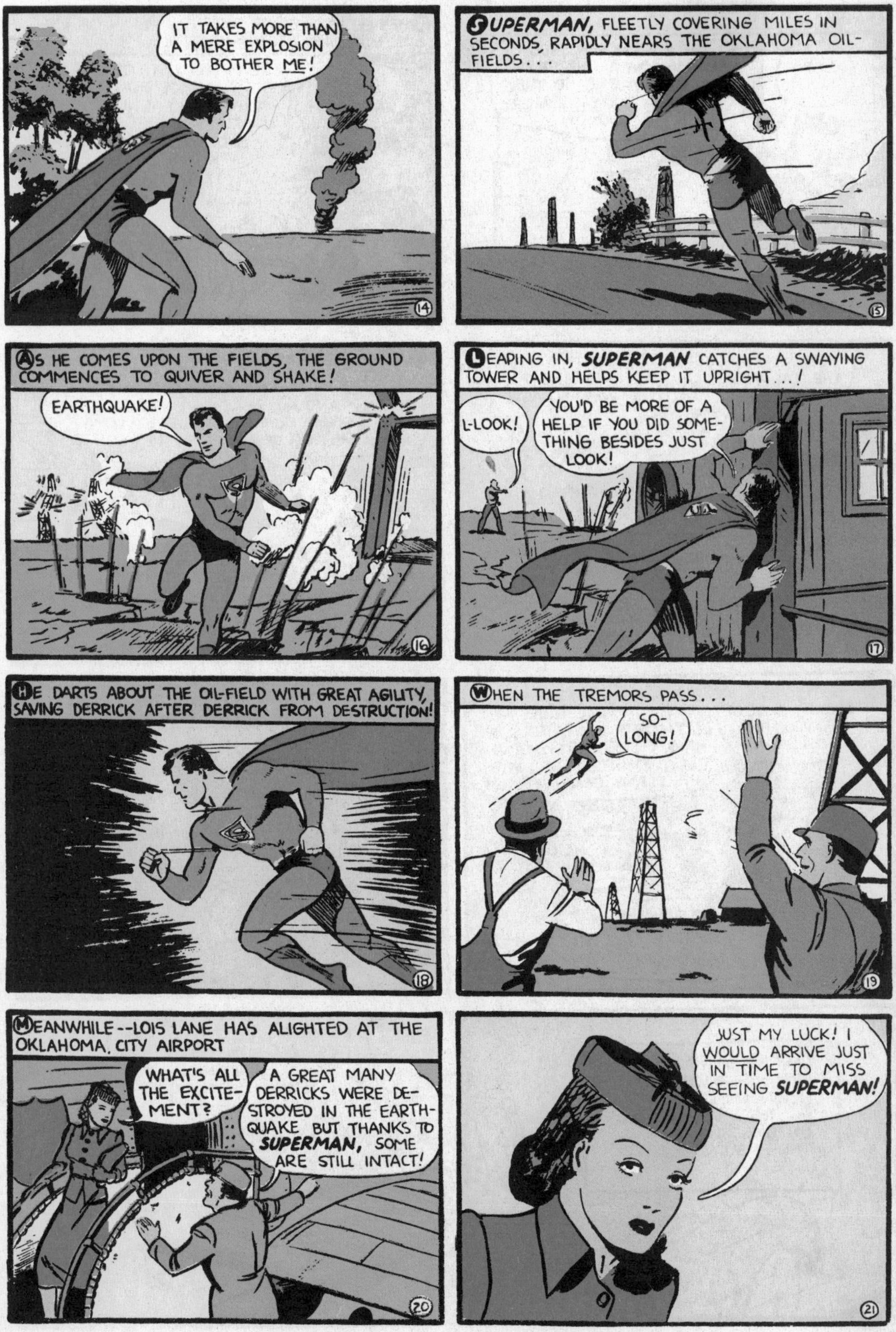
IT TAKES MORE THAN A MERE EXPLOSION TO BOTHER ME!
14
SUPERMAN, FLEETLY COVERING MILES IN SECONDS, RAPIDLY NEARS THE OKLAHOMA OIL-FIELDS...
15
AS HE COMES UPON THE FIELDS, THE GROUND COMMENCES TO QUIVER AND SHAKE!
EARTHQUAKE!
16
LEAPING IN, SUPERMAN CATCHES A SWAYING TOWER AND HELPS KEEP IT UPRIGHT...!
L-LOOK!
YOU'D BE MORE OF A HELP IF YOU DID SOMETHING BESIDES JUST LOOK!
17
HE DARTS ABOUT THE OIL-FIELD WITH GREAT AGILITY, SAVING DERRICK AFTER DERRICK FROM DESTRUCTION!
18
WHEN THE TREMORS PASS...
SO-LONG!
19
MEANWHILE--LOIS LANE HAS ALIGHTED AT THE OKLAHOMA CITY AIRPORT
WHAT'S ALL THE EXCITEMENT?
A GREAT MANY DERRICKS WERE DESTROYED IN THE EARTHQUAKE BUT THANKS TO SUPERMAN, SOME ARE STILL INTACT!
20
JUST MY LUCK! I WOULD ARRIVE JUST IN TIME TO MISS SEEING SUPERMAN!
21

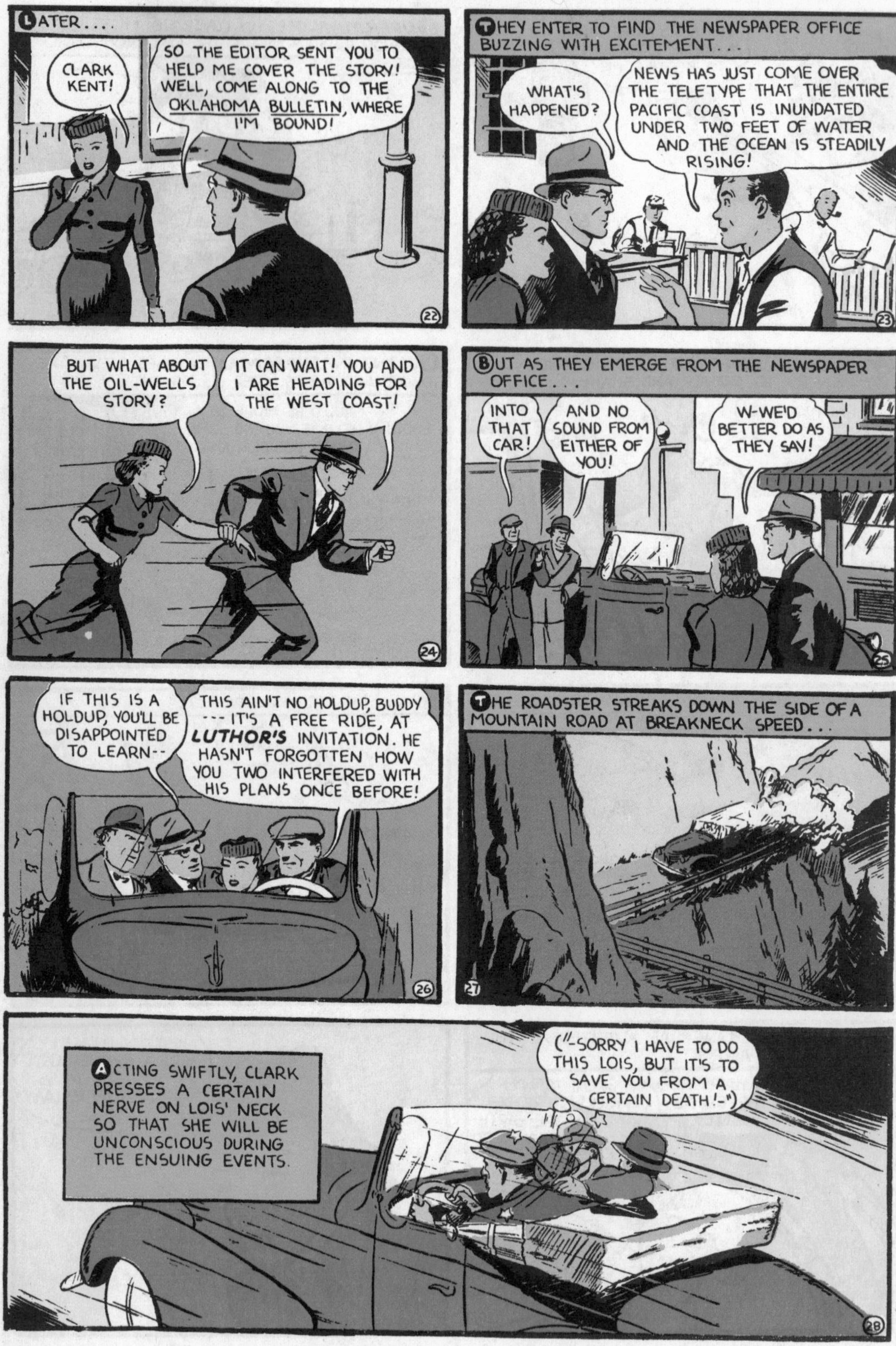
LATER....
CLARK KENT!
SO THE EDITOR SENT YOU TO HELP ME COVER THE STORY! WELL, COME ALONG TO THE OKLAHOMA BULLETIN, WHERE I'M BOUND!
THEY ENTER TO FIND THE NEWSPAPER OFFICE BUZZING WITH EXCITEMENT...
WHAT'S HAPPENED?
NEWS HAS JUST COME OVER THE TELETYPE THAT THE ENTIRE PACIFIC COAST IS INUNDATED UNDER TWO FEET OF WATER AND THE OCEAN IS STEADILY RISING!
BUT WHAT ABOUT THE OIL-WELLS STORY?
IT CAN WAIT! YOU AND I ARE HEADING FOR THE WEST COAST!
BUT AS THEY EMERGE FROM THE NEWSPAPER OFFICE...
INTO THAT CAR!
AND NO SOUND FROM EITHER OF YOU!
W-WE'D BETTER DO AS THEY SAY!
IF THIS IS A HOLDUP, YOU'LL BE DISAPPOINTED TO LEARN--
THIS AIN'T NO HOLDUP, BUDDY --- IT'S A FREE RIDE, AT LUTHOR'S INVITATION. HE HASN'T FORGOTTEN HOW YOU TWO INTERFERED WITH HIS PLANS ONCE BEFORE!
THE ROADSTER STREAKS DOWN THE SIDE OF A MOUNTAIN ROAD AT BREAKNECK SPEED...
ACTING SWIFTLY, CLARK PRESSES A CERTAIN NERVE ON LOIS' NECK SO THAT SHE WILL BE UNCONSCIOUS DURING THE ENSUING EVENTS.
("-SORRY I HAVE TO DO THIS LOIS, BUT IT'S TO SAVE YOU FROM A CERTAIN DEATH!-")

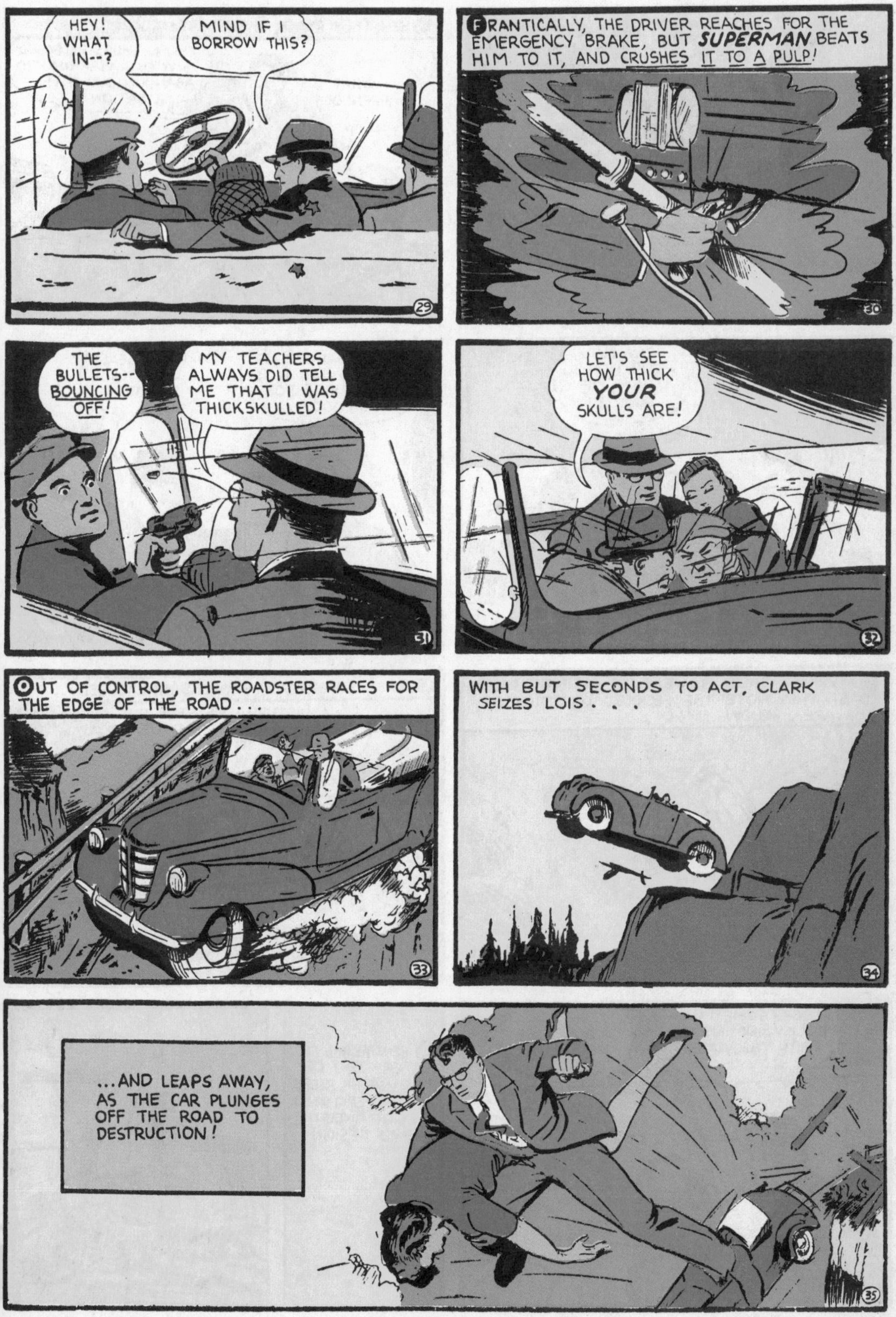
HEY! WHAT IN--?
MIND IF I BORROW THIS?
FRANTICALLY, THE DRIVER REACHES FOR THE EMERGENCY BRAKE, BUT SUPERMAN BEATS HIM TO IT, AND CRUSHES IT TO A PULP!
THE BULLETS--BOUNCING OFF!
MY TEACHERS ALWAYS DID TELL ME THAT I WAS THICKSKULLED!
LET'S SEE HOW THICK YOUR SKULLS ARE!
OUT OF CONTROL, THE ROADSTER RACES FOR THE EDGE OF THE ROAD...
WITH BUT SECONDS TO ACT, CLARK SEIZES LOIS . . .
...AND LEAPS AWAY, AS THE CAR PLUNGES OFF THE ROAD TO DESTRUCTION!

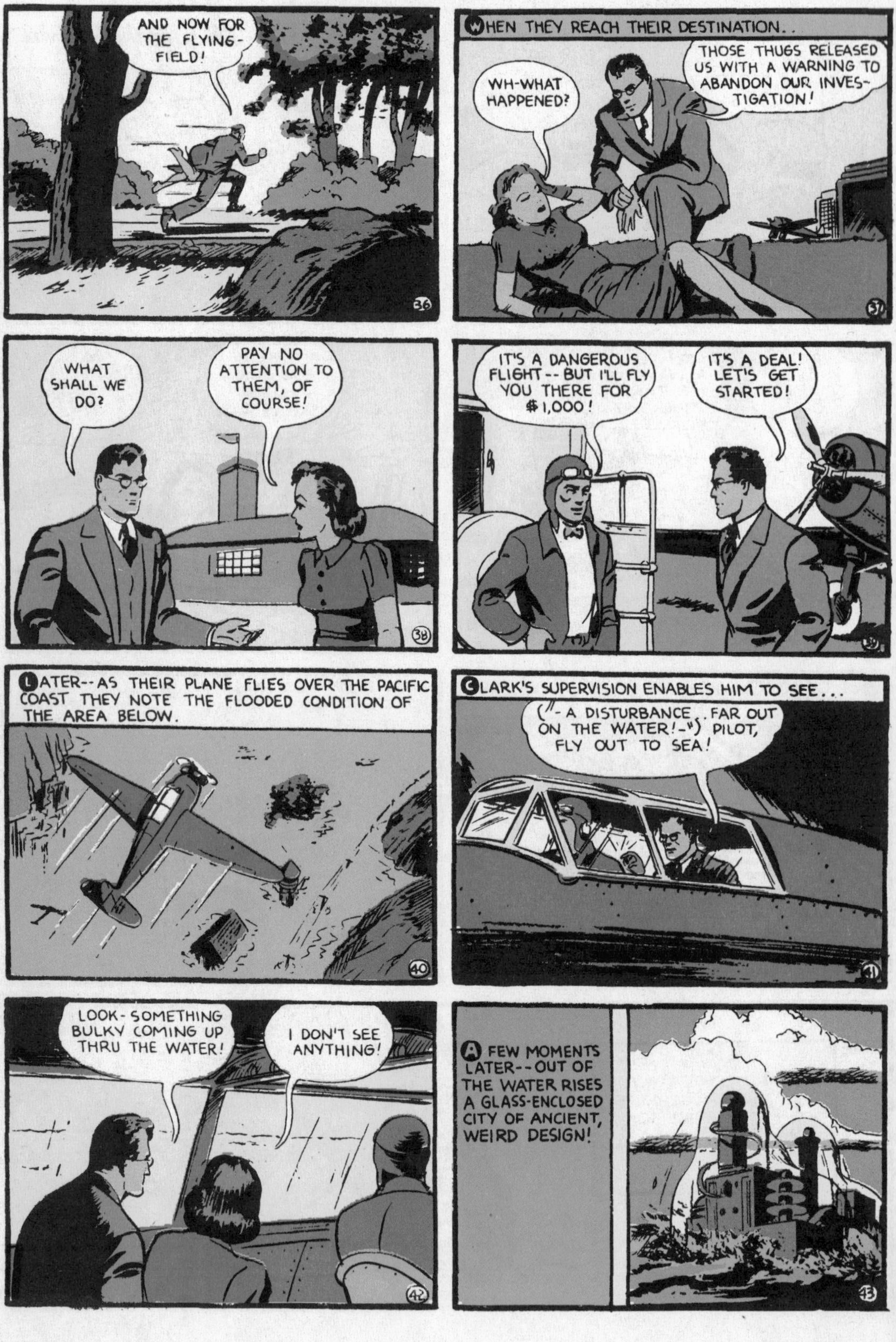
AND NOW FOR THE FLYING-FIELD!
WHEN THEY REACH THEIR DESTINATION..
WH-WHAT HAPPENED?
THOSE THUGS RELEASED US WITH A WARNING TO ABANDON OUR INVES-TIGATION!
WHAT SHALL WE DO?
PAY NO ATTENTION TO THEM, OF COURSE!
IT'S A DANGEROUS FLIGHT--BUT I'LL FLY YOU THERE FOR $1,000!
IT'S A DEAL! LET'S GET STARTED!
LATER--AS THEIR PLANE FLIES OVER THE PACIFIC COAST THEY NOTE THE FLOODED CONDITION OF THE AREA BELOW.
CLARK'S SUPERVISION ENABLES HIM TO SEE...
("- A DISTURBANCE..FAR OUT ON THE WATER!-") PILOT, FLY OUT TO SEA!
LOOK-SOMETHING BULKY COMING UP THRU THE WATER!
I DON'T SEE ANYTHING!
A FEW MOMENTS LATER--OUT OF THE WATER RISES A GLASS-ENCLOSED CITY OF ANCIENT, WEIRD DESIGN!

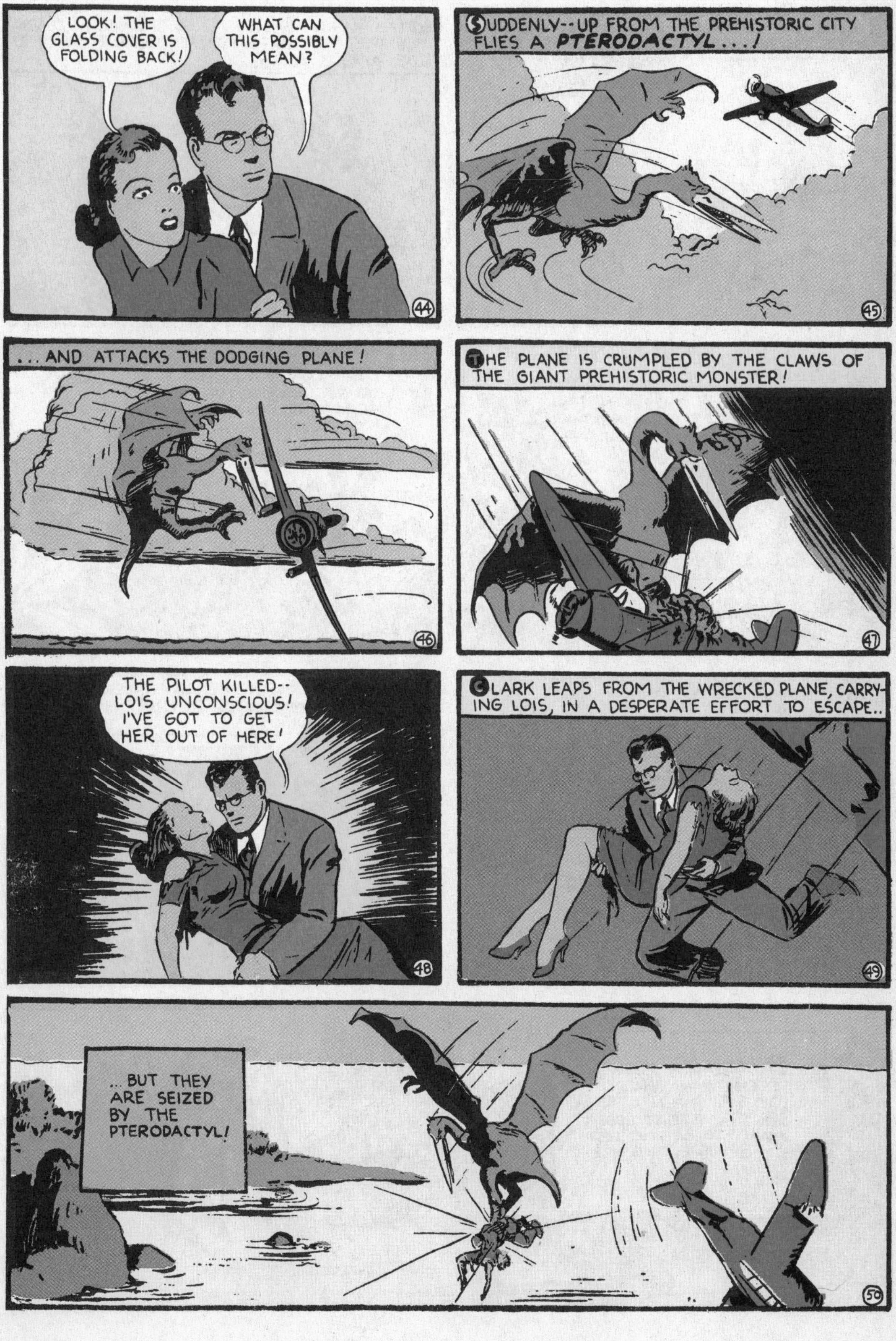
LOOK! THE GLASS COVER IS FOLDING BACK!
WHAT CAN THIS POSSIBLY MEAN?
SUDDENLY--UP FROM THE PREHISTORIC CITY FLIES A PTERODACTYL...!
...AND ATTACKS THE DODGING PLANE!
THE PLANE IS CRUMPLED BY THE CLAWS OF THE GIANT PREHISTORIC MONSTER!
THE PILOT KILLED--LOIS UNCONSCIOUS! I'VE GOT TO GET HER OUT OF HERE!
CLARK LEAPS FROM THE WRECKED PLANE, CARRYING LOIS, IN A DESPERATE EFFORT TO ESCAPE..
...BUT THEY ARE SEIZED BY THE PTERODACTYL!

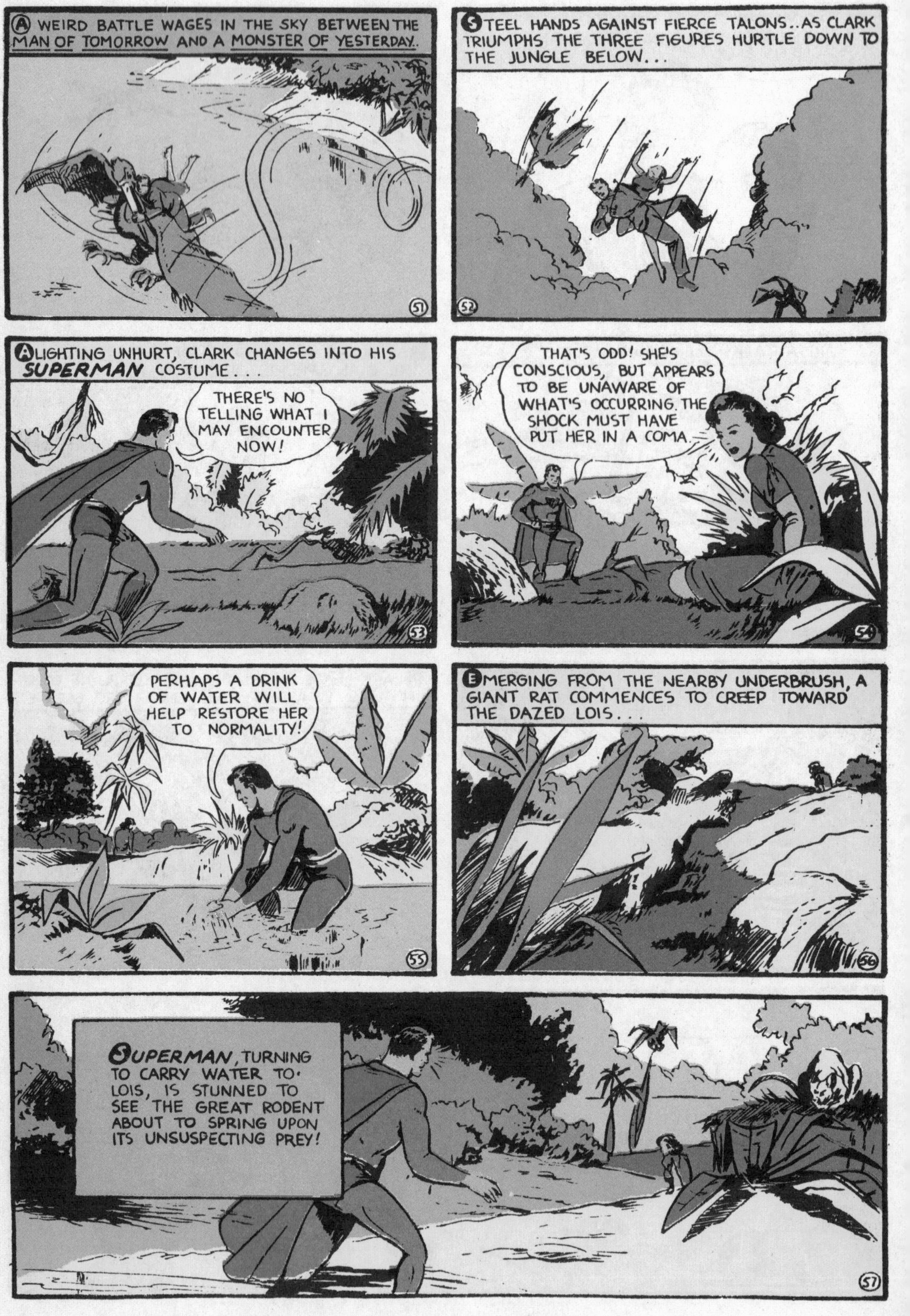
A WEIRD BATTLE WAGES IN THE SKY BETWEEN THE MAN OF TOMORROW AND A MONSTER OF YESTERDAY.
STEEL HANDS AGAINST FIERCE TALONS..AS CLARK TRIUMPHS THE THREE FIGURES HURTLE DOWN TO THE JUNGLE BELOW...
ALIGHTING UNHURT, CLARK CHANGES INTO HIS SUPERMAN COSTUME...
THERE'S NO TELLING WHAT I MAY ENCOUNTER NOW!
THAT'S ODD! SHE'S CONSCIOUS, BUT APPEARS TO BE UNAWARE OF WHAT'S OCCURRING. THE SHOCK MUST HAVE PUT HER IN A COMA.
PERHAPS A DRINK OF WATER WILL HELP RESTORE HER TO NORMALITY!
EMERGING FROM THE NEARBY UNDERBRUSH, A GIANT RAT COMMENCES TO CREEP TOWARD THE DAZED LOIS...
SUPERMAN, TURNING TO CARRY WATER TO LOIS, IS STUNNED TO SEE THE GREAT RODENT ABOUT TO SPRING UPON ITS UNSUSPECTING PREY!

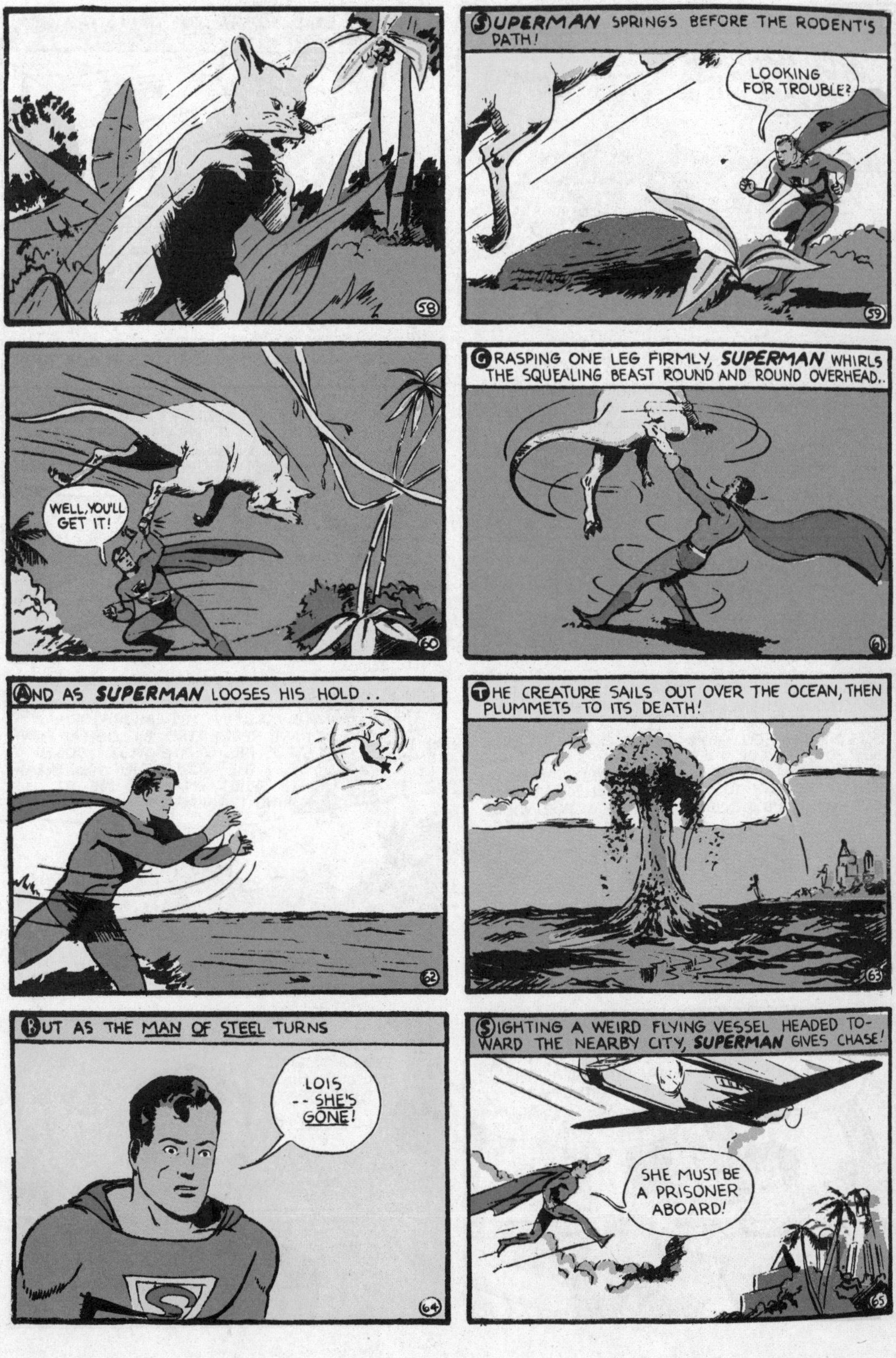
SUPERMAN SPRINGS BEFORE THE RODENT'S PATH!
LOOKING FOR TROUBLE?
WELL, YOU'LL GET IT!
GRASPING ONE LEG FIRMLY, SUPERMAN WHIRLS THE SQUEALING BEAST ROUND AND ROUND OVERHEAD..
AND AS SUPERMAN LOOSES HIS HOLD ..
THE CREATURE SAILS OUT OVER THE OCEAN, THEN PLUMMETS TO ITS DEATH!
BUT AS THE MAN OF STEEL TURNS
LOIS -- SHE'S GONE!
SIGHTING A WEIRD FLYING VESSEL HEADED TOWARD THE NEARBY CITY, SUPERMAN GIVES CHASE!
SHE MUST BE A PRISONER ABOARD!

As **SUPERMAN** NEARS THE CITY..

SUPERMAN! OFFER NO RESISTANCE--OR MISS LANE WILL BE DESTROYED!

LUTHOR'S VOICE!

66

FOR LOIS' SAKE, **SUPERMAN** STANDS PASSIVELY BY AS SHE LEAVES THE WEIRD VESSEL..

SO, MAN OF STEEL--WE MEET AGAIN!

SO-- IT'S .YOU AGAIN, LUTHOR! AND AS EVIL AS USUAL!

67

I DON'T CARE WHAT HAPPENS TO ME - BUT IF YOU HARM THAT GIRL--

ON THE CONTRARY, I WILL HAVE HER TREATED SO THAT HER SENSES RETURN--TAKE HER TO THE GREEN LABORATORY, MEN!

68

SUPERMAN ACCOMPANIES LUTHOR IN A TOUR OF THE CITY...

HOW DID YOU CREATE THIS WEIRD CITY?

IT WAS CREATED YEARS AGO --- I MERELY SALVAGED IT. WHAT YOU ARE WALKING UPON, IS A REMNANT OF THE SUNKEN CONTINENT, PACIFO!

YOU'LL ADMIT IT WAS A MIRACULOUS ACHIEVEMENT! WORKING UNDERWATER, I RAISED A GLASSOLITE-DOME OVER THE CITY, DRAINED OUT THE WATER, THEN RAISED THE CITY TO THE SURFACE OF THE OCEAN.

THEN IT WAS THIS TITANIC UNDERWATER UPHEAVAL THAT CAUSED THE OCEAN TO OVERFLOW! ...AND IT WAS YOU WHO TAPPED THE OIL-WELLS AND STOLE THE OIL FOR YOUR EVIL PURPOSES!

70

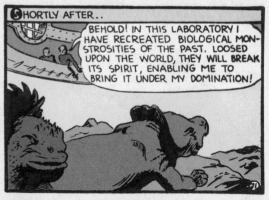

SHORTLY AFTER..

BEHOLD! IN THIS LABORATORY I HAVE RECREATED BIOLOGICAL MONSTROSITIES OF THE PAST. LOOSED UPON THE WORLD, THEY WILL BREAK ITS SPIRIT, ENABLING ME TO BRING IT UNDER MY DOMINATION!

71

BUT SURELY YOU WOULDN'T REALLY PERPETRATE SUCH AN INHUMAN CRIME ---!

IF YOU GIVE ME YOUR ASSISTANCE, I WILL BE INCLINED TO BE MORE MERCIFUL WITH THE WORLD, OTHERWISE...! WELL, WHAT IS YOUR DECISION?

72

GIVE ME A FEW MOMENTS! I MUST THINK-- THINK ...!

73

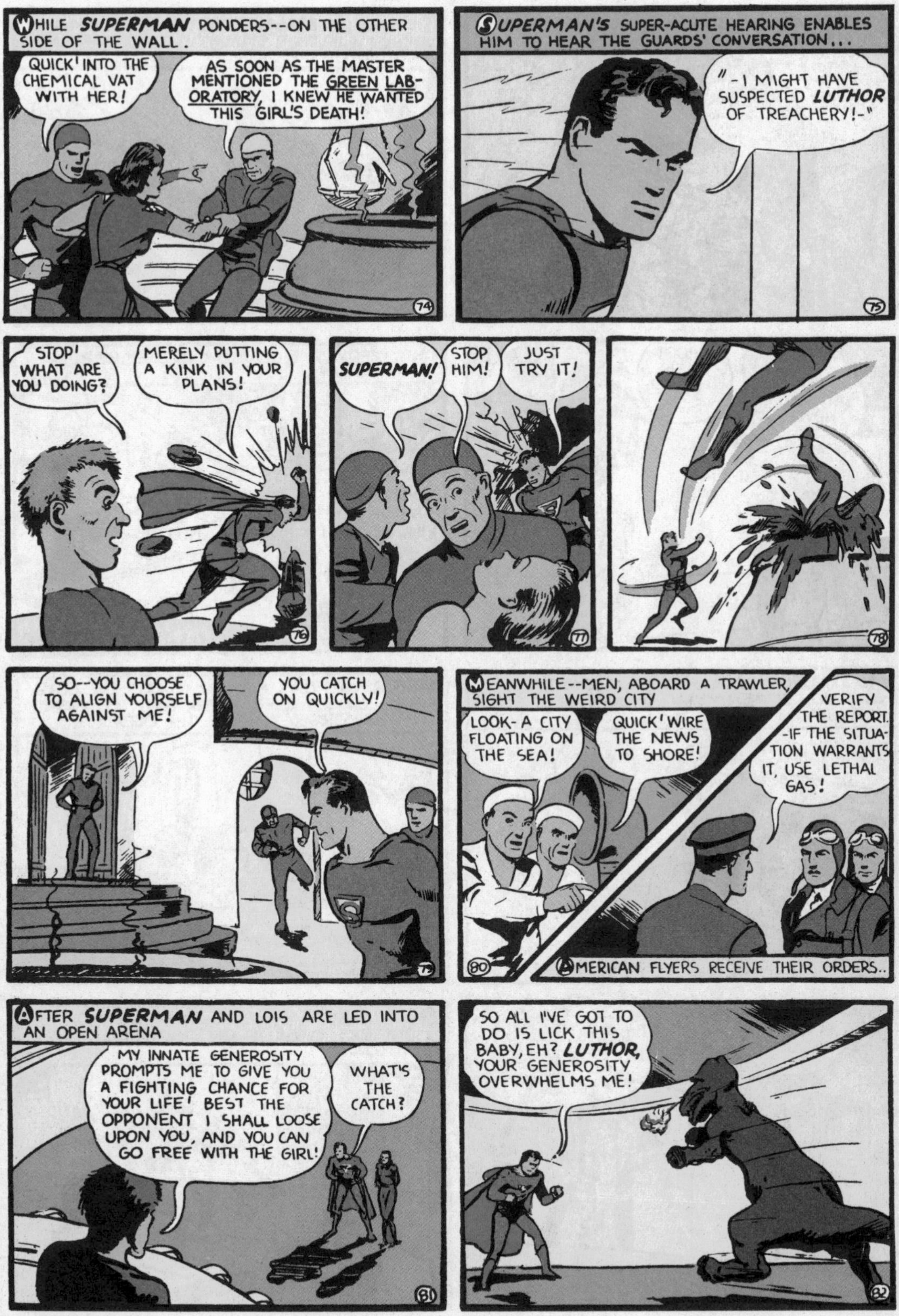
WHILE SUPERMAN PONDERS--ON THE OTHER SIDE OF THE WALL.
QUICK! INTO THE CHEMICAL VAT WITH HER!
AS SOON AS THE MASTER MENTIONED THE GREEN LABORATORY, I KNEW HE WANTED THIS GIRL'S DEATH!
74
SUPERMAN'S SUPER-ACUTE HEARING ENABLES HIM TO HEAR THE GUARDS' CONVERSATION...
"-I MIGHT HAVE SUSPECTED LUTHOR OF TREACHERY!-"
75
STOP! WHAT ARE YOU DOING?
MERELY PUTTING A KINK IN YOUR PLANS!
76
SUPERMAN!
STOP HIM!
JUST TRY IT!
77
78
SO--YOU CHOOSE TO ALIGN YOURSELF AGAINST ME!
YOU CATCH ON QUICKLY!
79
MEANWHILE--MEN, ABOARD A TRAWLER, SIGHT THE WEIRD CITY
LOOK- A CITY FLOATING ON THE SEA!
QUICK! WIRE THE NEWS TO SHORE!
VERIFY THE REPORT. -IF THE SITUATION WARRANTS IT, USE LETHAL GAS!
AMERICAN FLYERS RECEIVE THEIR ORDERS..
80
AFTER SUPERMAN AND LOIS ARE LED INTO AN OPEN ARENA
MY INNATE GENEROSITY PROMPTS ME TO GIVE YOU A FIGHTING CHANCE FOR YOUR LIFE! BEST THE OPPONENT I SHALL LOOSE UPON YOU, AND YOU CAN GO FREE WITH THE GIRL!
WHAT'S THE CATCH?
81
SO ALL I'VE GOT TO DO IS LICK THIS BABY, EH? LUTHOR, YOUR GENEROSITY OVERWHELMS ME!
82

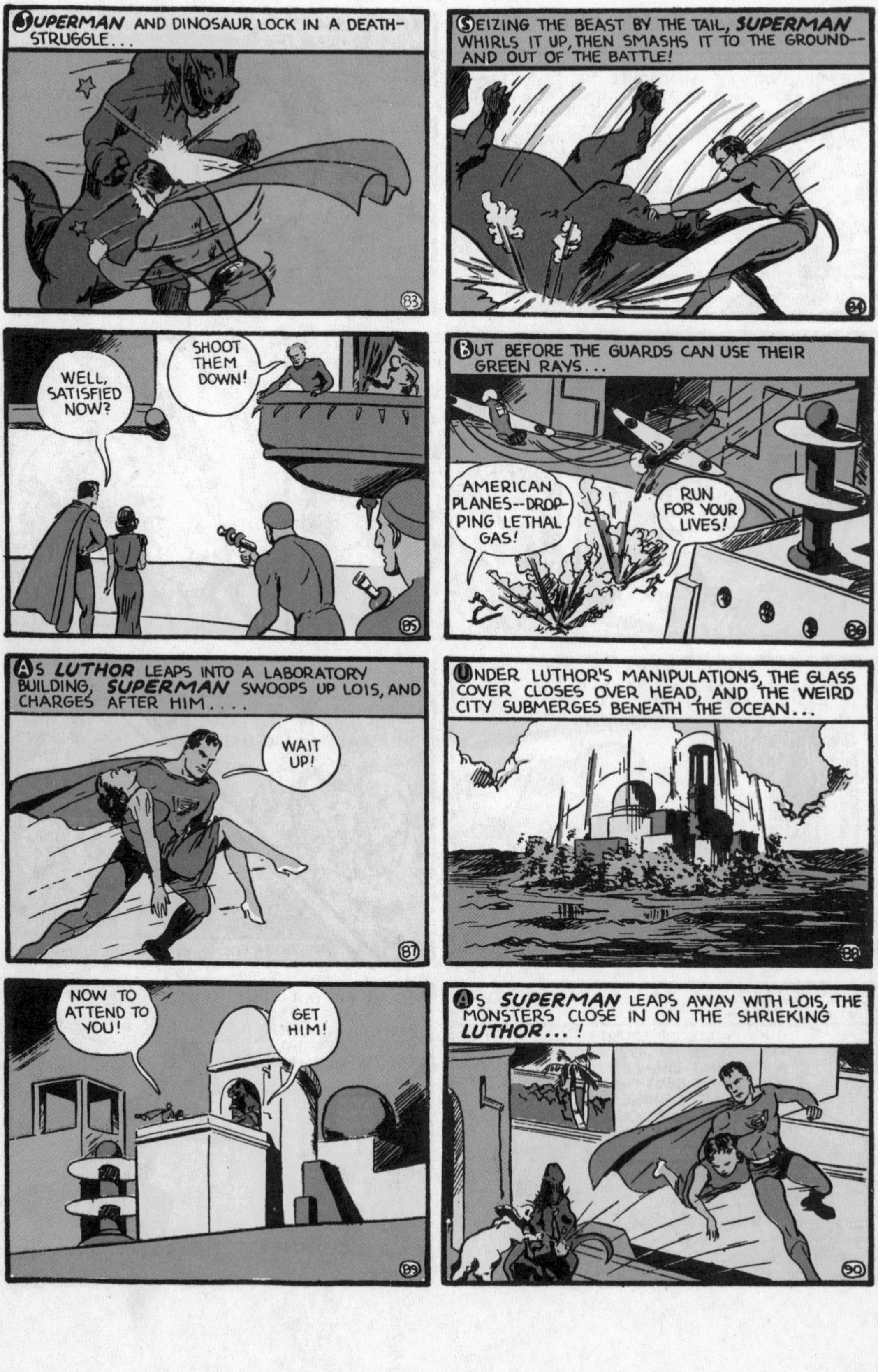
SUPERMAN AND DINOSAUR LOCK IN A DEATH-STRUGGLE...
83
SEIZING THE BEAST BY THE TAIL, SUPERMAN WHIRLS IT UP, THEN SMASHS IT TO THE GROUND--AND OUT OF THE BATTLE!
84
WELL, SATISFIED NOW?
SHOOT THEM DOWN!
85
BUT BEFORE THE GUARDS CAN USE THEIR GREEN RAYS...
AMERICAN PLANES--DROPPING LETHAL GAS!
RUN FOR YOUR LIVES!
86
AS LUTHOR LEAPS INTO A LABORATORY BUILDING, SUPERMAN SWOOPS UP LOIS, AND CHARGES AFTER HIM....
WAIT UP!
87
UNDER LUTHOR'S MANIPULATIONS, THE GLASS COVER CLOSES OVER HEAD, AND THE WEIRD CITY SUBMERGES BENEATH THE OCEAN...
88
NOW TO ATTEND TO YOU!
GET HIM!
89
AS SUPERMAN LEAPS AWAY WITH LOIS, THE MONSTERS CLOSE IN ON THE SHRIEKING LUTHOR...!
90

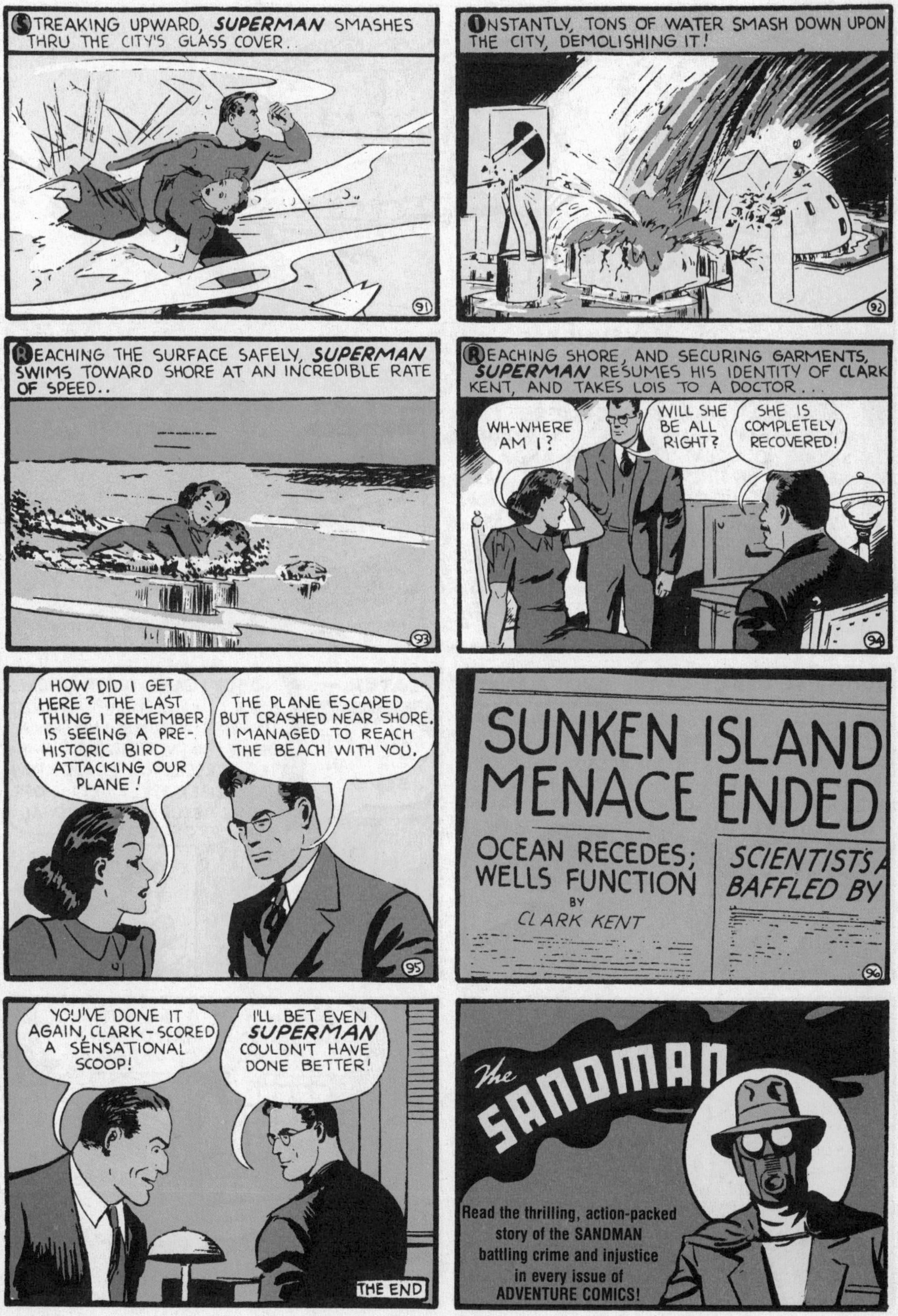
STREAKING UPWARD, SUPERMAN SMASHES THRU THE CITY'S GLASS COVER.
91
INSTANTLY, TONS OF WATER SMASH DOWN UPON THE CITY, DEMOLISHING IT!
92
REACHING THE SURFACE SAFELY, SUPERMAN SWIMS TOWARD SHORE AT AN INCREDIBLE RATE OF SPEED..
93
REACHING SHORE, AND SECURING GARMENTS, SUPERMAN RESUMES HIS IDENTITY OF CLARK KENT, AND TAKES LOIS TO A DOCTOR...
WH-WHERE AM I?
WILL SHE BE ALL RIGHT?
SHE IS COMPLETELY RECOVERED!
94
HOW DID I GET HERE? THE LAST THING I REMEMBER IS SEEING A PRE-HISTORIC BIRD ATTACKING OUR PLANE!
THE PLANE ESCAPED BUT CRASHED NEAR SHORE. I MANAGED TO REACH THE BEACH WITH YOU.
95
SUNKEN ISLAND MENACE ENDED
OCEAN RECEDES; WELLS FUNCTION
BY
CLARK KENT
SCIENTISTS A
BAFFLED BY
96
YOU'VE DONE IT AGAIN, CLARK-SCORED A SENSATIONAL SCOOP!
I'LL BET EVEN SUPERMAN COULDN'T HAVE DONE BETTER!
THE END
The SANDMAN
Read the thrilling, action-packed story of the SANDMAN battling crime and injustice in every issue of ADVENTURE COMICS!

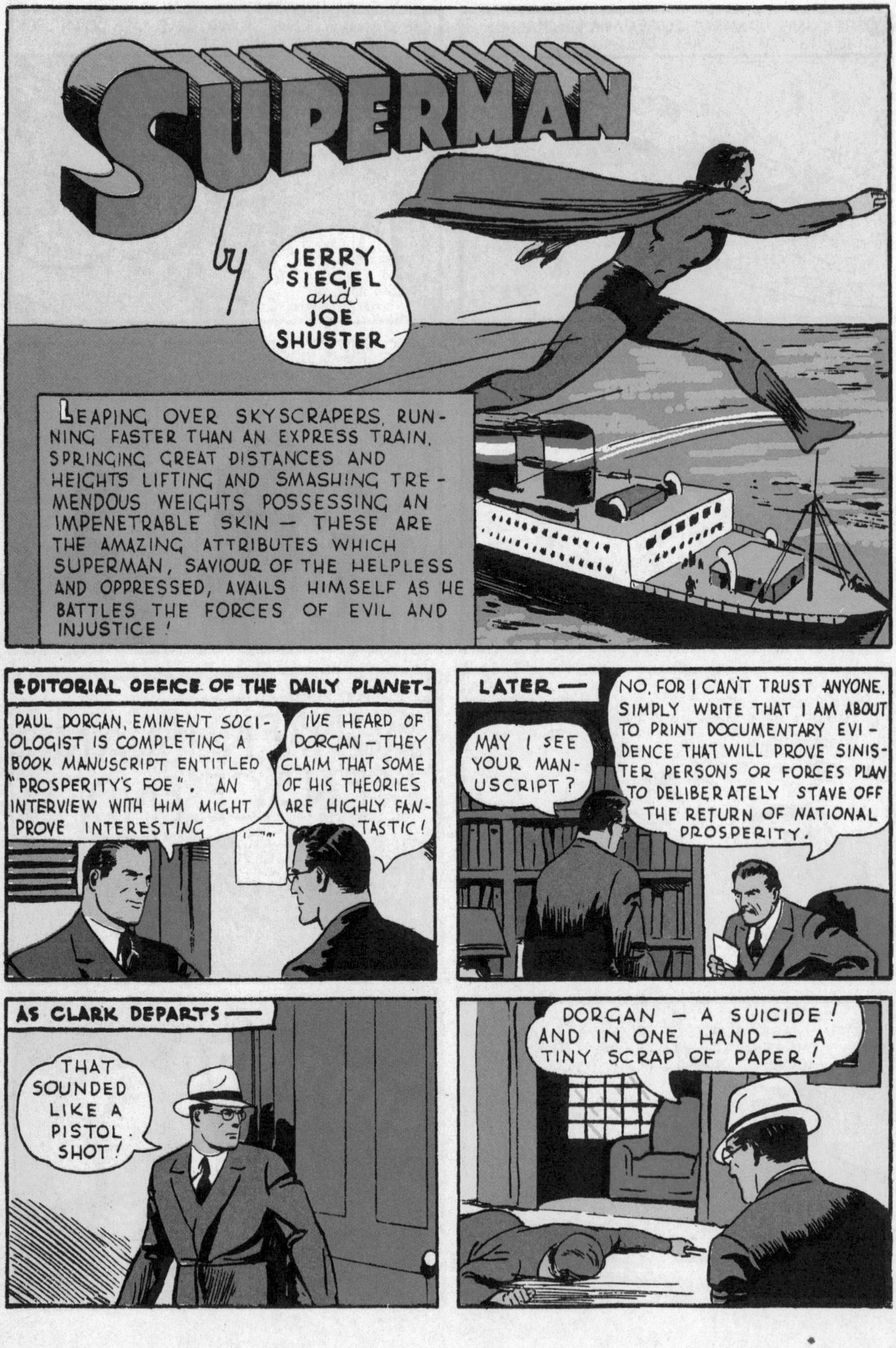
SUPERMAN
by
JERRY SIEGEL and JOE SHUSTER
LEAPING OVER SKYSCRAPERS, RUNNING FASTER THAN AN EXPRESS TRAIN, SPRINGING GREAT DISTANCES AND HEIGHTS LIFTING AND SMASHING TREMENDOUS WEIGHTS POSSESSING AN IMPENETRABLE SKIN — THESE ARE THE AMAZING ATTRIBUTES WHICH SUPERMAN, SAVIOUR OF THE HELPLESS AND OPPRESSED, AVAILS HIMSELF AS HE BATTLES THE FORCES OF EVIL AND INJUSTICE!
EDITORIAL OFFICE OF THE DAILY PLANET—
PAUL DORGAN, EMINENT SOCIOLOGIST IS COMPLETING A BOOK MANUSCRIPT ENTITLED "PROSPERITY'S FOE". AN INTERVIEW WITH HIM MIGHT PROVE INTERESTING
I'VE HEARD OF DORGAN — THEY CLAIM THAT SOME OF HIS THEORIES ARE HIGHLY FANTASTIC!
LATER —
MAY I SEE YOUR MANUSCRIPT?
NO, FOR I CAN'T TRUST ANYONE. SIMPLY WRITE THAT I AM ABOUT TO PRINT DOCUMENTARY EVIDENCE THAT WILL PROVE SINISTER PERSONS OR FORCES PLAN TO DELIBERATELY STAVE OFF THE RETURN OF NATIONAL PROSPERITY.
AS CLARK DEPARTS —
THAT SOUNDED LIKE A PISTOL SHOT!
DORGAN — A SUICIDE! AND IN ONE HAND — A TINY SCRAP OF PAPER!

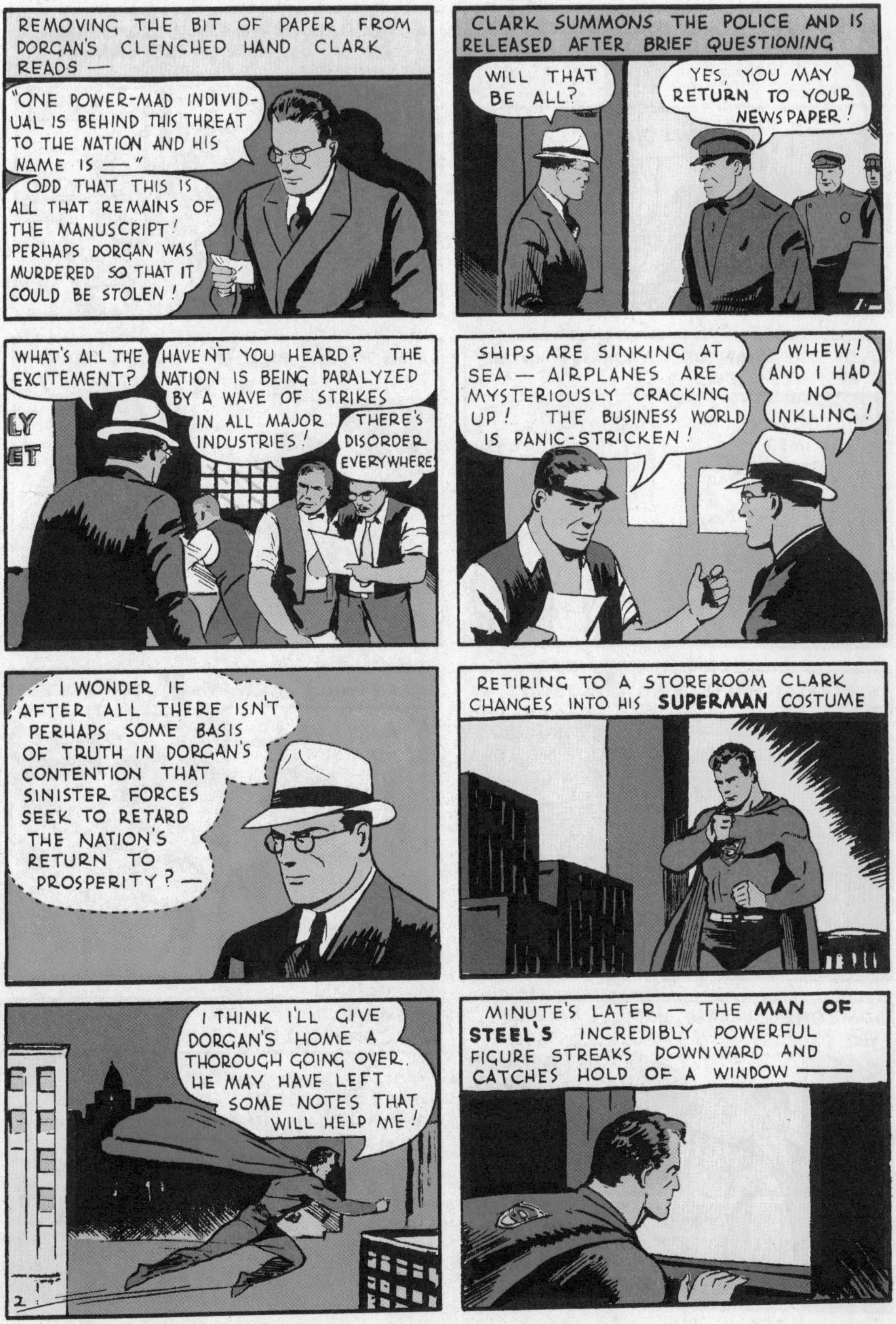

REMOVING THE BIT OF PAPER FROM DORGAN'S CLENCHED HAND CLARK READS —
"ONE POWER-MAD INDIVIDUAL IS BEHIND THIS THREAT TO THE NATION AND HIS NAME IS —"
ODD THAT THIS IS ALL THAT REMAINS OF THE MANUSCRIPT! PERHAPS DORGAN WAS MURDERED SO THAT IT COULD BE STOLEN!
CLARK SUMMONS THE POLICE AND IS RELEASED AFTER BRIEF QUESTIONING
WILL THAT BE ALL?
YES, YOU MAY RETURN TO YOUR NEWSPAPER!
WHAT'S ALL THE EXCITEMENT?
HAVEN'T YOU HEARD? THE NATION IS BEING PARALYZED BY A WAVE OF STRIKES IN ALL MAJOR INDUSTRIES!
THERE'S DISORDER EVERYWHERE!
SHIPS ARE SINKING AT SEA — AIRPLANES ARE MYSTERIOUSLY CRACKING UP! THE BUSINESS WORLD IS PANIC-STRICKEN!
WHEW! AND I HAD NO INKLING!
I WONDER IF AFTER ALL THERE ISN'T PERHAPS SOME BASIS OF TRUTH IN DORGAN'S CONTENTION THAT SINISTER FORCES SEEK TO RETARD THE NATION'S RETURN TO PROSPERITY? —
RETIRING TO A STOREROOM CLARK CHANGES INTO HIS SUPERMAN COSTUME
I THINK I'LL GIVE DORGAN'S HOME A THOROUGH GOING OVER. HE MAY HAVE LEFT SOME NOTES THAT WILL HELP ME!
MINUTE'S LATER — THE MAN OF STEEL'S INCREDIBLY POWERFUL FIGURE STREAKS DOWNWARD AND CATCHES HOLD OF A WINDOW ——

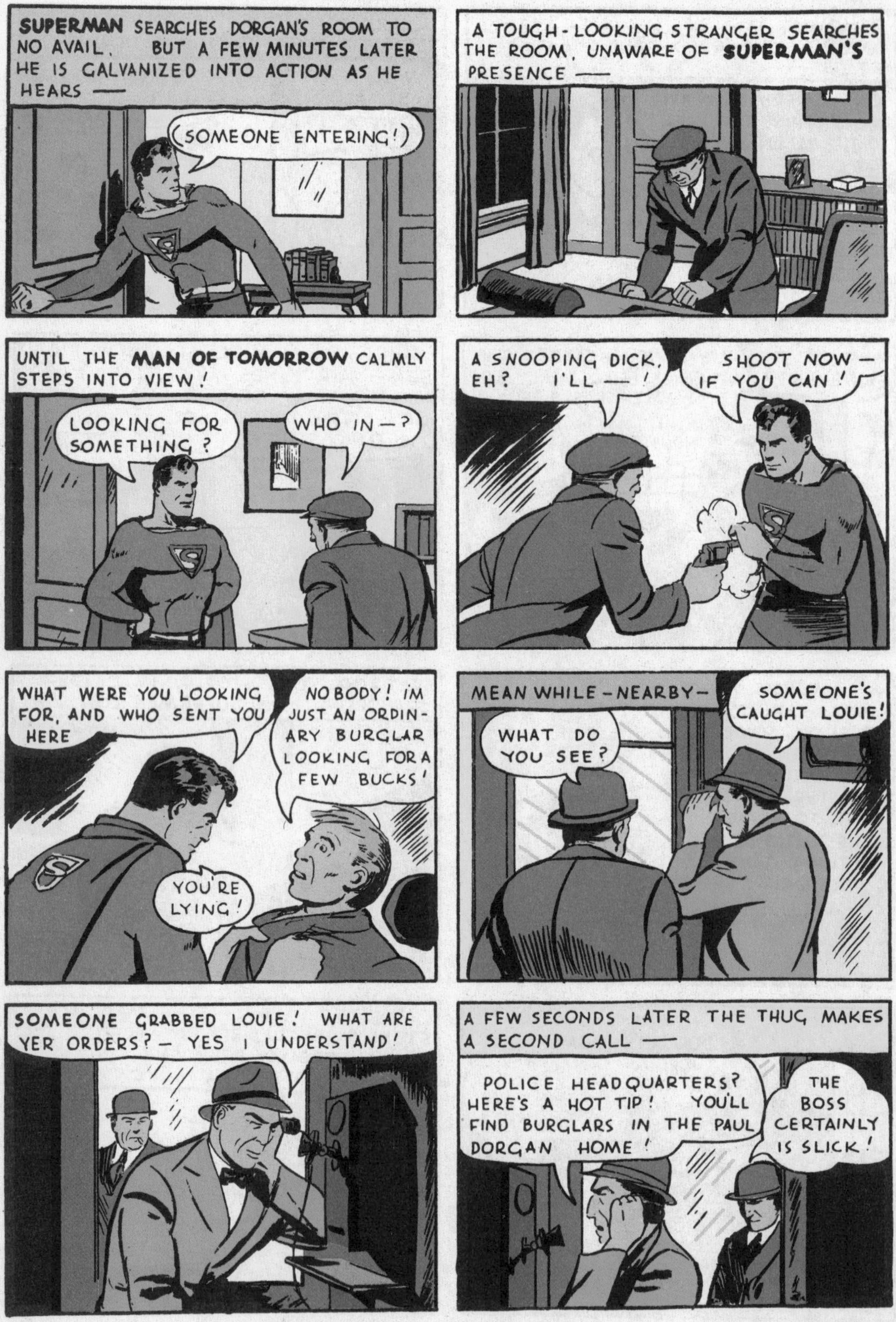

SUPERMAN SEARCHES DORGAN'S ROOM TO NO AVAIL. BUT A FEW MINUTES LATER HE IS GALVANIZED INTO ACTION AS HE HEARS —
(SOMEONE ENTERING!)
A TOUGH-LOOKING STRANGER SEARCHES THE ROOM, UNAWARE OF SUPERMAN'S PRESENCE —
UNTIL THE MAN OF TOMORROW CALMLY STEPS INTO VIEW!
LOOKING FOR SOMETHING?
WHO IN—?
A SNOOPING DICK, EH? I'LL —!
SHOOT NOW— IF YOU CAN!
WHAT WERE YOU LOOKING FOR, AND WHO SENT YOU HERE
NOBODY! I'M JUST AN ORDINARY BURGLAR LOOKING FOR A FEW BUCKS!
YOU'RE LYING!
MEAN WHILE-NEARBY-
WHAT DO YOU SEE?
SOMEONE'S CAUGHT LOUIE!
SOMEONE GRABBED LOUIE! WHAT ARE YER ORDERS?— YES I UNDERSTAND!
A FEW SECONDS LATER THE THUG MAKES A SECOND CALL —
POLICE HEADQUARTERS? HERE'S A HOT TIP! YOU'LL FIND BURGLARS IN THE PAUL DORGAN HOME!
THE BOSS CERTAINLY IS SLICK!

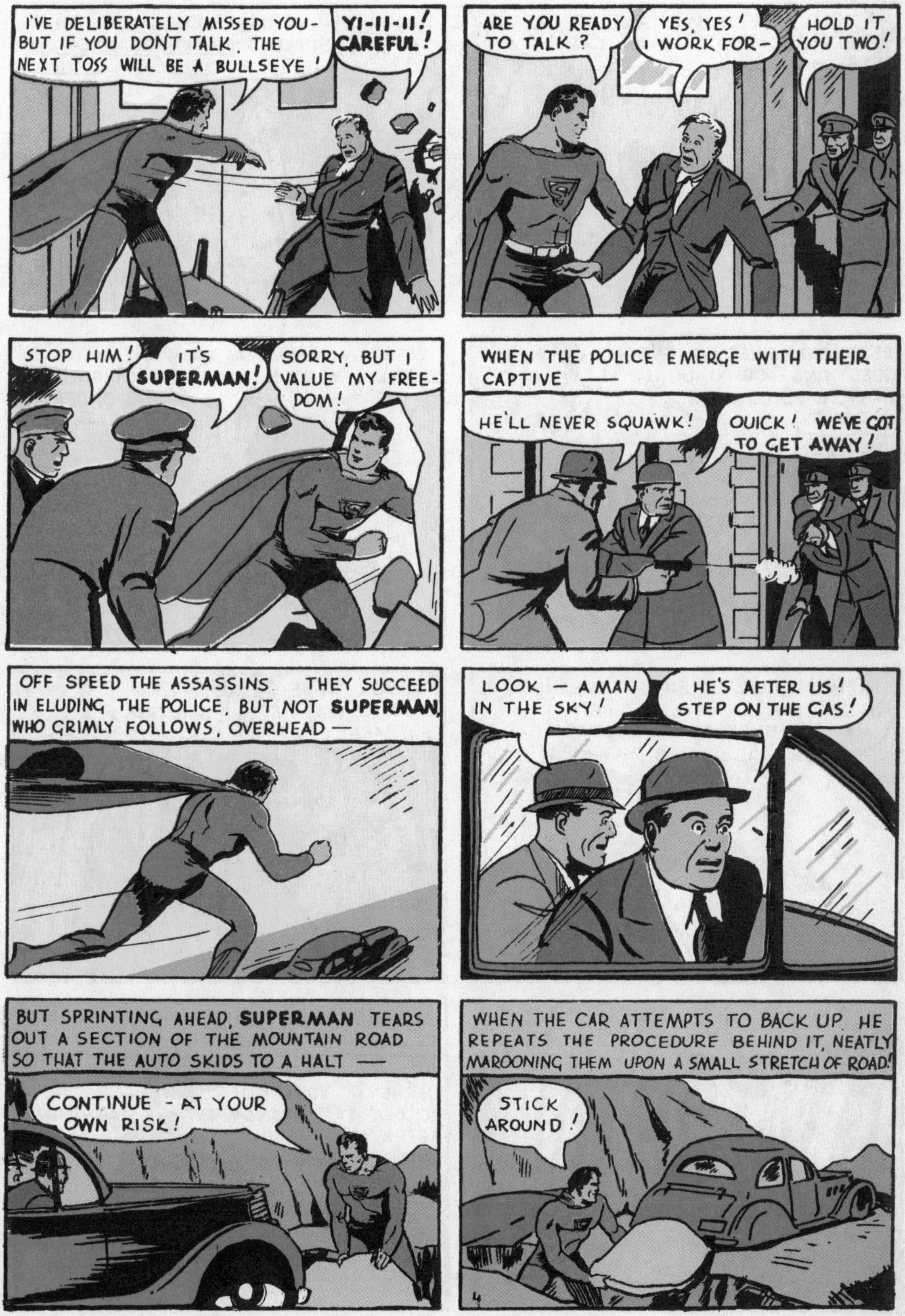
I'VE DELIBERATELY MISSED YOU- BUT IF YOU DON'T TALK, THE NEXT TOSS WILL BE A BULLSEYE!
YI-II-II! CAREFUL!
ARE YOU READY TO TALK?
YES, YES! I WORK FOR-
HOLD IT YOU TWO!
STOP HIM!
IT'S SUPERMAN!
SORRY, BUT I VALUE MY FREE-DOM!
WHEN THE POLICE EMERGE WITH THEIR CAPTIVE —
HE'LL NEVER SQUAWK!
QUICK! WE'VE GOT TO GET AWAY!
OFF SPEED THE ASSASSINS. THEY SUCCEED IN ELUDING THE POLICE, BUT NOT SUPERMAN, WHO GRIMLY FOLLOWS, OVERHEAD —
LOOK — A MAN IN THE SKY!
HE'S AFTER US! STEP ON THE GAS!
BUT SPRINTING AHEAD, SUPERMAN TEARS OUT A SECTION OF THE MOUNTAIN ROAD SO THAT THE AUTO SKIDS TO A HALT —
CONTINUE - AT YOUR OWN RISK!
WHEN THE CAR ATTEMPTS TO BACK UP, HE REPEATS THE PROCEDURE BEHIND IT, NEATLY MAROONING THEM UPON A SMALL STRETCH OF ROAD!
STICK AROUND!

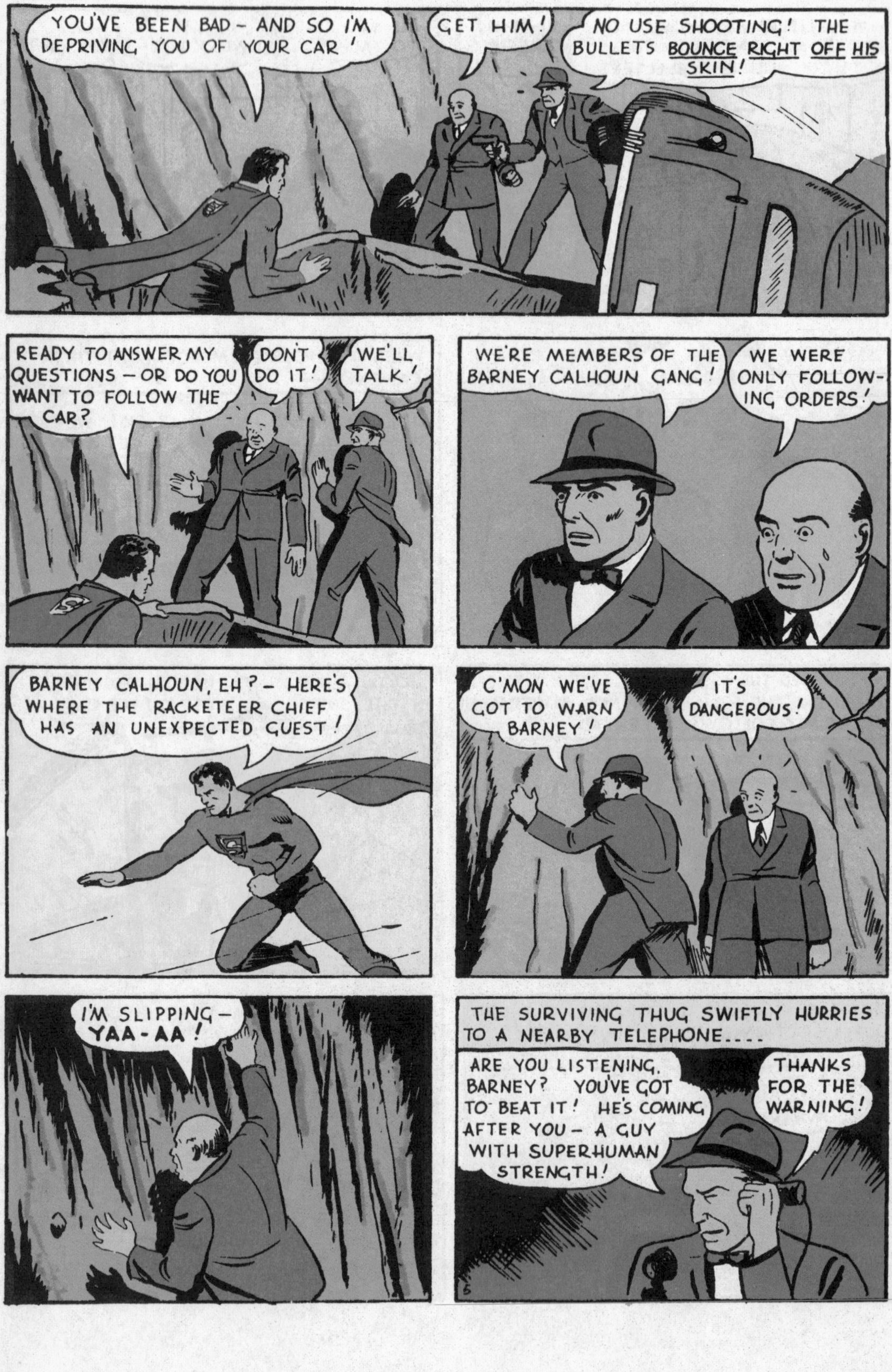
YOU'VE BEEN BAD - AND SO I'M DEPRIVING YOU OF YOUR CAR!
GET HIM!
NO USE SHOOTING! THE BULLETS BOUNCE RIGHT OFF HIS SKIN!
READY TO ANSWER MY QUESTIONS - OR DO YOU WANT TO FOLLOW THE CAR?
DON'T DO IT!
WE'LL TALK!
WE'RE MEMBERS OF THE BARNEY CALHOUN GANG!
WE WERE ONLY FOLLOWING ORDERS!
BARNEY CALHOUN, EH? - HERE'S WHERE THE RACKETEER CHIEF HAS AN UNEXPECTED GUEST!
C'MON WE'VE GOT TO WARN BARNEY!
IT'S DANGEROUS!
I'M SLIPPING - YAA - AA!
THE SURVIVING THUG SWIFTLY HURRIES TO A NEARBY TELEPHONE....
ARE YOU LISTENING, BARNEY? YOU'VE GOT TO BEAT IT! HE'S COMING AFTER YOU - A GUY WITH SUPERHUMAN STRENGTH!
THANKS FOR THE WARNING!

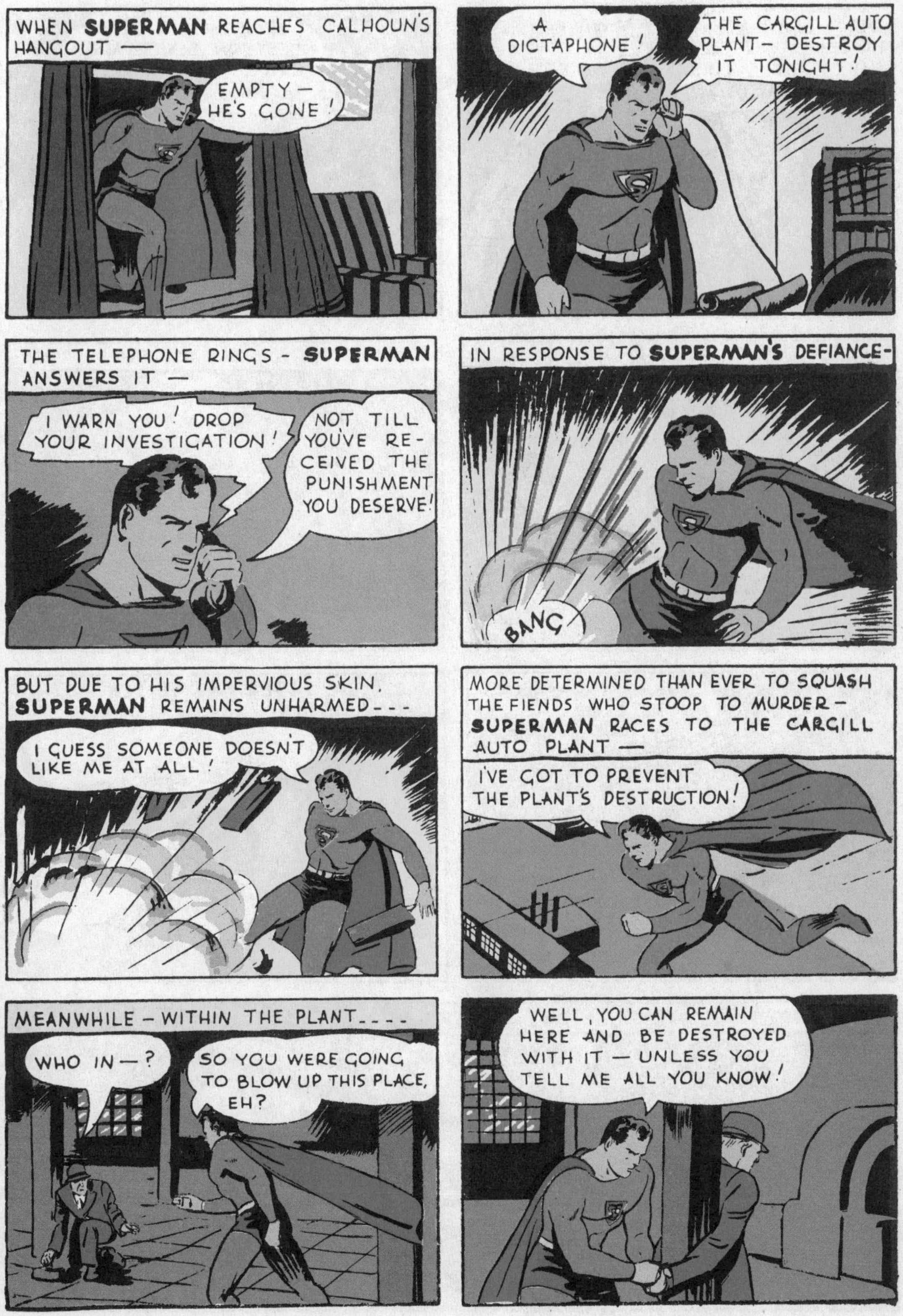
WHEN SUPERMAN REACHES CALHOUN'S HANGOUT —
EMPTY — HE'S GONE!
A DICTAPHONE!
THE CARGILL AUTO PLANT — DESTROY IT TONIGHT!
THE TELEPHONE RINGS - SUPERMAN ANSWERS IT —
I WARN YOU! DROP YOUR INVESTIGATION!
NOT TILL YOU'VE RECEIVED THE PUNISHMENT YOU DESERVE!
IN RESPONSE TO SUPERMAN'S DEFIANCE-
BANG
BUT DUE TO HIS IMPERVIOUS SKIN, SUPERMAN REMAINS UNHARMED---
I GUESS SOMEONE DOESN'T LIKE ME AT ALL!
MORE DETERMINED THAN EVER TO SQUASH THE FIENDS WHO STOOP TO MURDER — SUPERMAN RACES TO THE CARGILL AUTO PLANT —
I'VE GOT TO PREVENT THE PLANT'S DESTRUCTION!
MEANWHILE — WITHIN THE PLANT----
WHO IN —?
SO YOU WERE GOING TO BLOW UP THIS PLACE, EH?
WELL, YOU CAN REMAIN HERE AND BE DESTROYED WITH IT — UNLESS YOU TELL ME ALL YOU KNOW!

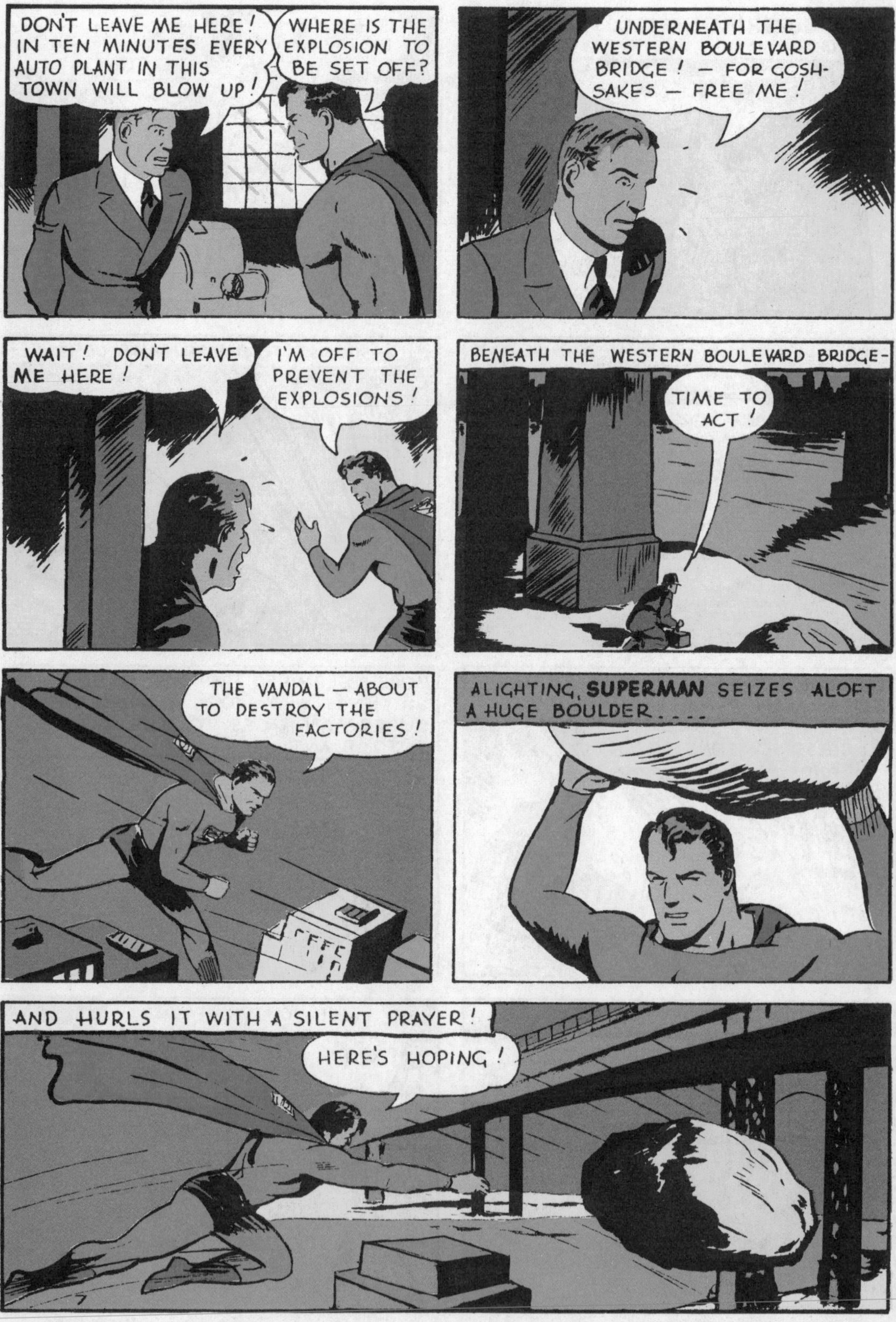

DON'T LEAVE ME HERE! IN TEN MINUTES EVERY AUTO PLANT IN THIS TOWN WILL BLOW UP!
WHERE IS THE EXPLOSION TO BE SET OFF?
UNDERNEATH THE WESTERN BOULEVARD BRIDGE! — FOR GOSH-SAKES — FREE ME!
WAIT! DON'T LEAVE ME HERE!
I'M OFF TO PREVENT THE EXPLOSIONS!
BENEATH THE WESTERN BOULEVARD BRIDGE-
TIME TO ACT!
THE VANDAL — ABOUT TO DESTROY THE FACTORIES!
ALIGHTING, SUPERMAN SEIZES ALOFT A HUGE BOULDER....
AND HURLS IT WITH A SILENT PRAYER!
HERE'S HOPING!

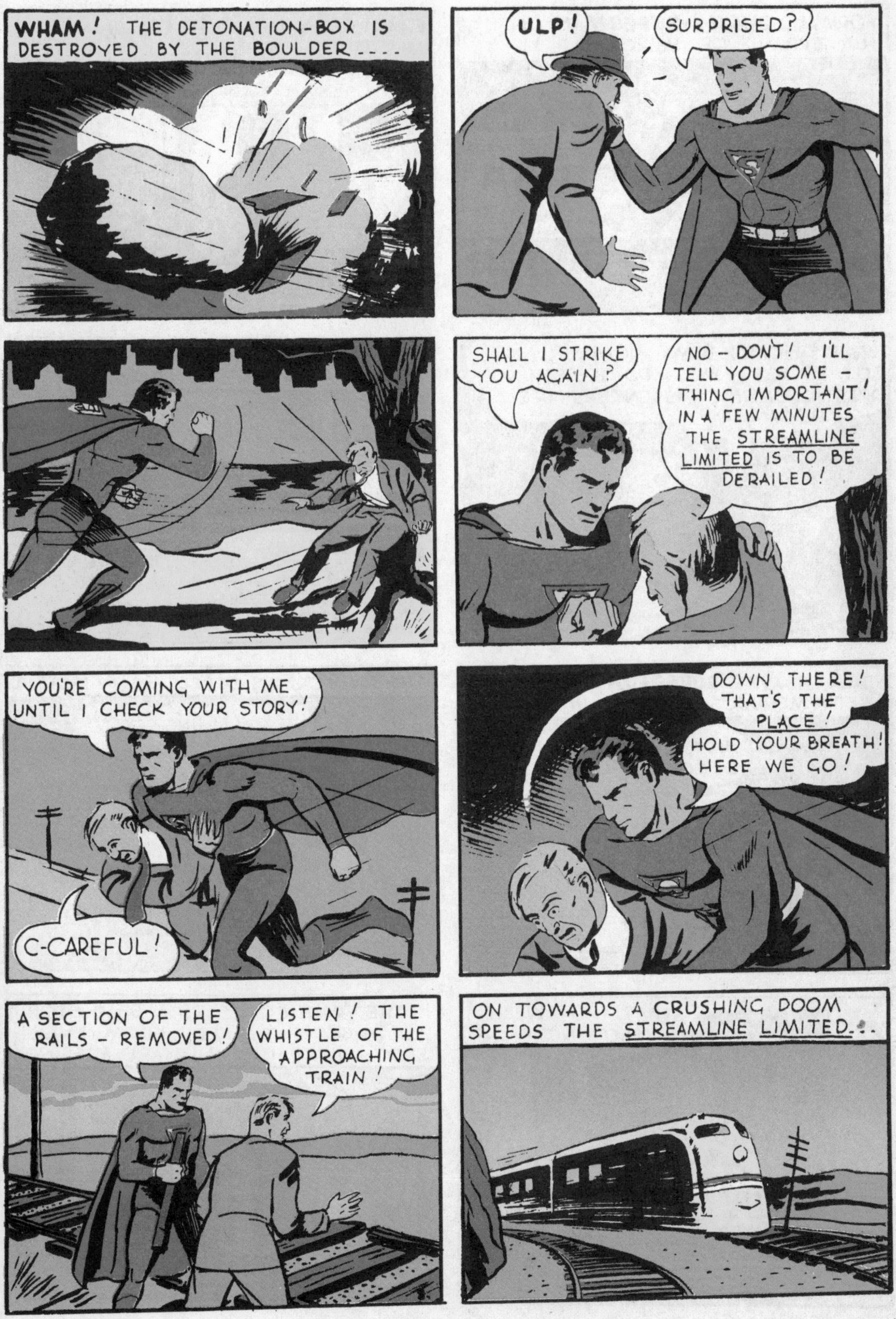
WHAM! THE DETONATION-BOX IS DESTROYED BY THE BOULDER....
ULP!
SURPRISED?
SHALL I STRIKE YOU AGAIN?
NO - DON'T! I'LL TELL YOU SOME - THING IMPORTANT! IN A FEW MINUTES THE STREAMLINE LIMITED IS TO BE DERAILED!
YOU'RE COMING WITH ME UNTIL I CHECK YOUR STORY!
C-CAREFUL!
DOWN THERE! THAT'S THE PLACE!
HOLD YOUR BREATH! HERE WE GO!
A SECTION OF THE RAILS - REMOVED!
LISTEN! THE WHISTLE OF THE APPROACHING TRAIN!
ON TOWARDS A CRUSHING DOOM SPEEDS THE STREAMLINE LIMITED...

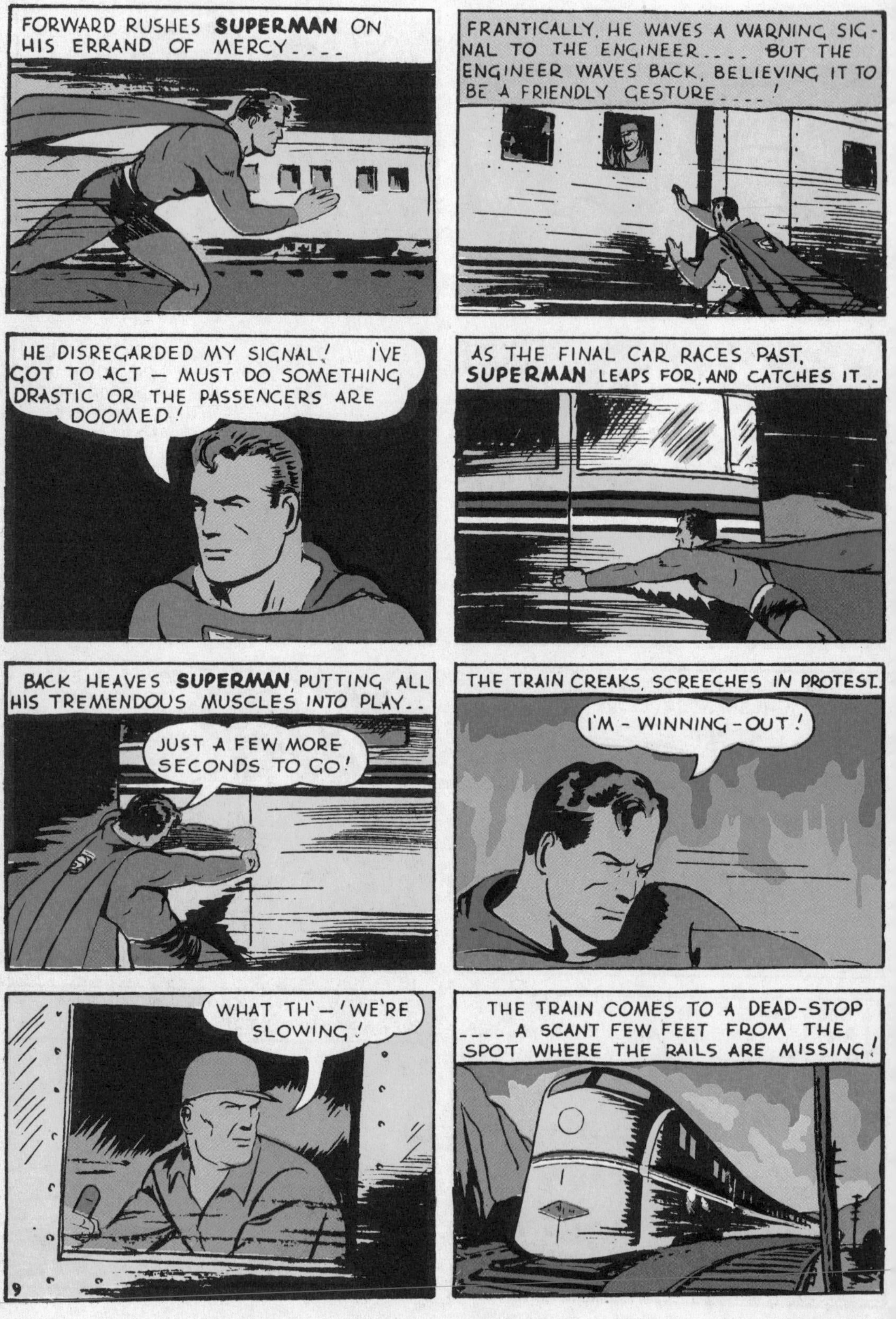
FORWARD RUSHES SUPERMAN ON HIS ERRAND OF MERCY----
FRANTICALLY, HE WAVES A WARNING SIGNAL TO THE ENGINEER.... BUT THE ENGINEER WAVES BACK, BELIEVING IT TO BE A FRIENDLY GESTURE....!
HE DISREGARDED MY SIGNAL! I'VE GOT TO ACT — MUST DO SOMETHING DRASTIC OR THE PASSENGERS ARE DOOMED!
AS THE FINAL CAR RACES PAST, SUPERMAN LEAPS FOR, AND CATCHES IT..
BACK HEAVES SUPERMAN, PUTTING ALL HIS TREMENDOUS MUSCLES INTO PLAY..
JUST A FEW MORE SECONDS TO GO!
THE TRAIN CREAKS, SCREECHES IN PROTEST.
I'M - WINNING - OUT!
WHAT TH'—'WE'RE SLOWING!
THE TRAIN COMES TO A DEAD-STOP ---- A SCANT FEW FEET FROM THE SPOT WHERE THE RAILS ARE MISSING!

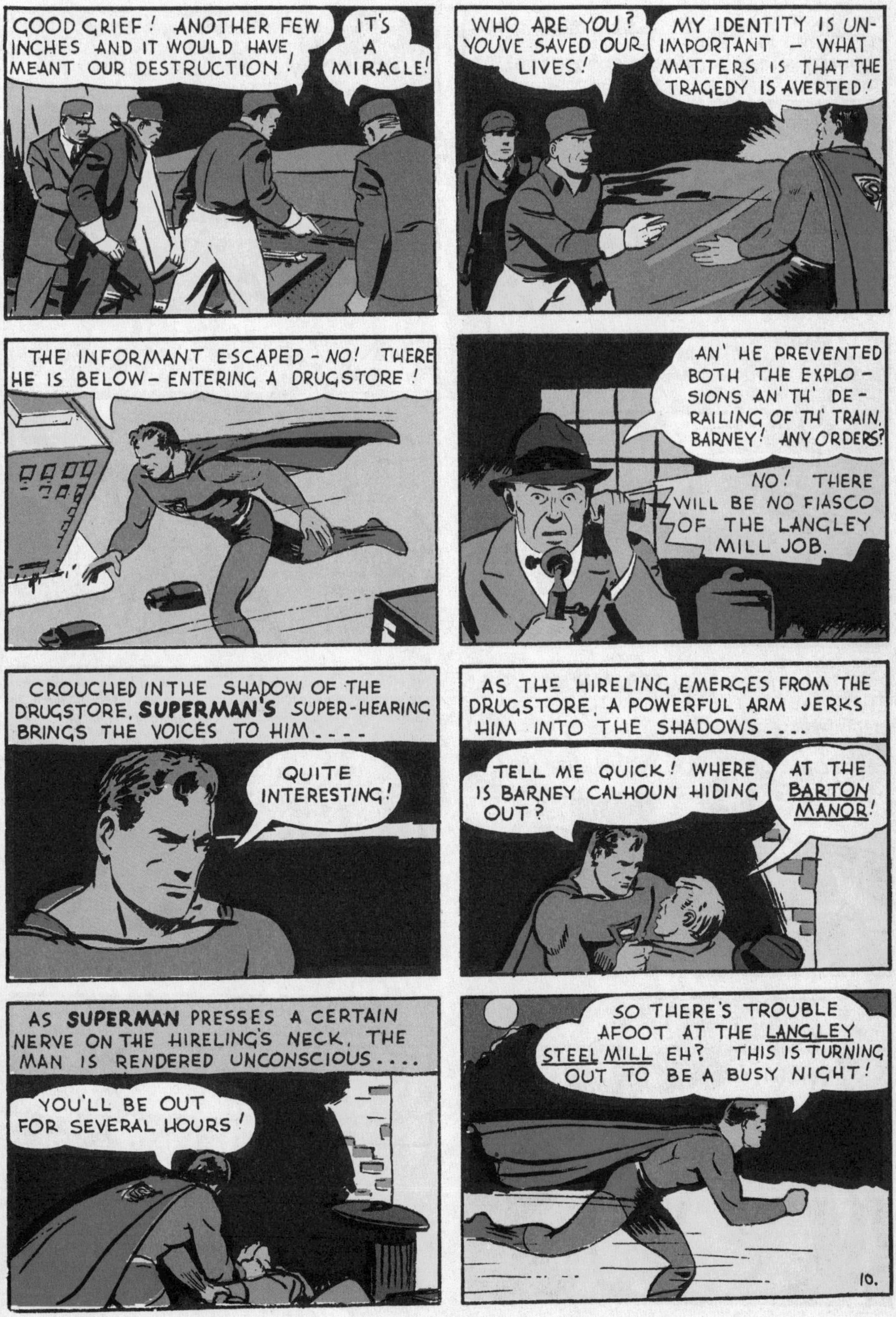
GOOD GRIEF! ANOTHER FEW INCHES AND IT WOULD HAVE MEANT OUR DESTRUCTION!
IT'S A MIRACLE!
WHO ARE YOU? YOU'VE SAVED OUR LIVES!
MY IDENTITY IS UNIMPORTANT - WHAT MATTERS IS THAT THE TRAGEDY IS AVERTED!
THE INFORMANT ESCAPED - NO! THERE HE IS BELOW - ENTERING A DRUGSTORE!
AN' HE PREVENTED BOTH THE EXPLOSIONS AN' TH' DERAILING OF TH' TRAIN, BARNEY! ANY ORDERS?
NO! THERE WILL BE NO FIASCO OF THE LANGLEY MILL JOB.
CROUCHED IN THE SHADOW OF THE DRUGSTORE, SUPERMAN'S SUPER-HEARING BRINGS THE VOICES TO HIM....
QUITE INTERESTING!
AS THE HIRELING EMERGES FROM THE DRUGSTORE, A POWERFUL ARM JERKS HIM INTO THE SHADOWS....
TELL ME QUICK! WHERE IS BARNEY CALHOUN HIDING OUT?
AT THE BARTON MANOR!
AS SUPERMAN PRESSES A CERTAIN NERVE ON THE HIRELING'S NECK, THE MAN IS RENDERED UNCONSCIOUS....
YOU'LL BE OUT FOR SEVERAL HOURS!
SO THERE'S TROUBLE AFOOT AT THE LANGLEY STEEL MILL EH? THIS IS TURNING OUT TO BE A BUSY NIGHT!
10.

WITHIN THE LANGLEY STEEL MILLS, THE THUG WHO HAD ESCAPED FROM THE MOUNTAIN ROAD GLOATS, FOR HE HAS TAMPERED WITH THE MILL'S MECHANISMS...

A COUPLE "ACCIDENTS", AND TH' MEN WILL REFUSE TO WORK HERE!

AS THE GREAT STEEL DIPPER TURNS, IT'S WEAKENED SUPPORTS BREAK, AND IT CRASHES DOWN TOWARD WORKERS BELOW, SPEWING MOLTEN METAL....!

LOOK OUT!

IT'S FALLING!

RACING AT AN INCREDIBLE SPEED, A CLOAKED FIGURE DARTS FORWARD, TOSSES THE TERRIFIED MEN TO SAFETY....

ONE SIDE, PLEASE!

....AND CATCHES THE GREAT, FALLING DIPPER!

B-BUT — IT'S IMPOSSIBLE!

COME TO THINK OF IT, IT IS!

AS THE EYES OF SUPERMAN AND THE THUG MEET, THERE IS MUTUAL RECOGNITION....

YOU!

YOU WON'T GET ME!

THE THUG UNEXPECTEDLY TRIPS AND —

— HE TUMBLES INTO A HUGE BOWL OF MOLTEN ORE!

YI-II-II!

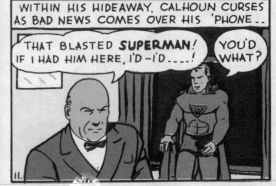

WITHIN HIS HIDEAWAY, CALHOUN CURSES AS BAD NEWS COMES OVER HIS 'PHONE..

THAT BLASTED SUPERMAN! IF I HAD HIM HERE, I'D–I'D....!

YOU'D WHAT?

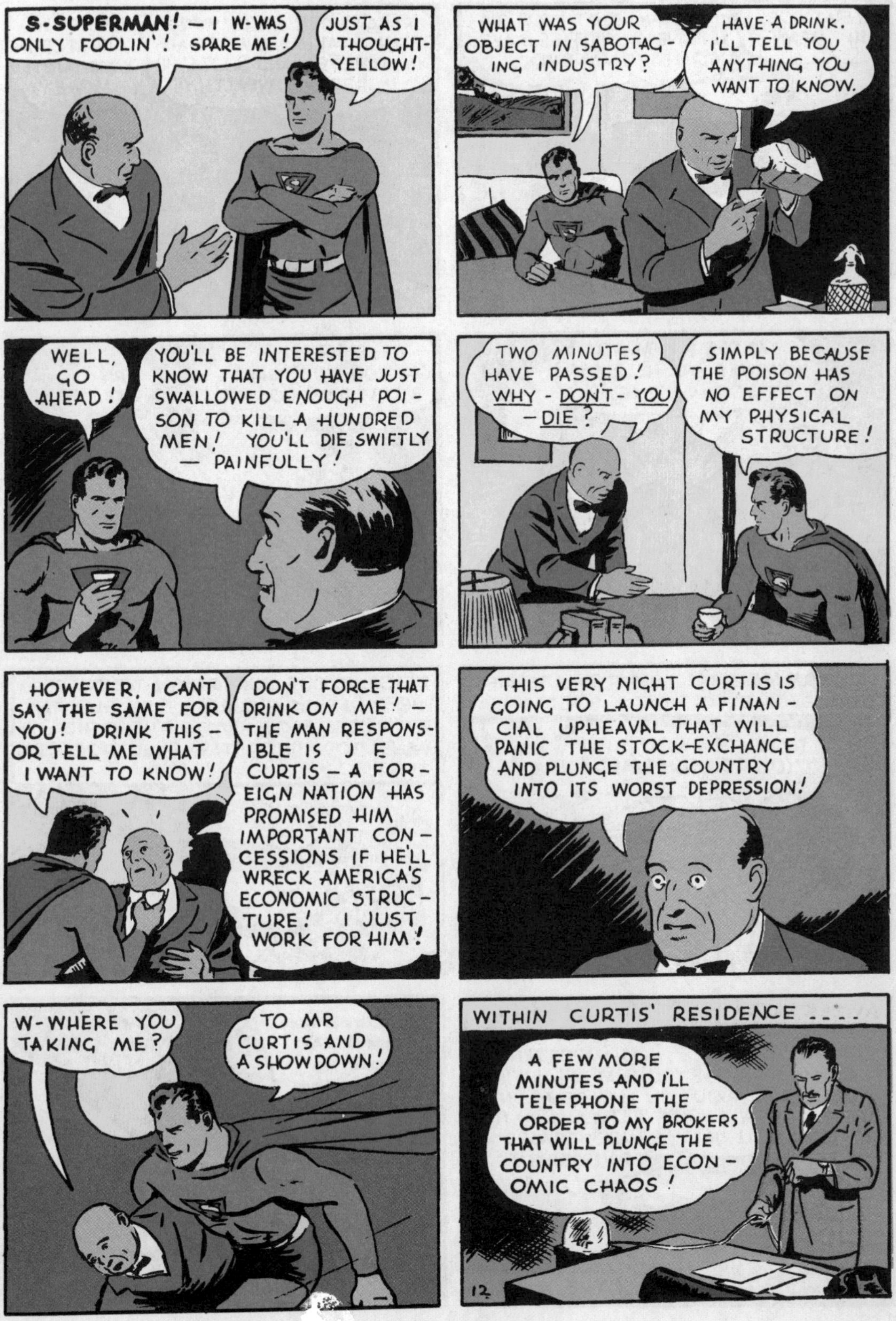

S-SUPERMAN! — I W-WAS ONLY FOOLIN'! SPARE ME!
JUST AS I THOUGHT- YELLOW!
WHAT WAS YOUR OBJECT IN SABOTAGING INDUSTRY?
HAVE A DRINK. I'LL TELL YOU ANYTHING YOU WANT TO KNOW.
WELL, GO AHEAD!
YOU'LL BE INTERESTED TO KNOW THAT YOU HAVE JUST SWALLOWED ENOUGH POISON TO KILL A HUNDRED MEN! YOU'LL DIE SWIFTLY — PAINFULLY!
TWO MINUTES HAVE PASSED! WHY - DON'T - YOU - DIE?
SIMPLY BECAUSE THE POISON HAS NO EFFECT ON MY PHYSICAL STRUCTURE!
HOWEVER, I CAN'T SAY THE SAME FOR YOU! DRINK THIS - OR TELL ME WHAT I WANT TO KNOW!
DON'T FORCE THAT DRINK ON ME! — THE MAN RESPONSIBLE IS J E CURTIS — A FOREIGN NATION HAS PROMISED HIM IMPORTANT CONCESSIONS IF HE'LL WRECK AMERICA'S ECONOMIC STRUCTURE! I JUST WORK FOR HIM!
THIS VERY NIGHT CURTIS IS GOING TO LAUNCH A FINANCIAL UPHEAVAL THAT WILL PANIC THE STOCK-EXCHANGE AND PLUNGE THE COUNTRY INTO ITS WORST DEPRESSION!
W-WHERE YOU TAKING ME?
TO MR CURTIS AND A SHOWDOWN!
WITHIN CURTIS' RESIDENCE ....
A FEW MORE MINUTES AND I'LL TELEPHONE THE ORDER TO MY BROKERS THAT WILL PLUNGE THE COUNTRY INTO ECONOMIC CHAOS!
12

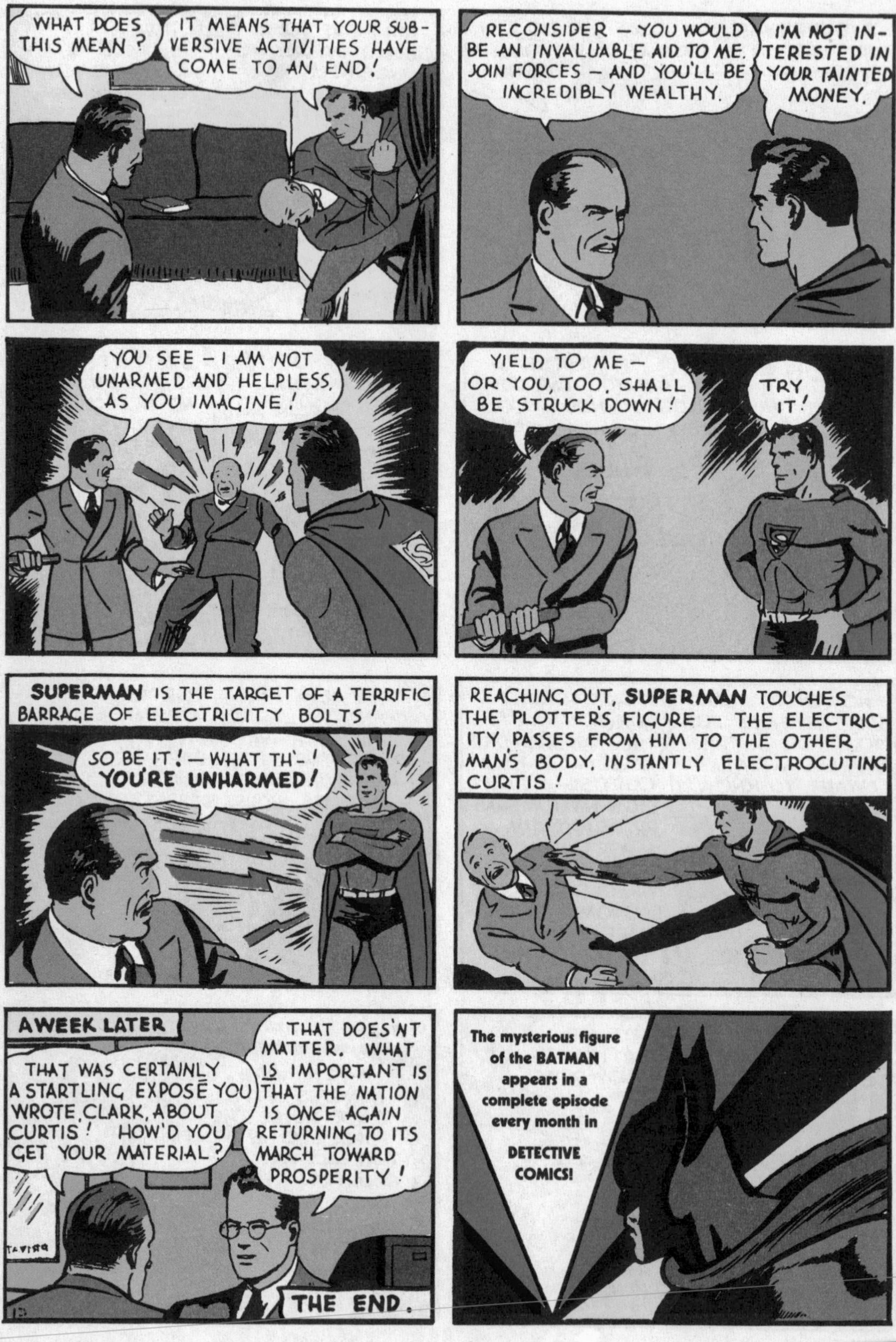
WHAT DOES THIS MEAN ?
IT MEANS THAT YOUR SUB-VERSIVE ACTIVITIES HAVE COME TO AN END!
RECONSIDER — YOU WOULD BE AN INVALUABLE AID TO ME. JOIN FORCES — AND YOU'LL BE INCREDIBLY WEALTHY.
I'M NOT INTERESTED IN YOUR TAINTED MONEY.
YOU SEE — I AM NOT UNARMED AND HELPLESS, AS YOU IMAGINE!
YIELD TO ME — OR YOU, TOO, SHALL BE STRUCK DOWN!
TRY IT!
SUPERMAN IS THE TARGET OF A TERRIFIC BARRAGE OF ELECTRICITY BOLTS!
SO BE IT! — WHAT TH'-! YOU'RE UNHARMED!
REACHING OUT, SUPERMAN TOUCHES THE PLOTTER'S FIGURE — THE ELECTRICITY PASSES FROM HIM TO THE OTHER MAN'S BODY, INSTANTLY ELECTROCUTING CURTIS!
A WEEK LATER
THAT WAS CERTAINLY A STARTLING EXPOSÉ YOU WROTE, CLARK, ABOUT CURTIS! HOW'D YOU GET YOUR MATERIAL?
THAT DOES'NT MATTER. WHAT IS IMPORTANT IS THAT THE NATION IS ONCE AGAIN RETURNING TO ITS MARCH TOWARD PROSPERITY!
THE END.
The mysterious figure of the BATMAN appears in a complete episode every month in DETECTIVE COMICS!

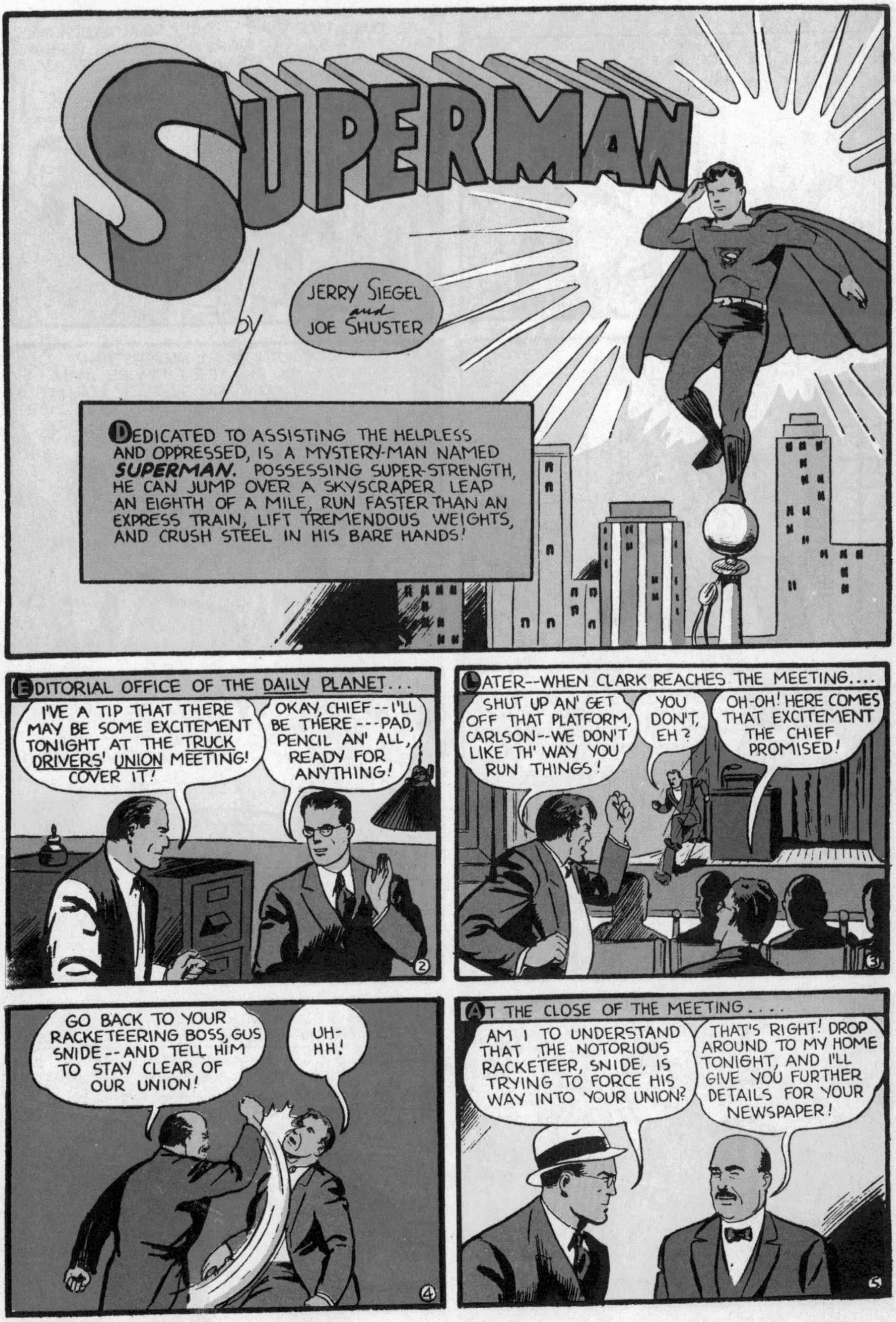
SUPERMAN
by JERRY SIEGEL and JOE SHUSTER
DEDICATED TO ASSISTING THE HELPLESS AND OPPRESSED, IS A MYSTERY-MAN NAMED SUPERMAN. POSSESSING SUPER-STRENGTH, HE CAN JUMP OVER A SKYSCRAPER LEAP AN EIGHTH OF A MILE, RUN FASTER THAN AN EXPRESS TRAIN, LIFT TREMENDOUS WEIGHTS, AND CRUSH STEEL IN HIS BARE HANDS!
EDITORIAL OFFICE OF THE DAILY PLANET...
I'VE A TIP THAT THERE MAY BE SOME EXCITEMENT TONIGHT AT THE TRUCK DRIVERS' UNION MEETING! COVER IT!
OKAY, CHIEF--I'LL BE THERE---PAD, PENCIL AN' ALL, READY FOR ANYTHING!
2
LATER--WHEN CLARK REACHES THE MEETING....
SHUT UP AN' GET OFF THAT PLATFORM, CARLSON--WE DON'T LIKE TH' WAY YOU RUN THINGS!
YOU DON'T, EH?
OH-OH! HERE COMES THAT EXCITEMENT THE CHIEF PROMISED!
3
GO BACK TO YOUR RACKETEERING BOSS, GUS SNIDE--AND TELL HIM TO STAY CLEAR OF OUR UNION!
UH-HH!
4
AT THE CLOSE OF THE MEETING....
AM I TO UNDERSTAND THAT THE NOTORIOUS RACKETEER, SNIDE, IS TRYING TO FORCE HIS WAY INTO YOUR UNION?
THAT'S RIGHT! DROP AROUND TO MY HOME TONIGHT, AND I'LL GIVE YOU FURTHER DETAILS FOR YOUR NEWSPAPER!
5

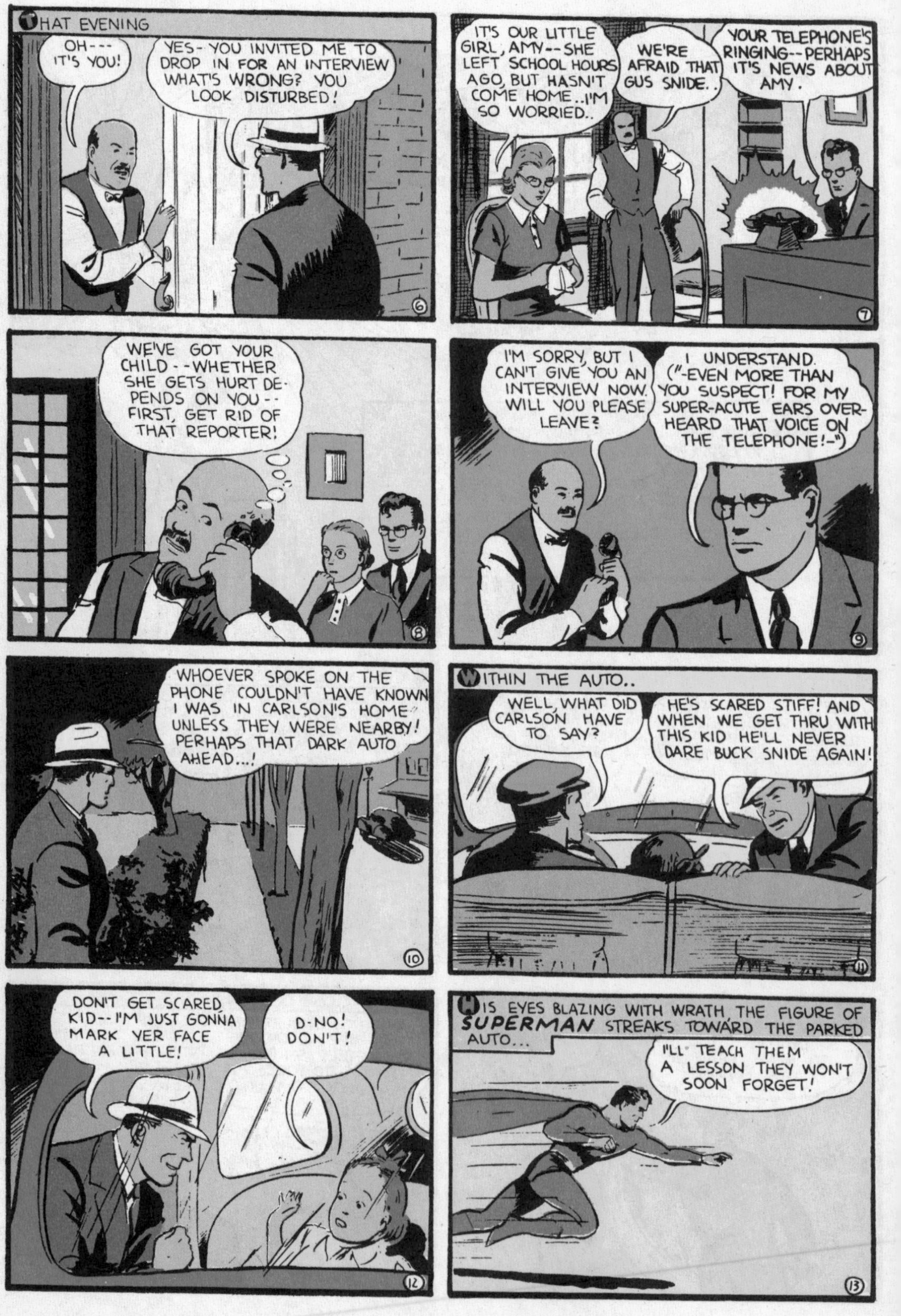

THAT EVENING
OH--- IT'S YOU!
YES- YOU INVITED ME TO DROP IN FOR AN INTERVIEW WHAT'S WRONG? YOU LOOK DISTURBED!
IT'S OUR LITTLE GIRL, AMY--SHE LEFT SCHOOL HOURS AGO, BUT HASN'T COME HOME..I'M SO WORRIED..
WE'RE AFRAID THAT GUS SNIDE..
YOUR TELEPHONE'S RINGING--PERHAPS IT'S NEWS ABOUT AMY.
WE'VE GOT YOUR CHILD--WHETHER SHE GETS HURT DE-PENDS ON YOU--FIRST, GET RID OF THAT REPORTER!
I'M SORRY, BUT I CAN'T GIVE YOU AN INTERVIEW NOW. WILL YOU PLEASE LEAVE?
I UNDERSTAND. ("-EVEN MORE THAN YOU SUSPECT! FOR MY SUPER-ACUTE EARS OVER-HEARD THAT VOICE ON THE TELEPHONE!-")
WHOEVER SPOKE ON THE PHONE COULDN'T HAVE KNOWN I WAS IN CARLSON'S HOME UNLESS THEY WERE NEARBY! PERHAPS THAT DARK AUTO AHEAD...!
WITHIN THE AUTO..
WELL, WHAT DID CARLSON HAVE TO SAY?
HE'S SCARED STIFF! AND WHEN WE GET THRU WITH THIS KID HE'LL NEVER DARE BUCK SNIDE AGAIN!
DON'T GET SCARED KID--I'M JUST GONNA MARK YER FACE A LITTLE!
D-NO! DON'T!
HIS EYES BLAZING WITH WRATH THE FIGURE OF SUPERMAN STREAKS TOWARD THE PARKED AUTO...
I'LL TEACH THEM A LESSON THEY WON'T SOON FORGET!

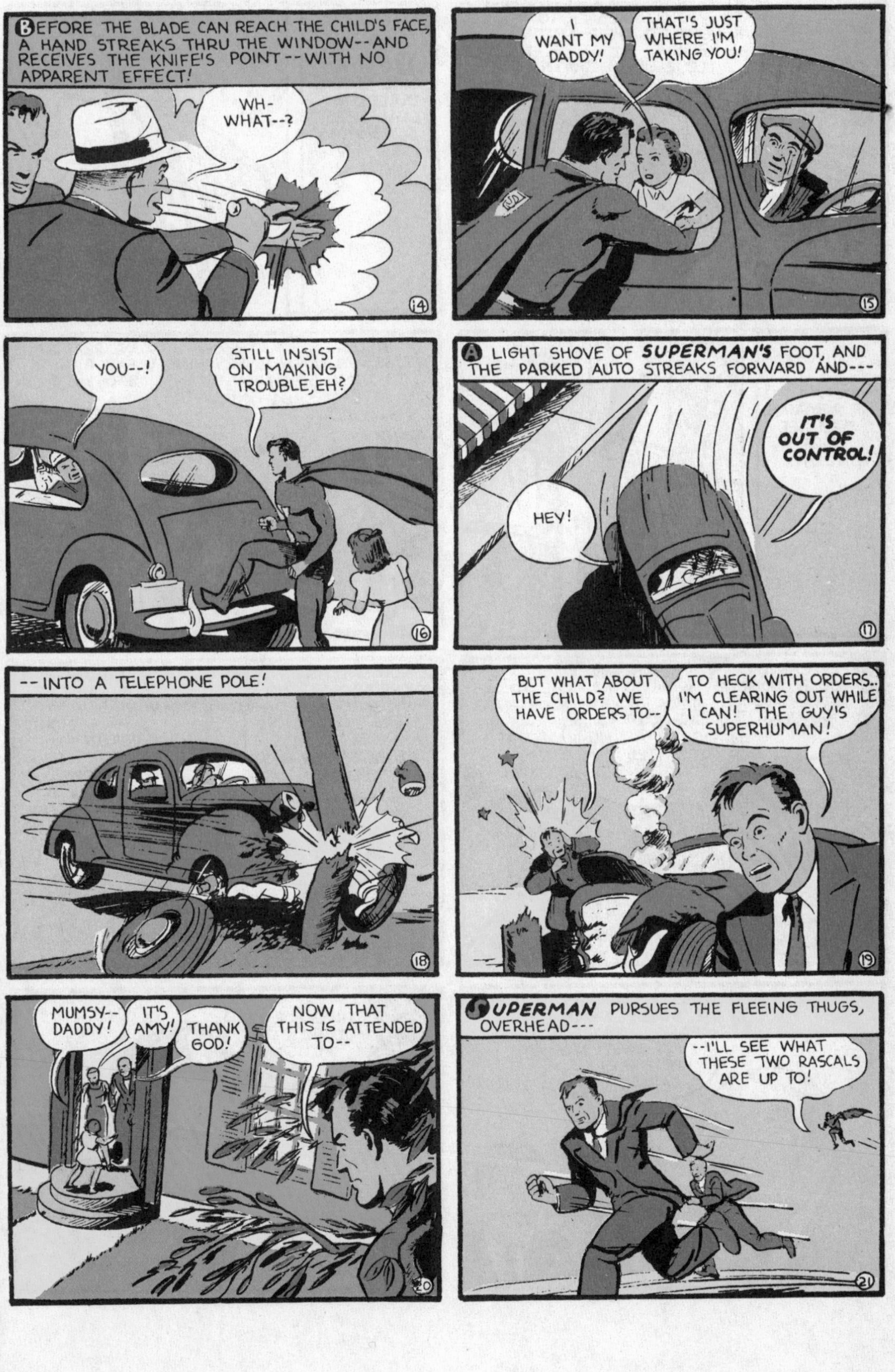

BEFORE THE BLADE CAN REACH THE CHILD'S FACE, A HAND STREAKS THRU THE WINDOW--AND RECEIVES THE KNIFE'S POINT--WITH NO APPARENT EFFECT!
WH- WHAT--?
14
I WANT MY DADDY!
THAT'S JUST WHERE I'M TAKING YOU!
15
YOU--!
STILL INSIST ON MAKING TROUBLE, EH?
16
A LIGHT SHOVE OF SUPERMAN'S FOOT, AND THE PARKED AUTO STREAKS FORWARD AND---
IT'S OUT OF CONTROL!
HEY!
17
--INTO A TELEPHONE POLE!
18
BUT WHAT ABOUT THE CHILD? WE HAVE ORDERS TO--
TO HECK WITH ORDERS.. I'M CLEARING OUT WHILE I CAN! THE GUY'S SUPERHUMAN!
19
MUMSY-- DADDY!
IT'S AMY!
THANK GOD!
NOW THAT THIS IS ATTENDED TO--
20
SUPERMAN PURSUES THE FLEEING THUGS, OVERHEAD---
--I'LL SEE WHAT THESE TWO RASCALS ARE UP TO!
21

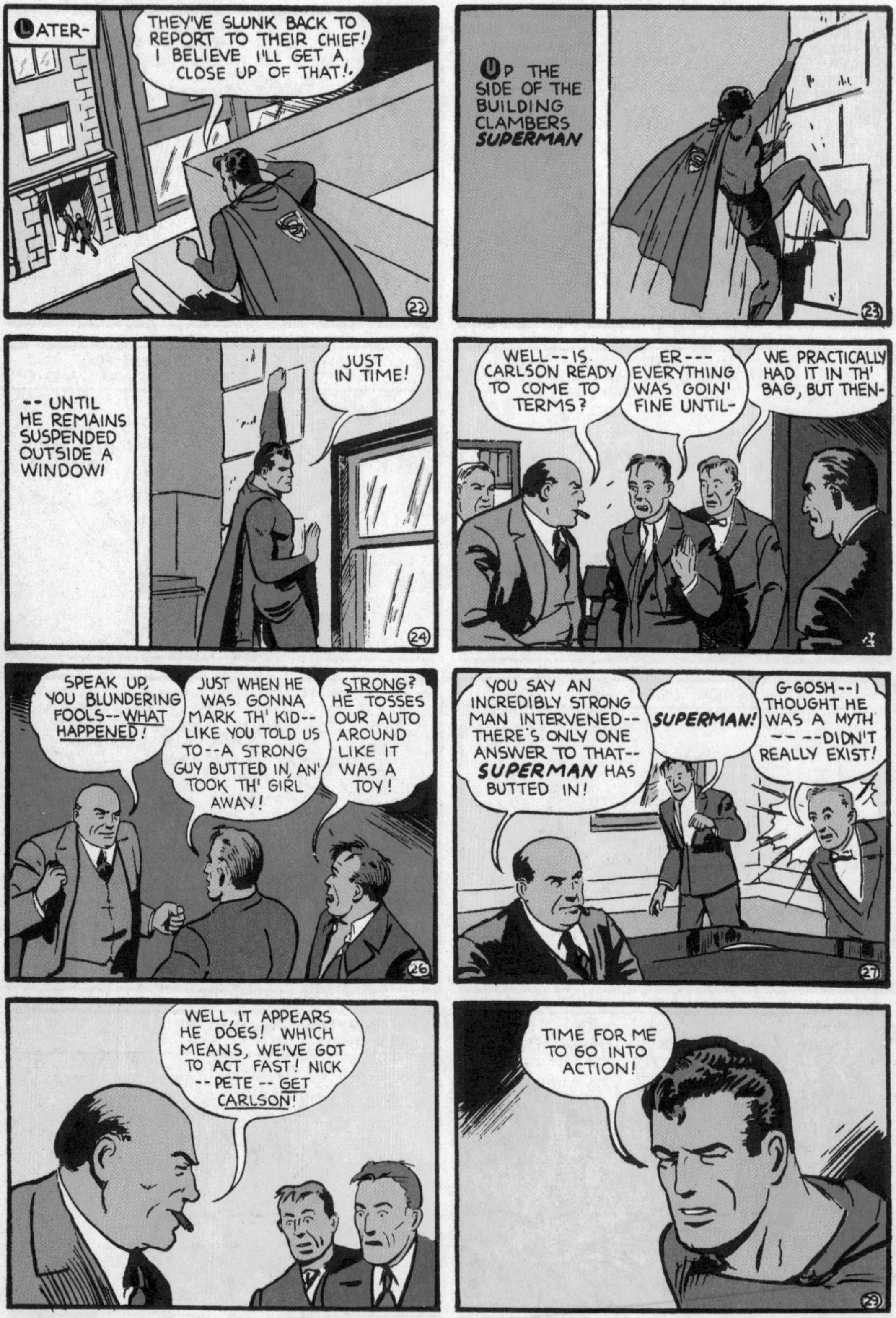
LATER-
THEY'VE SLUNK BACK TO REPORT TO THEIR CHIEF! I BELIEVE I'LL GET A CLOSE UP OF THAT!.
22
UP THE SIDE OF THE BUILDING CLAMBERS SUPERMAN
23
--UNTIL HE REMAINS SUSPENDED OUTSIDE A WINDOW!
JUST IN TIME!
24
WELL--IS CARLSON READY TO COME TO TERMS?
ER--- EVERYTHING WAS GOIN' FINE UNTIL-
WE PRACTICALLY HAD IT IN TH' BAG, BUT THEN-
SPEAK UP, YOU BLUNDERING FOOLS--WHAT HAPPENED!
JUST WHEN HE WAS GONNA MARK TH' KID--LIKE YOU TOLD US TO--A STRONG GUY BUTTED IN, AN' TOOK TH' GIRL AWAY!
STRONG? HE TOSSES OUR AUTO AROUND LIKE IT WAS A TOY!
26
YOU SAY AN INCREDIBLY STRONG MAN INTERVENED--THERE'S ONLY ONE ANSWER TO THAT--SUPERMAN HAS BUTTED IN!
SUPERMAN!
G-GOSH--I THOUGHT HE WAS A MYTH ----DIDN'T REALLY EXIST!
27
WELL, IT APPEARS HE DOES! WHICH MEANS, WE'VE GOT TO ACT FAST! NICK --PETE--GET CARLSON!
TIME FOR ME TO GO INTO ACTION!
29

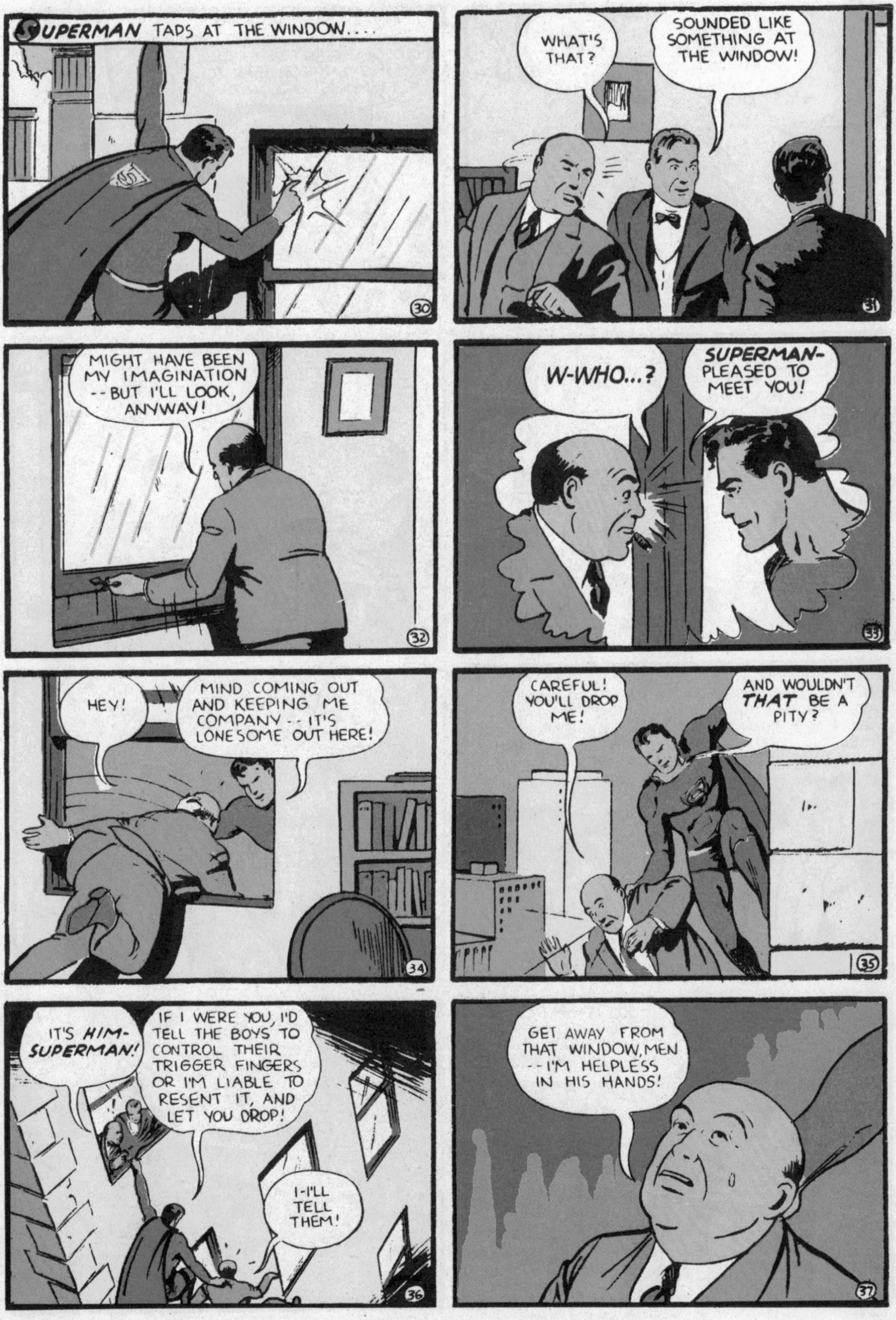
SUPERMAN TAPS AT THE WINDOW....
WHAT'S THAT?
SOUNDED LIKE SOMETHING AT THE WINDOW!
MIGHT HAVE BEEN MY IMAGINATION --BUT I'LL LOOK, ANYWAY!
W-WHO...?
SUPERMAN- PLEASED TO MEET YOU!
HEY!
MIND COMING OUT AND KEEPING ME COMPANY--IT'S LONESOME OUT HERE!
CAREFUL! YOU'LL DROP ME!
AND WOULDN'T THAT BE A PITY?
IT'S HIM- SUPERMAN!
IF I WERE YOU, I'D TELL THE BOYS TO CONTROL THEIR TRIGGER FINGERS OR I'M LIABLE TO RESENT IT, AND LET YOU DROP!
I-I'LL TELL THEM!
GET AWAY FROM THAT WINDOW, MEN --I'M HELPLESS IN HIS HANDS!

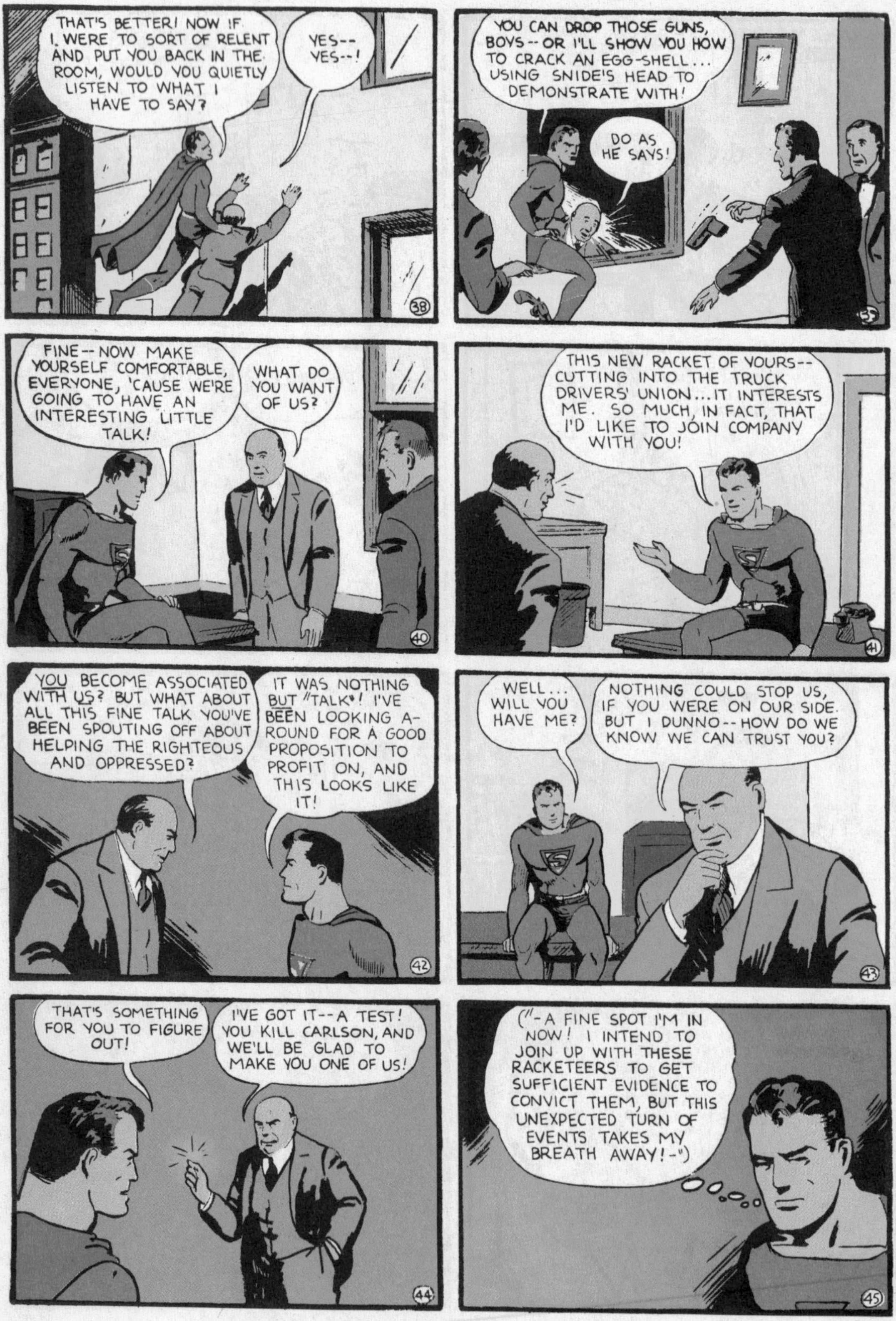
THAT'S BETTER! NOW IF I WERE TO SORT OF RELENT AND PUT YOU BACK IN THE ROOM, WOULD YOU QUIETLY LISTEN TO WHAT I HAVE TO SAY?
YES-- YES--!
38
YOU CAN DROP THOSE GUNS, BOYS -- OR I'LL SHOW YOU HOW TO CRACK AN EGG-SHELL... USING SNIDE'S HEAD TO DEMONSTRATE WITH!
DO AS HE SAYS!
FINE -- NOW MAKE YOURSELF COMFORTABLE, EVERYONE, 'CAUSE WE'RE GOING TO HAVE AN INTERESTING LITTLE TALK!
WHAT DO YOU WANT OF US?
40
THIS NEW RACKET OF YOURS-- CUTTING INTO THE TRUCK DRIVERS' UNION... IT INTERESTS ME. SO MUCH, IN FACT, THAT I'D LIKE TO JOIN COMPANY WITH YOU!
41
YOU BECOME ASSOCIATED WITH US? BUT WHAT ABOUT ALL THIS FINE TALK YOU'VE BEEN SPOUTING OFF ABOUT HELPING THE RIGHTEOUS AND OPPRESSED?
IT WAS NOTHING BUT "TALK"! I'VE BEEN LOOKING A-ROUND FOR A GOOD PROPOSITION TO PROFIT ON, AND THIS LOOKS LIKE IT!
42
WELL... WILL YOU HAVE ME?
NOTHING COULD STOP US, IF YOU WERE ON OUR SIDE. BUT I DUNNO -- HOW DO WE KNOW WE CAN TRUST YOU?
43
THAT'S SOMETHING FOR YOU TO FIGURE OUT!
I'VE GOT IT -- A TEST! YOU KILL CARLSON, AND WE'LL BE GLAD TO MAKE YOU ONE OF US!
44
("- A FINE SPOT I'M IN NOW! I INTEND TO JOIN UP WITH THESE RACKETEERS TO GET SUFFICIENT EVIDENCE TO CONVICT THEM, BUT THIS UNEXPECTED TURN OF EVENTS TAKES MY BREATH AWAY! -")
45

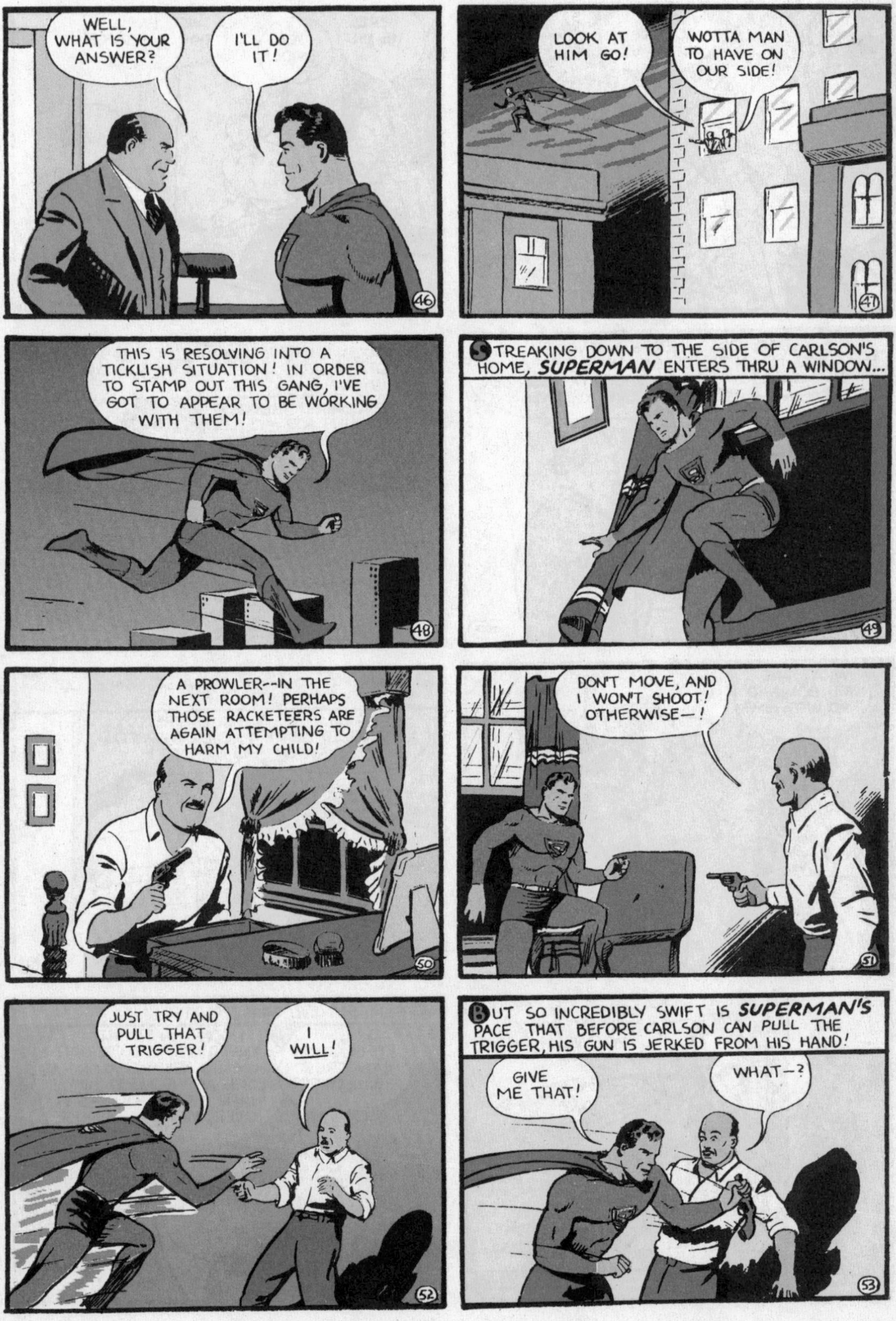
WELL, WHAT IS YOUR ANSWER?
I'LL DO IT!
46
LOOK AT HIM GO!
WOTTA MAN TO HAVE ON OUR SIDE!
47
THIS IS RESOLVING INTO A TICKLISH SITUATION! IN ORDER TO STAMP OUT THIS GANG, I'VE GOT TO APPEAR TO BE WORKING WITH THEM!
48
STREAKING DOWN TO THE SIDE OF CARLSON'S HOME, SUPERMAN ENTERS THRU A WINDOW...
49
A PROWLER--IN THE NEXT ROOM! PERHAPS THOSE RACKETEERS ARE AGAIN ATTEMPTING TO HARM MY CHILD!
50
DON'T MOVE, AND I WON'T SHOOT! OTHERWISE—!
51
JUST TRY AND PULL THAT TRIGGER!
I WILL!
52
BUT SO INCREDIBLY SWIFT IS SUPERMAN'S PACE THAT BEFORE CARLSON CAN PULL THE TRIGGER, HIS GUN IS JERKED FROM HIS HAND!
GIVE ME THAT!
WHAT—?
53

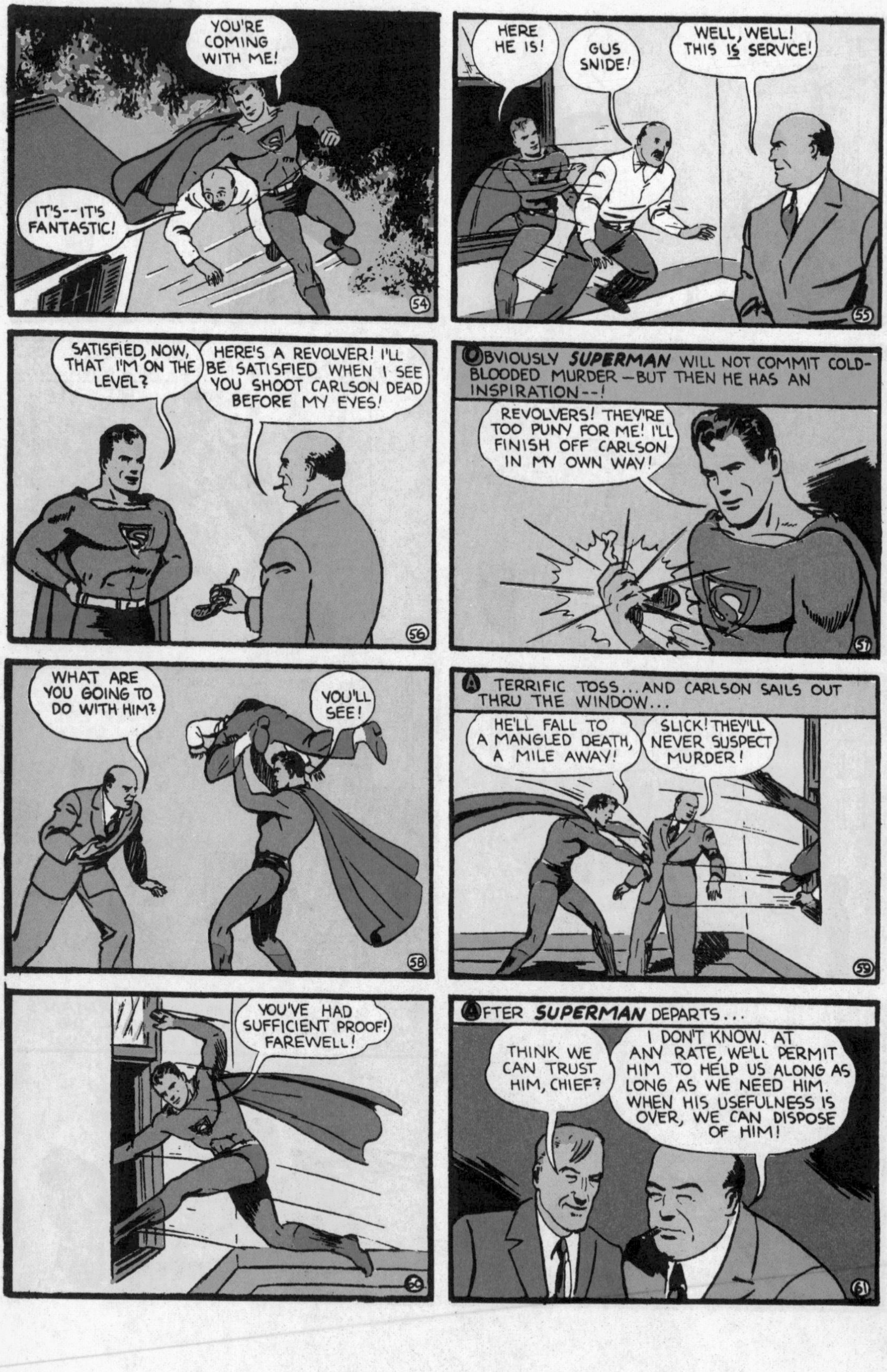
YOU'RE COMING WITH ME!
IT'S--IT'S FANTASTIC!
HERE HE IS!
GUS SNIDE!
WELL, WELL! THIS IS SERVICE!
SATISFIED, NOW, THAT I'M ON THE LEVEL?
HERE'S A REVOLVER! I'LL BE SATISFIED WHEN I SEE YOU SHOOT CARLSON DEAD BEFORE MY EYES!
OBVIOUSLY SUPERMAN WILL NOT COMMIT COLD-BLOODED MURDER—BUT THEN HE HAS AN INSPIRATION--!
REVOLVERS! THEY'RE TOO PUNY FOR ME! I'LL FINISH OFF CARLSON IN MY OWN WAY!
WHAT ARE YOU GOING TO DO WITH HIM?
YOU'LL SEE!
A TERRIFIC TOSS... AND CARLSON SAILS OUT THRU THE WINDOW...
HE'LL FALL TO A MANGLED DEATH, A MILE AWAY!
SLICK! THEY'LL NEVER SUSPECT MURDER!
YOU'VE HAD SUFFICIENT PROOF! FAREWELL!
AFTER SUPERMAN DEPARTS...
THINK WE CAN TRUST HIM, CHIEF?
I DON'T KNOW. AT ANY RATE, WE'LL PERMIT HIM TO HELP US ALONG AS LONG AS WE NEED HIM. WHEN HIS USEFULNESS IS OVER, WE CAN DISPOSE OF HIM!

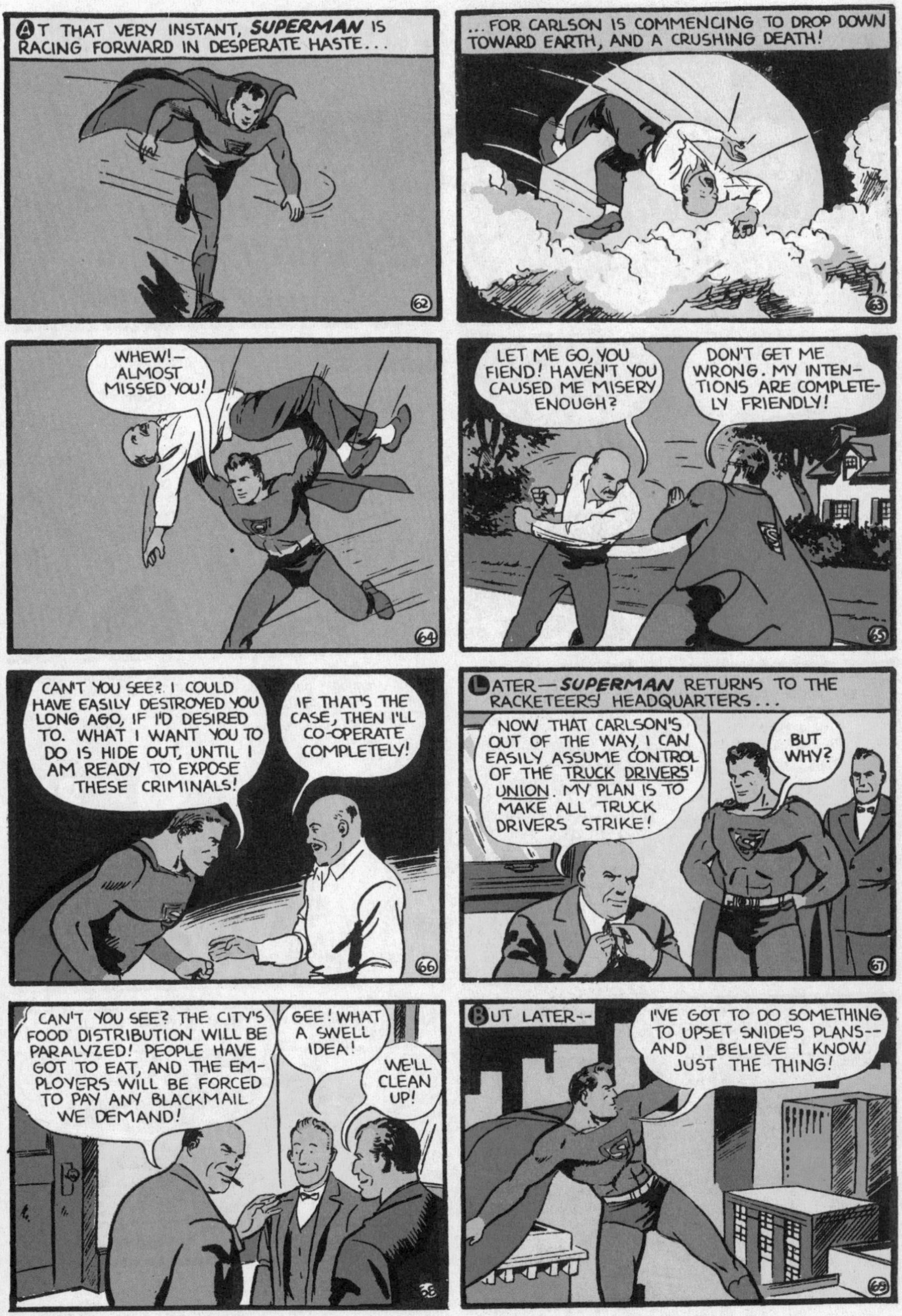
AT THAT VERY INSTANT, SUPERMAN IS RACING FORWARD IN DESPERATE HASTE...
...FOR CARLSON IS COMMENCING TO DROP DOWN TOWARD EARTH, AND A CRUSHING DEATH!
WHEW!— ALMOST MISSED YOU!
LET ME GO, YOU FIEND! HAVEN'T YOU CAUSED ME MISERY ENOUGH?
DON'T GET ME WRONG. MY INTENTIONS ARE COMPLETELY FRIENDLY!
CAN'T YOU SEE? I COULD HAVE EASILY DESTROYED YOU LONG AGO, IF I'D DESIRED TO. WHAT I WANT YOU TO DO IS HIDE OUT, UNTIL I AM READY TO EXPOSE THESE CRIMINALS!
IF THAT'S THE CASE, THEN I'LL CO-OPERATE COMPLETELY!
LATER—SUPERMAN RETURNS TO THE RACKETEERS' HEADQUARTERS...
NOW THAT CARLSON'S OUT OF THE WAY, I CAN EASILY ASSUME CONTROL OF THE TRUCK DRIVERS' UNION. MY PLAN IS TO MAKE ALL TRUCK DRIVERS STRIKE!
BUT WHY?
CAN'T YOU SEE? THE CITY'S FOOD DISTRIBUTION WILL BE PARALYZED! PEOPLE HAVE GOT TO EAT, AND THE EMPLOYERS WILL BE FORCED TO PAY ANY BLACKMAIL WE DEMAND!
GEE! WHAT A SWELL IDEA!
WE'LL CLEAN UP!
BUT LATER--
I'VE GOT TO DO SOMETHING TO UPSET SNIDE'S PLANS-- AND I BELIEVE I KNOW JUST THE THING!

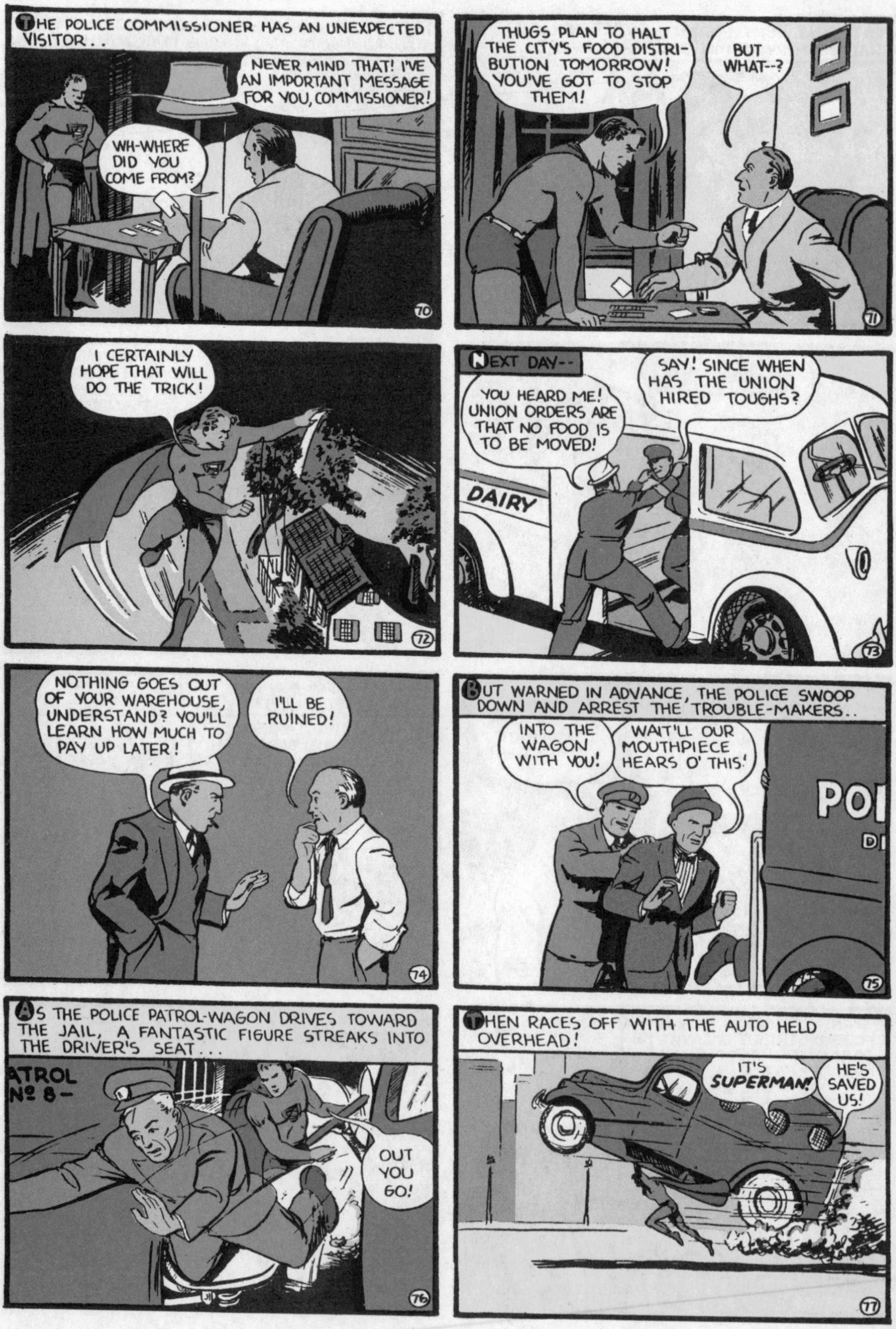
THE POLICE COMMISSIONER HAS AN UNEXPECTED VISITOR..
NEVER MIND THAT! I'VE AN IMPORTANT MESSAGE FOR YOU, COMMISSIONER!
WH-WHERE DID YOU COME FROM?
70
THUGS PLAN TO HALT THE CITY'S FOOD DISTRIBUTION TOMORROW! YOU'VE GOT TO STOP THEM!
BUT WHAT--?
71
I CERTAINLY HOPE THAT WILL DO THE TRICK!
72
NEXT DAY--
YOU HEARD ME! UNION ORDERS ARE THAT NO FOOD IS TO BE MOVED!
SAY! SINCE WHEN HAS THE UNION HIRED TOUGHS?
DAIRY
73
NOTHING GOES OUT OF YOUR WAREHOUSE, UNDERSTAND? YOU'LL LEARN HOW MUCH TO PAY UP LATER!
I'LL BE RUINED!
74
BUT WARNED IN ADVANCE, THE POLICE SWOOP DOWN AND ARREST THE TROUBLE-MAKERS..
INTO THE WAGON WITH YOU!
WAIT'LL OUR MOUTHPIECE HEARS O' THIS!
75
AS THE POLICE PATROL-WAGON DRIVES TOWARD THE JAIL, A FANTASTIC FIGURE STREAKS INTO THE DRIVER'S SEAT...
ATROL Nº 8-
OUT YOU GO!
76
THEN RACES OFF WITH THE AUTO HELD OVERHEAD!
IT'S SUPERMAN!
HE'S SAVED US!
77

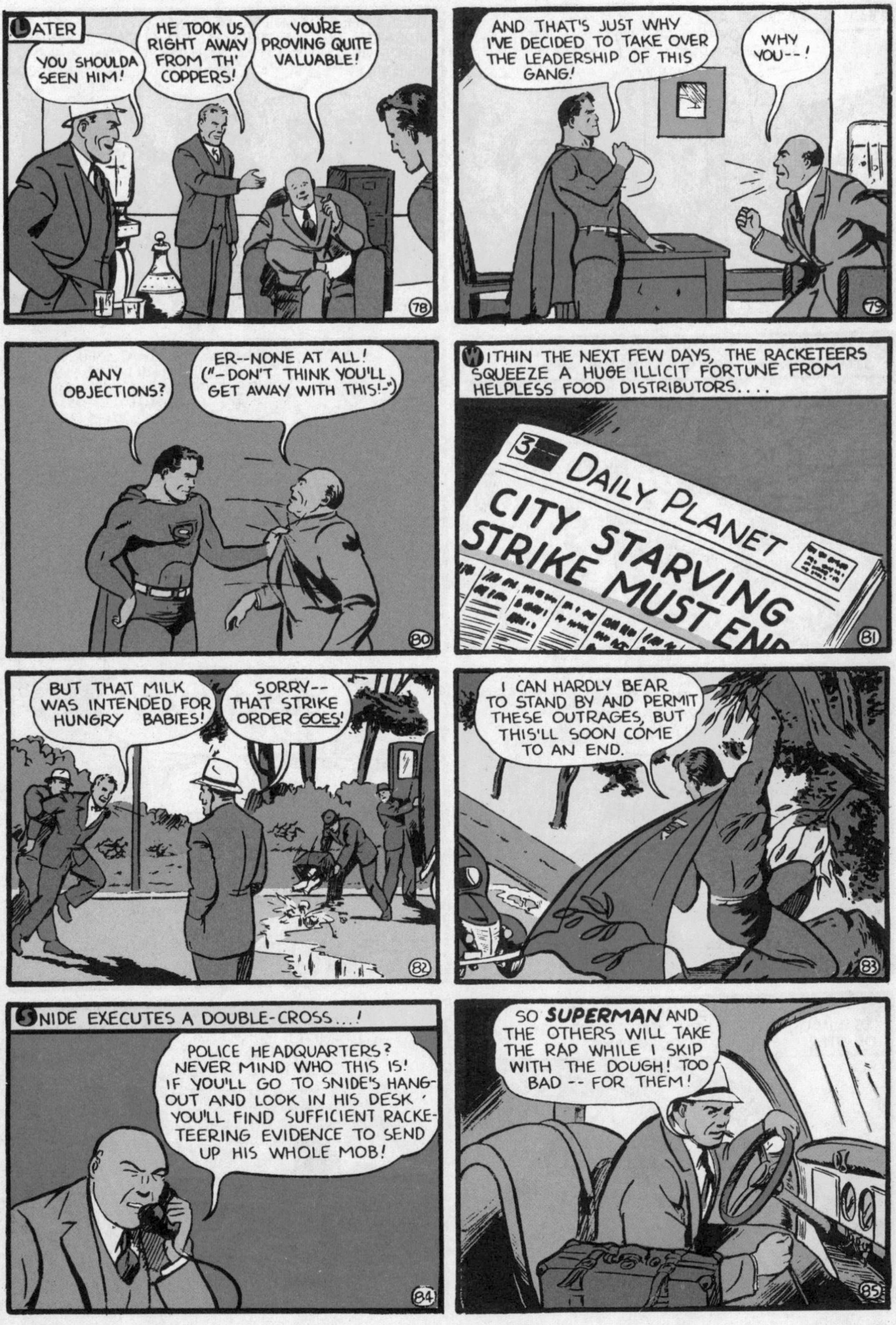
LATER
YOU SHOULDA SEEN HIM!
HE TOOK US RIGHT AWAY FROM TH' COPPERS!
YOU'RE PROVING QUITE VALUABLE!
AND THAT'S JUST WHY I'VE DECIDED TO TAKE OVER THE LEADERSHIP OF THIS GANG!
WHY YOU--!
ANY OBJECTIONS?
ER--NONE AT ALL! ("-DON'T THINK YOU'LL GET AWAY WITH THIS!-")
WITHIN THE NEXT FEW DAYS, THE RACKETEERS SQUEEZE A HUGE ILLICIT FORTUNE FROM HELPLESS FOOD DISTRIBUTORS....
DAILY PLANET
CITY STARVING
STRIKE MUST END
BUT THAT MILK WAS INTENDED FOR HUNGRY BABIES!
SORRY--THAT STRIKE ORDER GOES!
I CAN HARDLY BEAR TO STAND BY AND PERMIT THESE OUTRAGES, BUT THIS'LL SOON COME TO AN END.
SNIDE EXECUTES A DOUBLE-CROSS...!
POLICE HEADQUARTERS? NEVER MIND WHO THIS IS! IF YOU'LL GO TO SNIDE'S HANG-OUT AND LOOK IN HIS DESK YOU'LL FIND SUFFICIENT RACKE-TEERING EVIDENCE TO SEND UP HIS WHOLE MOB!
SO SUPERMAN AND THE OTHERS WILL TAKE THE RAP WHILE I SKIP WITH THE DOUGH! TOO BAD -- FOR THEM!

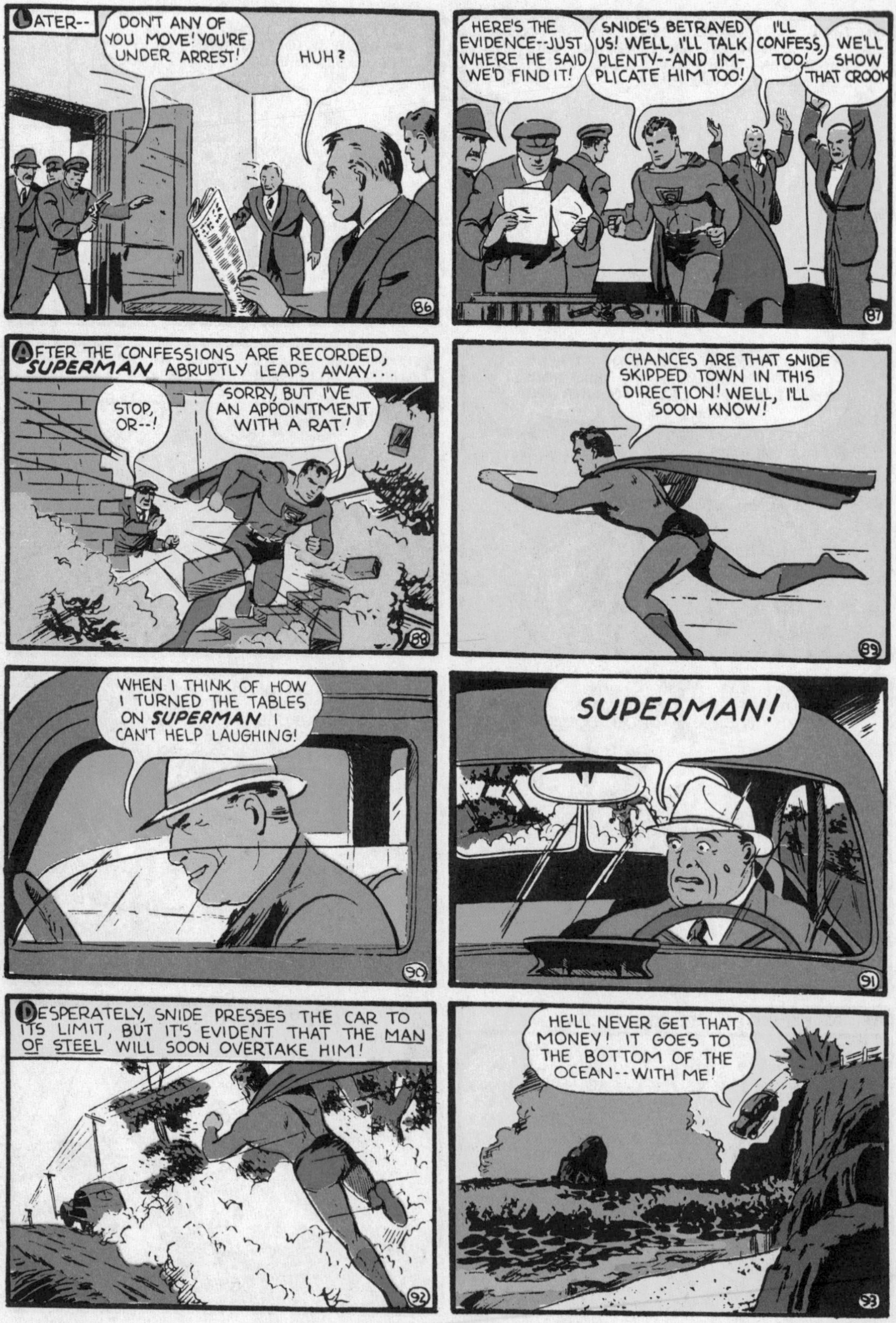
LATER--
DON'T ANY OF YOU MOVE! YOU'RE UNDER ARREST!
HUH?
HERE'S THE EVIDENCE--JUST WHERE HE SAID WE'D FIND IT!
SNIDE'S BETRAYED US! WELL, I'LL TALK PLENTY--AND IMPLICATE HIM TOO!
I'LL CONFESS, TOO!
WE'LL SHOW THAT CROOK
AFTER THE CONFESSIONS ARE RECORDED, SUPERMAN ABRUPTLY LEAPS AWAY...
STOP, OR--!
SORRY, BUT I'VE AN APPOINTMENT WITH A RAT!
CHANCES ARE THAT SNIDE SKIPPED TOWN IN THIS DIRECTION! WELL, I'LL SOON KNOW!
WHEN I THINK OF HOW I TURNED THE TABLES ON SUPERMAN I CAN'T HELP LAUGHING!
SUPERMAN!
DESPERATELY, SNIDE PRESSES THE CAR TO ITS LIMIT, BUT IT'S EVIDENT THAT THE MAN OF STEEL WILL SOON OVERTAKE HIM!
HE'LL NEVER GET THAT MONEY! IT GOES TO THE BOTTOM OF THE OCEAN--WITH ME!

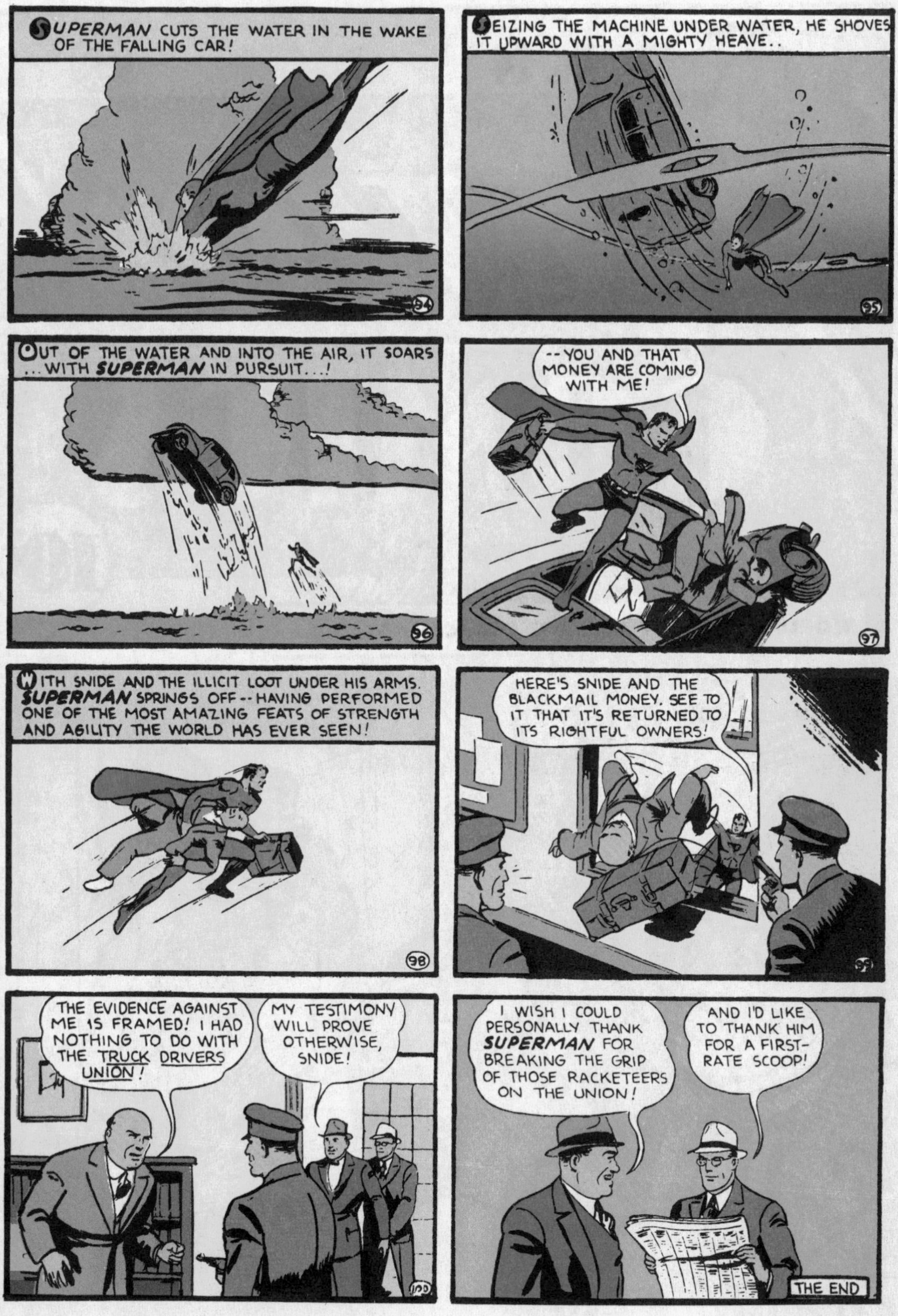
SUPERMAN CUTS THE WATER IN THE WAKE OF THE FALLING CAR!
SEIZING THE MACHINE UNDER WATER, HE SHOVES IT UPWARD WITH A MIGHTY HEAVE..
OUT OF THE WATER AND INTO THE AIR, IT SOARS ...WITH SUPERMAN IN PURSUIT...!
--YOU AND THAT MONEY ARE COMING WITH ME!
WITH SNIDE AND THE ILLICIT LOOT UNDER HIS ARMS, SUPERMAN SPRINGS OFF--HAVING PERFORMED ONE OF THE MOST AMAZING FEATS OF STRENGTH AND AGILITY THE WORLD HAS EVER SEEN!
HERE'S SNIDE AND THE BLACKMAIL MONEY. SEE TO IT THAT IT'S RETURNED TO ITS RIGHTFUL OWNERS!
THE EVIDENCE AGAINST ME IS FRAMED! I HAD NOTHING TO DO WITH THE TRUCK DRIVERS UNION!
MY TESTIMONY WILL PROVE OTHERWISE, SNIDE!
I WISH I COULD PERSONALLY THANK SUPERMAN FOR BREAKING THE GRIP OF THOSE RACKETEERS ON THE UNION!
AND I'D LIKE TO THANK HIM FOR A FIRST-RATE SCOOP!
THE END

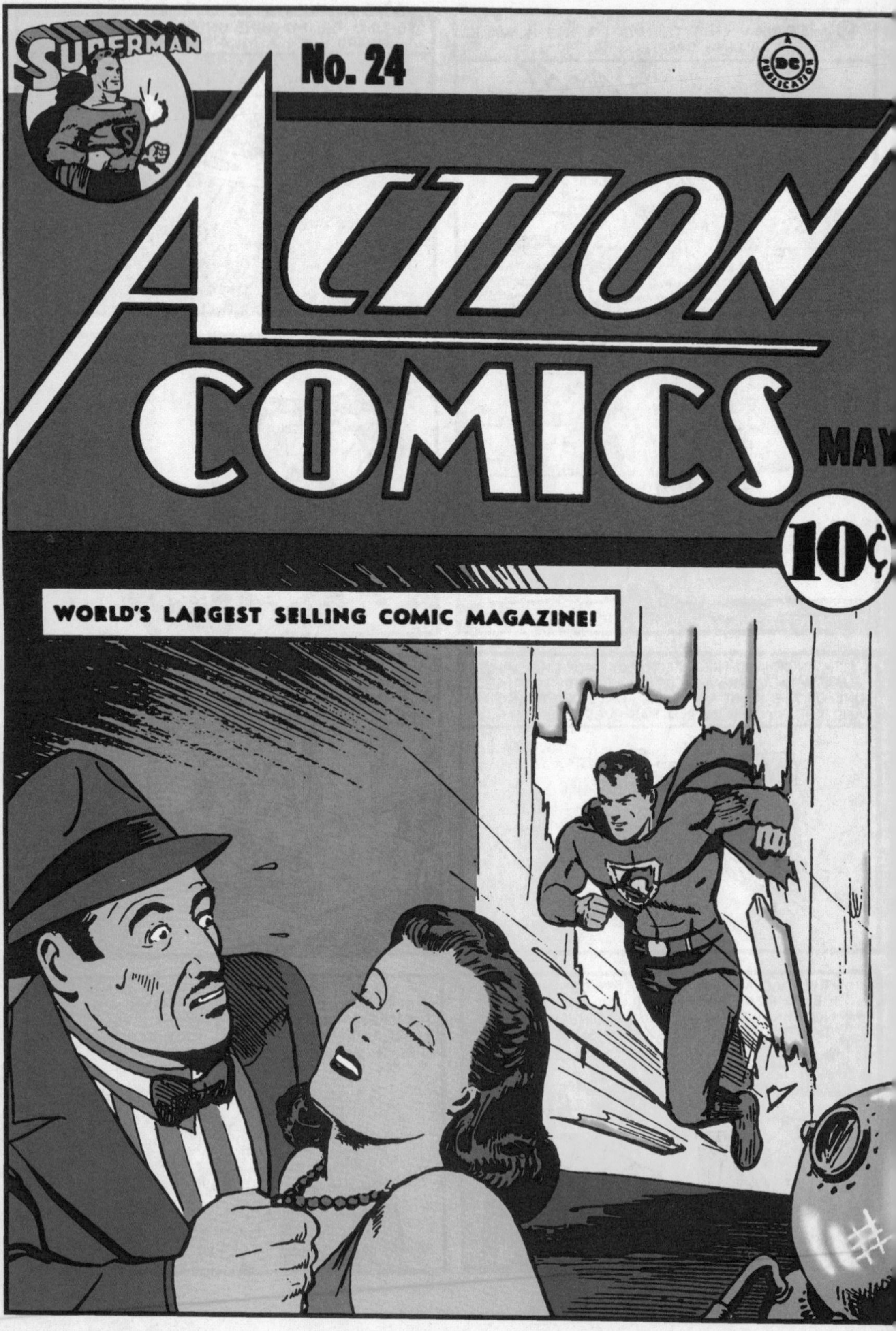
SUPERMAN
No. 24
A DC PUBLICATION
ACTION COMICS
MAY
10¢
WORLD'S LARGEST SELLING COMIC MAGAZINE!

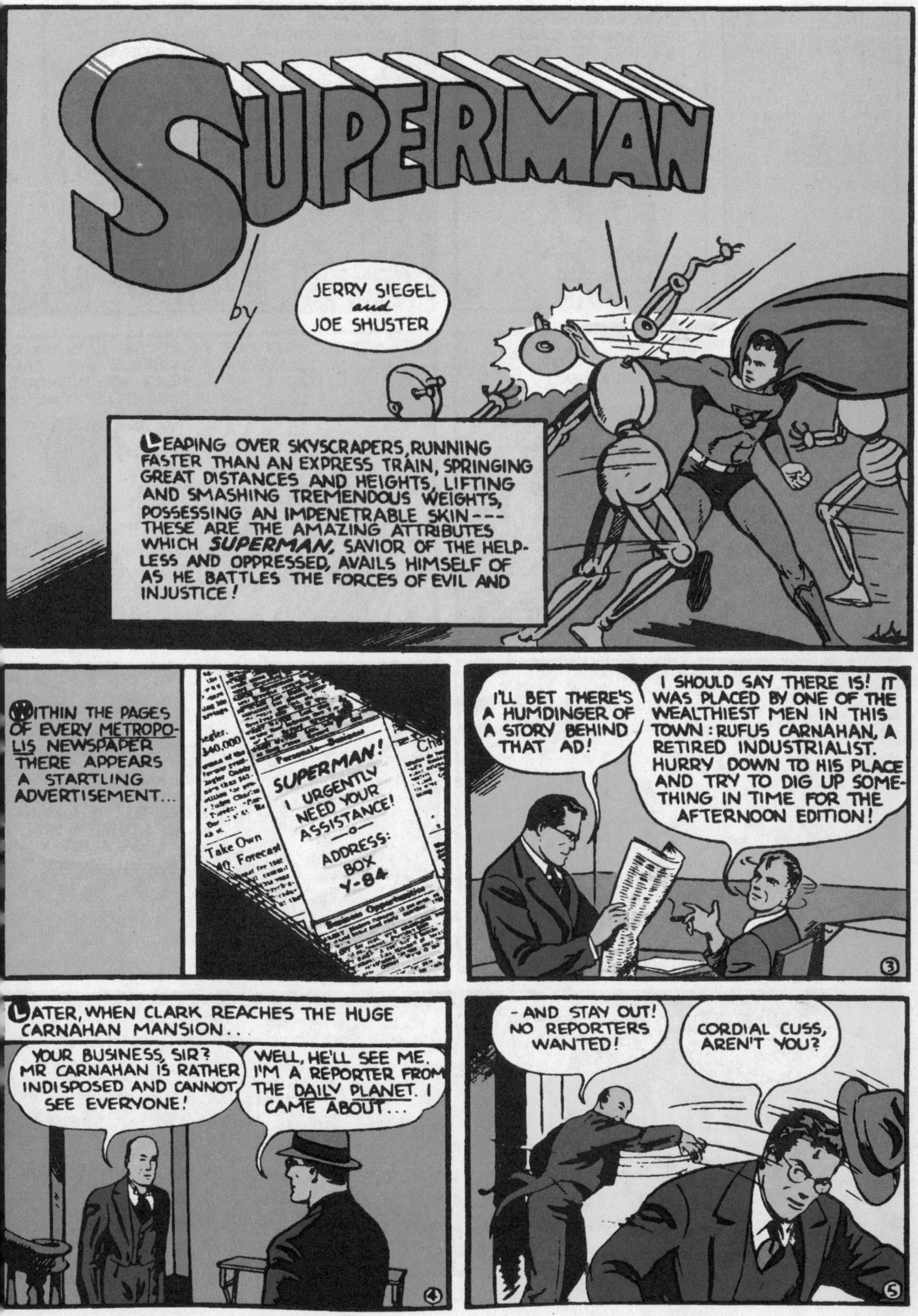
SUPERMAN
by
JERRY SIEGEL and JOE SHUSTER
LEAPING OVER SKYSCRAPERS, RUNNING FASTER THAN AN EXPRESS TRAIN, SPRINGING GREAT DISTANCES AND HEIGHTS, LIFTING AND SMASHING TREMENDOUS WEIGHTS, POSSESSING AN IMPENETRABLE SKIN--- THESE ARE THE AMAZING ATTRIBUTES WHICH SUPERMAN, SAVIOR OF THE HELPLESS AND OPPRESSED, AVAILS HIMSELF OF AS HE BATTLES THE FORCES OF EVIL AND INJUSTICE!
WITHIN THE PAGES OF EVERY METROPOLIS NEWSPAPER THERE APPEARS A STARTLING ADVERTISEMENT...
SUPERMAN! I URGENTLY NEED YOUR ASSISTANCE! ADDRESS: BOX Y-84
I'LL BET THERE'S A HUMDINGER OF A STORY BEHIND THAT AD!
I SHOULD SAY THERE IS! IT WAS PLACED BY ONE OF THE WEALTHIEST MEN IN THIS TOWN: RUFUS CARNAHAN, A RETIRED INDUSTRIALIST. HURRY DOWN TO HIS PLACE AND TRY TO DIG UP SOMETHING IN TIME FOR THE AFTERNOON EDITION!
3
LATER, WHEN CLARK REACHES THE HUGE CARNAHAN MANSION..
YOUR BUSINESS, SIR? MR CARNAHAN IS RATHER INDISPOSED AND CANNOT SEE EVERYONE!
WELL, HE'LL SEE ME. I'M A REPORTER FROM THE DAILY PLANET. I CAME ABOUT...
4
-AND STAY OUT! NO REPORTERS WANTED!
CORDIAL CUSS, AREN'T YOU?
5

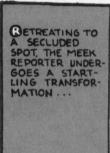

RETREATING TO A SECLUDED SPOT, THE MEEK REPORTER UNDER-GOES A START-LING TRANSFOR-MATION...

CARNAHAN NEEDS ME--AND NO BUTLER IS GOING TO KEEP US APART!

(6)

YOU MUST HAVE THE WRONG ADDRESS. THERE'S NO MASQUERADE BALL HERE.

SINCE YOU INSIST, I'LL COME IN!

BUT I DIDN'T INVITE YOU TO--!

NOT GOING TO DENY IT, ARE YOU?

(8)

GET OUT! GET OUT OR I'LL TELEPHONE THE POLICE!

AT THE RATE YOU'RE SHOUTING THEY CAN HEAR YOU WITHOUT THE TELEPHONE!

(9)

JENKINS! WHAT'S THE MEANING OF THIS DISTURBANCE?

MR CARNAHAN!

(10)

YOU MUST GET BACK TO BED, SIR! THE DOCTOR SAID---!

HANG THE DOCTOR AND HIS INFERNAL ORDERS! IF I WANT TO STRETCH MY LEGS A BIT---

(11)

THE BUTLER'S RIGHT! YOUR BED IS THE PLACE FOR YOU!

(12)

ALIGHTING AT THE TOP OF THE GREAT STAIRS, *SUPERMAN* TENDERLY LIFTS THE ELDERLY MAN IN HIS ARMS.

WH-WHAT-?

YOU HEARD ME! BACK TO BED WITH YOU!

DOCTOR KNOWS BEST!

HOW DARE Y---!

POLICE HEADQUARTERS? SEND A POLICEMAN-- NO! AN ENTIRE SQUAD OF THEM--TO THE CARNAHAN RESIDENCE! A MADMAN IS MENACING OUR LIVES!

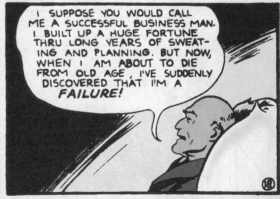

AND -WHO IN TARNATION ARE YOU?

SUPERMAN -- AT YOUR SERVICE!

IT'S ALMOST TOO GOOD TO BE TRUE! YOU SAW MY AD! YOU'VE COME!

JUST WHY DO YOU, A MULTI-MILLIONAIRE, NEED MY ASSISTANCE?

I SUPPOSE YOU WOULD CALL ME A SUCCESSFUL BUSINESS MAN. I BUILT UP A HUGE FORTUNE THRU LONG YEARS OF SWEATING AND PLANNING. BUT NOW, WHEN I AM ABOUT TO DIE FROM OLD AGE, I'VE SUDDENLY DISCOVERED THAT I'M A *FAILURE!*

I'VE LEARNED THAT PETER, THE SON I'VE NEGLECTED AND INDULGED THRU THE YEARS, IS A WEAK-KNEED SOP AND SPENDTHRIFT-- THAT HE SUFFERS HUGE GAMBLING LOSSES!

I'VE HEARD OF YOUR GREAT SENSE OF HUMANITY! ASSIST ME, I IMPLORE YOU! STRAIGHTEN OUT MY SON'S CHARACTER SO THAT HE WILL BE A *MAN!* I'LL PAY YOU ANY AMOUNT!

I GIVE YOU MY WORD --- BUT I ABSOLUTELY RE-FUSE TO ACCEPT ANY COMPENSATION

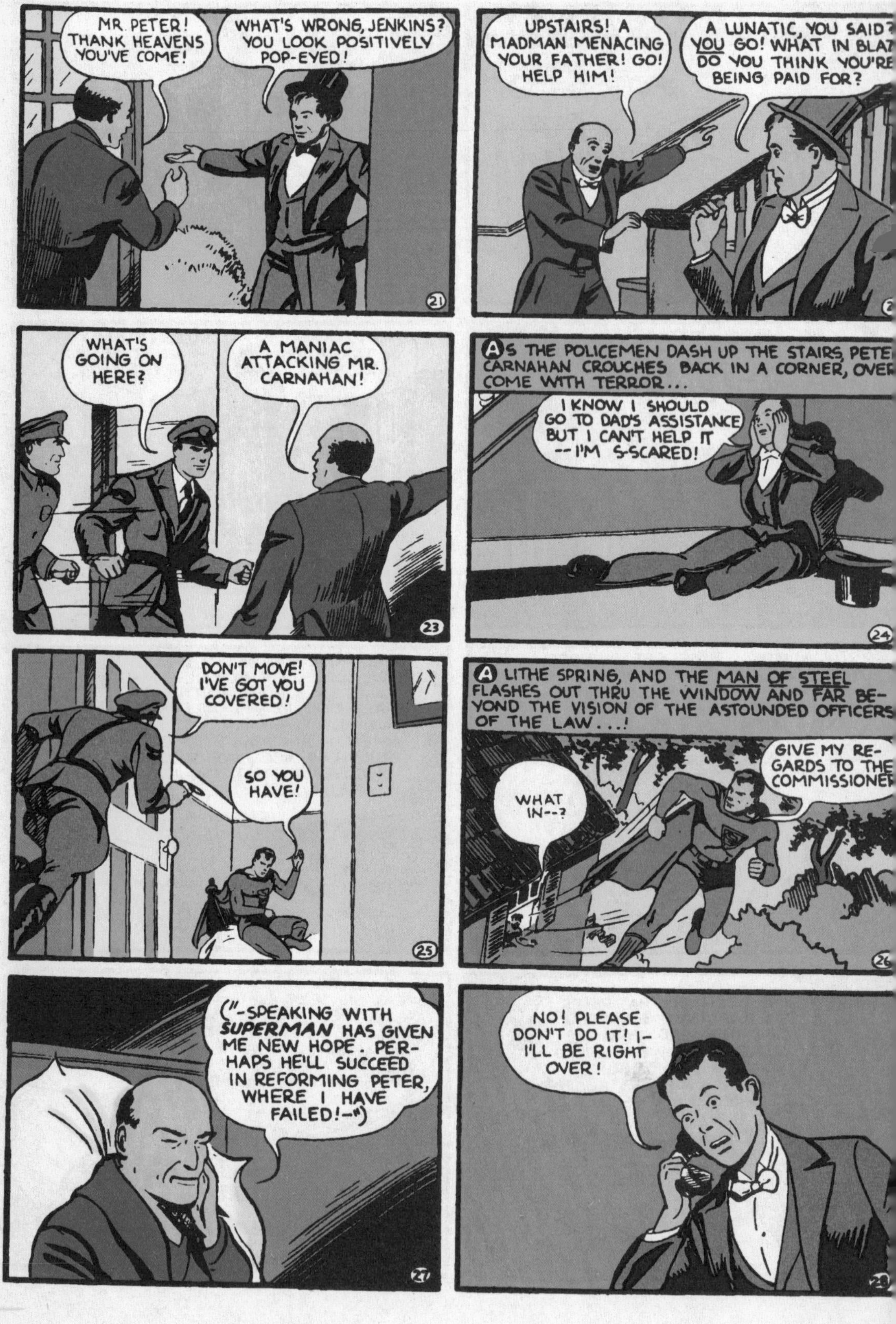
MR. PETER! THANK HEAVENS YOU'VE COME!
WHAT'S WRONG, JENKINS? YOU LOOK POSITIVELY POP-EYED!
UPSTAIRS! A MADMAN MENACING YOUR FATHER! GO! HELP HIM!
A LUNATIC, YOU SAID? YOU GO! WHAT IN BLAZ DO YOU THINK YOU'RE BEING PAID FOR?
WHAT'S GOING ON HERE?
A MANIAC ATTACKING MR. CARNAHAN!
AS THE POLICEMEN DASH UP THE STAIRS, PETE CARNAHAN CROUCHES BACK IN A CORNER, OVER COME WITH TERROR...
I KNOW I SHOULD GO TO DAD'S ASSISTANCE BUT I CAN'T HELP IT --I'M S-SCARED!
DON'T MOVE! I'VE GOT YOU COVERED!
SO YOU HAVE!
A LITHE SPRING, AND THE MAN OF STEEL FLASHES OUT THRU THE WINDOW AND FAR BEYOND THE VISION OF THE ASTOUNDED OFFICERS OF THE LAW...!
WHAT IN--?
GIVE MY REGARDS TO THE COMMISSIONER
("-SPEAKING WITH SUPERMAN HAS GIVEN ME NEW HOPE. PERHAPS HE'LL SUCCEED IN REFORMING PETER, WHERE I HAVE FAILED!-")
NO! PLEASE DON'T DO IT! I-I'LL BE RIGHT OVER!

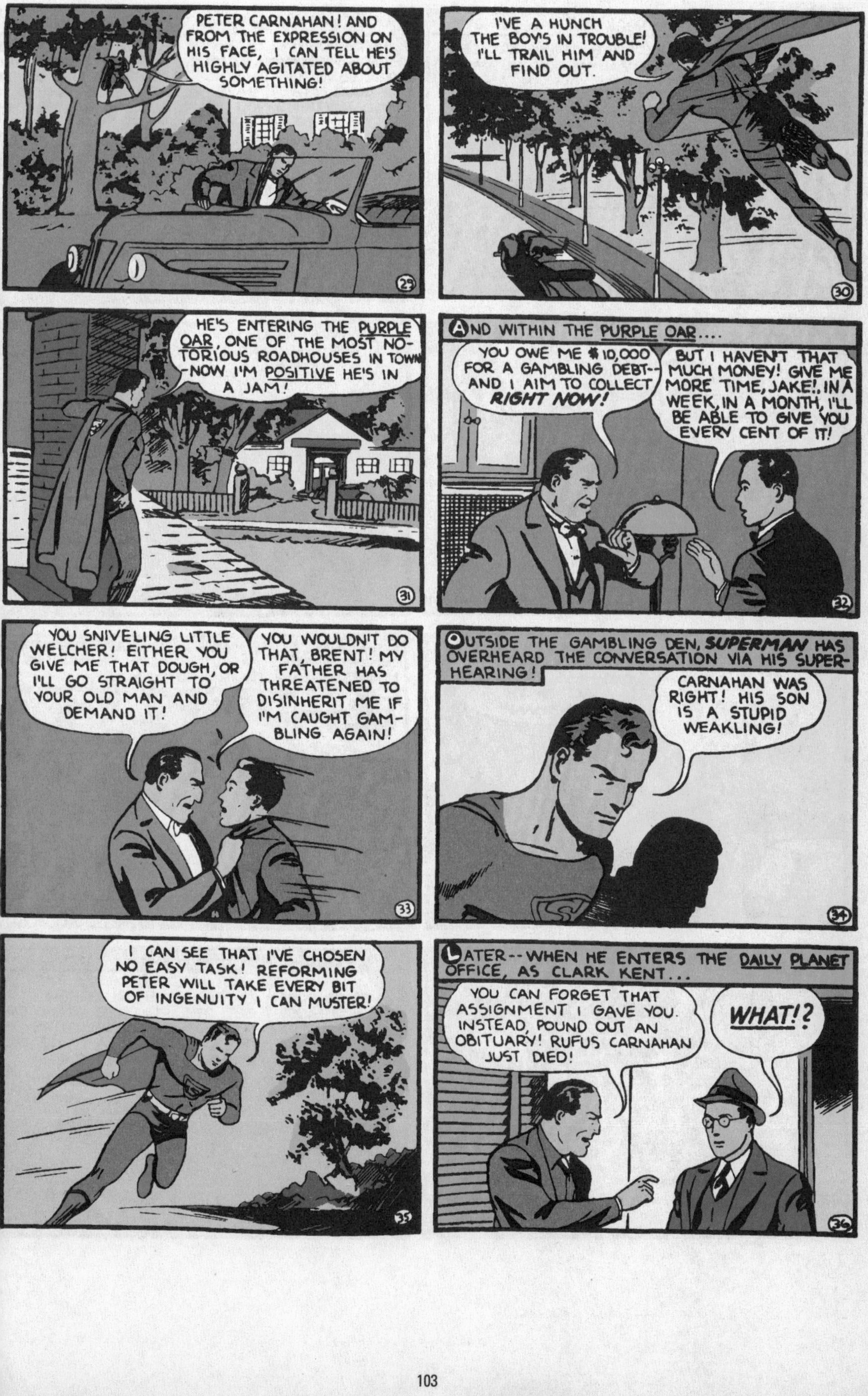
PETER CARNAHAN! AND FROM THE EXPRESSION ON HIS FACE, I CAN TELL HE'S HIGHLY AGITATED ABOUT SOMETHING!
I'VE A HUNCH THE BOY'S IN TROUBLE! I'LL TRAIL HIM AND FIND OUT.
HE'S ENTERING THE PURPLE OAR, ONE OF THE MOST NOTORIOUS ROADHOUSES IN TOWN -NOW I'M POSITIVE HE'S IN A JAM!
AND WITHIN THE PURPLE OAR....
YOU OWE ME $10,000 FOR A GAMBLING DEBT--AND I AIM TO COLLECT RIGHT NOW!
BUT I HAVEN'T THAT MUCH MONEY! GIVE ME MORE TIME, JAKE!, IN A WEEK, IN A MONTH, I'LL BE ABLE TO GIVE YOU EVERY CENT OF IT!
YOU SNIVELING LITTLE WELCHER! EITHER YOU GIVE ME THAT DOUGH, OR I'LL GO STRAIGHT TO YOUR OLD MAN AND DEMAND IT!
YOU WOULDN'T DO THAT, BRENT! MY FATHER HAS THREATENED TO DISINHERIT ME IF I'M CAUGHT GAMBLING AGAIN!
OUTSIDE THE GAMBLING DEN, SUPERMAN HAS OVERHEARD THE CONVERSATION VIA HIS SUPER-HEARING!
CARNAHAN WAS RIGHT! HIS SON IS A STUPID WEAKLING!
I CAN SEE THAT I'VE CHOSEN NO EASY TASK! REFORMING PETER WILL TAKE EVERY BIT OF INGENUITY I CAN MUSTER!
LATER--WHEN HE ENTERS THE DAILY PLANET OFFICE, AS CLARK KENT...
YOU CAN FORGET THAT ASSIGNMENT I GAVE YOU. INSTEAD, POUND OUT AN OBITUARY! RUFUS CARNAHAN JUST DIED!
WHAT!?

A S CLARK TYPES CARNAHAN'S OBITUARY, HE NOTES--

HM-MM! ACCORDING TO THIS ARTICLE, RUFUS CARNAHAN HAS AN UNUSUAL PROVISION IN HIS WILL. IN CASE HIS SON IS INVOLVED IN A GAMBLING SCANDAL, PETER IS NOT TO RECEIVE ONE CENT!

L ATER-AT THE CARNAHAN MANSION...

WE'RE RUNNING STATE-MENTS FROM MANY NOTABLES DEPLORING THE PASSING OF YOUR FATHER. HAVE YOU ANYTHING YOU WISH TO SAY?

ONLY THIS. I'M TERRIBLY GRIEF-STRICKEN. AND I INTEND TO LIVE UP TO THE IDEALS WHICH MADE MY FATHER THE GREAT MAN HE WAS!

JAKE! JAKE BRENT!

BUT YOU CAN'T COME IN!

OUTA MY WAY!

JAKE! WHAT ARE YOU DOING <u>HERE</u>?

SCRAM, YOU!

BUT--!

BUT I WAS IN THE MIDDLE OF AN INTERVIEW!

GET OUT! I HAVE STRICTLY PRIVATE BUSINESS TO TRANS-ACT WITH CARNAHAN!

B UT OUTSIDE THE MANSION, CLARK TAKES REFUGE BEHIND A TREE. HIS EYES GLOW WEIRDLY AS HE MAKES USE OF THEIR X-RAY ABILITY...

T HE SIDE OF THE MANSION SEEMS TO MELT AWAY!

...REVEALING THE TENSE SCENE WITHIN!

$100,000! YOU MUST BE MAD!

NOT MAD--*SMART!* THE ANTE'S GONE UP! EITHER I GET THE HUNDRED GRAND OR I TIP OFF THE EXECUTORS OF THE WILL ABOUT A LITTLE BILL YOU OWE ME--AND THEN, YOU'LL RECEIVE <u>NOTHING</u>!

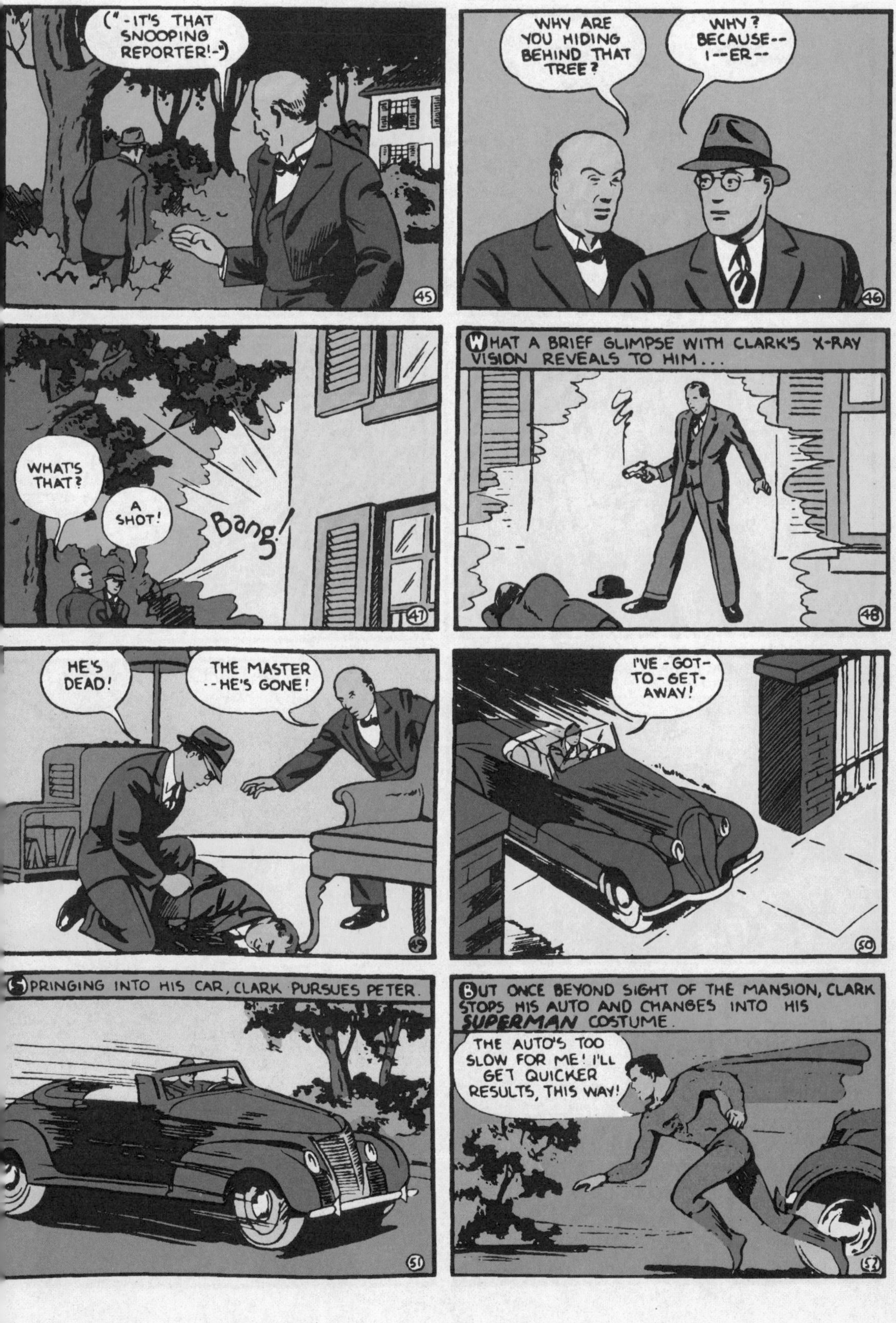
("-IT'S THAT SNOOPING REPORTER!-")
WHY ARE YOU HIDING BEHIND THAT TREE?
WHY? BECAUSE-- I--ER--
WHAT'S THAT?
A SHOT!
Bang!
WHAT A BRIEF GLIMPSE WITH CLARK'S X-RAY VISION REVEALS TO HIM...
HE'S DEAD!
THE MASTER --HE'S GONE!
I'VE-GOT-TO-GET-AWAY!
SPRINGING INTO HIS CAR, CLARK PURSUES PETER.
BUT ONCE BEYOND SIGHT OF THE MANSION, CLARK STOPS HIS AUTO AND CHANGES INTO HIS SUPERMAN COSTUME.
THE AUTO'S TOO SLOW FOR ME! I'LL GET QUICKER RESULTS, THIS WAY!

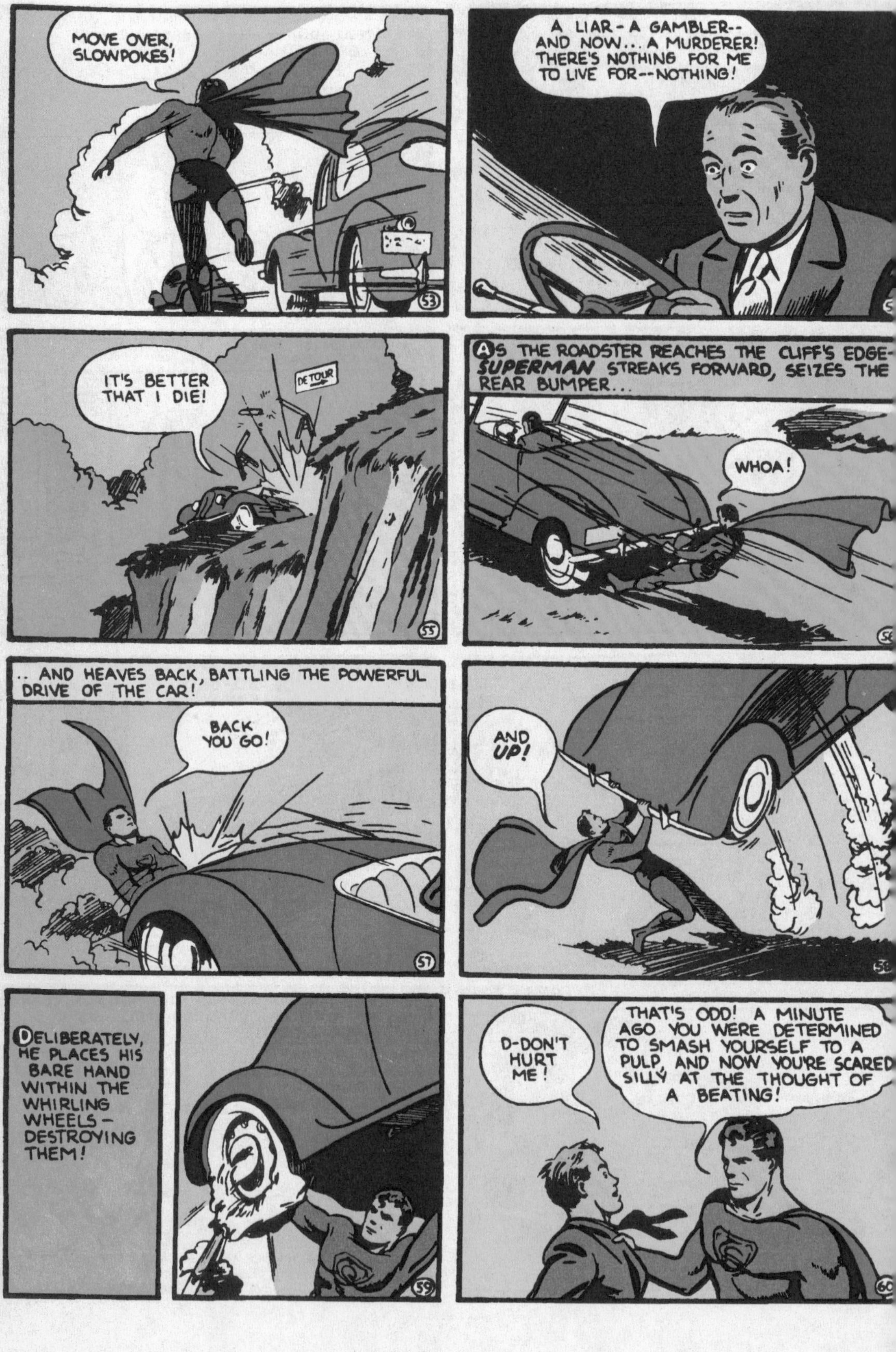
MOVE OVER, SLOWPOKES!
A LIAR - A GAMBLER-- AND NOW... A MURDERER! THERE'S NOTHING FOR ME TO LIVE FOR--NOTHING!
IT'S BETTER THAT I DIE!
DETOUR
AS THE ROADSTER REACHES THE CLIFF'S EDGE- SUPERMAN STREAKS FORWARD, SEIZES THE REAR BUMPER...
WHOA!
.. AND HEAVES BACK, BATTLING THE POWERFUL DRIVE OF THE CAR!
BACK YOU GO!
AND UP!
DELIBERATELY, HE PLACES HIS BARE HAND WITHIN THE WHIRLING WHEELS- DESTROYING THEM!
D-DON'T HURT ME!
THAT'S ODD! A MINUTE AGO YOU WERE DETERMINED TO SMASH YOURSELF TO A PULP, AND NOW YOU'RE SCARED SILLY AT THE THOUGHT OF A BEATING!

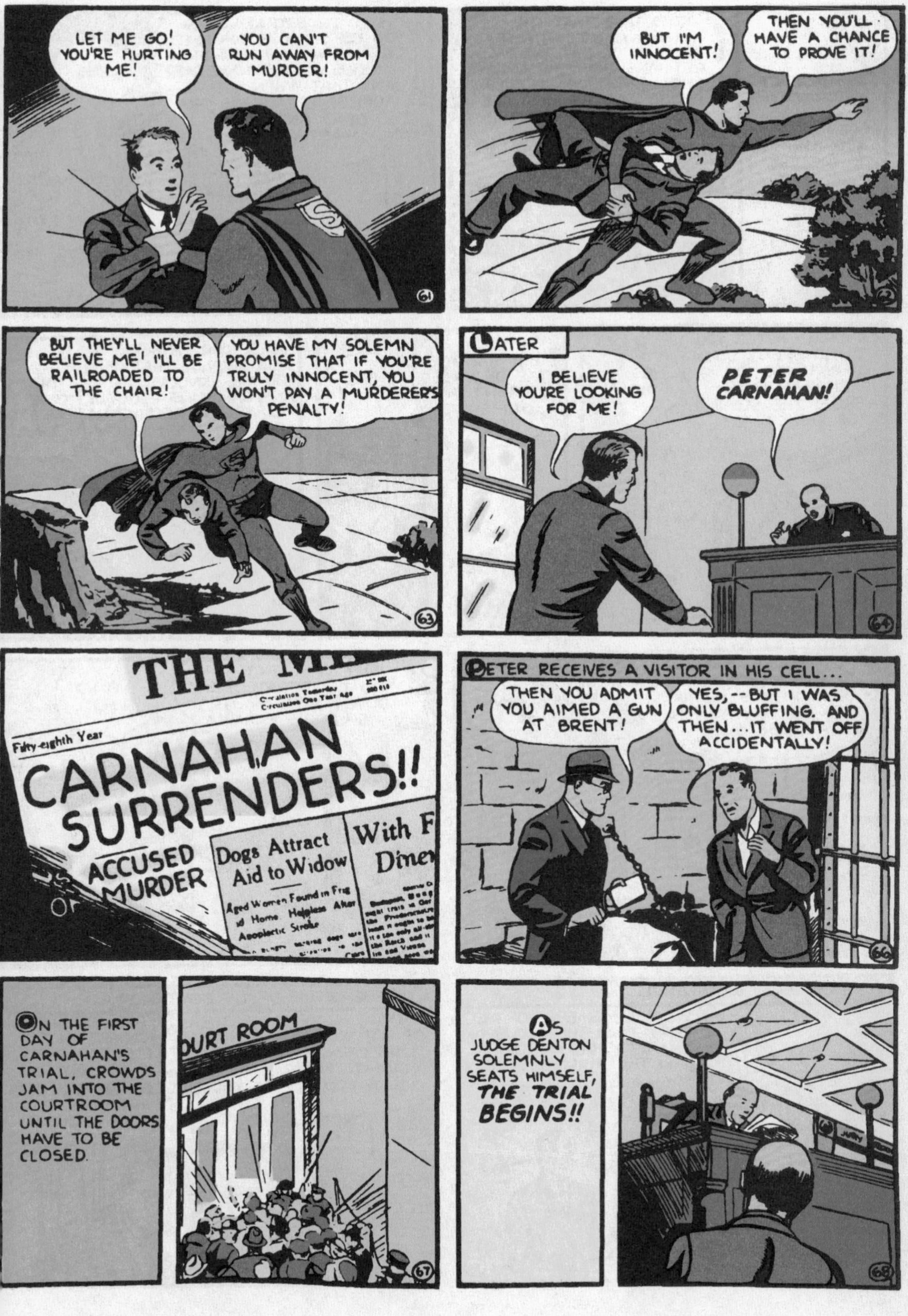
LET ME GO! YOU'RE HURTING ME!
YOU CAN'T RUN AWAY FROM MURDER!
BUT I'M INNOCENT!
THEN YOU'LL HAVE A CHANCE TO PROVE IT!
BUT THEY'LL NEVER BELIEVE ME! I'LL BE RAILROADED TO THE CHAIR!
YOU HAVE MY SOLEMN PROMISE THAT IF YOU'RE TRULY INNOCENT, YOU WON'T PAY A MURDERER'S PENALTY!
LATER
I BELIEVE YOU'RE LOOKING FOR ME!
PETER CARNAHAN!
THE
Fifty-eighth Year
CARNAHAN SURRENDERS!!
ACCUSED MURDER
Dogs Attract Aid to Widow
Aged Women Found in Frig id Home Helpless After Apoplectic Stroke
PETER RECEIVES A VISITOR IN HIS CELL...
THEN YOU ADMIT YOU AIMED A GUN AT BRENT!
YES,--BUT I WAS ONLY BLUFFING. AND THEN...IT WENT OFF ACCIDENTALLY!
ON THE FIRST DAY OF CARNAHAN'S TRIAL, CROWDS JAM INTO THE COURTROOM UNTIL THE DOORS HAVE TO BE CLOSED.
OURT ROOM
AS JUDGE DENTON SOLEMNLY SEATS HIMSELF, THE TRIAL BEGINS!!
JURY

THE DISTRICT ATTORNEY MAKES HIS OPENING ADDRESS TO THE JURY

IT IS TRUE THAT THE VICTIM WAS NOT AN ASSET TO SOCIETY, BUT THE FACT REMAINS THAT THE ACCUSED SHOT HIM DOWN IN COLD BLOOD AND WE MUST SEE TO IT THAT HE PAYS THE SUPREME PENALTY!

IS IT TRUE THAT WHEN YOU LEFT THE ROOM PETER CARNAHAN AND JAKE BRENT WERE ALONE TOGETHER AND THAT WHEN YOU RETURNED, BRENT WAS SHOT DEAD AND YOUR MASTER GONE?

YES.

SHORTLY AFTER YOU FOUND BRENT SLAIN DID YOU SEE YOUNG CARNAHAN FLEE FROM THE SCENE OF THE CRIME?

YES, I DID!

DID YOU OWE THE DECEASED BRENT A GAMBLING DEBT?

YES, BUT--!

DOES YOUR FATHER'S WILL PROVIDE THAT IF YOU ARE INVOLVED IN ANY GAMBLING ESCAPADE, YOU ARE TO RECEIVE NO PART OF THE MILLIONS HE LEFT BEHIND HIM?

THAT'S TRUE... ONLY TOO TRUE!

DID BRENT THREATEN TO EXPOSE YOUR GAMBLING DEBT TO HIM IF YOU FAILED TO PAY HIM A HUGE SUM?

YES. HE TRIED TO BLACKMAIL ME. HE...

ISN'T IT A FACT THAT YOU DELIBERATELY SHOT DOWN JAKE BRENT TO SHUT HIS MOUTH?

NO! NO! NO!

AND SEVERAL DAYS LATER...!

WE, THE MEMBERS OF THE JURY, FIND THE ACCUSED-- *GUILTY*, OF MURDER IN THE FIRST DEGREE!

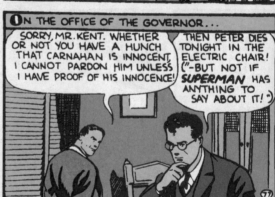

ON THE OFFICE OF THE GOVERNOR...

SORRY, MR. KENT. WHETHER OR NOT YOU HAVE A HUNCH THAT CARNAHAN IS INNOCENT, I CANNOT PARDON HIM UNLESS I HAVE PROOF OF HIS INNOCENCE!

THEN PETER DIES TONIGHT IN THE ELECTRIC CHAIR! ("-BUT NOT IF *SUPERMAN* HAS ANYTHING TO SAY ABOUT IT!")

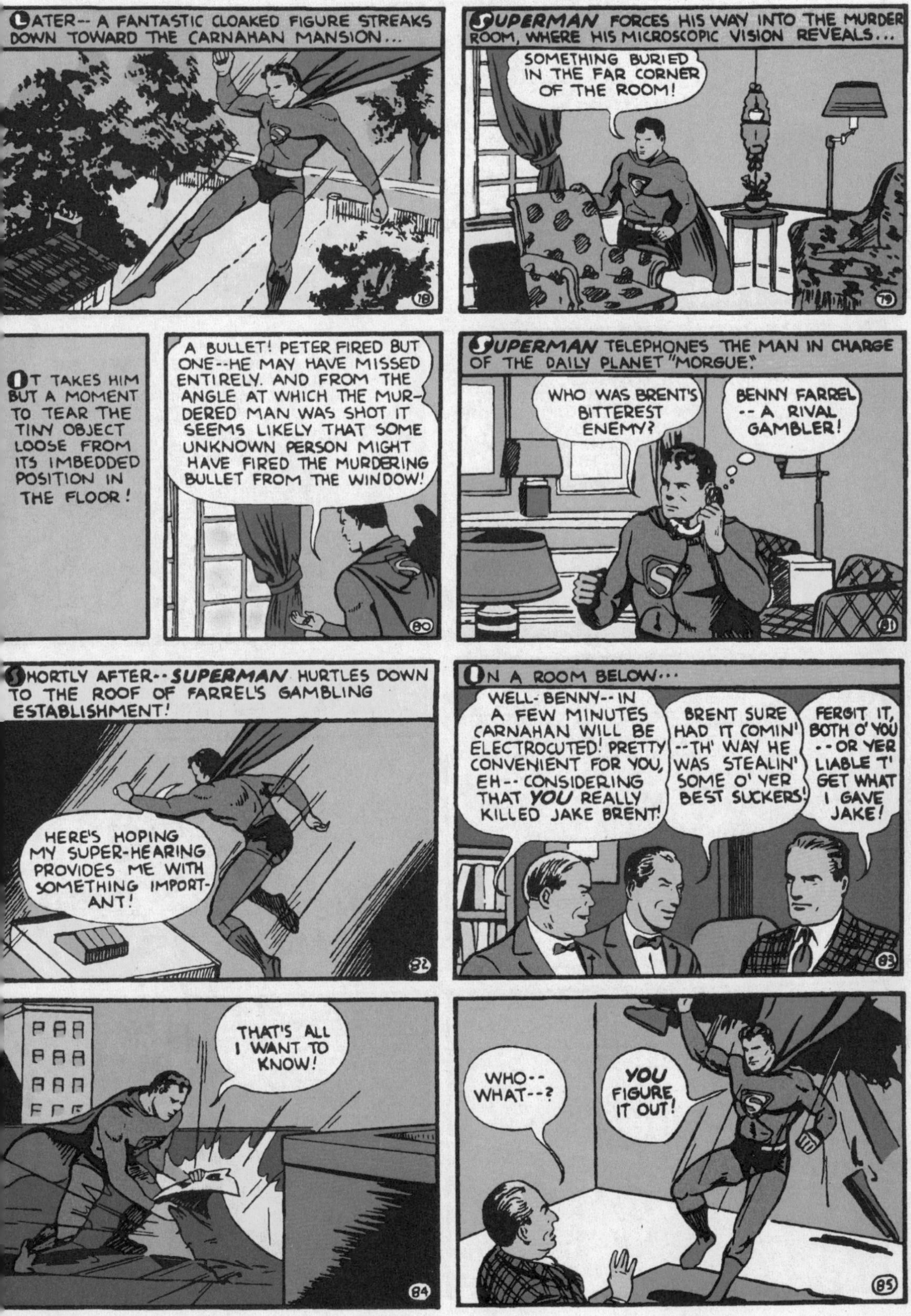
LATER-- A FANTASTIC CLOAKED FIGURE STREAKS DOWN TOWARD THE CARNAHAN MANSION...
SUPERMAN FORCES HIS WAY INTO THE MURDER ROOM, WHERE HIS MICROSCOPIC VISION REVEALS...
SOMETHING BURIED IN THE FAR CORNER OF THE ROOM!
IT TAKES HIM BUT A MOMENT TO TEAR THE TINY OBJECT LOOSE FROM ITS IMBEDDED POSITION IN THE FLOOR!
A BULLET! PETER FIRED BUT ONE--HE MAY HAVE MISSED ENTIRELY. AND FROM THE ANGLE AT WHICH THE MURDERED MAN WAS SHOT IT SEEMS LIKELY THAT SOME UNKNOWN PERSON MIGHT HAVE FIRED THE MURDERING BULLET FROM THE WINDOW!
SUPERMAN TELEPHONES THE MAN IN CHARGE OF THE DAILY PLANET "MORGUE."
WHO WAS BRENT'S BITTEREST ENEMY?
BENNY FARREL -- A RIVAL GAMBLER!
SHORTLY AFTER--SUPERMAN HURTLES DOWN TO THE ROOF OF FARREL'S GAMBLING ESTABLISHMENT!
HERE'S HOPING MY SUPER-HEARING PROVIDES ME WITH SOMETHING IMPORTANT!
IN A ROOM BELOW...
WELL- BENNY--IN A FEW MINUTES CARNAHAN WILL BE ELECTROCUTED! PRETTY CONVENIENT FOR YOU, EH-- CONSIDERING THAT YOU REALLY KILLED JAKE BRENT!
BRENT SURE HAD IT COMIN' --TH' WAY HE WAS STEALIN' SOME O' YER BEST SUCKERS!
FERGIT IT, BOTH O' YOU --OR YER LIABLE T' GET WHAT I GAVE JAKE!
THAT'S ALL I WANT TO KNOW!
WHO-- WHAT--?
YOU FIGURE IT OUT!

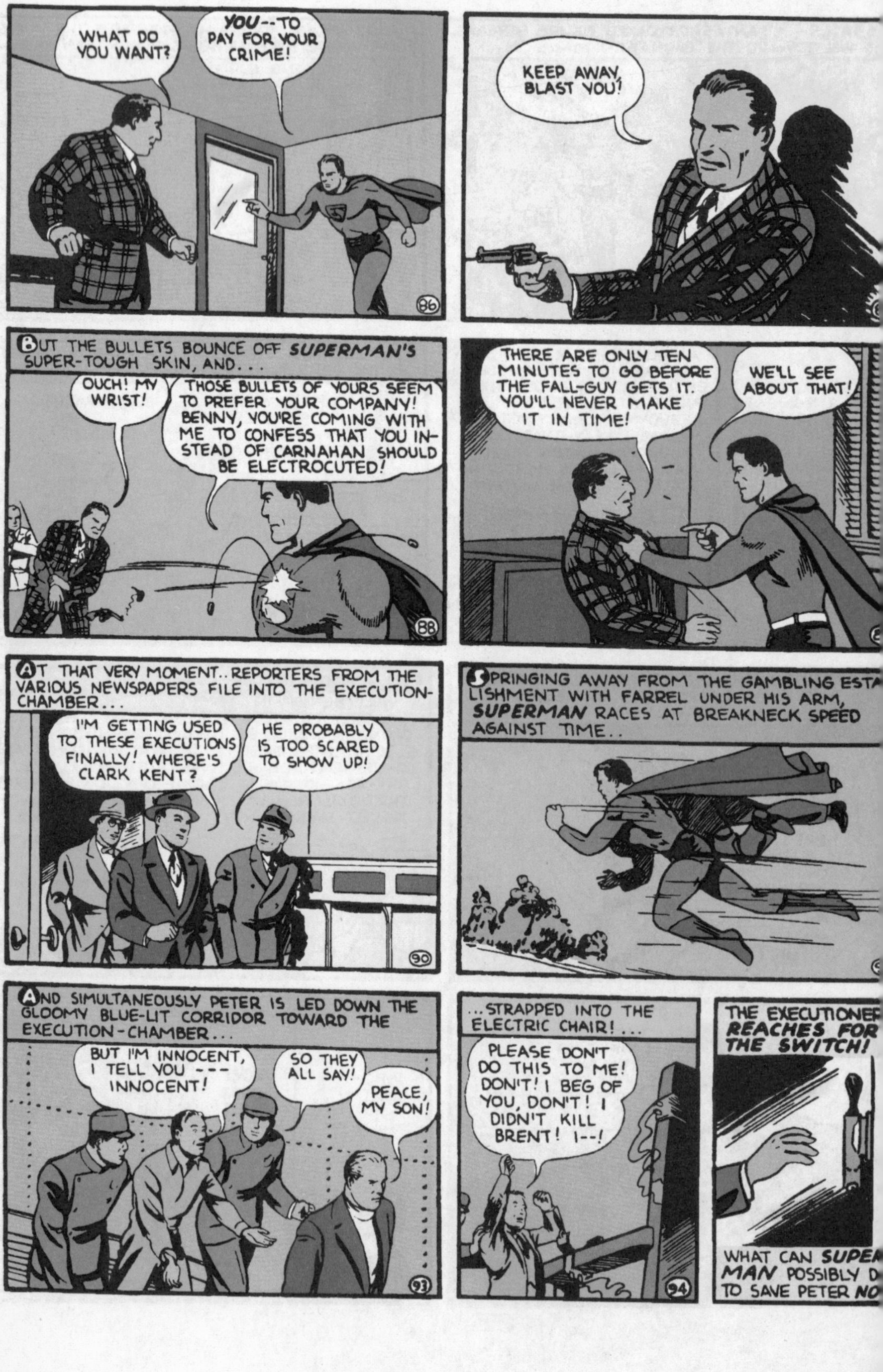
WHAT DO YOU WANT?
YOU--TO PAY FOR YOUR CRIME!
86
KEEP AWAY, BLAST YOU!
BUT THE BULLETS BOUNCE OFF SUPERMAN'S SUPER-TOUGH SKIN, AND...
OUCH! MY WRIST!
THOSE BULLETS OF YOURS SEEM TO PREFER YOUR COMPANY! BENNY, YOU'RE COMING WITH ME TO CONFESS THAT YOU IN-STEAD OF CARNAHAN SHOULD BE ELECTROCUTED!
88
THERE ARE ONLY TEN MINUTES TO GO BEFORE THE FALL-GUY GETS IT. YOU'LL NEVER MAKE IT IN TIME!
WE'LL SEE ABOUT THAT!
AT THAT VERY MOMENT.. REPORTERS FROM THE VARIOUS NEWSPAPERS FILE INTO THE EXECUTION-CHAMBER...
I'M GETTING USED TO THESE EXECUTIONS FINALLY! WHERE'S CLARK KENT?
HE PROBABLY IS TOO SCARED TO SHOW UP!
90
SPRINGING AWAY FROM THE GAMBLING ESTA LISHMENT WITH FARREL UNDER HIS ARM, SUPERMAN RACES AT BREAKNECK SPEED AGAINST TIME..
AND SIMULTANEOUSLY PETER IS LED DOWN THE GLOOMY BLUE-LIT CORRIDOR TOWARD THE EXECUTION-CHAMBER...
BUT I'M INNOCENT, I TELL YOU --- INNOCENT!
SO THEY ALL SAY!
PEACE, MY SON!
93
...STRAPPED INTO THE ELECTRIC CHAIR! ...
PLEASE DON'T DO THIS TO ME! DON'T! I BEG OF YOU, DON'T! I DIDN'T KILL BRENT! I--!
94
THE EXECUTIONE REACHES FOR THE SWITCH!
WHAT CAN SUPE MAN POSSIBLY D TO SAVE PETER NO

ONTO THE POWER-HOUSE WHICH SUPPLIES ELECTRICITY TO METROPOLIS AND THE PRISON STREAKS THE MAN OF TOMORROW!

WITH A BURST OF AMAZING STRENGTH, HE RIPS AN INTEGRAL PIECE FROM THE DYNAMO...

I HATE TO BE DESTRUCTIVE--BUT THE SITUATION DEMANDS IT!

WITHIN THE ELECTROCUTION-CHAMBER...

THE LIGHTS-- THEY'RE OUT!

NO ELECTRICITY-- WE'LL HAVE TO POSTPONE THE ELECTROCUTION!

LATER--AT THE GOVERNOR'S HOME...

GO AHEAD-- CONFESS, OR I'LL SHAKE YOUR TEETH LOOSE!

MAKE HIM STOP! I DID IT! I CONFESS I KILLED JAKE!

THIS IS MOST IRREGULAR!

YOU HEARD ME! THIS IS THE GOVERNOR!-- CARNAHAN IS PARDONED!

NO NEED FOR ME TO HANG AROUND ANY FURTHER. SO-LONG!

SEVERAL DAYS LATER--WITHIN THE OFFICE OF CARNAHAN'S LAWYERS...

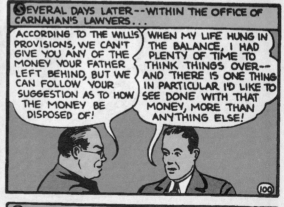

ACCORDING TO THE WILL'S PROVISIONS, WE CAN'T GIVE YOU ANY OF THE MONEY YOUR FATHER LEFT BEHIND, BUT WE CAN FOLLOW YOUR SUGGESTION AS TO HOW THE MONEY BE DISPOSED OF!

WHEN MY LIFE HUNG IN THE BALANCE, I HAD PLENTY OF TIME TO THINK THINGS OVER-- AND THERE IS ONE THING IN PARTICULAR I'D LIKE TO SEE DONE WITH THAT MONEY, MORE THAN ANYTHING ELSE!

I'D LIKE TO ESTABLISH A HOME FOR WAYWARD UNDERPRIVILEGED YOUTHS-SEE THAT THEY DON'T SUCCUMB TO THE PITFALLS I FACED! AND I WOULD LIKE NOTHING BETTER THAN TO DIRECT IT!

SIX MONTHS LATER--

CONGRATULATIONS, PETER! YOU'VE ACCOMPLISHED MIRACLES IN GUIDING THE CHARACTER OF YOUR CHARGES!

THANK YOU! I'M TRYING HARD TO ATONE FOR THE MESS I MADE OF MY LIFE. I ONLY REGRET THAT I COULDN'T HAVE MADE MY FATHER PROUD OF ME WHILE HE LIVED!

RUFUS CARNAHAN HOME FOR YOUTH

THE END

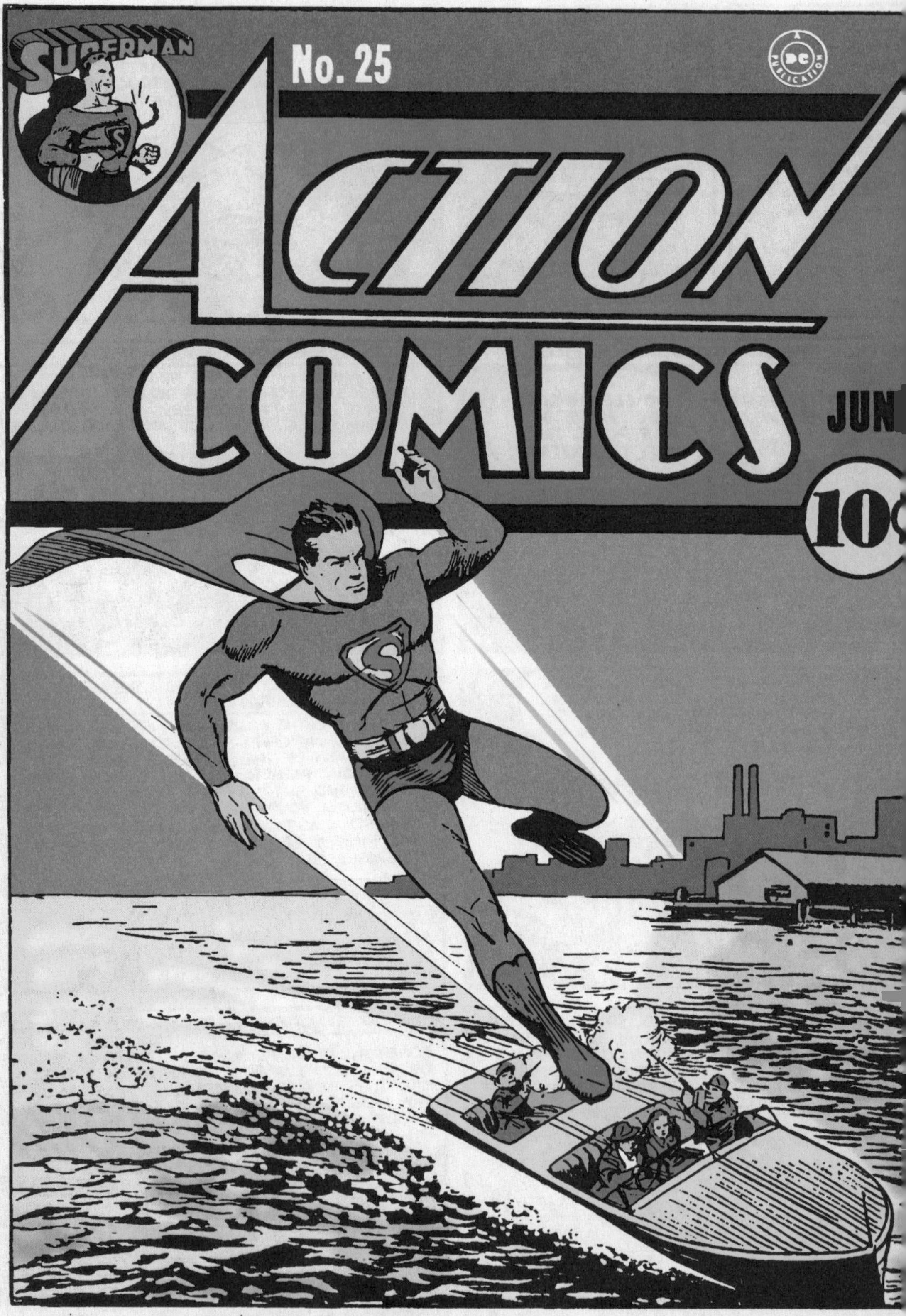
SUPERMAN
No. 25
A DC PUBLICATION
ACTION COMICS
JUN
10

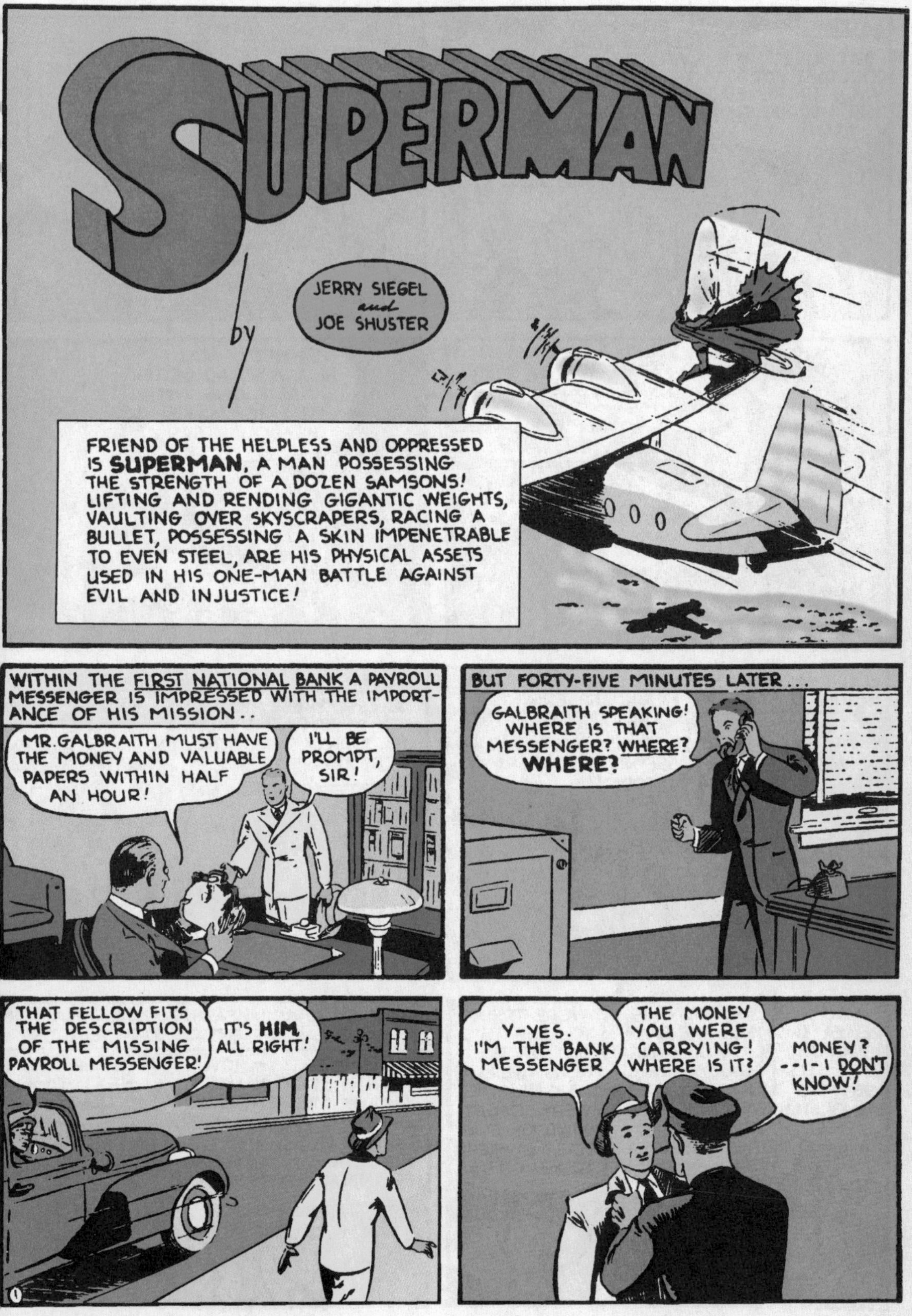
SUPERMAN
by
JERRY SIEGEL and JOE SHUSTER
FRIEND OF THE HELPLESS AND OPPRESSED IS SUPERMAN, A MAN POSSESSING THE STRENGTH OF A DOZEN SAMSONS! LIFTING AND RENDING GIGANTIC WEIGHTS, VAULTING OVER SKYSCRAPERS, RACING A BULLET, POSSESSING A SKIN IMPENETRABLE TO EVEN STEEL, ARE HIS PHYSICAL ASSETS USED IN HIS ONE-MAN BATTLE AGAINST EVIL AND INJUSTICE!
WITHIN THE FIRST NATIONAL BANK A PAYROLL MESSENGER IS IMPRESSED WITH THE IMPORTANCE OF HIS MISSION..
MR.GALBRAITH MUST HAVE THE MONEY AND VALUABLE PAPERS WITHIN HALF AN HOUR!
I'LL BE PROMPT, SIR!
BUT FORTY-FIVE MINUTES LATER...
GALBRAITH SPEAKING! WHERE IS THAT MESSENGER? WHERE? WHERE?
THAT FELLOW FITS THE DESCRIPTION OF THE MISSING PAYROLL MESSENGER!
IT'S HIM, ALL RIGHT!
Y-YES. I'M THE BANK MESSENGER
THE MONEY YOU WERE CARRYING! WHERE IS IT?
MONEY? --I-I DON'T KNOW!

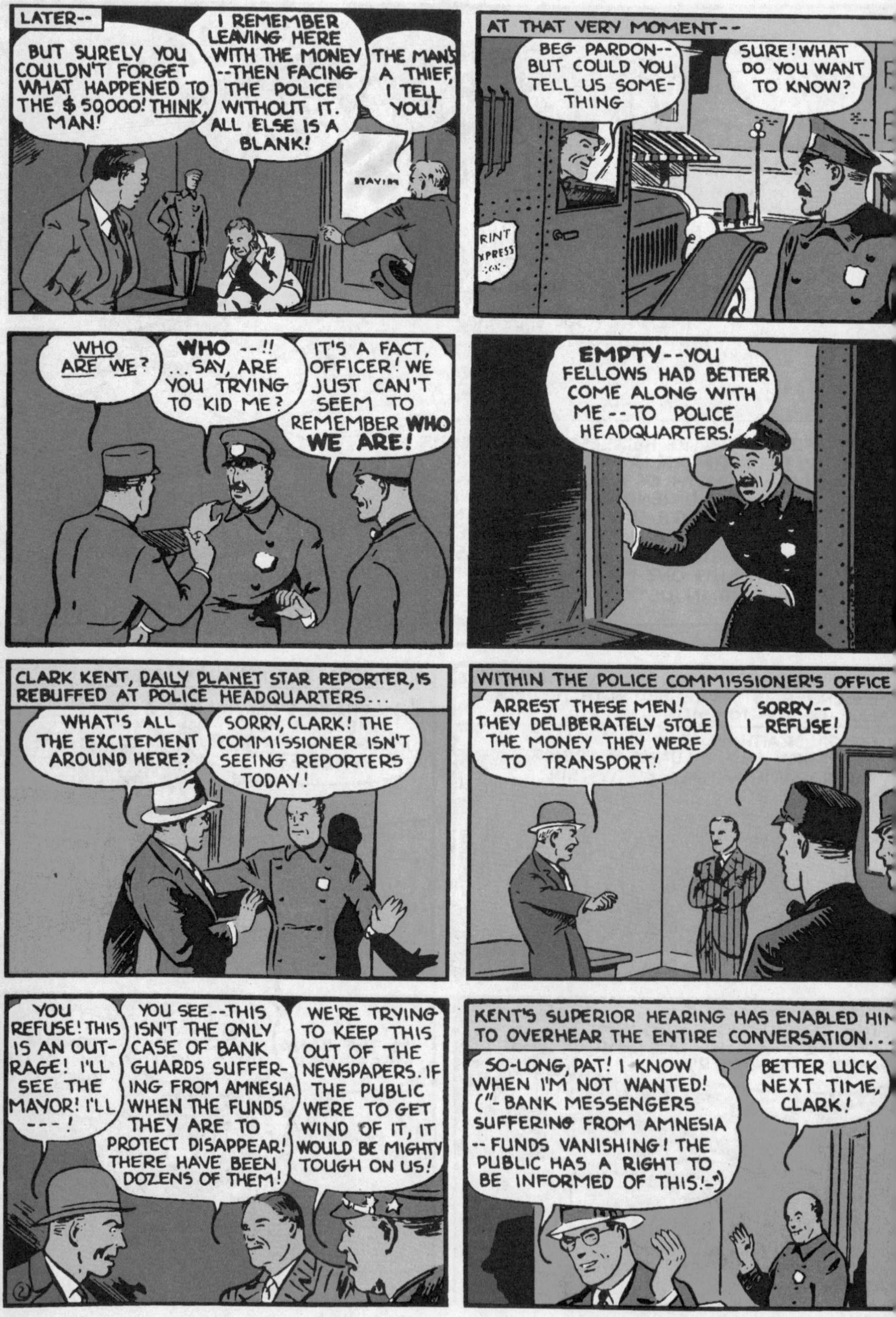
LATER--
BUT SURELY YOU COULDN'T FORGET WHAT HAPPENED TO THE $ 50000! THINK, MAN!
I REMEMBER LEAVING HERE WITH THE MONEY --THEN FACING THE POLICE WITHOUT IT. ALL ELSE IS A BLANK!
THE MAN'S A THIEF, I TELL YOU!
AT THAT VERY MOMENT--
BEG PARDON-- BUT COULD YOU TELL US SOMETHING
SURE! WHAT DO YOU WANT TO KNOW?
WHO ARE WE?
WHO --!! ... SAY, ARE YOU TRYING TO KID ME?
IT'S A FACT, OFFICER! WE JUST CAN'T SEEM TO REMEMBER WHO WE ARE!
EMPTY--YOU FELLOWS HAD BETTER COME ALONG WITH ME--TO POLICE HEADQUARTERS!
CLARK KENT, DAILY PLANET STAR REPORTER, IS REBUFFED AT POLICE HEADQUARTERS...
WHAT'S ALL THE EXCITEMENT AROUND HERE?
SORRY, CLARK! THE COMMISSIONER ISN'T SEEING REPORTERS TODAY!
WITHIN THE POLICE COMMISSIONER'S OFFICE
ARREST THESE MEN! THEY DELIBERATELY STOLE THE MONEY THEY WERE TO TRANSPORT!
SORRY-- I REFUSE!
YOU REFUSE! THIS IS AN OUTRAGE! I'LL SEE THE MAYOR! I'LL ---!
YOU SEE--THIS ISN'T THE ONLY CASE OF BANK GUARDS SUFFERING FROM AMNESIA WHEN THE FUNDS THEY ARE TO PROTECT DISAPPEAR! THERE HAVE BEEN DOZENS OF THEM!
WE'RE TRYING TO KEEP THIS OUT OF THE NEWSPAPERS. IF THE PUBLIC WERE TO GET WIND OF IT, IT WOULD BE MIGHTY TOUGH ON US!
KENT'S SUPERIOR HEARING HAS ENABLED HIM TO OVERHEAR THE ENTIRE CONVERSATION...
SO-LONG, PAT! I KNOW WHEN I'M NOT WANTED! ("- BANK MESSENGERS SUFFERING FROM AMNESIA -- FUNDS VANISHING! THE PUBLIC HAS A RIGHT TO BE INFORMED OF THIS!-")
BETTER LUCK NEXT TIME, CLARK!

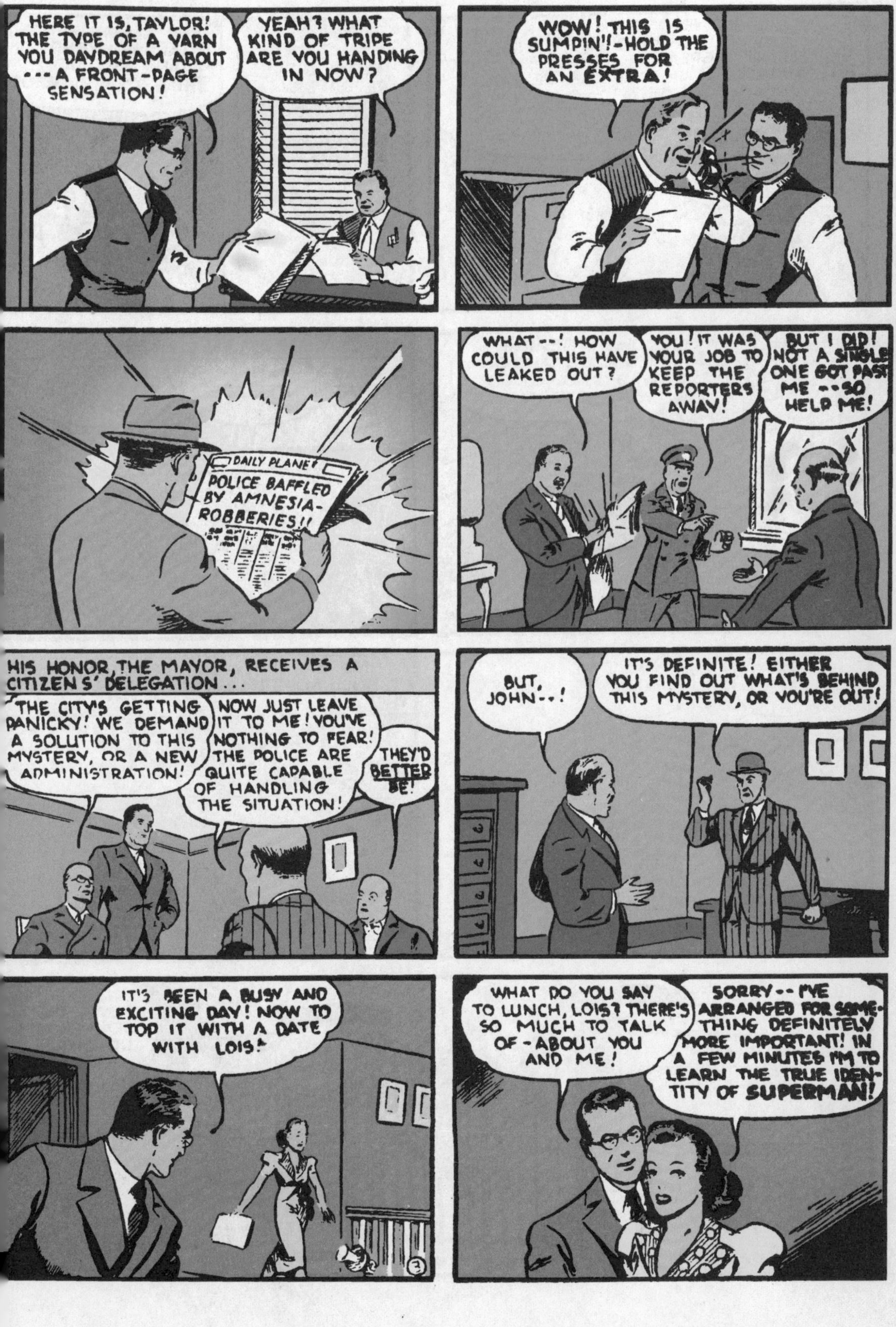
HERE IT IS, TAYLOR! THE TYPE OF A YARN YOU DAYDREAM ABOUT --- A FRONT-PAGE SENSATION!
YEAH? WHAT KIND OF TRIPE ARE YOU HANDING IN NOW?
WOW! THIS IS SUMPIN'!-HOLD THE PRESSES FOR AN EXTRA!
DAILY PLANET
POLICE BAFFLED BY AMNESIA-ROBBERIES!!
WHAT--! HOW COULD THIS HAVE LEAKED OUT?
YOU! IT WAS YOUR JOB TO KEEP THE REPORTERS AWAY!
BUT I DID! NOT A SINGLE ONE GOT PAST ME --SO HELP ME!
HIS HONOR, THE MAYOR, RECEIVES A CITIZENS' DELEGATION...
THE CITY'S GETTING PANICKY! WE DEMAND A SOLUTION TO THIS MYSTERY, OR A NEW ADMINISTRATION!
NOW JUST LEAVE IT TO ME! YOU'VE NOTHING TO FEAR! THE POLICE ARE QUITE CAPABLE OF HANDLING THE SITUATION!
THEY'D BETTER BE!
BUT, JOHN--!
IT'S DEFINITE! EITHER YOU FIND OUT WHAT'S BEHIND THIS MYSTERY, OR YOU'RE OUT!
IT'S BEEN A BUSY AND EXCITING DAY! NOW TO TOP IT WITH A DATE WITH LOIS!
WHAT DO YOU SAY TO LUNCH, LOIS? THERE'S SO MUCH TO TALK OF - ABOUT YOU AND ME!
SORRY-- I'VE ARRANGED FOR SOMETHING DEFINITELY MORE IMPORTANT! IN A FEW MINUTES I'M TO LEARN THE TRUE IDENTITY OF SUPERMAN!

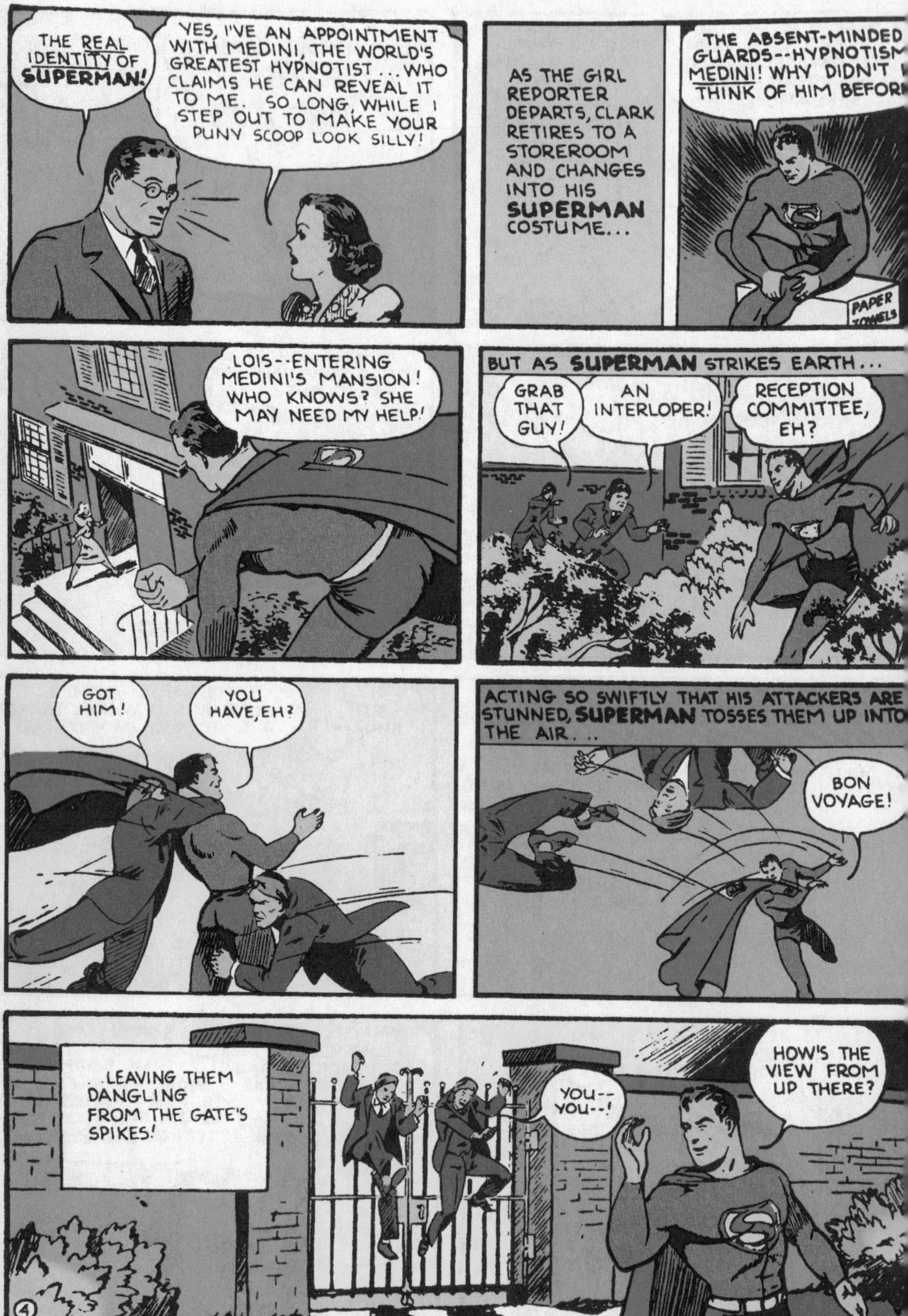

THE REAL IDENTITY OF SUPERMAN!
YES, I'VE AN APPOINTMENT WITH MEDINI, THE WORLD'S GREATEST HYPNOTIST ... WHO CLAIMS HE CAN REVEAL IT TO ME. SO LONG, WHILE I STEP OUT TO MAKE YOUR PUNY SCOOP LOOK SILLY!
AS THE GIRL REPORTER DEPARTS, CLARK RETIRES TO A STOREROOM AND CHANGES INTO HIS SUPERMAN COSTUME...
THE ABSENT-MINDED GUARDS--HYPNOTISM MEDINI! WHY DIDN'T I THINK OF HIM BEFOR
PAPER TOWELS
LOIS--ENTERING MEDINI'S MANSION! WHO KNOWS? SHE MAY NEED MY HELP!
BUT AS SUPERMAN STRIKES EARTH...
GRAB THAT GUY!
AN INTERLOPER!
RECEPTION COMMITTEE, EH?
GOT HIM!
YOU HAVE, EH?
ACTING SO SWIFTLY THAT HIS ATTACKERS ARE STUNNED, SUPERMAN TOSSES THEM UP INTO THE AIR...
BON VOYAGE!
...LEAVING THEM DANGLING FROM THE GATE'S SPIKES!
YOU--YOU--!
HOW'S THE VIEW FROM UP THERE?
4

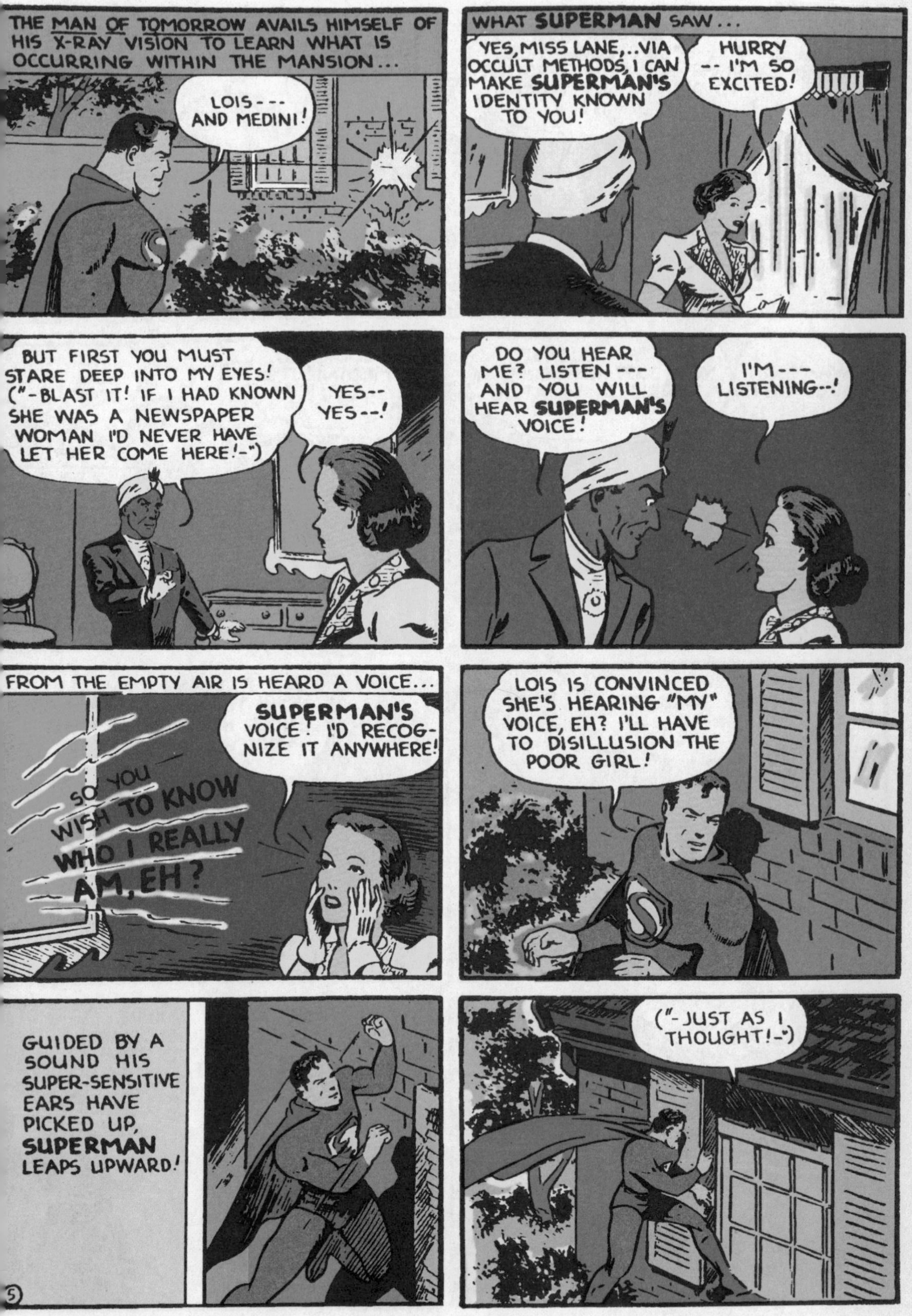
THE MAN OF TOMORROW AVAILS HIMSELF OF HIS X-RAY VISION TO LEARN WHAT IS OCCURRING WITHIN THE MANSION...
LOIS--- AND MEDINI!
WHAT SUPERMAN SAW...
YES, MISS LANE,..VIA OCCULT METHODS, I CAN MAKE SUPERMAN'S IDENTITY KNOWN TO YOU!
HURRY -- I'M SO EXCITED!
BUT FIRST YOU MUST STARE DEEP INTO MY EYES! ("-BLAST IT! IF I HAD KNOWN SHE WAS A NEWSPAPER WOMAN I'D NEVER HAVE LET HER COME HERE!-")
YES-- YES--!
DO YOU HEAR ME? LISTEN --- AND YOU WILL HEAR SUPERMAN'S VOICE!
I'M--- LISTENING--!
FROM THE EMPTY AIR IS HEARD A VOICE...
SO YOU WISH TO KNOW WHO I REALLY AM, EH?
SUPERMAN'S VOICE! I'D RECOGNIZE IT ANYWHERE!
LOIS IS CONVINCED SHE'S HEARING "MY" VOICE, EH? I'LL HAVE TO DISILLUSION THE POOR GIRL!
GUIDED BY A SOUND HIS SUPER-SENSITIVE EARS HAVE PICKED UP, SUPERMAN LEAPS UPWARD!
5
("-JUST AS I THOUGHT!-")

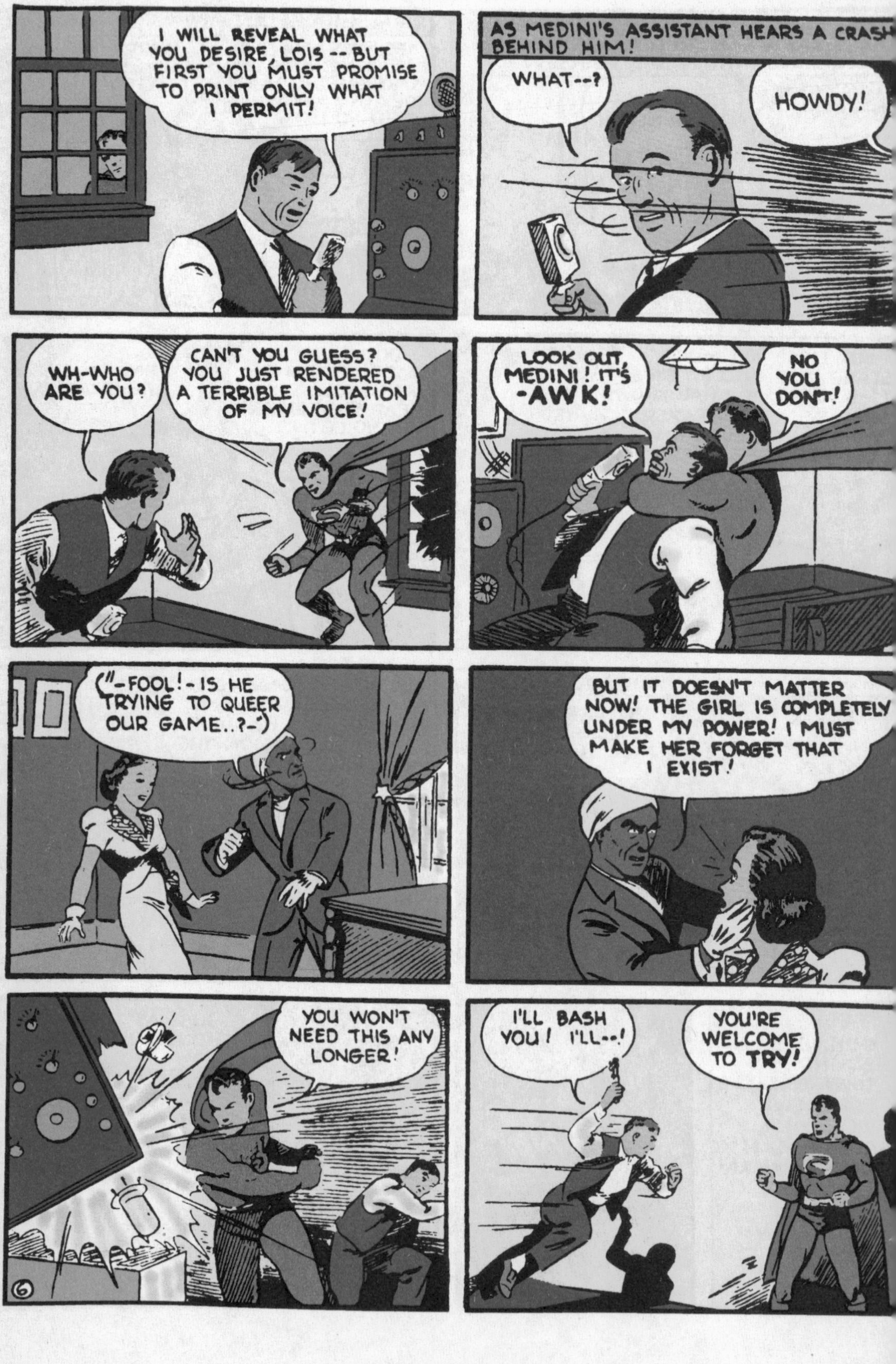
I WILL REVEAL WHAT YOU DESIRE, LOIS -- BUT FIRST YOU MUST PROMISE TO PRINT ONLY WHAT I PERMIT!
AS MEDINI'S ASSISTANT HEARS A CRASH BEHIND HIM!
WHAT--?
HOWDY!
WH-WHO ARE YOU?
CAN'T YOU GUESS? YOU JUST RENDERED A TERRIBLE IMITATION OF MY VOICE!
LOOK OUT, MEDINI! IT'S -AWK!
NO YOU DON'T!
("-FOOL!-IS HE TRYING TO QUEER OUR GAME..?-")
BUT IT DOESN'T MATTER NOW! THE GIRL IS COMPLETELY UNDER MY POWER! I MUST MAKE HER FORGET THAT I EXIST!
YOU WON'T NEED THIS ANY LONGER!
6
I'LL BASH YOU! I'LL--!
YOU'RE WELCOME TO TRY!

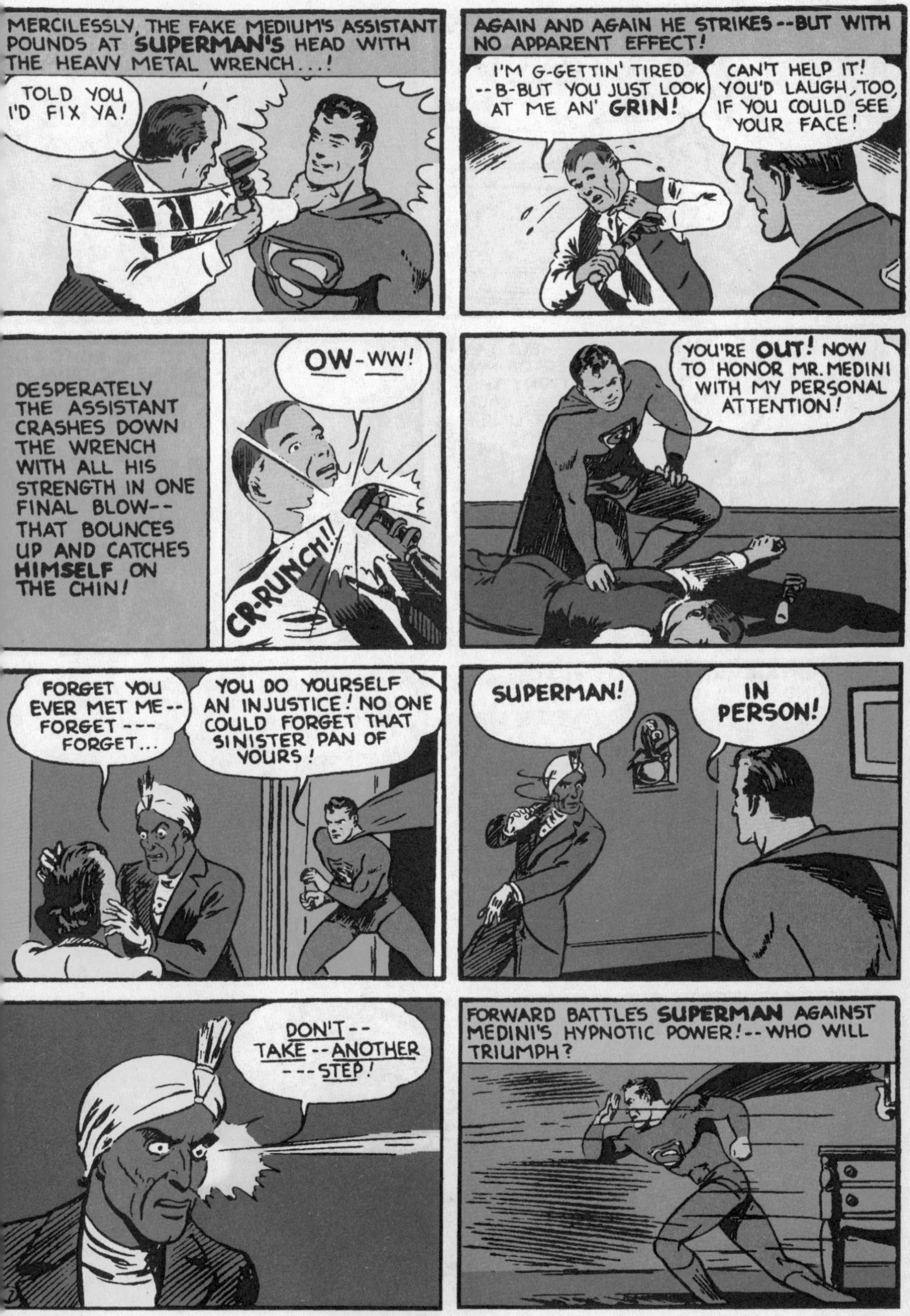
MERCILESSLY, THE FAKE MEDIUM'S ASSISTANT POUNDS AT SUPERMAN'S HEAD WITH THE HEAVY METAL WRENCH...!
TOLD YOU I'D FIX YA!
AGAIN AND AGAIN HE STRIKES--BUT WITH NO APPARENT EFFECT!
I'M G-GETTIN' TIRED --B-BUT YOU JUST LOOK AT ME AN' GRIN!
CAN'T HELP IT! YOU'D LAUGH, TOO, IF YOU COULD SEE YOUR FACE!
DESPERATELY THE ASSISTANT CRASHES DOWN THE WRENCH WITH ALL HIS STRENGTH IN ONE FINAL BLOW-- THAT BOUNCES UP AND CATCHES HIMSELF ON THE CHIN!
OW-WW!
CR-RUNCH!!
YOU'RE OUT! NOW TO HONOR MR. MEDINI WITH MY PERSONAL ATTENTION!
FORGET YOU EVER MET ME-- FORGET--- FORGET...
YOU DO YOURSELF AN INJUSTICE! NO ONE COULD FORGET THAT SINISTER PAN OF YOURS!
SUPERMAN!
IN PERSON!
DON'T-- TAKE--ANOTHER ---STEP!
FORWARD BATTLES SUPERMAN AGAINST MEDINI'S HYPNOTIC POWER!--WHO WILL TRIUMPH?

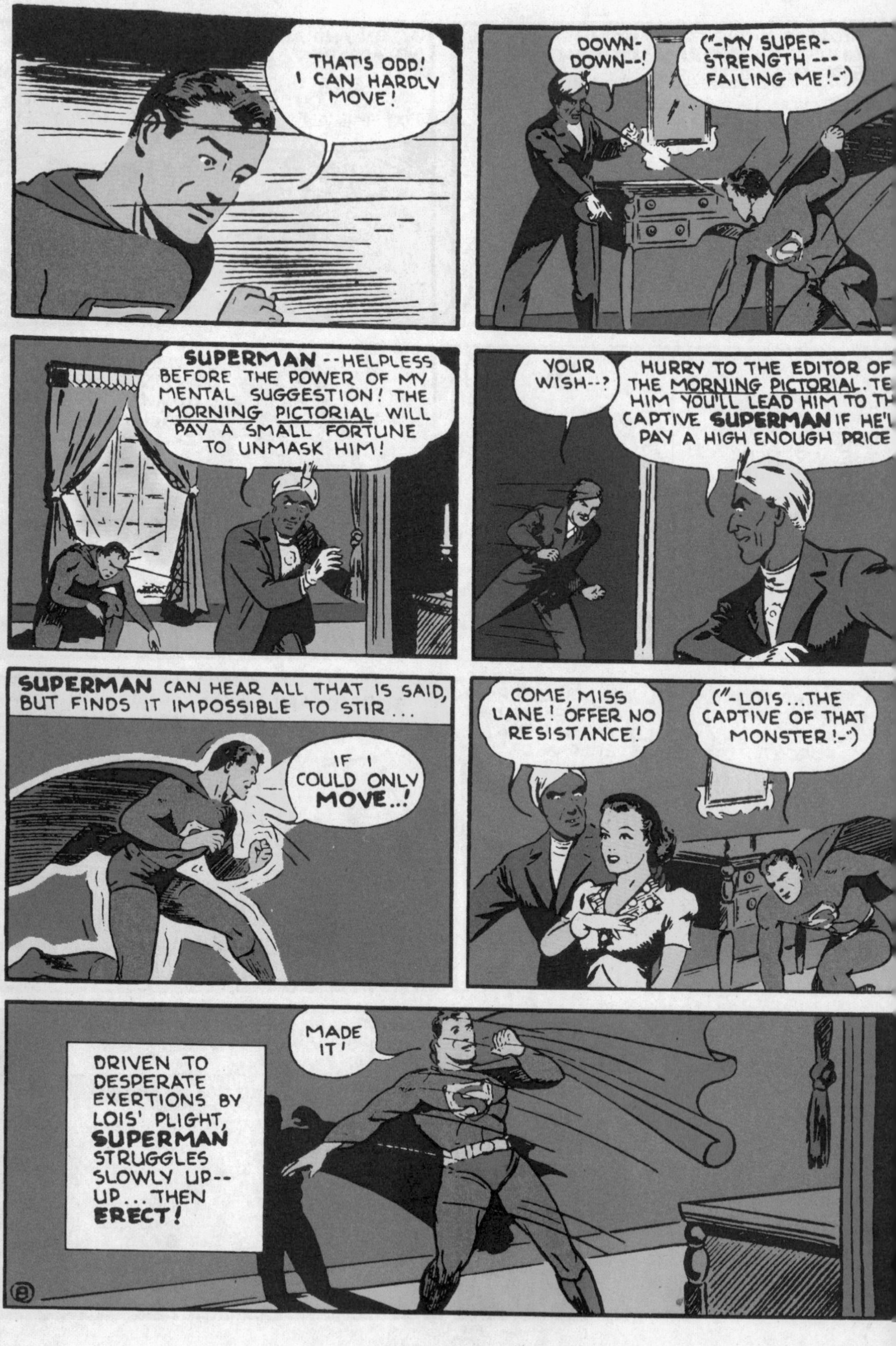

THAT'S ODD! I CAN HARDLY MOVE!
DOWN-DOWN--!
("-MY SUPER-STRENGTH --- FAILING ME!-")
SUPERMAN --HELPLESS BEFORE THE POWER OF MY MENTAL SUGGESTION! THE MORNING PICTORIAL WILL PAY A SMALL FORTUNE TO UNMASK HIM!
YOUR WISH--?
HURRY TO THE EDITOR OF THE MORNING PICTORIAL. TE HIM YOU'LL LEAD HIM TO TH CAPTIVE SUPERMAN IF HE' PAY A HIGH ENOUGH PRICE
SUPERMAN CAN HEAR ALL THAT IS SAID, BUT FINDS IT IMPOSSIBLE TO STIR...
IF I COULD ONLY MOVE..!
COME, MISS LANE! OFFER NO RESISTANCE!
("-LOIS...THE CAPTIVE OF THAT MONSTER!-")
DRIVEN TO DESPERATE EXERTIONS BY LOIS' PLIGHT, SUPERMAN STRUGGLES SLOWLY UP-- UP... THEN ERECT!
MADE IT!
8

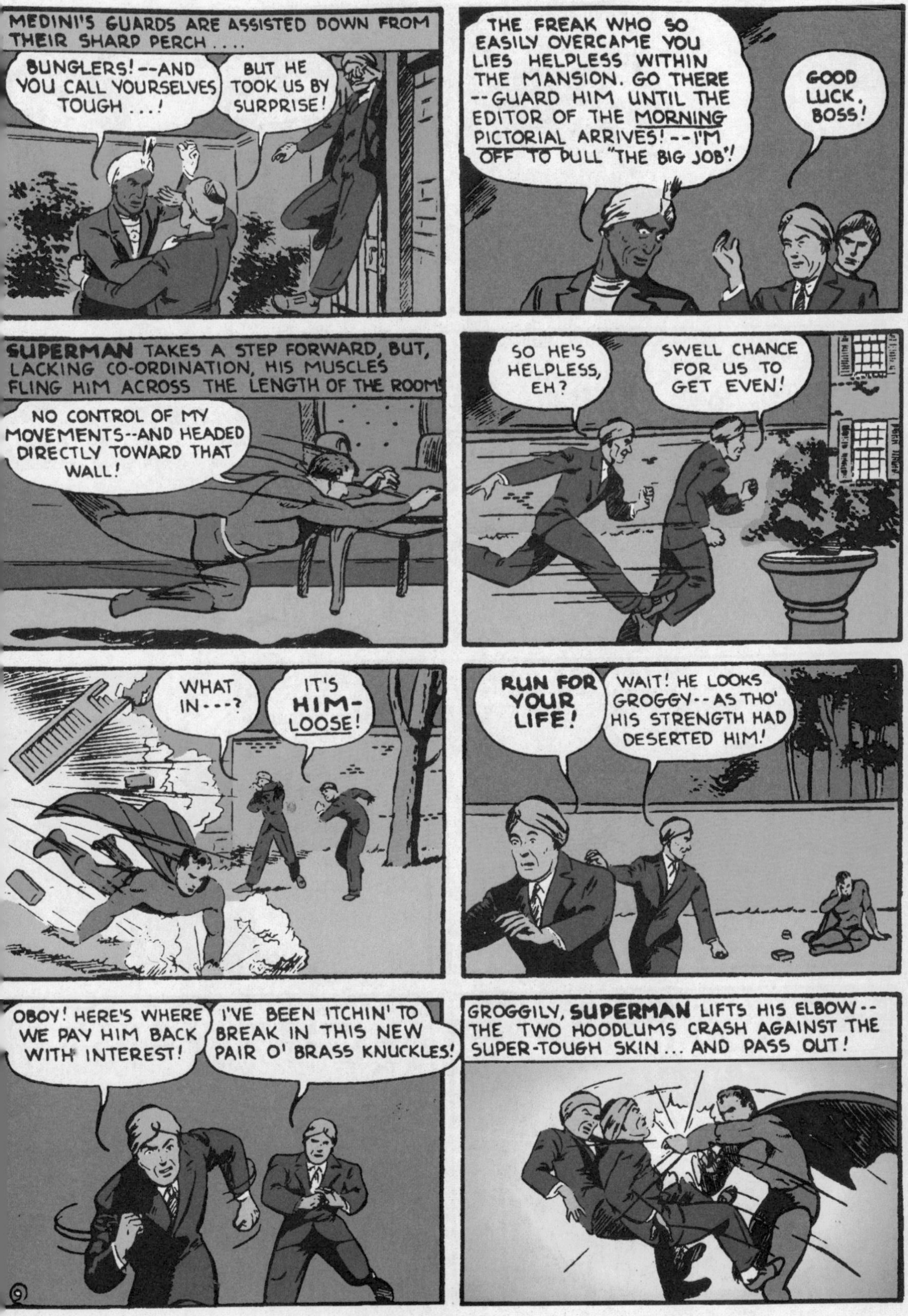
MEDINI'S GUARDS ARE ASSISTED DOWN FROM THEIR SHARP PERCH....
BUNGLERS!--AND YOU CALL YOURSELVES TOUGH...!
BUT HE TOOK US BY SURPRISE!
THE FREAK WHO SO EASILY OVERCAME YOU LIES HELPLESS WITHIN THE MANSION. GO THERE --GUARD HIM UNTIL THE EDITOR OF THE MORNING PICTORIAL ARRIVES!--I'M OFF TO PULL "THE BIG JOB"!
GOOD LUCK, BOSS!
SUPERMAN TAKES A STEP FORWARD, BUT, LACKING CO-ORDINATION, HIS MUSCLES FLING HIM ACROSS THE LENGTH OF THE ROOM!
NO CONTROL OF MY MOVEMENTS--AND HEADED DIRECTLY TOWARD THAT WALL!
SO HE'S HELPLESS, EH?
SWELL CHANCE FOR US TO GET EVEN!
WHAT IN---?
IT'S HIM-LOOSE!
RUN FOR YOUR LIFE!
WAIT! HE LOOKS GROGGY--AS THO' HIS STRENGTH HAD DESERTED HIM!
OBOY! HERE'S WHERE WE PAY HIM BACK WITH INTEREST!
I'VE BEEN ITCHIN' TO BREAK IN THIS NEW PAIR O' BRASS KNUCKLES!
GROGGILY, SUPERMAN LIFTS HIS ELBOW--THE TWO HOODLUMS CRASH AGAINST THE SUPER-TOUGH SKIN... AND PASS OUT!
9

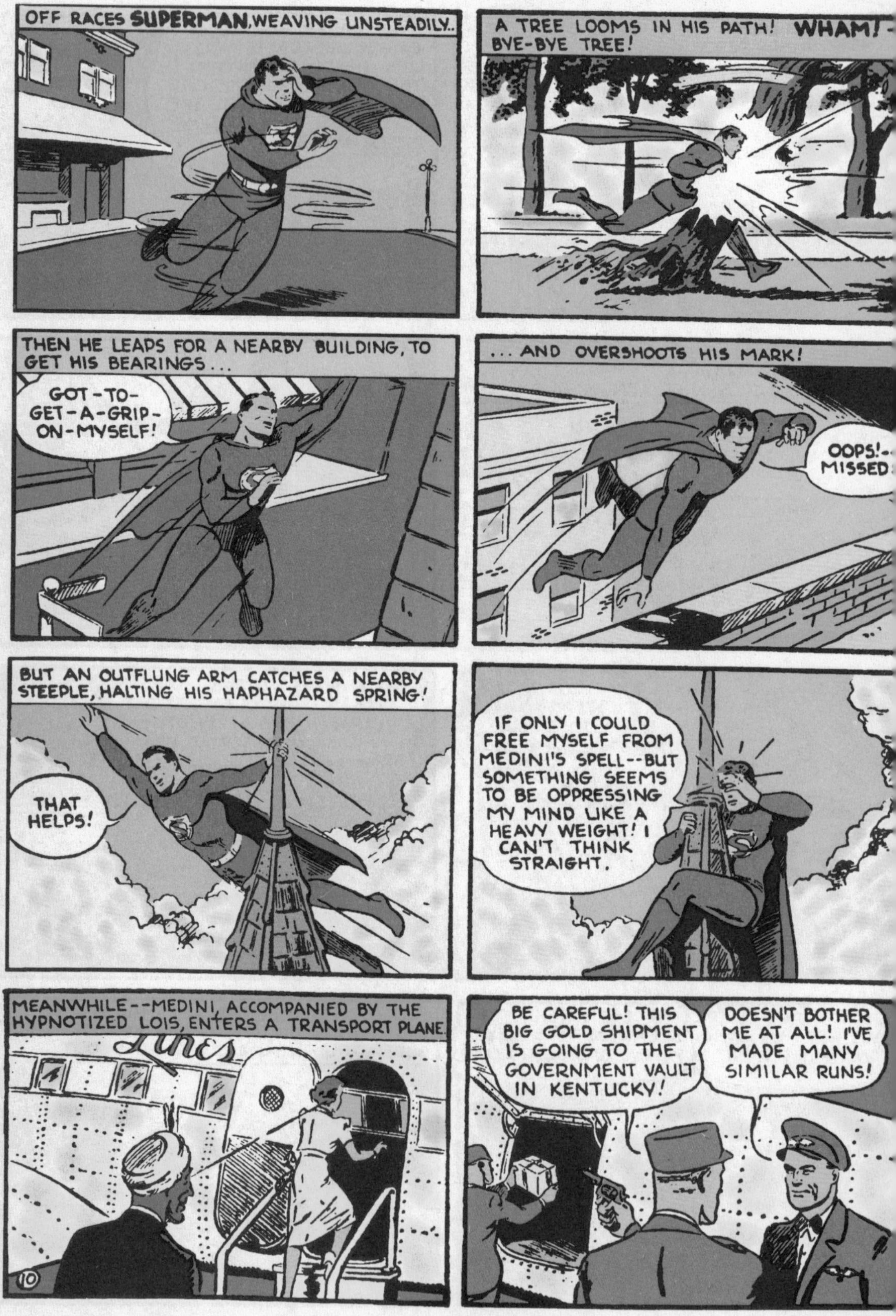
OFF RACES SUPERMAN, WEAVING UNSTEADILY..
A TREE LOOMS IN HIS PATH! WHAM!-BYE-BYE TREE!
THEN HE LEAPS FOR A NEARBY BUILDING, TO GET HIS BEARINGS...
GOT-TO-GET-A-GRIP-ON-MYSELF!
...AND OVERSHOOTS HIS MARK!
OOPS!--MISSED
BUT AN OUTFLUNG ARM CATCHES A NEARBY STEEPLE, HALTING HIS HAPHAZARD SPRING!
THAT HELPS!
IF ONLY I COULD FREE MYSELF FROM MEDINI'S SPELL--BUT SOMETHING SEEMS TO BE OPPRESSING MY MIND LIKE A HEAVY WEIGHT! I CAN'T THINK STRAIGHT.
MEANWHILE--MEDINI, ACCOMPANIED BY THE HYPNOTIZED LOIS, ENTERS A TRANSPORT PLANE.
Lines
10
BE CAREFUL! THIS BIG GOLD SHIPMENT IS GOING TO THE GOVERNMENT VAULT IN KENTUCKY!
DOESN'T BOTHER ME AT ALL! I'VE MADE MANY SIMILAR RUNS!

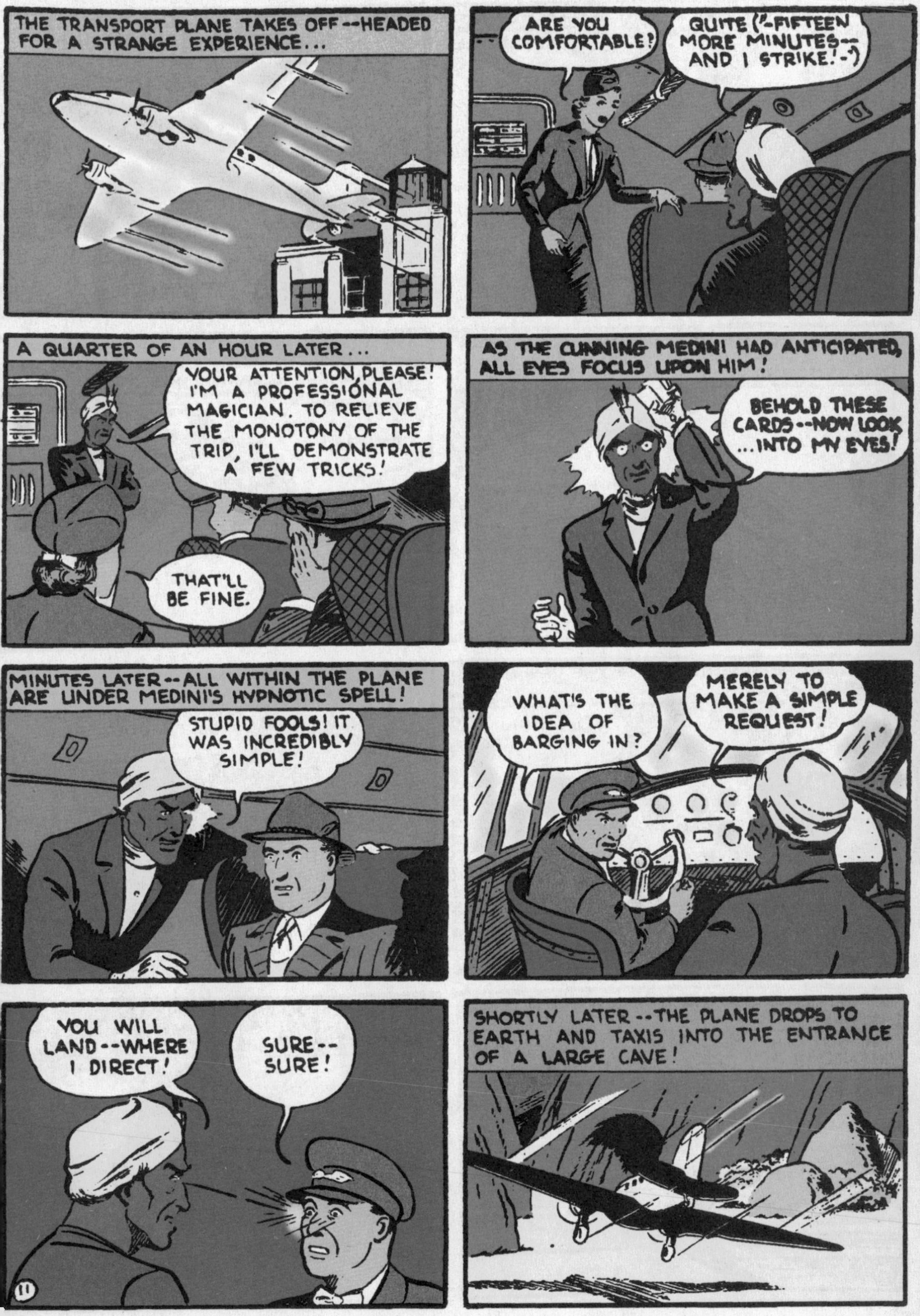
THE TRANSPORT PLANE TAKES OFF--HEADED FOR A STRANGE EXPERIENCE...
ARE YOU COMFORTABLE?
QUITE ("-FIFTEEN MORE MINUTES--AND I STRIKE!-")
A QUARTER OF AN HOUR LATER...
YOUR ATTENTION, PLEASE! I'M A PROFESSIONAL MAGICIAN. TO RELIEVE THE MONOTONY OF THE TRIP, I'LL DEMONSTRATE A FEW TRICKS!
THAT'LL BE FINE.
AS THE CUNNING MEDINI HAD ANTICIPATED, ALL EYES FOCUS UPON HIM!
BEHOLD THESE CARDS--NOW LOOK ...INTO MY EYES!
MINUTES LATER--ALL WITHIN THE PLANE ARE UNDER MEDINI'S HYPNOTIC SPELL!
STUPID FOOLS! IT WAS INCREDIBLY SIMPLE!
WHAT'S THE IDEA OF BARGING IN?
MERELY TO MAKE A SIMPLE REQUEST!
YOU WILL LAND--WHERE I DIRECT!
SURE--SURE!
11
SHORTLY LATER--THE PLANE DROPS TO EARTH AND TAXIS INTO THE ENTRANCE OF A LARGE CAVE!

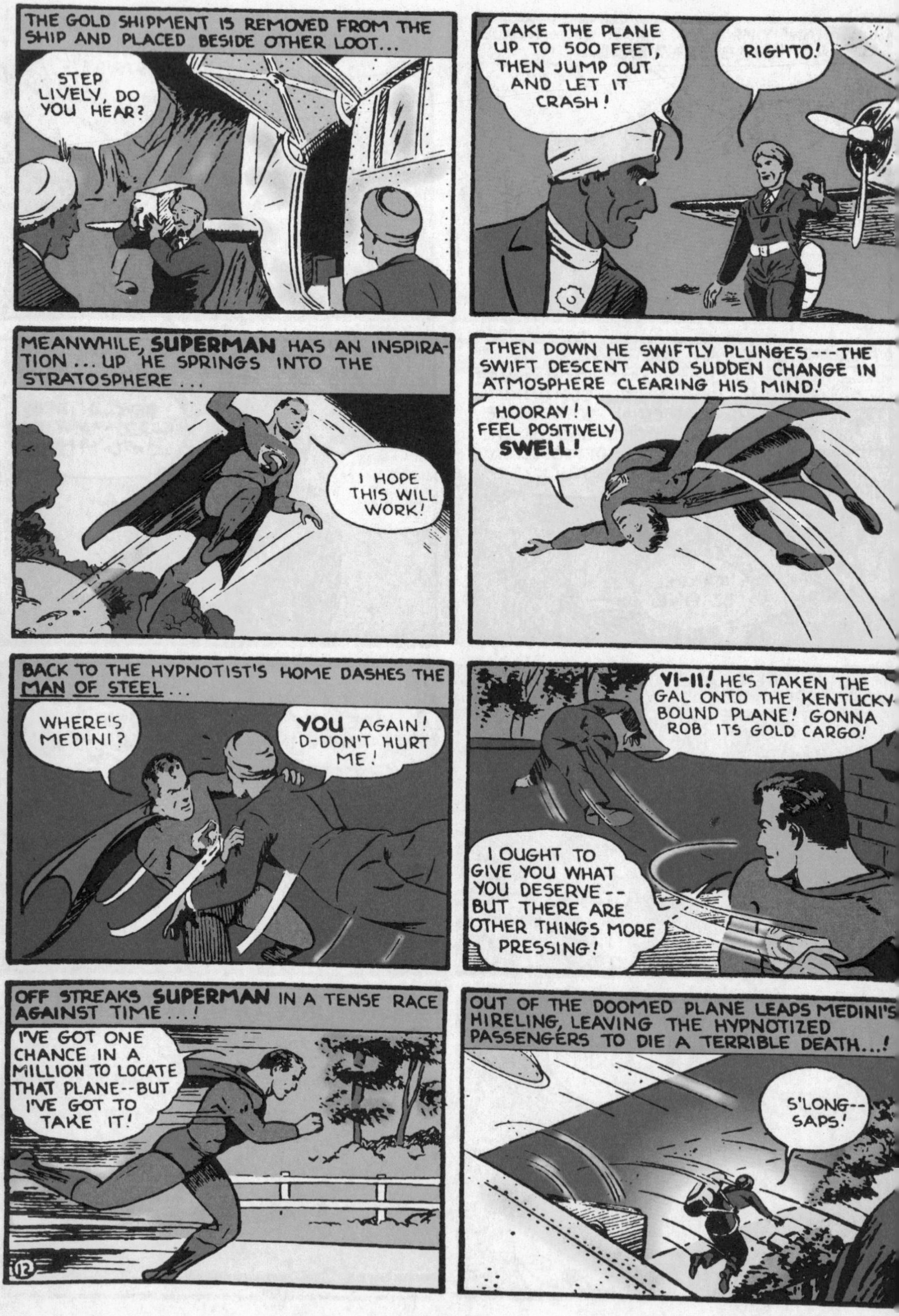
THE GOLD SHIPMENT IS REMOVED FROM THE SHIP AND PLACED BESIDE OTHER LOOT...
STEP LIVELY, DO YOU HEAR?
TAKE THE PLANE UP TO 500 FEET, THEN JUMP OUT AND LET IT CRASH!
RIGHTO!
MEANWHILE, SUPERMAN HAS AN INSPIRATION ... UP HE SPRINGS INTO THE STRATOSPHERE ...
I HOPE THIS WILL WORK!
THEN DOWN HE SWIFTLY PLUNGES---THE SWIFT DESCENT AND SUDDEN CHANGE IN ATMOSPHERE CLEARING HIS MIND!
HOORAY! I FEEL POSITIVELY SWELL!
BACK TO THE HYPNOTIST'S HOME DASHES THE MAN OF STEEL...
WHERE'S MEDINI?
YOU AGAIN! D-DON'T HURT ME!
YI-II! HE'S TAKEN THE GAL ONTO THE KENTUCKY-BOUND PLANE! GONNA ROB ITS GOLD CARGO!
I OUGHT TO GIVE YOU WHAT YOU DESERVE-- BUT THERE ARE OTHER THINGS MORE PRESSING!
OFF STREAKS SUPERMAN IN A TENSE RACE AGAINST TIME...!
I'VE GOT ONE CHANCE IN A MILLION TO LOCATE THAT PLANE--BUT I'VE GOT TO TAKE IT!
12
OUT OF THE DOOMED PLANE LEAPS MEDINI'S HIRELING, LEAVING THE HYPNOTIZED PASSENGERS TO DIE A TERRIBLE DEATH...!
S'LONG-- SAPS!

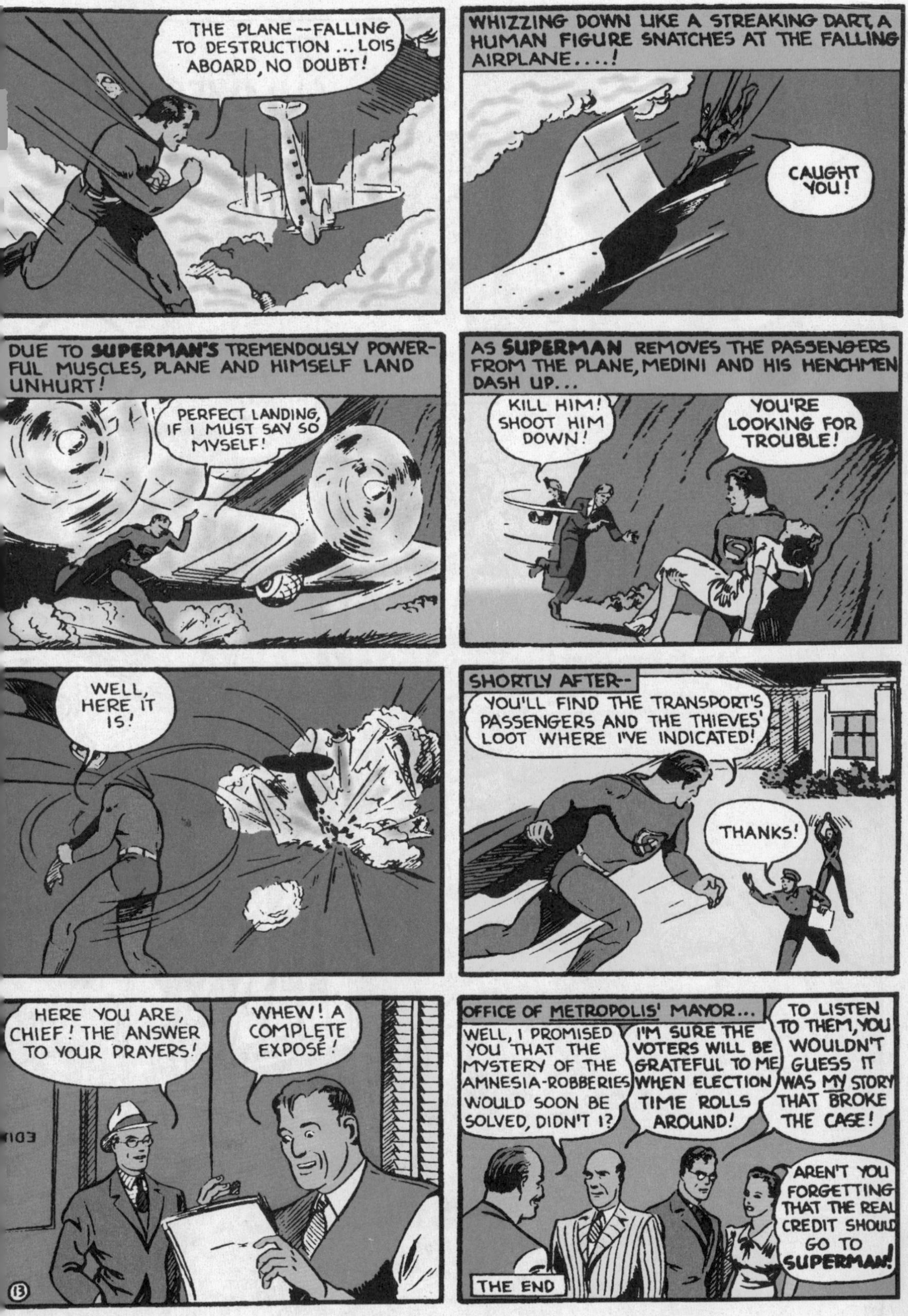
THE PLANE --FALLING TO DESTRUCTION ... LOIS ABOARD, NO DOUBT!
WHIZZING DOWN LIKE A STREAKING DART, A HUMAN FIGURE SNATCHES AT THE FALLING AIRPLANE....!
CAUGHT YOU!
DUE TO SUPERMAN'S TREMENDOUSLY POWERFUL MUSCLES, PLANE AND HIMSELF LAND UNHURT!
PERFECT LANDING, IF I MUST SAY SO MYSELF!
AS SUPERMAN REMOVES THE PASSENGERS FROM THE PLANE, MEDINI AND HIS HENCHMEN DASH UP...
KILL HIM! SHOOT HIM DOWN!
YOU'RE LOOKING FOR TROUBLE!
WELL, HERE IT IS!
SHORTLY AFTER--
YOU'LL FIND THE TRANSPORT'S PASSENGERS AND THE THIEVES' LOOT WHERE I'VE INDICATED!
THANKS!
HERE YOU ARE, CHIEF! THE ANSWER TO YOUR PRAYERS!
WHEW! A COMPLETE EXPOSÉ!
13
OFFICE OF METROPOLIS' MAYOR...
WELL, I PROMISED YOU THAT THE MYSTERY OF THE AMNESIA-ROBBERIES WOULD SOON BE SOLVED, DIDN'T I?
I'M SURE THE VOTERS WILL BE GRATEFUL TO ME WHEN ELECTION TIME ROLLS AROUND!
TO LISTEN TO THEM, YOU WOULDN'T GUESS IT WAS MY STORY THAT BROKE THE CASE!
AREN'T YOU FORGETTING THAT THE REAL CREDIT SHOULD GO TO SUPERMAN!
THE END

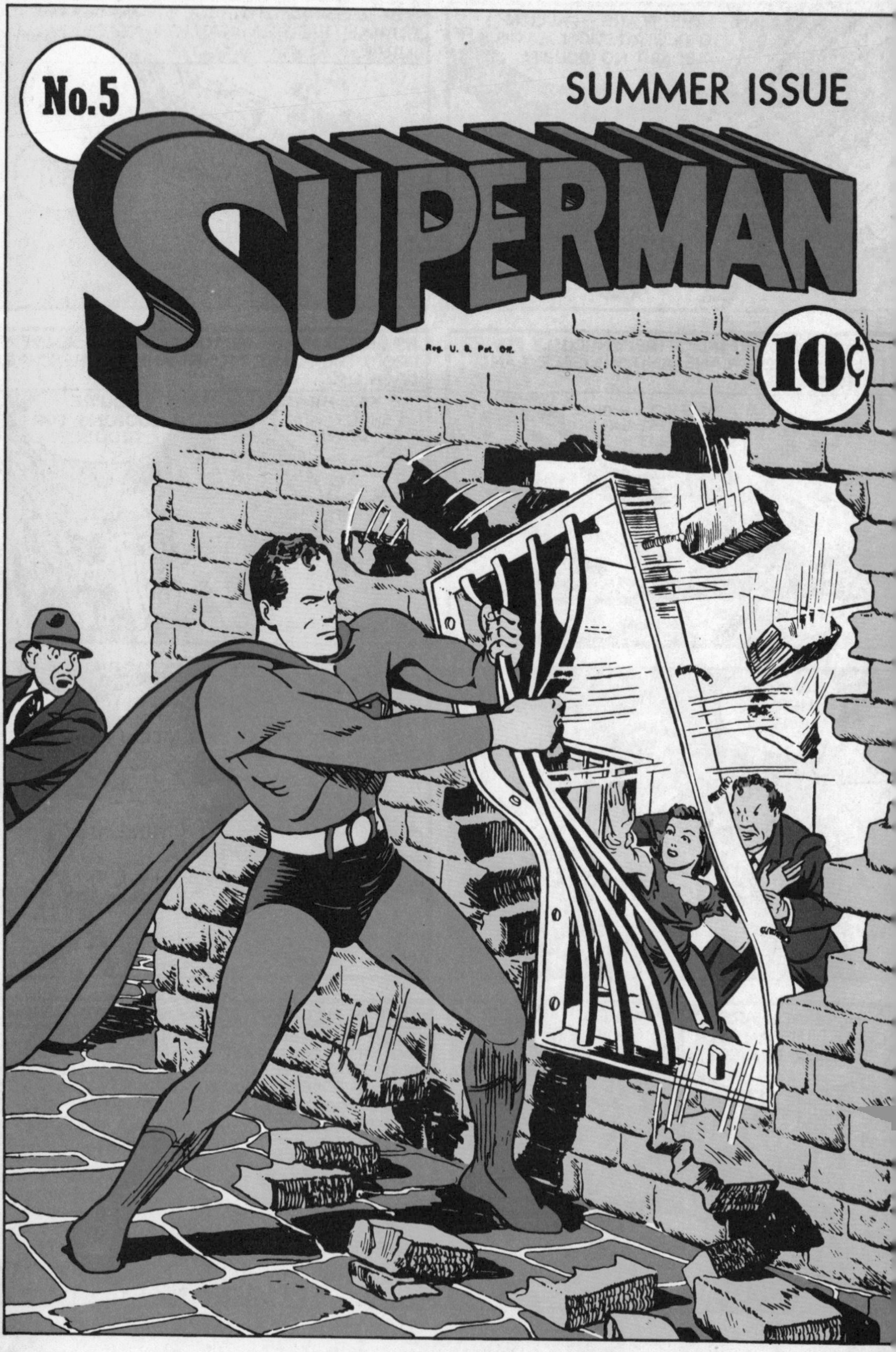
No.5
SUMMER ISSUE
SUPERMAN
Reg. U. S. Pat. Off.
10¢

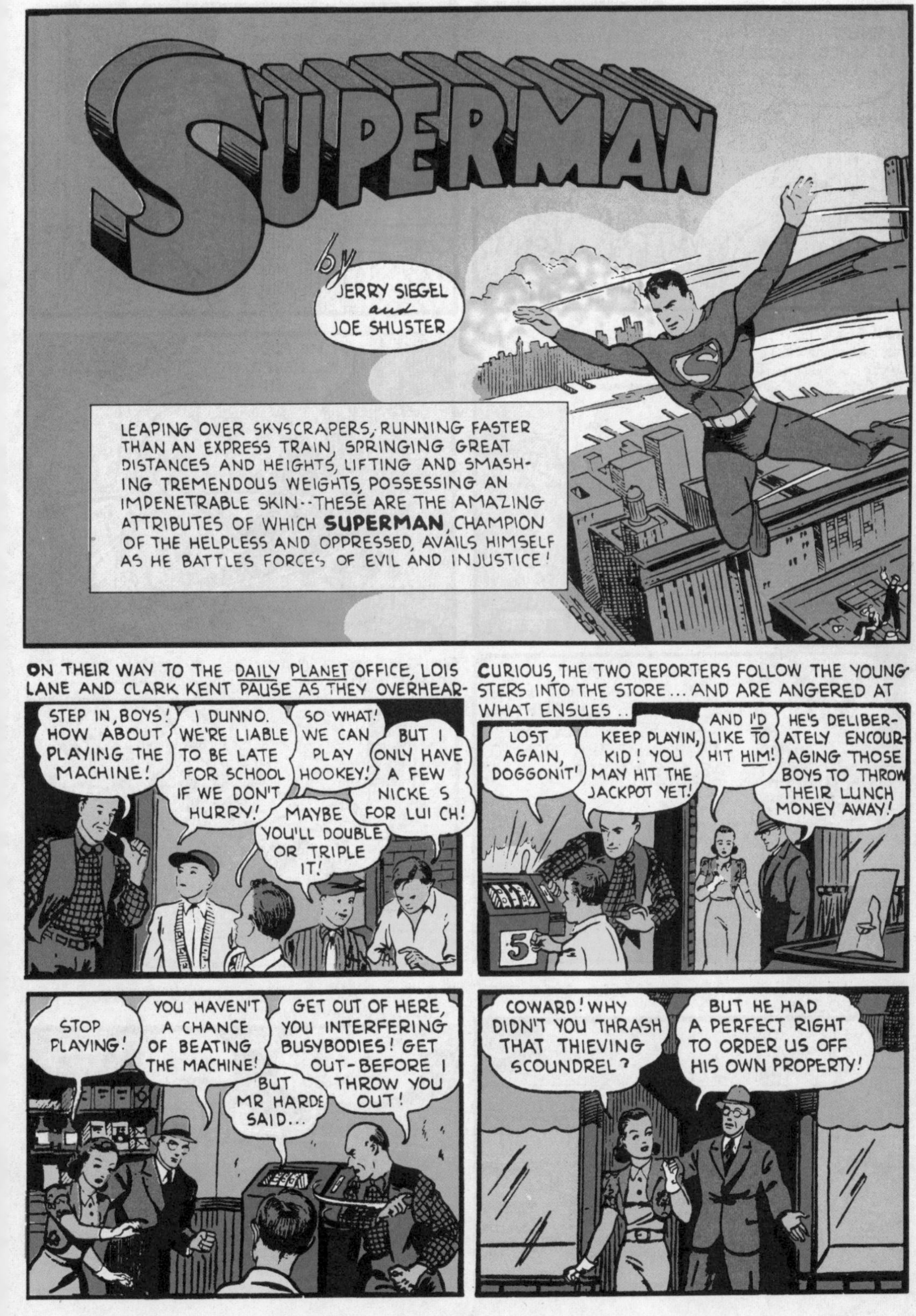
SUPERMAN
by
JERRY SIEGEL and JOE SHUSTER
LEAPING OVER SKYSCRAPERS, RUNNING FASTER THAN AN EXPRESS TRAIN, SPRINGING GREAT DISTANCES AND HEIGHTS, LIFTING AND SMASHING TREMENDOUS WEIGHTS, POSSESSING AN IMPENETRABLE SKIN--THESE ARE THE AMAZING ATTRIBUTES OF WHICH SUPERMAN, CHAMPION OF THE HELPLESS AND OPPRESSED, AVAILS HIMSELF AS HE BATTLES FORCES OF EVIL AND INJUSTICE!
ON THEIR WAY TO THE DAILY PLANET OFFICE, LOIS LANE AND CLARK KENT PAUSE AS THEY OVERHEAR-
STEP IN, BOYS! HOW ABOUT PLAYING THE MACHINE!
I DUNNO. WE'RE LIABLE TO BE LATE FOR SCHOOL IF WE DON'T HURRY!
SO WHAT! WE CAN PLAY HOOKEY!
BUT I ONLY HAVE A FEW NICKE S FOR LUI CH!
MAYBE YOU'LL DOUBLE OR TRIPLE IT!
CURIOUS, THE TWO REPORTERS FOLLOW THE YOUNGSTERS INTO THE STORE... AND ARE ANGERED AT WHAT ENSUES..
LOST AGAIN, DOGGONIT!
KEEP PLAYIN, KID! YOU MAY HIT THE JACKPOT YET!
AND I'D LIKE TO HIT HIM!
HE'S DELIBERATELY ENCOURAGING THOSE BOYS TO THROW THEIR LUNCH MONEY AWAY!
5
STOP PLAYING!
YOU HAVEN'T A CHANCE OF BEATING THE MACHINE!
GET OUT OF HERE, YOU INTERFERING BUSYBODIES! GET OUT-BEFORE I THROW YOU OUT!
BUT MR HARDE SAID...
COWARD! WHY DIDN'T YOU THRASH THAT THIEVING SCOUNDREL?
BUT HE HAD A PERFECT RIGHT TO ORDER US OFF HIS OWN PROPERTY!

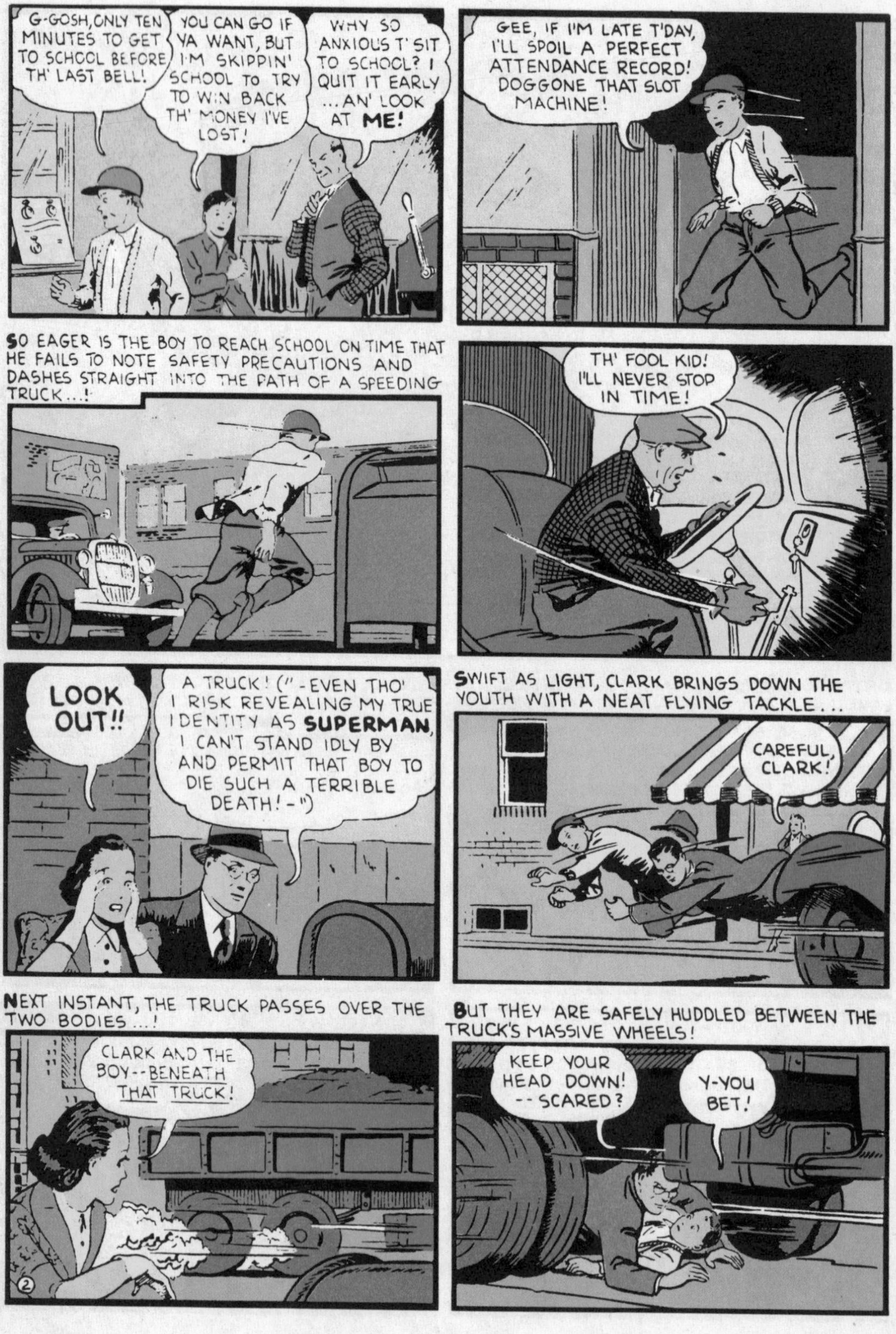
G-GOSH, ONLY TEN MINUTES TO GET TO SCHOOL BEFORE TH' LAST BELL!
YOU CAN GO IF YA WANT, BUT I'M SKIPPIN' SCHOOL TO TRY TO WIN BACK TH' MONEY I'VE LOST!
WHY SO ANXIOUS T' SIT TO SCHOOL? I QUIT IT EARLY ... AN' LOOK AT ME!
GEE, IF I'M LATE T'DAY, I'LL SPOIL A PERFECT ATTENDANCE RECORD! DOGGONE THAT SLOT MACHINE!
SO EAGER IS THE BOY TO REACH SCHOOL ON TIME THAT HE FAILS TO NOTE SAFETY PRECAUTIONS AND DASHES STRAIGHT INTO THE PATH OF A SPEEDING TRUCK...!
TH' FOOL KID! I'LL NEVER STOP IN TIME!
LOOK OUT!!
A TRUCK! ("-EVEN THO' I RISK REVEALING MY TRUE IDENTITY AS SUPERMAN, I CAN'T STAND IDLY BY AND PERMIT THAT BOY TO DIE SUCH A TERRIBLE DEATH!-")
SWIFT AS LIGHT, CLARK BRINGS DOWN THE YOUTH WITH A NEAT FLYING TACKLE...
CAREFUL, CLARK!
NEXT INSTANT, THE TRUCK PASSES OVER THE TWO BODIES...!
CLARK AND THE BOY--BENEATH THAT TRUCK!
2
BUT THEY ARE SAFELY HUDDLED BETWEEN THE TRUCK'S MASSIVE WHEELS!
KEEP YOUR HEAD DOWN! --SCARED?
Y-YOU BET!

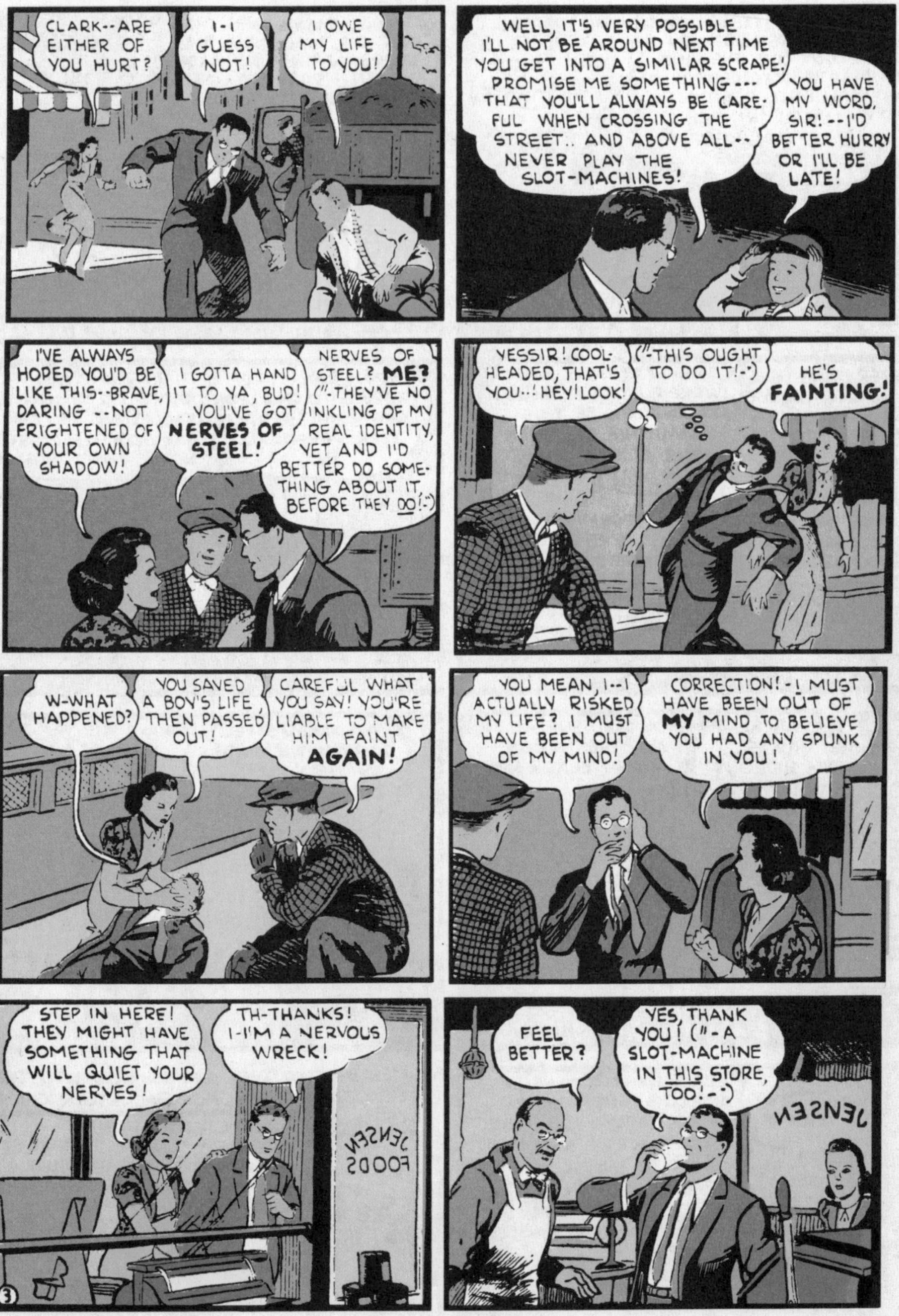
CLARK--ARE EITHER OF YOU HURT?
I-I GUESS NOT!
I OWE MY LIFE TO YOU!
WELL, IT'S VERY POSSIBLE I'LL NOT BE AROUND NEXT TIME YOU GET INTO A SIMILAR SCRAPE! PROMISE ME SOMETHING--- THAT YOU'LL ALWAYS BE CAREFUL WHEN CROSSING THE STREET.. AND ABOVE ALL-- NEVER PLAY THE SLOT-MACHINES!
YOU HAVE MY WORD, SIR! --I'D BETTER HURRY OR I'LL BE LATE!
I'VE ALWAYS HOPED YOU'D BE LIKE THIS--BRAVE, DARING --NOT FRIGHTENED OF YOUR OWN SHADOW!
I GOTTA HAND IT TO YA, BUD! ..YOU'VE GOT **NERVES OF STEEL!**
NERVES OF STEEL? **ME?** ("-THEY'VE NO INKLING OF MY REAL IDENTITY, YET AND I'D BETTER DO SOMETHING ABOUT IT, BEFORE THEY DO!-")
YESSIR! COOL-HEADED, THAT'S YOU..! HEY! LOOK!
("-THIS OUGHT TO DO IT!-")
HE'S **FAINTING!**
W-WHAT HAPPENED?
YOU SAVED A BOY'S LIFE, THEN PASSED OUT!
CAREFUL WHAT YOU SAY! YOU'RE LIABLE TO MAKE HIM FAINT **AGAIN!**
YOU MEAN, I--I ACTUALLY RISKED MY LIFE? I MUST HAVE BEEN OUT OF MY MIND!
CORRECTION! -I MUST HAVE BEEN OUT OF **MY** MIND TO BELIEVE YOU HAD ANY SPUNK IN YOU!
STEP IN HERE! THEY MIGHT HAVE SOMETHING THAT WILL QUIET YOUR NERVES!
TH-THANKS! I-I'M A NERVOUS WRECK!
3
FEEL BETTER?
YES, THANK YOU! ("-A SLOT-MACHINE IN THIS STORE, TOO!-")

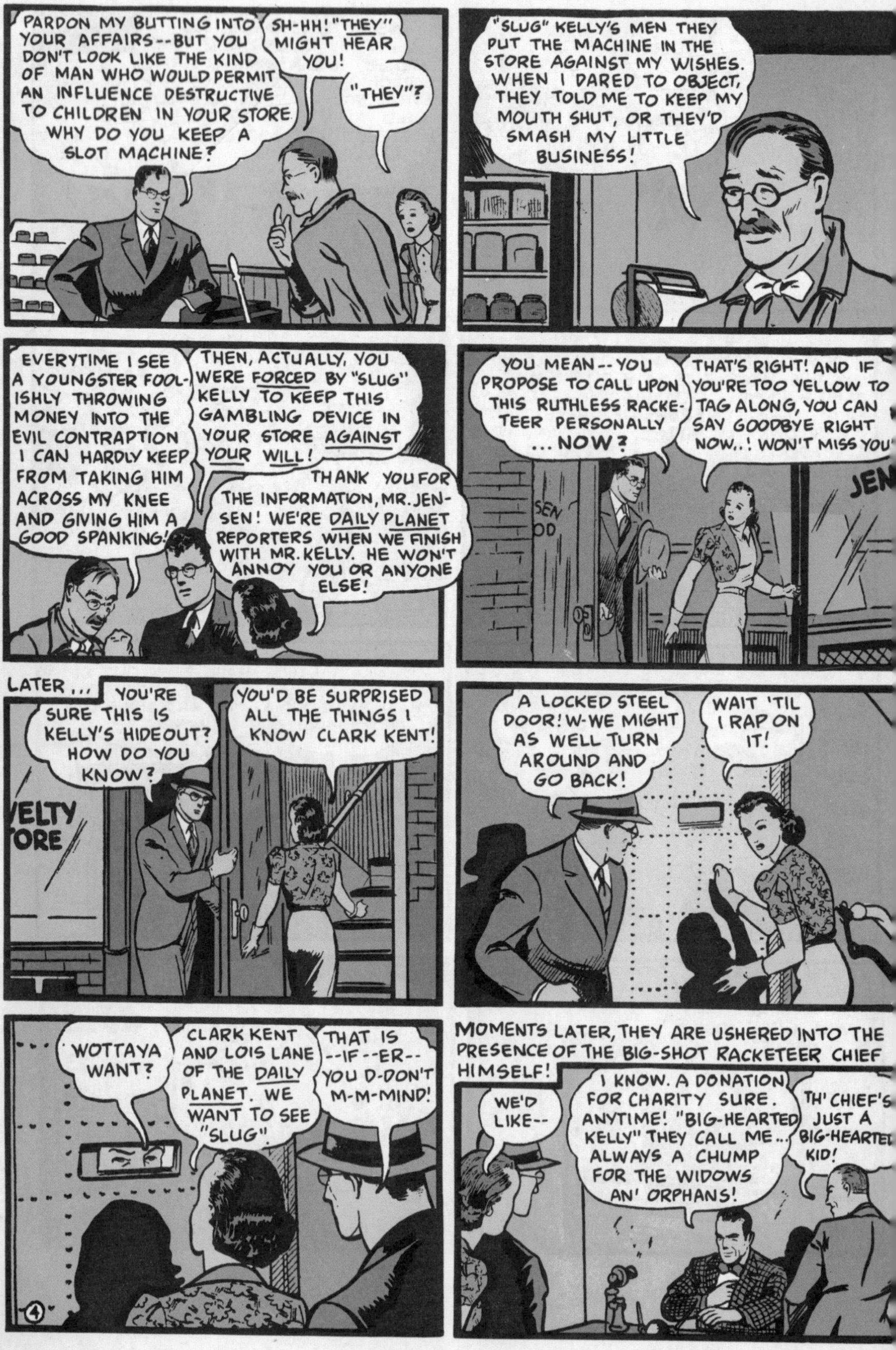
PARDON MY BUTTING INTO YOUR AFFAIRS--BUT YOU DON'T LOOK LIKE THE KIND OF MAN WHO WOULD PERMIT AN INFLUENCE DESTRUCTIVE TO CHILDREN IN YOUR STORE. WHY DO YOU KEEP A SLOT MACHINE?
SH-HH! "THEY" MIGHT HEAR YOU!
"THEY"?
"SLUG" KELLY'S MEN THEY PUT THE MACHINE IN THE STORE AGAINST MY WISHES. WHEN I DARED TO OBJECT, THEY TOLD ME TO KEEP MY MOUTH SHUT, OR THEY'D SMASH MY LITTLE BUSINESS!
EVERYTIME I SEE A YOUNGSTER FOOLISHLY THROWING MONEY INTO THE EVIL CONTRAPTION I CAN HARDLY KEEP FROM TAKING HIM ACROSS MY KNEE AND GIVING HIM A GOOD SPANKING!
THEN, ACTUALLY, YOU WERE FORCED BY "SLUG" KELLY TO KEEP THIS GAMBLING DEVICE IN YOUR STORE AGAINST YOUR WILL!
THANK YOU FOR THE INFORMATION, MR. JENSEN! WE'RE DAILY PLANET REPORTERS WHEN WE FINISH WITH MR. KELLY. HE WON'T ANNOY YOU OR ANYONE ELSE!
YOU MEAN--YOU PROPOSE TO CALL UPON THIS RUTHLESS RACKETEER PERSONALLY ...NOW?
THAT'S RIGHT! AND IF YOU'RE TOO YELLOW TO TAG ALONG, YOU CAN SAY GOODBYE RIGHT NOW..! WON'T MISS YOU
LATER...
YOU'RE SURE THIS IS KELLY'S HIDEOUT? HOW DO YOU KNOW?
YOU'D BE SURPRISED ALL THE THINGS I KNOW CLARK KENT!
A LOCKED STEEL DOOR! W-WE MIGHT AS WELL TURN AROUND AND GO BACK!
WAIT 'TIL I RAP ON IT!
WOTTAYA WANT?
CLARK KENT AND LOIS LANE OF THE DAILY PLANET. WE WANT TO SEE "SLUG".
THAT IS --IF--ER-- YOU D-DON'T M-M-MIND!
MOMENTS LATER, THEY ARE USHERED INTO THE PRESENCE OF THE BIG-SHOT RACKETEER CHIEF HIMSELF!
WE'D LIKE--
I KNOW. A DONATION FOR CHARITY SURE. ANYTIME! "BIG-HEARTED KELLY" THEY CALL ME... ALWAYS A CHUMP FOR THE WIDOWS AN' ORPHANS!
TH' CHIEF'S JUST A BIG-HEARTED KID!

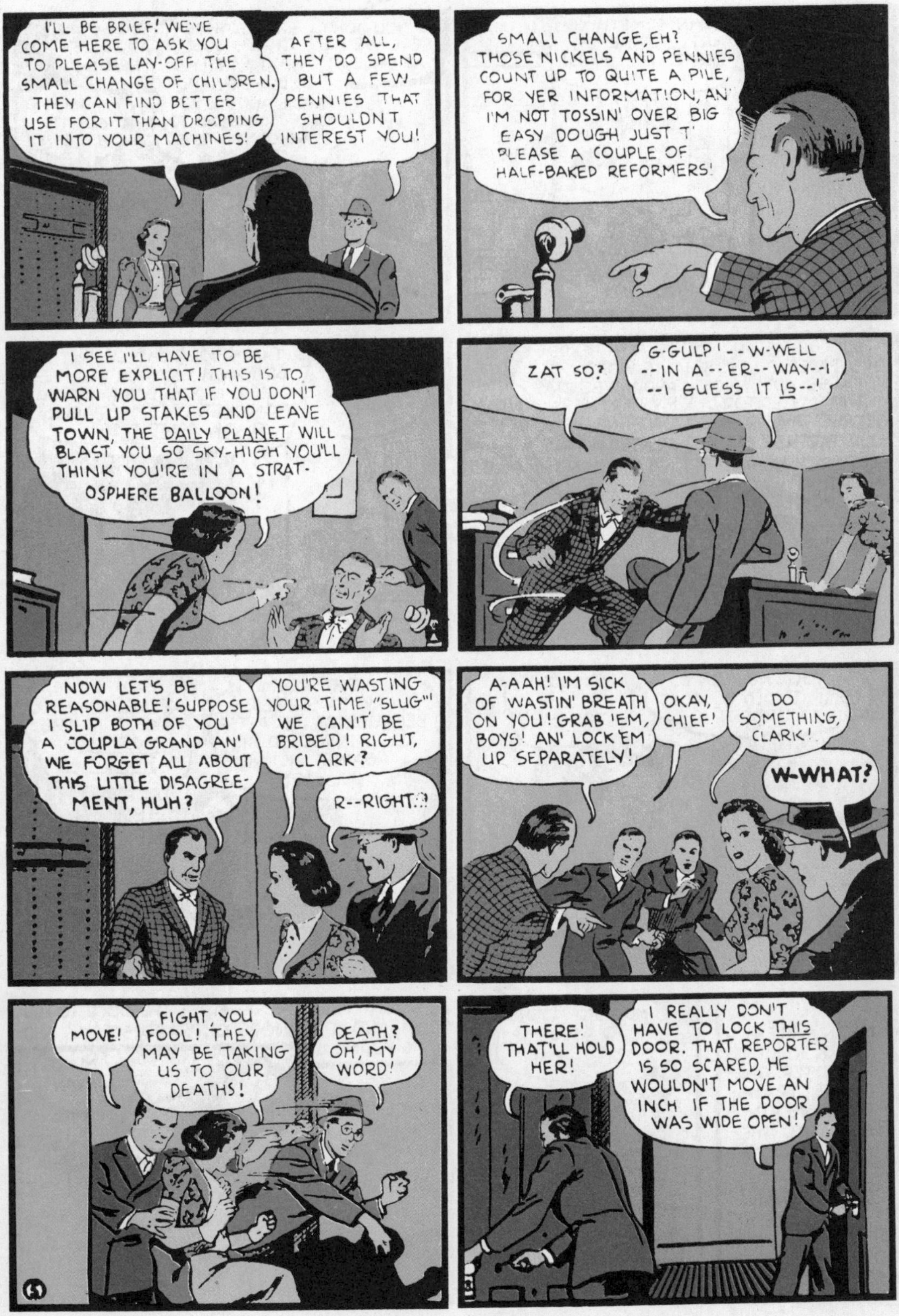
I'LL BE BRIEF! WE'VE COME HERE TO ASK YOU TO PLEASE LAY-OFF THE SMALL CHANGE OF CHILDREN. THEY CAN FIND BETTER USE FOR IT THAN DROPPING IT INTO YOUR MACHINES!
AFTER ALL, THEY DO SPEND BUT A FEW PENNIES THAT SHOULDN'T INTEREST YOU!
SMALL CHANGE, EH? THOSE NICKELS AND PENNIES COUNT UP TO QUITE A PILE, FOR YER INFORMATION, AN' I'M NOT TOSSIN' OVER BIG EASY DOUGH JUST T' PLEASE A COUPLE OF HALF-BAKED REFORMERS!
I SEE I'LL HAVE TO BE MORE EXPLICIT! THIS IS TO WARN YOU THAT IF YOU DON'T PULL UP STAKES AND LEAVE TOWN, THE DAILY PLANET WILL BLAST YOU SO SKY-HIGH YOU'LL THINK YOU'RE IN A STRAT-OSPHERE BALLOON!
ZAT SO?
G-GULP! --W-WELL --IN A --ER-- WAY--I --I GUESS IT IS--!
NOW LET'S BE REASONABLE! SUPPOSE I SLIP BOTH OF YOU A COUPLA GRAND AN' WE FORGET ALL ABOUT THIS LITTLE DISAGREE-MENT, HUH?
YOU'RE WASTING YOUR TIME "SLUG"! WE CAN'T BE BRIBED! RIGHT, CLARK?
R--RIGHT!?
A-AAH! I'M SICK OF WASTIN' BREATH ON YOU! GRAB 'EM, BOYS! AN' LOCK 'EM UP SEPARATELY!
OKAY, CHIEF!
DO SOMETHING, CLARK!
W-WHAT?
MOVE!
FIGHT, YOU FOOL! THEY MAY BE TAKING US TO OUR DEATHS!
DEATH? OH, MY WORD!
THERE! THAT'LL HOLD HER!
I REALLY DON'T HAVE TO LOCK THIS DOOR. THAT REPORTER IS SO SCARED, HE WOULDN'T MOVE AN INCH IF THE DOOR WAS WIDE OPEN!

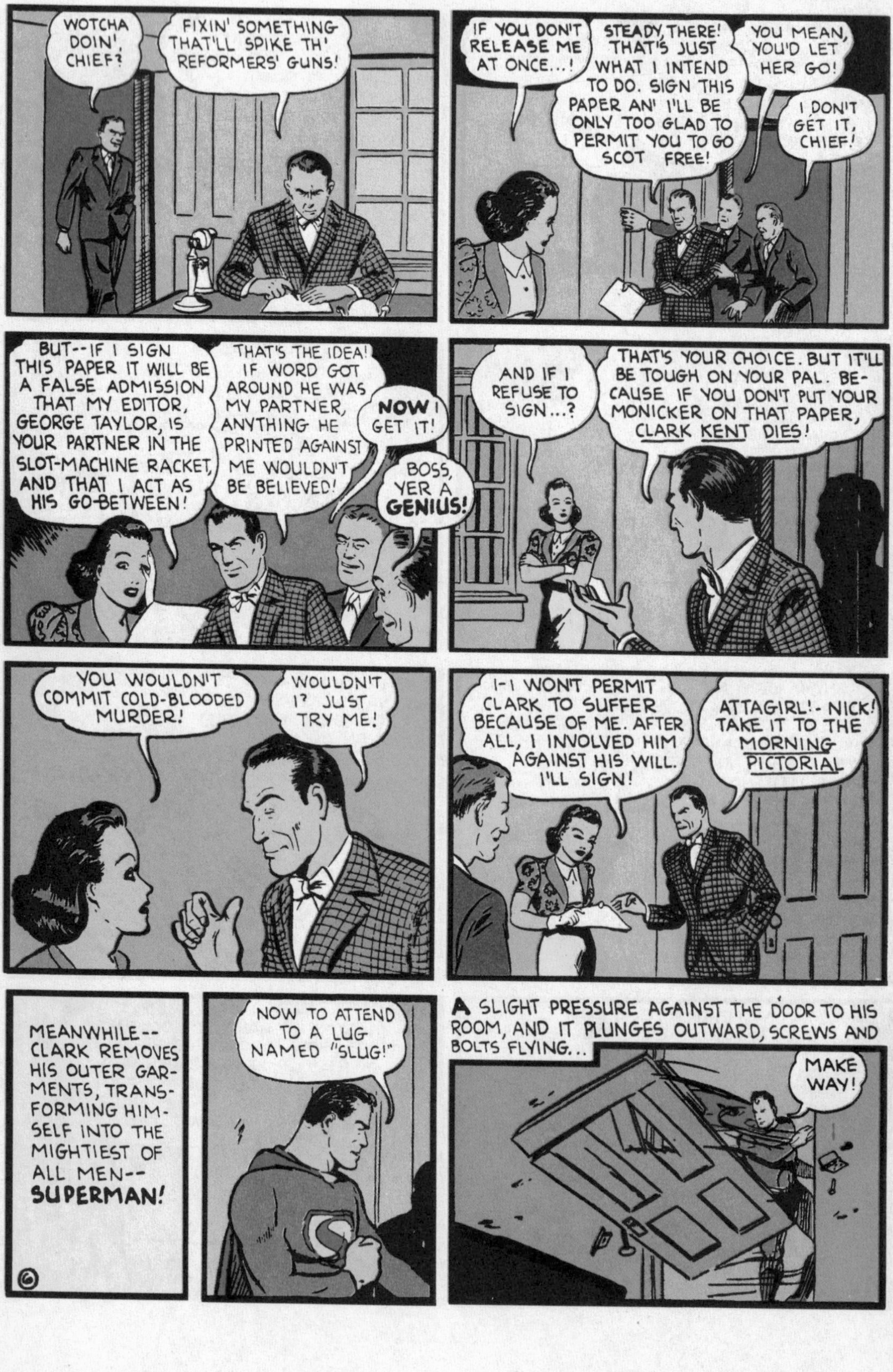

WOTCHA DOIN', CHIEF?
FIXIN' SOMETHING THAT'LL SPIKE TH' REFORMERS' GUNS!
IF YOU DON'T RELEASE ME AT ONCE...!
STEADY, THERE! THAT'S JUST WHAT I INTEND TO DO. SIGN THIS PAPER AN' I'LL BE ONLY TOO GLAD TO PERMIT YOU TO GO SCOT FREE!
YOU MEAN, YOU'D LET HER GO!
I DON'T GET IT, CHIEF!
BUT--IF I SIGN THIS PAPER IT WILL BE A FALSE ADMISSION THAT MY EDITOR, GEORGE TAYLOR, IS YOUR PARTNER IN THE SLOT-MACHINE RACKET, AND THAT I ACT AS HIS GO-BETWEEN!
THAT'S THE IDEA! IF WORD GOT AROUND HE WAS MY PARTNER, ANYTHING HE PRINTED AGAINST ME WOULDN'T BE BELIEVED!
NOW I GET IT!
BOSS, YER A GENIUS!
AND IF I REFUSE TO SIGN...?
THAT'S YOUR CHOICE. BUT IT'LL BE TOUGH ON YOUR PAL. BECAUSE IF YOU DON'T PUT YOUR MONICKER ON THAT PAPER, CLARK KENT DIES!
YOU WOULDN'T COMMIT COLD-BLOODED MURDER!
WOULDN'T I? JUST TRY ME!
I-I WON'T PERMIT CLARK TO SUFFER BECAUSE OF ME. AFTER ALL, I INVOLVED HIM AGAINST HIS WILL. I'LL SIGN!
ATTAGIRL!- NICK! TAKE IT TO THE MORNING PICTORIAL
MEANWHILE-- CLARK REMOVES HIS OUTER GARMENTS, TRANSFORMING HIMSELF INTO THE MIGHTIEST OF ALL MEN-- SUPERMAN!
NOW TO ATTEND TO A LUG NAMED "SLUG!"
A SLIGHT PRESSURE AGAINST THE DOOR TO HIS ROOM, AND IT PLUNGES OUTWARD, SCREWS AND BOLTS FLYING...
MAKE WAY!

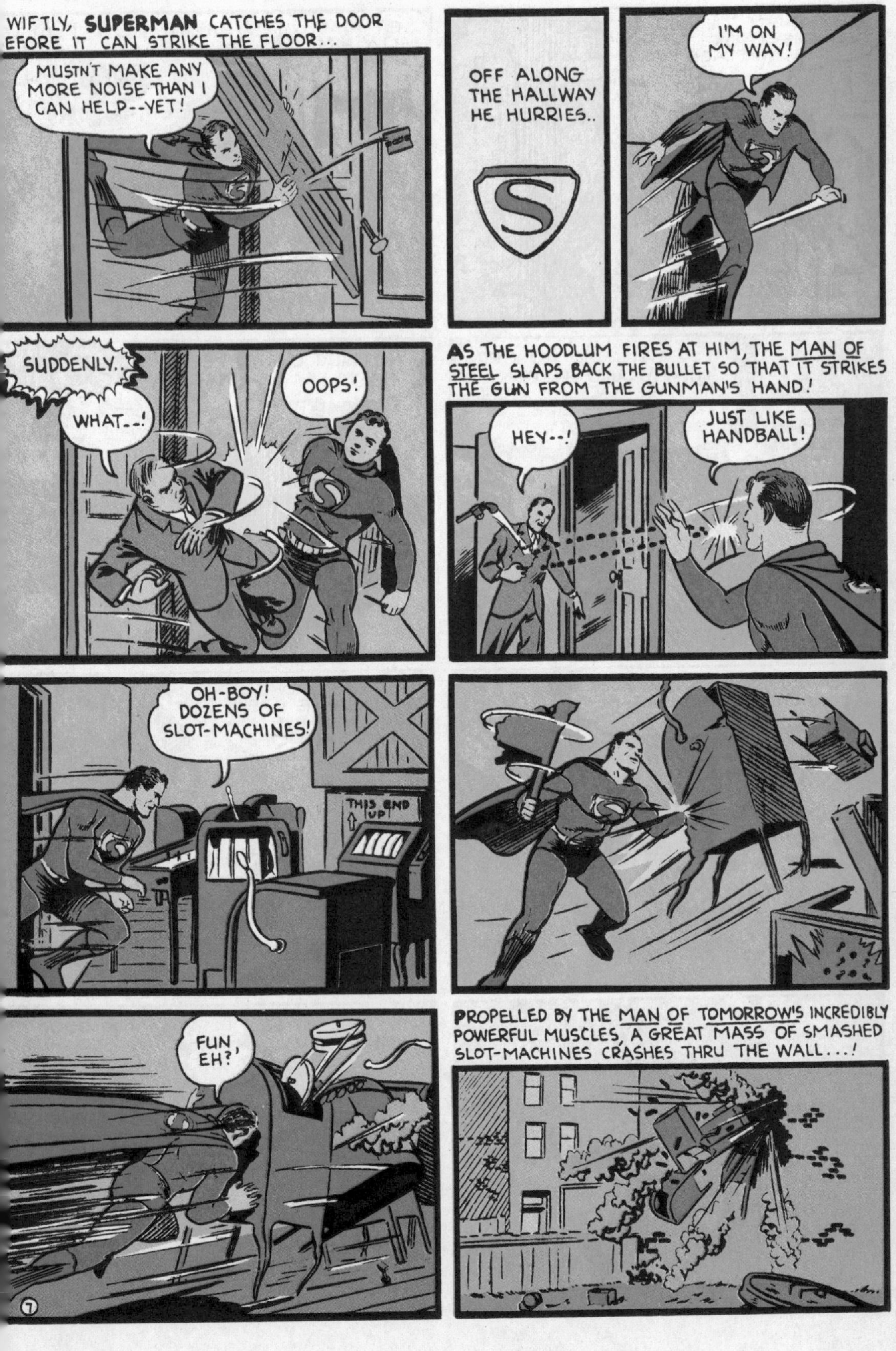
WIFTLY, SUPERMAN CATCHES THE DOOR
EFORE IT CAN STRIKE THE FLOOR...
MUSTN'T MAKE ANY MORE NOISE THAN I CAN HELP--YET!
OFF ALONG THE HALLWAY HE HURRIES..
I'M ON MY WAY!
SUDDENLY..
WHAT--!
OOPS!
AS THE HOODLUM FIRES AT HIM, THE MAN OF STEEL SLAPS BACK THE BULLET SO THAT IT STRIKES THE GUN FROM THE GUNMAN'S HAND!
HEY--!
JUST LIKE HANDBALL!
OH-BOY! DOZENS OF SLOT-MACHINES!
THIS END UP
FUN, EH?
7
PROPELLED BY THE MAN OF TOMORROW'S INCREDIBLY POWERFUL MUSCLES, A GREAT MASS OF SMASHED SLOT-MACHINES CRASHES THRU THE WALL...!

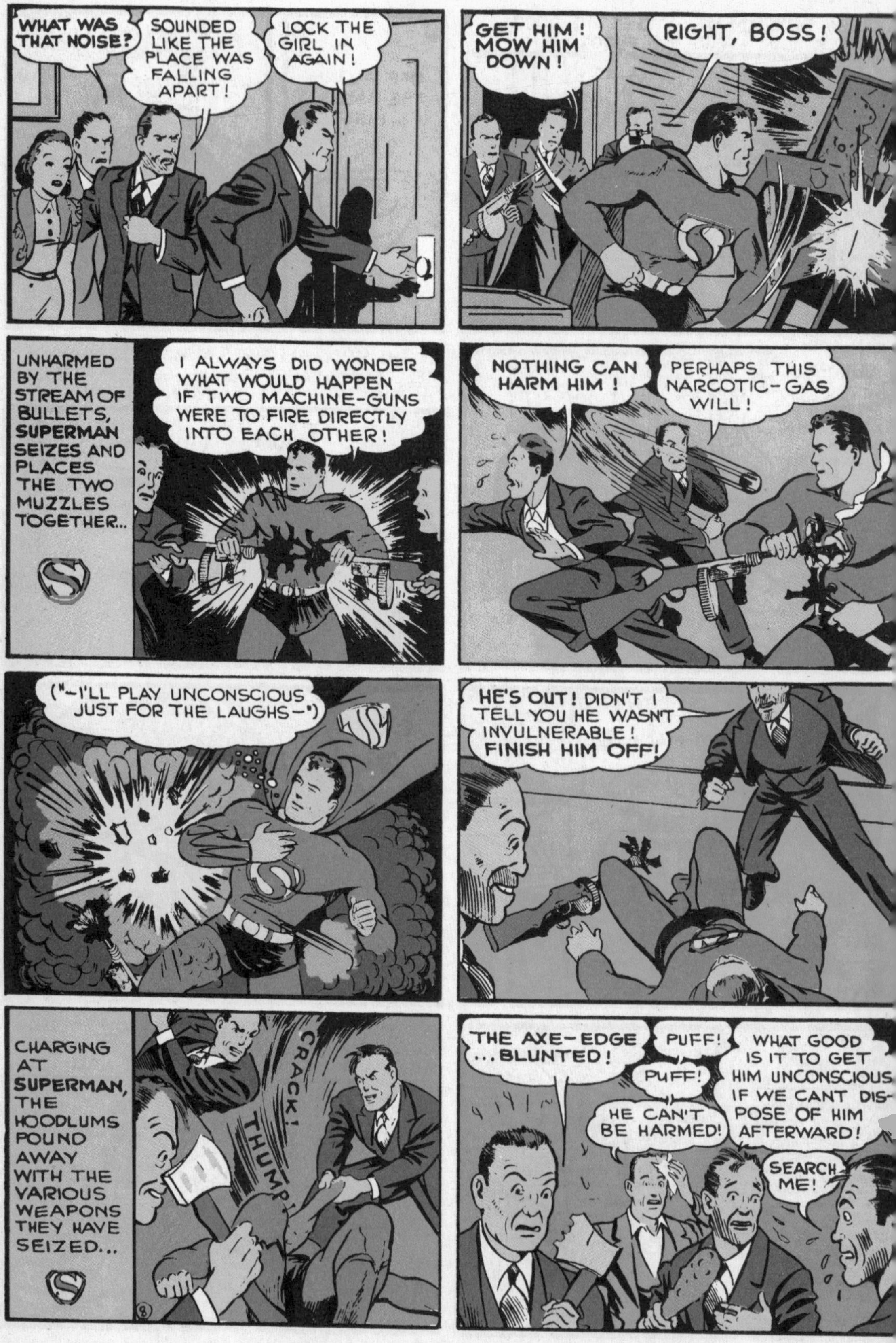

WHAT WAS THAT NOISE?
SOUNDED LIKE THE PLACE WAS FALLING APART!
LOCK THE GIRL IN AGAIN!
GET HIM! MOW HIM DOWN!
RIGHT, BOSS!
UNHARMED BY THE STREAM OF BULLETS, SUPERMAN SEIZES AND PLACES THE TWO MUZZLES TOGETHER...
I ALWAYS DID WONDER WHAT WOULD HAPPEN IF TWO MACHINE-GUNS WERE TO FIRE DIRECTLY INTO EACH OTHER!
NOTHING CAN HARM HIM!
PERHAPS THIS NARCOTIC-GAS WILL!
("-I'LL PLAY UNCONSCIOUS JUST FOR THE LAUGHS-")
HE'S OUT! DIDN'T I TELL YOU HE WASN'T INVULNERABLE! FINISH HIM OFF!
CHARGING AT SUPERMAN, THE HOODLUMS POUND AWAY WITH THE VARIOUS WEAPONS THEY HAVE SEIZED...
CRACK!
THUMP!
THE AXE-EDGE ...BLUNTED!
PUFF!
PUFF!
HE CAN'T BE HARMED!
WHAT GOOD IS IT TO GET HIM UNCONSCIOUS IF WE CANT DISPOSE OF HIM AFTERWARD!
SEARCH ME!

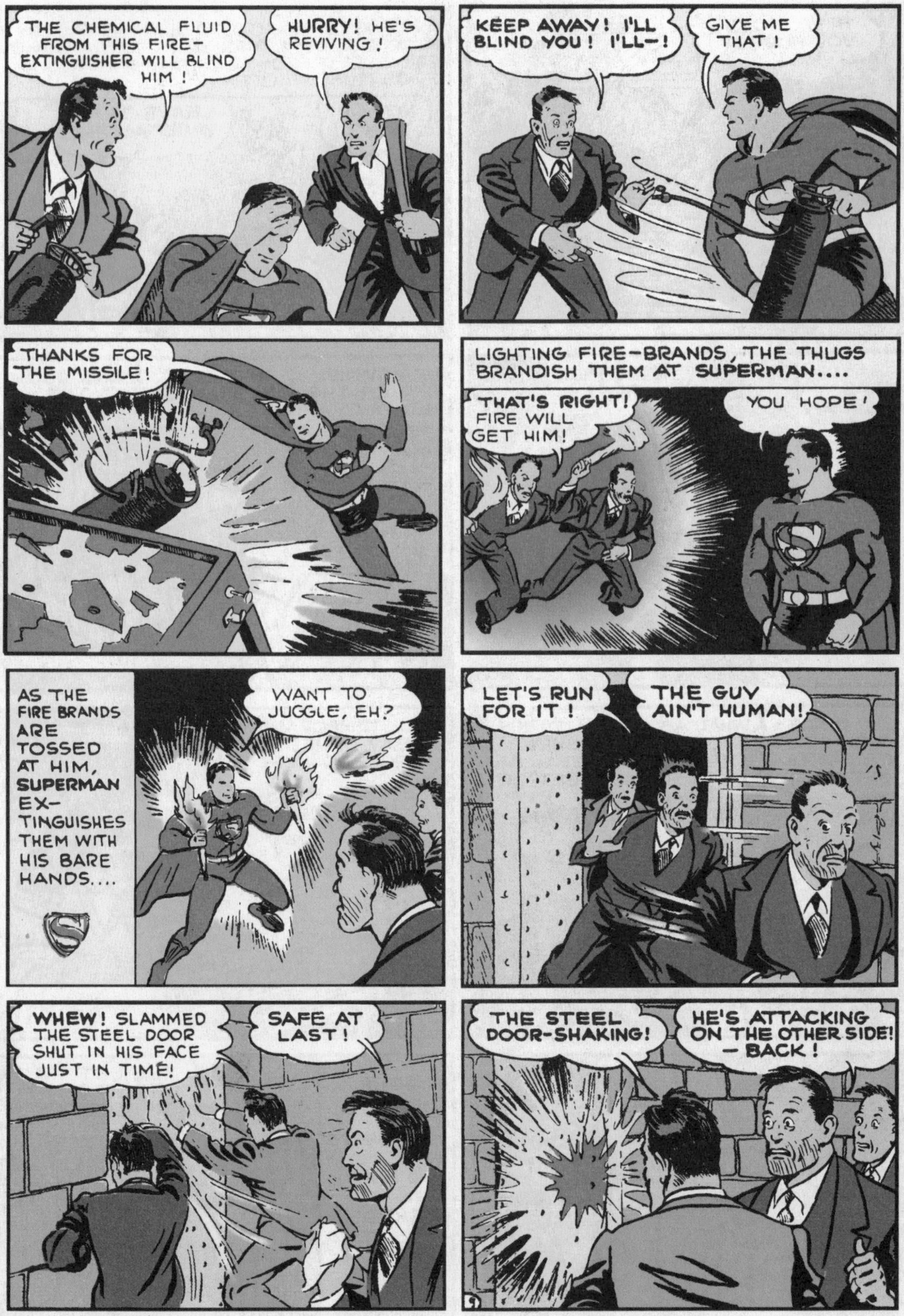
THE CHEMICAL FLUID FROM THIS FIRE-EXTINGUISHER WILL BLIND HIM!
HURRY! HE'S REVIVING!
KEEP AWAY! I'LL BLIND YOU! I'LL--!
GIVE ME THAT!
THANKS FOR THE MISSILE!
LIGHTING FIRE-BRANDS, THE THUGS BRANDISH THEM AT SUPERMAN....
THAT'S RIGHT! FIRE WILL GET HIM!
YOU HOPE!
AS THE FIRE BRANDS ARE TOSSED AT HIM, SUPERMAN EX-TINGUISHES THEM WITH HIS BARE HANDS....
WANT TO JUGGLE, EH?
LET'S RUN FOR IT!
THE GUY AIN'T HUMAN!
WHEW! SLAMMED THE STEEL DOOR SHUT IN HIS FACE JUST IN TIME!
SAFE AT LAST!
THE STEEL DOOR-SHAKING!
HE'S ATTACKING ON THE OTHER SIDE! - BACK!

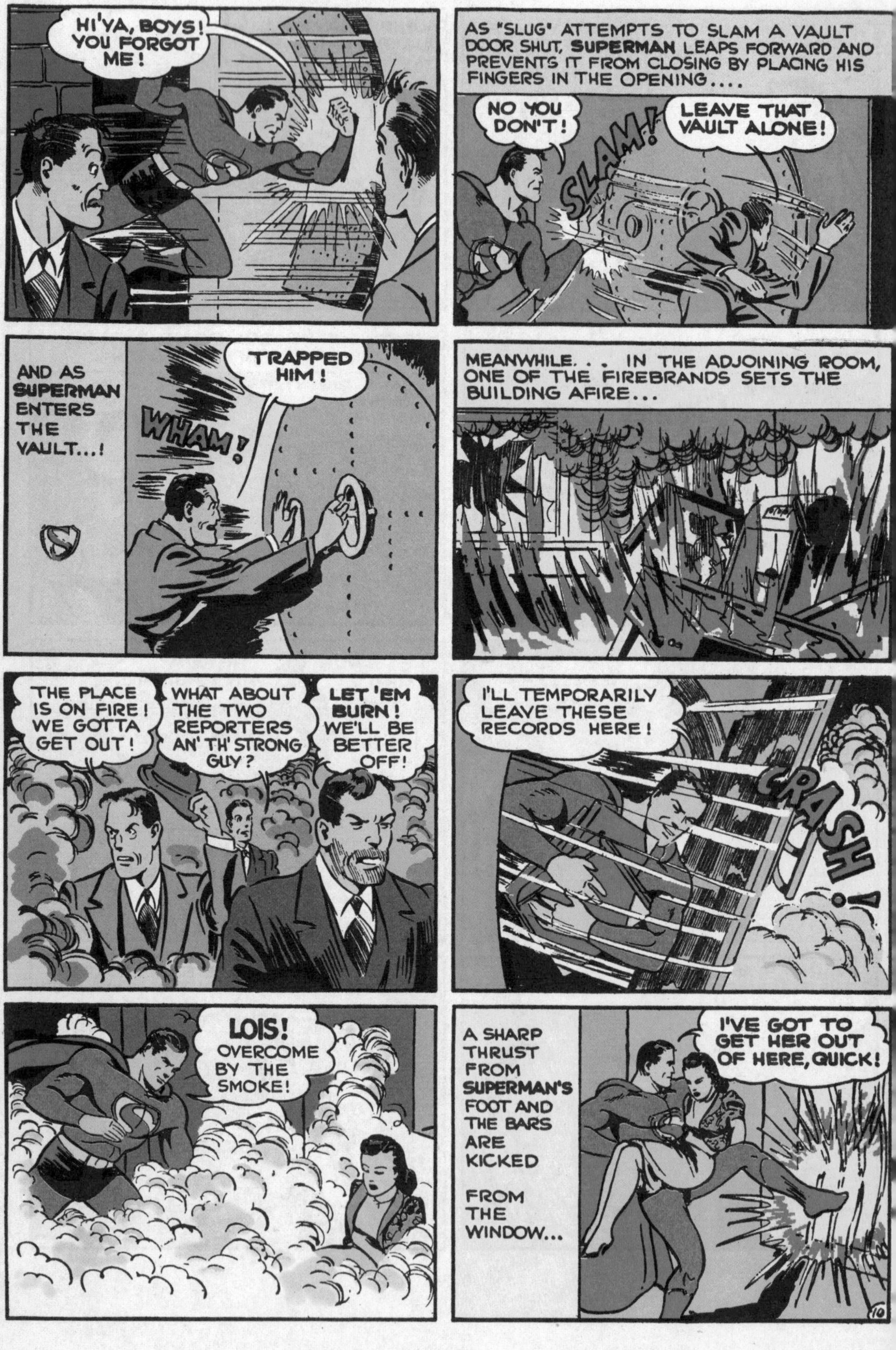
HI'YA, BOYS! YOU FORGOT ME!
AS "SLUG" ATTEMPTS TO SLAM A VAULT DOOR SHUT, SUPERMAN LEAPS FORWARD AND PREVENTS IT FROM CLOSING BY PLACING HIS FINGERS IN THE OPENING....
NO YOU DON'T!
SLAM!
LEAVE THAT VAULT ALONE!
AND AS SUPERMAN ENTERS THE VAULT...!
TRAPPED HIM!
WHAM!
MEANWHILE. . . IN THE ADJOINING ROOM, ONE OF THE FIREBRANDS SETS THE BUILDING AFIRE...
THE PLACE IS ON FIRE! WE GOTTA GET OUT!
WHAT ABOUT THE TWO REPORTERS AN' TH' STRONG GUY?
LET 'EM BURN! WE'LL BE BETTER OFF!
I'LL TEMPORARILY LEAVE THESE RECORDS HERE!
CRASH!
LOIS! OVERCOME BY THE SMOKE!
A SHARP THRUST FROM SUPERMAN'S FOOT AND THE BARS ARE KICKED
FROM THE WINDOW...
I'VE GOT TO GET HER OUT OF HERE, QUICK!
10

DOWN TOWARD EARTH LEAPS THE MAN OF STEEL WITH HIS PRECIOUS BURDEN

WH-WHERE AM I?

ON YOUR WAY TO TERRA FIRMA, MY DEAR!

BUT WHAT OF CLARK?

I'M ON MY WAY BACK TO RESCUE HIM!

SHORTLY AFTER.

SUPERMAN GUIDED ME OUT-- BUT WHAT ARE THESE LEDGER BOOKS HE GAVE ME?

"SLUG'S" SECRET RECORDS!

MEANWHILE-- --IN THE EDITORIAL OFFICE OF THE DAILY PLANET...

HAVE YOU SEEN THE MORNING PICTORIAL'S EXTRA?

WHAT IN BLAZES--?

MORNING PICTORIAL

PLANET EDITOR AND REPORTER IN LEAGUE WITH RACKETEER

REPORTERS SIGNED STORY SENT TO MORNING PICTORIAL

NO DOUBT OF THE SIGNATURE ON THAT STATEMENT! IT'S LOIS'! BUT WHY SHOULD SHE--?

I CAN EXPLAIN, CHIEF!

"SLUG" FORCED ME TO SIGN THAT PAPER AGAINST MY WILL! HE THINKS THAT YOU'LL NOW BE HANDICAPPED IN A FIGHT AGAINST HIM!

HE THINKS SO, EH? WELL, WITH THE AID OF HIS SECRET RECORDS, WE'LL SETTLE MR. KELLY'S HASH!

("ONE QUICK GLANCE AND MY PHOTOGRAPHIC MEMORY WILL ENABLE ME TO REMEMBER ALL THESE NAMES AND ADDRESSES!")

SLIPPING AWAY INTO A STOREROOM, CLARK ONCE AGAIN CHANGES INTO HIS SUPERMAN COSTUME...

NOW TO VISIT THE VARIOUS STORES WHERE "SLUG" PLACED HIS SLOT MACHINES!

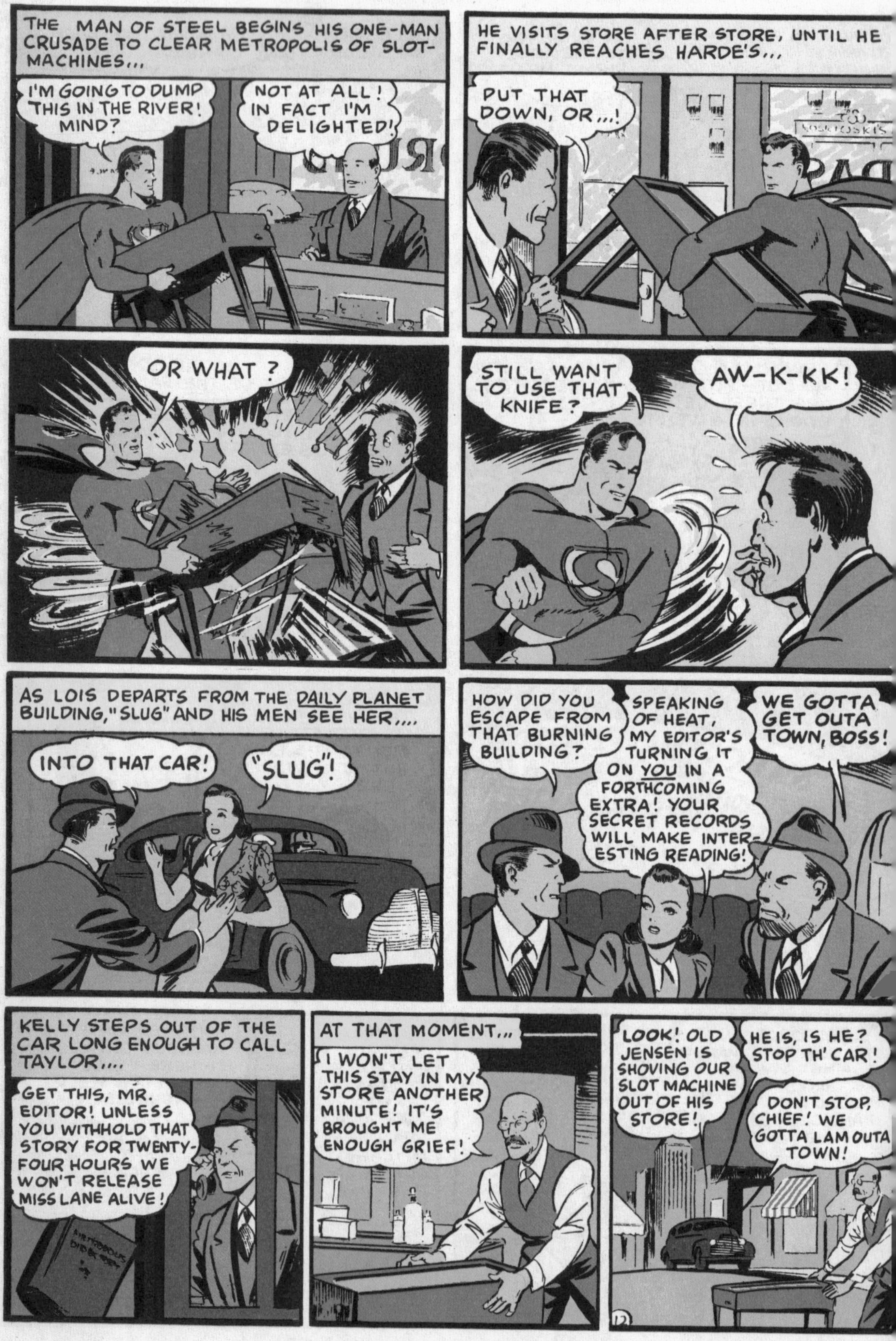

THE MAN OF STEEL BEGINS HIS ONE-MAN CRUSADE TO CLEAR METROPOLIS OF SLOT-MACHINES...
I'M GOING TO DUMP THIS IN THE RIVER! MIND?
NOT AT ALL! IN FACT I'M DELIGHTED!
HE VISITS STORE AFTER STORE, UNTIL HE FINALLY REACHES HARDE'S...
PUT THAT DOWN, OR...!
OR WHAT ?
STILL WANT TO USE THAT KNIFE?
AW-K-KK!
AS LOIS DEPARTS FROM THE DAILY PLANET BUILDING, "SLUG" AND HIS MEN SEE HER....
INTO THAT CAR!
"SLUG"!
HOW DID YOU ESCAPE FROM THAT BURNING BUILDING?
SPEAKING OF HEAT, MY EDITOR'S TURNING IT ON YOU IN A FORTHCOMING EXTRA! YOUR SECRET RECORDS WILL MAKE INTER-ESTING READING!
WE GOTTA GET OUTA TOWN, BOSS!
KELLY STEPS OUT OF THE CAR LONG ENOUGH TO CALL TAYLOR....
GET THIS, MR. EDITOR! UNLESS YOU WITHHOLD THAT STORY FOR TWENTY-FOUR HOURS WE WON'T RELEASE MISS LANE ALIVE!
AT THAT MOMENT...
I WON'T LET THIS STAY IN MY STORE ANOTHER MINUTE! IT'S BROUGHT ME ENOUGH GRIEF!
LOOK! OLD JENSEN IS SHOVING OUR SLOT MACHINE OUT OF HIS STORE!
HE IS, IS HE? STOP TH' CAR!
DON'T STOP, CHIEF! WE GOTTA LAM OUTA TOWN!
12

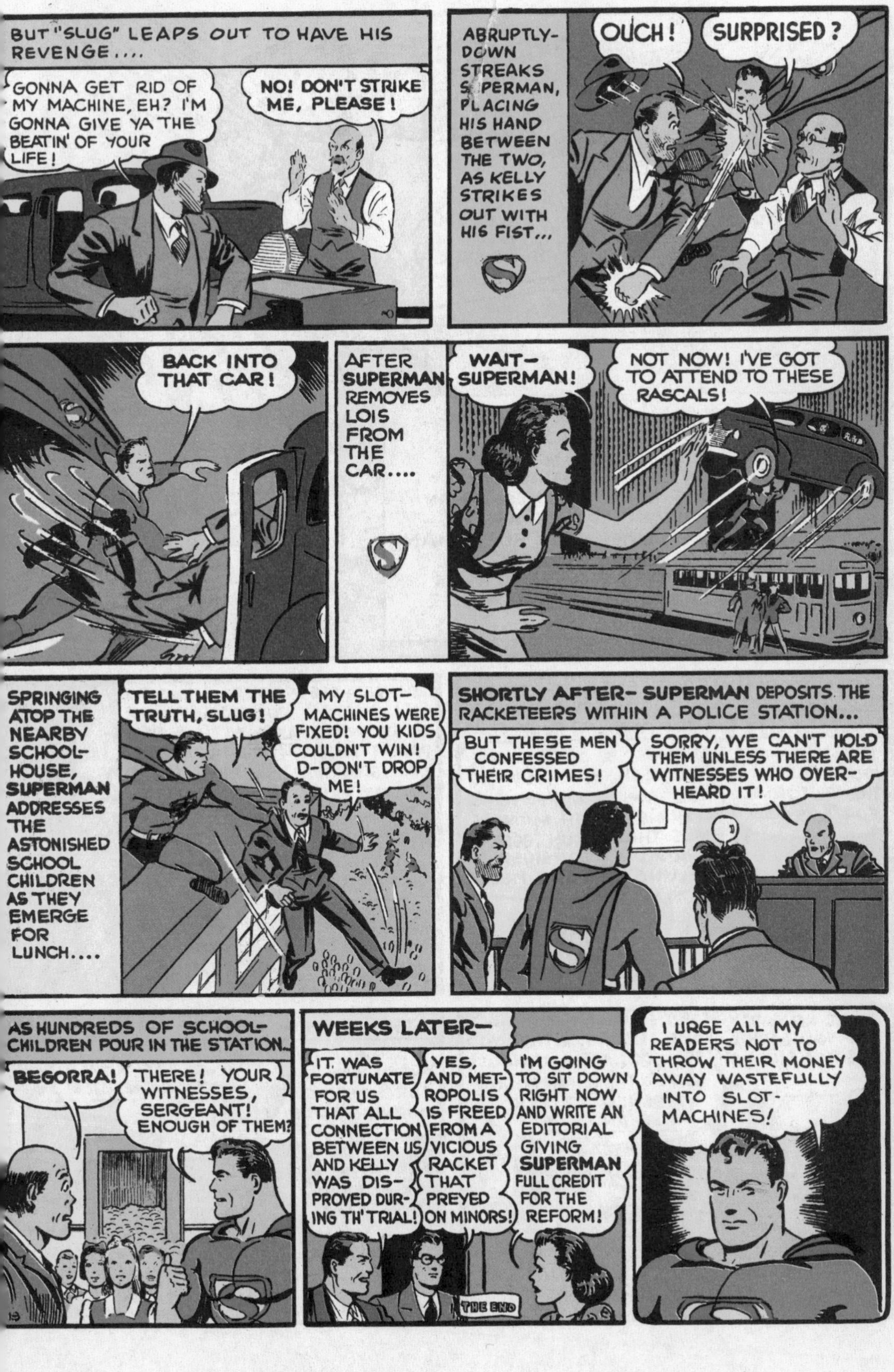
BUT "SLUG" LEAPS OUT TO HAVE HIS REVENGE....
GONNA GET RID OF MY MACHINE, EH? I'M GONNA GIVE YA THE BEATIN' OF YOUR LIFE!
NO! DON'T STRIKE ME, PLEASE!
ABRUPTLY-DOWN STREAKS SUPERMAN, PLACING HIS HAND BETWEEN THE TWO, AS KELLY STRIKES OUT WITH HIS FIST...
OUCH!
SURPRISED?
BACK INTO THAT CAR!
AFTER SUPERMAN REMOVES LOIS FROM THE CAR....
WAIT-SUPERMAN!
NOT NOW! I'VE GOT TO ATTEND TO THESE RASCALS!
SPRINGING ATOP THE NEARBY SCHOOL-HOUSE, SUPERMAN ADDRESSES THE ASTONISHED SCHOOL CHILDREN AS THEY EMERGE FOR LUNCH....
TELL THEM THE TRUTH, SLUG!
MY SLOT-MACHINES WERE FIXED! YOU KIDS COULDN'T WIN! D-DON'T DROP ME!
SHORTLY AFTER- SUPERMAN DEPOSITS THE RACKETEERS WITHIN A POLICE STATION...
BUT THESE MEN CONFESSED THEIR CRIMES!
SORRY, WE CAN'T HOLD THEM UNLESS THERE ARE WITNESSES WHO OVER-HEARD IT!
AS HUNDREDS OF SCHOOL-CHILDREN POUR IN THE STATION...
BEGORRA!
THERE! YOUR WITNESSES, SERGEANT! ENOUGH OF THEM?
WEEKS LATER-
IT WAS FORTUNATE FOR US THAT ALL CONNECTION BETWEEN US AND KELLY WAS DIS-PROVED DUR-ING TH' TRIAL!
YES, AND MET-ROPOLIS IS FREED FROM A VICIOUS RACKET THAT PREYED ON MINORS!
I'M GOING TO SIT DOWN RIGHT NOW AND WRITE AN EDITORIAL GIVING SUPERMAN FULL CREDIT FOR THE REFORM!
THE END
I URGE ALL MY READERS NOT TO THROW THEIR MONEY AWAY WASTEFULLY INTO SLOT-MACHINES!

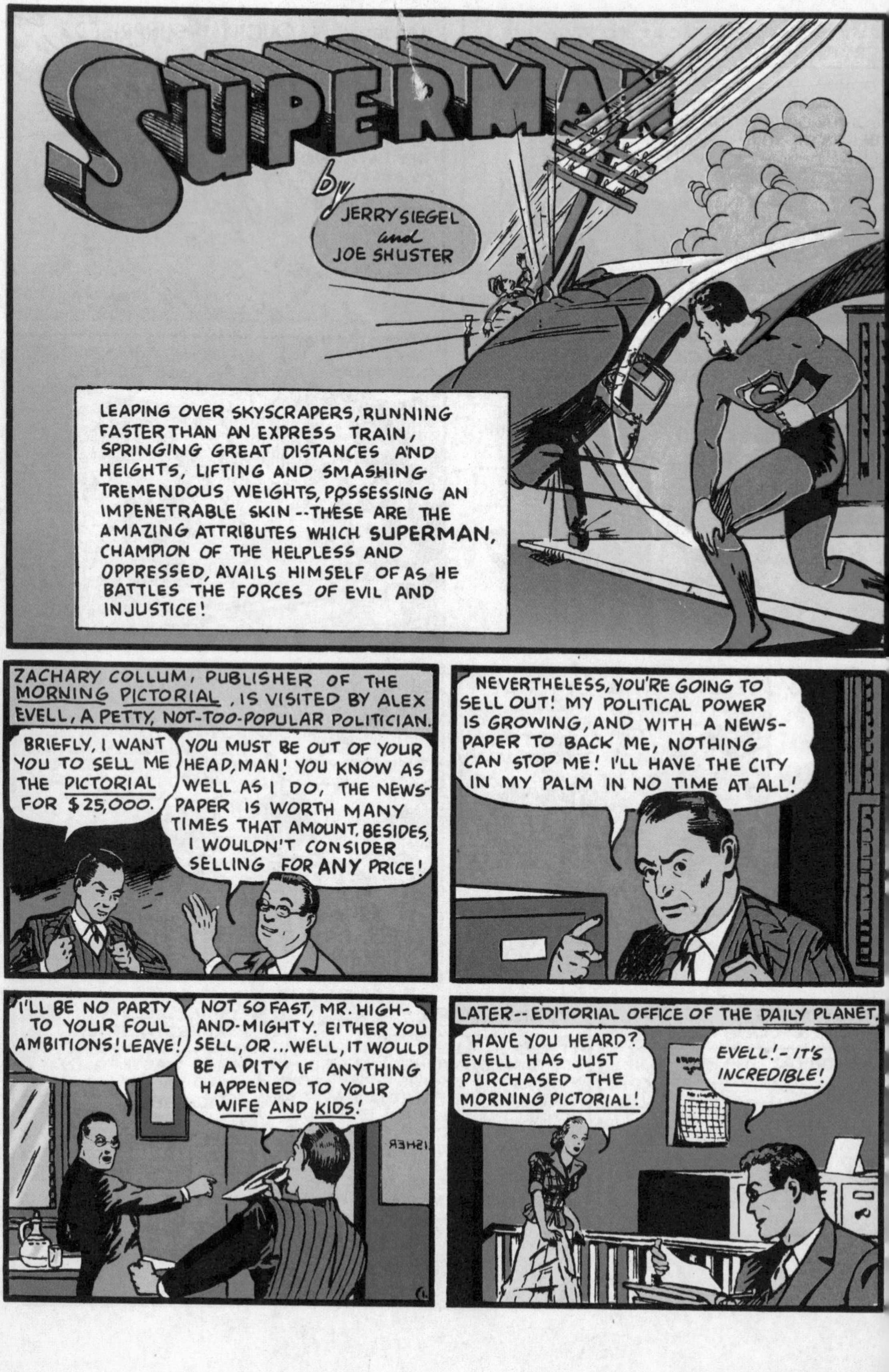
SUPERMAN
by JERRY SIEGEL and JOE SHUSTER
LEAPING OVER SKYSCRAPERS, RUNNING FASTER THAN AN EXPRESS TRAIN, SPRINGING GREAT DISTANCES AND HEIGHTS, LIFTING AND SMASHING TREMENDOUS WEIGHTS, POSSESSING AN IMPENETRABLE SKIN --THESE ARE THE AMAZING ATTRIBUTES WHICH SUPERMAN, CHAMPION OF THE HELPLESS AND OPPRESSED, AVAILS HIMSELF OF AS HE BATTLES THE FORCES OF EVIL AND INJUSTICE!
ZACHARY COLLUM, PUBLISHER OF THE MORNING PICTORIAL, IS VISITED BY ALEX EVELL, A PETTY, NOT-TOO-POPULAR POLITICIAN.
BRIEFLY, I WANT YOU TO SELL ME THE PICTORIAL FOR $25,000.
YOU MUST BE OUT OF YOUR HEAD, MAN! YOU KNOW AS WELL AS I DO, THE NEWSPAPER IS WORTH MANY TIMES THAT AMOUNT. BESIDES, I WOULDN'T CONSIDER SELLING FOR ANY PRICE!
NEVERTHELESS, YOU'RE GOING TO SELL OUT! MY POLITICAL POWER IS GROWING, AND WITH A NEWSPAPER TO BACK ME, NOTHING CAN STOP ME! I'LL HAVE THE CITY IN MY PALM IN NO TIME AT ALL!
I'LL BE NO PARTY TO YOUR FOUL AMBITIONS! LEAVE!
NOT SO FAST, MR. HIGH-AND-MIGHTY. EITHER YOU SELL, OR... WELL, IT WOULD BE A PITY IF ANYTHING HAPPENED TO YOUR WIFE AND KIDS!
LATER-- EDITORIAL OFFICE OF THE DAILY PLANET.
HAVE YOU HEARD? EVELL HAS JUST PURCHASED THE MORNING PICTORIAL!
EVELL! - IT'S INCREDIBLE!

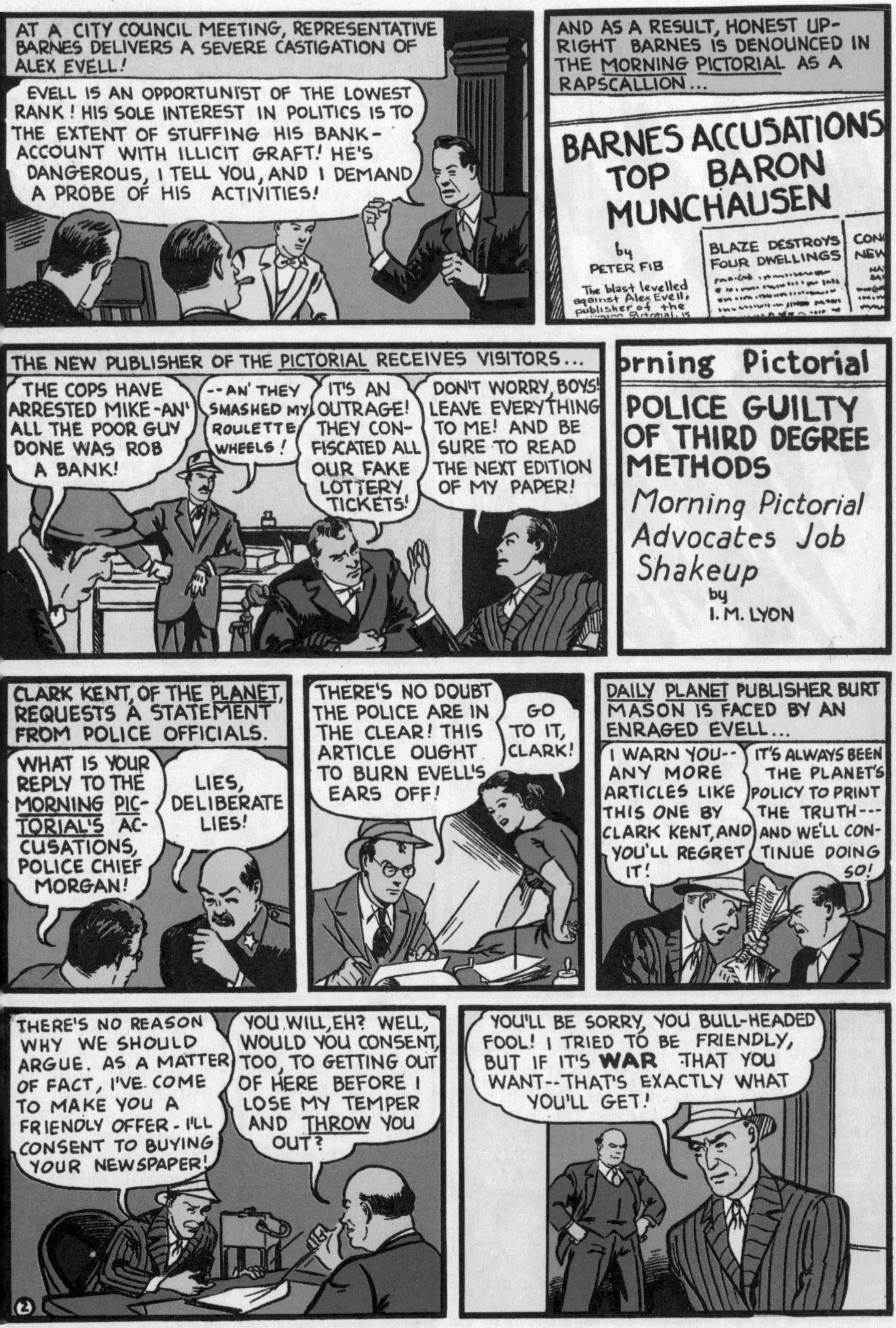
AT A CITY COUNCIL MEETING, REPRESENTATIVE BARNES DELIVERS A SEVERE CASTIGATION OF ALEX EVELL!
EVELL IS AN OPPORTUNIST OF THE LOWEST RANK! HIS SOLE INTEREST IN POLITICS IS TO THE EXTENT OF STUFFING HIS BANK-ACCOUNT WITH ILLICIT GRAFT! HE'S DANGEROUS, I TELL YOU, AND I DEMAND A PROBE OF HIS ACTIVITIES!
AND AS A RESULT, HONEST UP-RIGHT BARNES IS DENOUNCED IN THE MORNING PICTORIAL AS A RAPSCALLION...
BARNES ACCUSATIONS TOP BARON MUNCHAUSEN
by PETER FIB
The blast levelled against Alex Evell, publisher of the
BLAZE DESTROYS FOUR DWELLINGS
THE NEW PUBLISHER OF THE PICTORIAL RECEIVES VISITORS...
THE COPS HAVE ARRESTED MIKE-AN' ALL THE POOR GUY DONE WAS ROB A BANK!
--AN' THEY SMASHED MY ROULETTE WHEELS!
IT'S AN OUTRAGE! THEY CONFISCATED ALL OUR FAKE LOTTERY TICKETS!
DON'T WORRY, BOYS! LEAVE EVERYTHING TO ME! AND BE SURE TO READ THE NEXT EDITION OF MY PAPER!
orning Pictorial
POLICE GUILTY OF THIRD DEGREE METHODS
Morning Pictorial Advocates Job Shakeup
by I. M. LYON
CLARK KENT, OF THE PLANET, REQUESTS A STATEMENT FROM POLICE OFFICIALS.
WHAT IS YOUR REPLY TO THE MORNING PICTORIAL'S ACCUSATIONS, POLICE CHIEF MORGAN!
LIES, DELIBERATE LIES!
THERE'S NO DOUBT THE POLICE ARE IN THE CLEAR! THIS ARTICLE OUGHT TO BURN EVELL'S EARS OFF!
GO TO IT, CLARK!
DAILY PLANET PUBLISHER BURT MASON IS FACED BY AN ENRAGED EVELL...
I WARN YOU-- ANY MORE ARTICLES LIKE THIS ONE BY CLARK KENT, AND YOU'LL REGRET IT!
IT'S ALWAYS BEEN THE PLANET'S POLICY TO PRINT THE TRUTH--- AND WE'LL CONTINUE DOING SO!
THERE'S NO REASON WHY WE SHOULD ARGUE. AS A MATTER OF FACT, I'VE COME TO MAKE YOU A FRIENDLY OFFER - I'LL CONSENT TO BUYING YOUR NEWSPAPER!
YOU WILL, EH? WELL, WOULD YOU CONSENT, TOO, TO GETTING OUT OF HERE BEFORE I LOSE MY TEMPER AND THROW YOU OUT?
2
YOU'LL BE SORRY, YOU BULL-HEADED FOOL! I TRIED TO BE FRIENDLY, BUT IF IT'S WAR THAT YOU WANT--THAT'S EXACTLY WHAT YOU'LL GET!

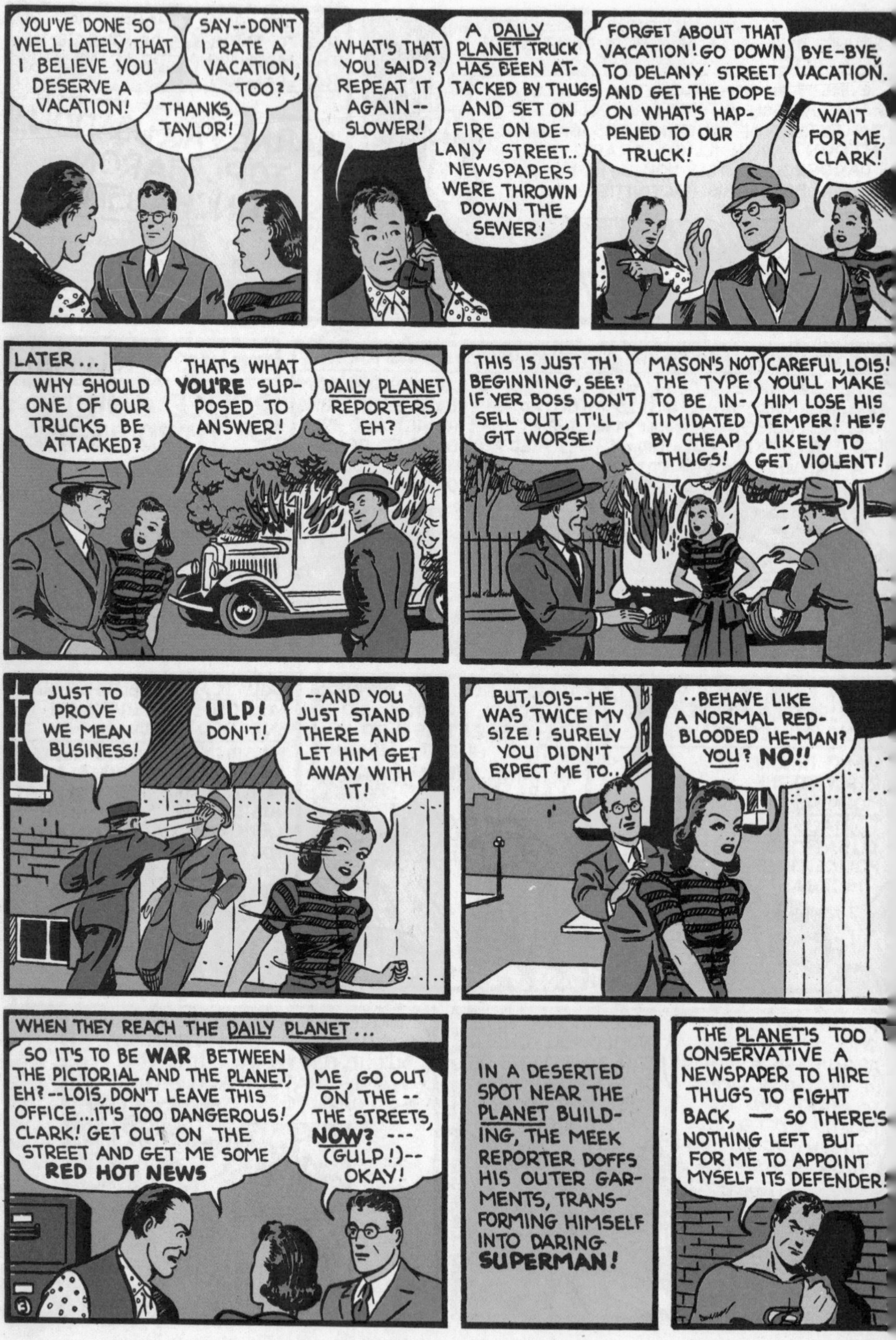
YOU'VE DONE SO WELL LATELY THAT I BELIEVE YOU DESERVE A VACATION!
SAY--DON'T I RATE A VACATION, TOO?
THANKS, TAYLOR!
WHAT'S THAT YOU SAID? REPEAT IT AGAIN-- SLOWER!
A DAILY PLANET TRUCK HAS BEEN ATTACKED BY THUGS AND SET ON FIRE ON DELANY STREET.. NEWSPAPERS WERE THROWN DOWN THE SEWER!
FORGET ABOUT THAT VACATION! GO DOWN TO DELANY STREET AND GET THE DOPE ON WHAT'S HAPPENED TO OUR TRUCK!
BYE-BYE, VACATION.
WAIT FOR ME, CLARK!
LATER...
WHY SHOULD ONE OF OUR TRUCKS BE ATTACKED?
THAT'S WHAT YOU'RE SUPPOSED TO ANSWER!
DAILY PLANET REPORTERS, EH?
THIS IS JUST TH' BEGINNING, SEE? IF YER BOSS DON'T SELL OUT, IT'LL GIT WORSE!
MASON'S NOT THE TYPE TO BE INTIMIDATED BY CHEAP THUGS!
CAREFUL, LOIS! YOU'LL MAKE HIM LOSE HIS TEMPER! HE'S LIKELY TO GET VIOLENT!
JUST TO PROVE WE MEAN BUSINESS!
ULP! DON'T!
--AND YOU JUST STAND THERE AND LET HIM GET AWAY WITH IT!
BUT, LOIS--HE WAS TWICE MY SIZE! SURELY YOU DIDN'T EXPECT ME TO..
..BEHAVE LIKE A NORMAL RED-BLOODED HE-MAN? YOU? NO!!
WHEN THEY REACH THE DAILY PLANET...
SO IT'S TO BE WAR BETWEEN THE PICTORIAL AND THE PLANET, EH? --LOIS, DON'T LEAVE THIS OFFICE...IT'S TOO DANGEROUS! CLARK! GET OUT ON THE STREET AND GET ME SOME RED HOT NEWS
ME, GO OUT ON THE -- THE STREETS, NOW? --- (GULP!)-- OKAY!
IN A DESERTED SPOT NEAR THE PLANET BUILDING, THE MEEK REPORTER DOFFS HIS OUTER GARMENTS, TRANSFORMING HIMSELF INTO DARING SUPERMAN!
THE PLANET'S TOO CONSERVATIVE A NEWSPAPER TO HIRE THUGS TO FIGHT BACK, — SO THERE'S NOTHING LEFT BUT FOR ME TO APPOINT MYSELF ITS DEFENDER!

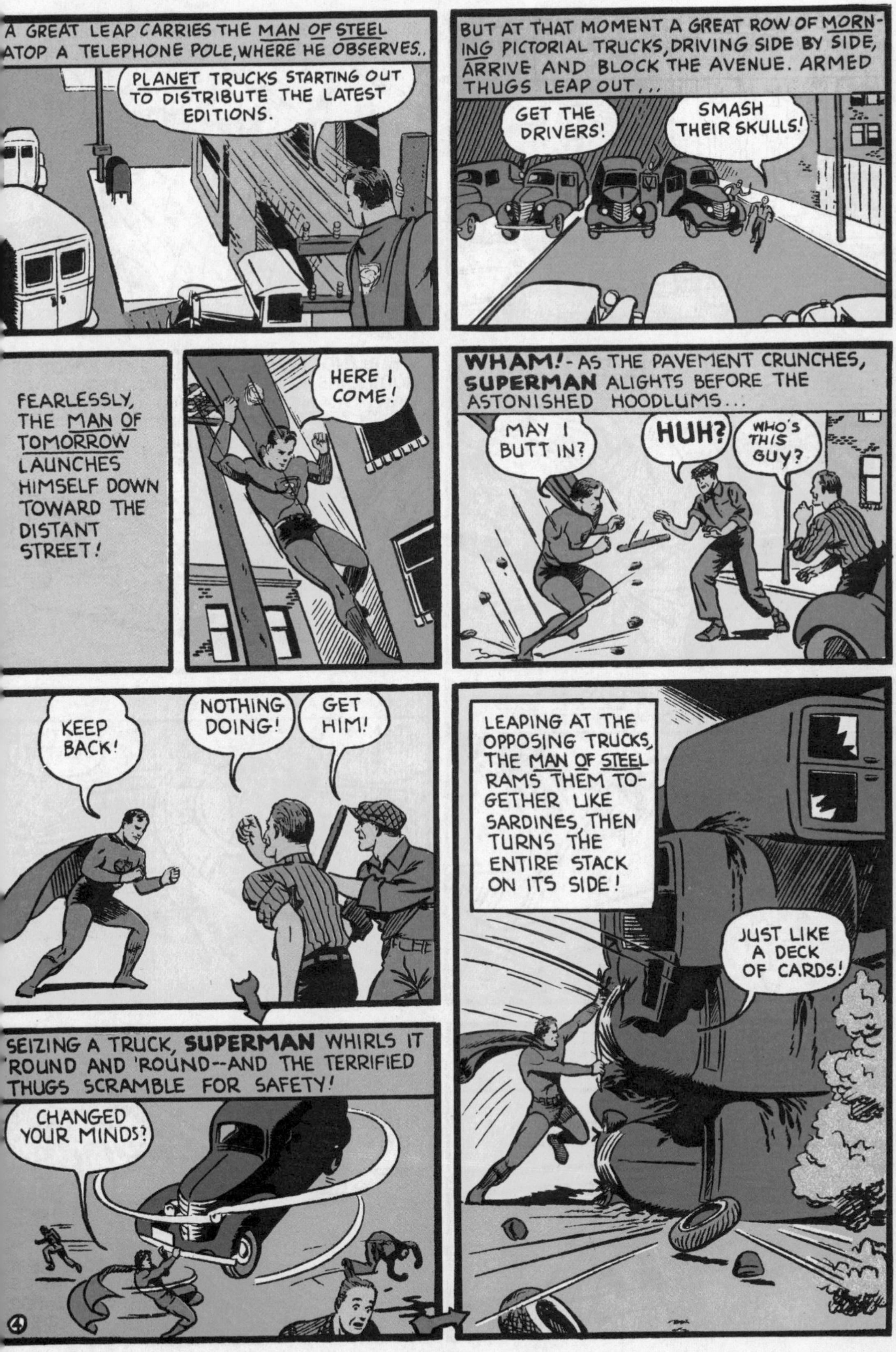
A GREAT LEAP CARRIES THE MAN OF STEEL ATOP A TELEPHONE POLE, WHERE HE OBSERVES..
PLANET TRUCKS STARTING OUT TO DISTRIBUTE THE LATEST EDITIONS.
BUT AT THAT MOMENT A GREAT ROW OF MORNING PICTORIAL TRUCKS, DRIVING SIDE BY SIDE, ARRIVE AND BLOCK THE AVENUE. ARMED THUGS LEAP OUT...
GET THE DRIVERS!
SMASH THEIR SKULLS!
FEARLESSLY, THE MAN OF TOMORROW LAUNCHES HIMSELF DOWN TOWARD THE DISTANT STREET!
HERE I COME!
WHAM! - AS THE PAVEMENT CRUNCHES, SUPERMAN ALIGHTS BEFORE THE ASTONISHED HOODLUMS...
MAY I BUTT IN?
HUH?
WHO'S THIS GUY?
KEEP BACK!
NOTHING DOING!
GET HIM!
SEIZING A TRUCK, SUPERMAN WHIRLS IT 'ROUND AND 'ROUND--AND THE TERRIFIED THUGS SCRAMBLE FOR SAFETY!
CHANGED YOUR MINDS?
4
LEAPING AT THE OPPOSING TRUCKS, THE MAN OF STEEL RAMS THEM TOGETHER LIKE SARDINES, THEN TURNS THE ENTIRE STACK ON ITS SIDE!
JUST LIKE A DECK OF CARDS!

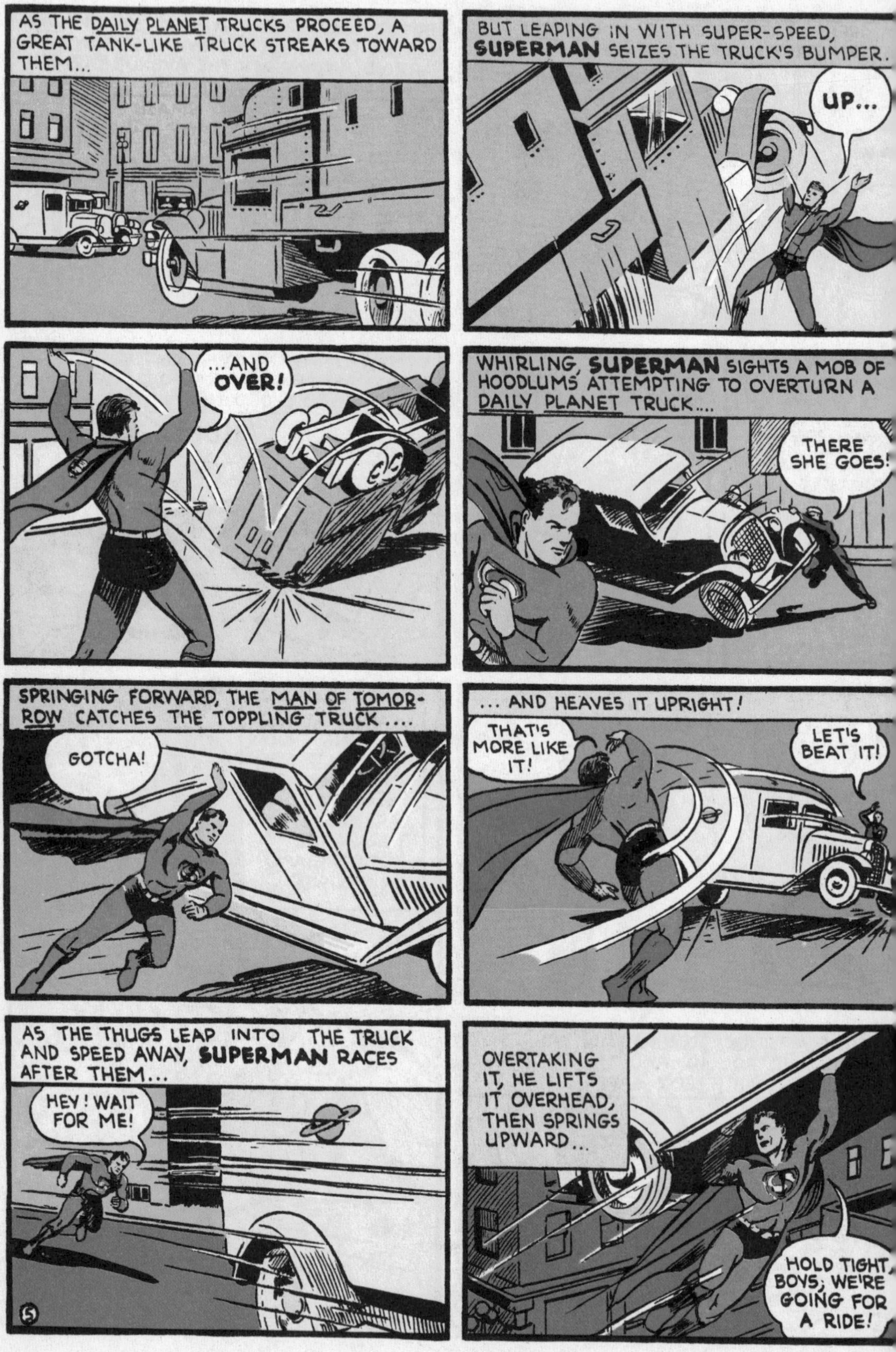
AS THE DAILY PLANET TRUCKS PROCEED, A GREAT TANK-LIKE TRUCK STREAKS TOWARD THEM...
BUT LEAPING IN WITH SUPER-SPEED, SUPERMAN SEIZES THE TRUCK'S BUMPER.
UP...
...AND OVER!
WHIRLING, SUPERMAN SIGHTS A MOB OF HOODLUMS ATTEMPTING TO OVERTURN A DAILY PLANET TRUCK....
THERE SHE GOES!
SPRINGING FORWARD, THE MAN OF TOMORROW CATCHES THE TOPPLING TRUCK....
GOTCHA!
... AND HEAVES IT UPRIGHT!
THAT'S MORE LIKE IT!
LET'S BEAT IT!
AS THE THUGS LEAP INTO THE TRUCK AND SPEED AWAY, SUPERMAN RACES AFTER THEM...
HEY! WAIT FOR ME!
5
OVERTAKING IT, HE LIFTS IT OVERHEAD, THEN SPRINGS UPWARD...
HOLD TIGHT, BOYS; WE'RE GOING FOR A RIDE!

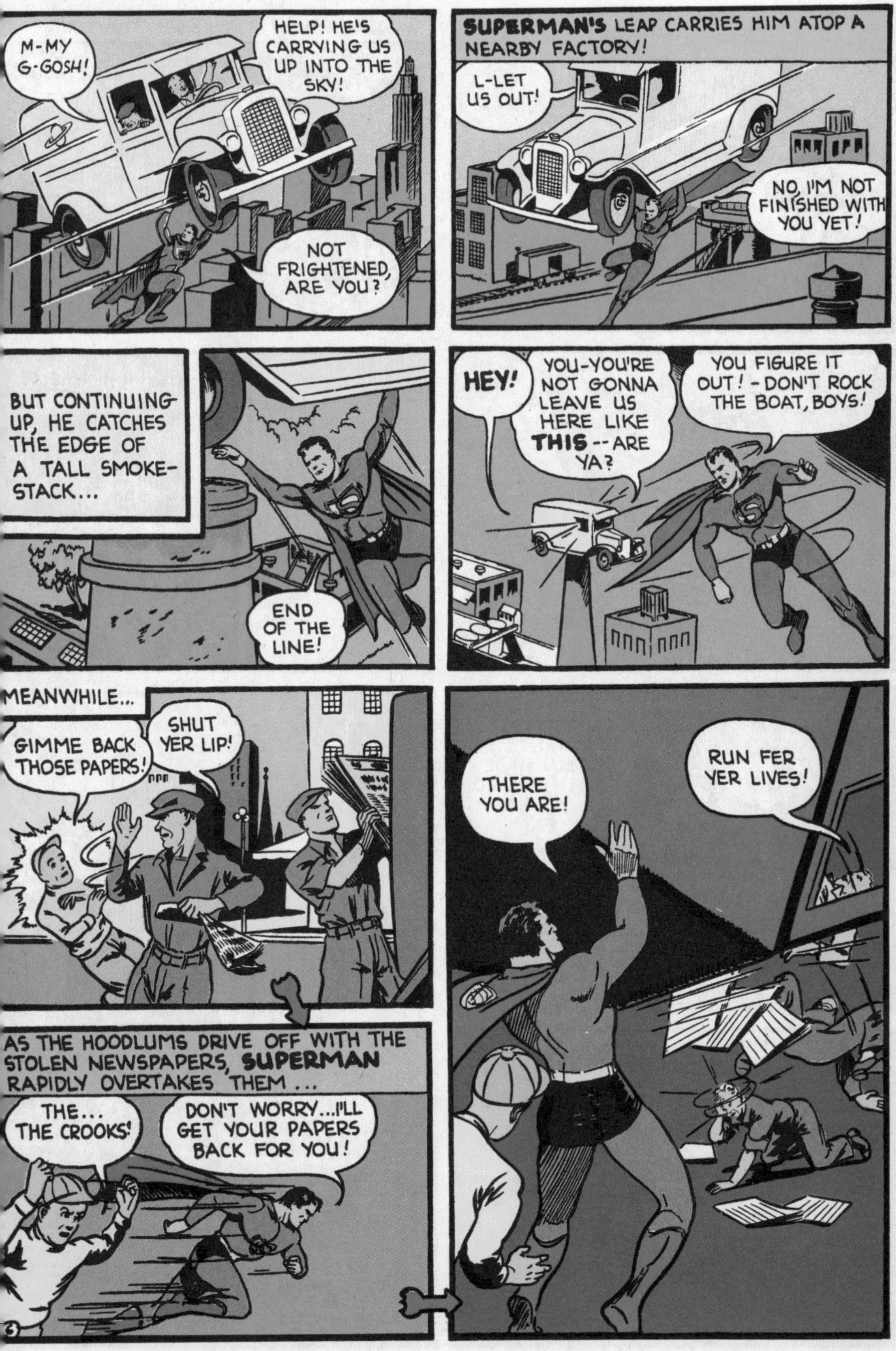
M-MY G-GOSH!
HELP! HE'S CARRYING US UP INTO THE SKY!
NOT FRIGHTENED, ARE YOU?
SUPERMAN'S LEAP CARRIES HIM ATOP A NEARBY FACTORY!
L-LET US OUT!
NO, I'M NOT FINISHED WITH YOU YET!
BUT CONTINUING UP, HE CATCHES THE EDGE OF A TALL SMOKE-STACK...
END OF THE LINE!
HEY!
YOU-YOU'RE NOT GONNA LEAVE US HERE LIKE THIS --ARE YA?
YOU FIGURE IT OUT! - DON'T ROCK THE BOAT, BOYS!
MEANWHILE...
GIMME BACK THOSE PAPERS!
SHUT YER LIP!
AS THE HOODLUMS DRIVE OFF WITH THE STOLEN NEWSPAPERS, SUPERMAN RAPIDLY OVERTAKES THEM ...
THE... THE CROOKS!
DON'T WORRY...I'LL GET YOUR PAPERS BACK FOR YOU!
THERE YOU ARE!
RUN FER YER LIVES!

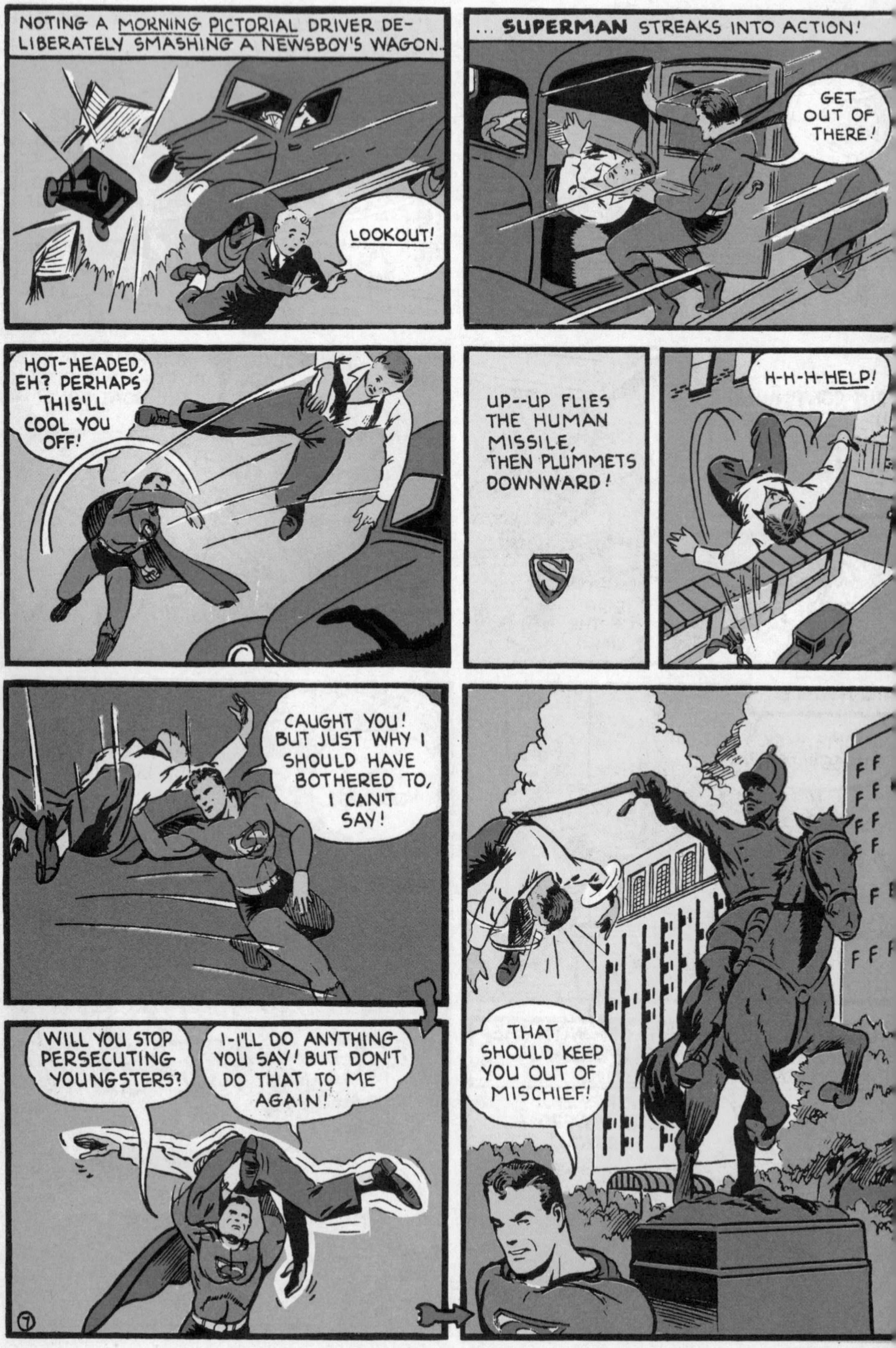
NOTING A MORNING PICTORIAL DRIVER DELIBERATELY SMASHING A NEWSBOY'S WAGON...
LOOKOUT!
... SUPERMAN STREAKS INTO ACTION!
GET OUT OF THERE!
HOT-HEADED, EH? PERHAPS THIS'LL COOL YOU OFF!
UP--UP FLIES THE HUMAN MISSILE, THEN PLUMMETS DOWNWARD!
H-H-H-HELP!
CAUGHT YOU! BUT JUST WHY I SHOULD HAVE BOTHERED TO, I CAN'T SAY!
WILL YOU STOP PERSECUTING YOUNGSTERS?
I-I'LL DO ANYTHING YOU SAY! BUT DON'T DO THAT TO ME AGAIN!
7
THAT SHOULD KEEP YOU OUT OF MISCHIEF!

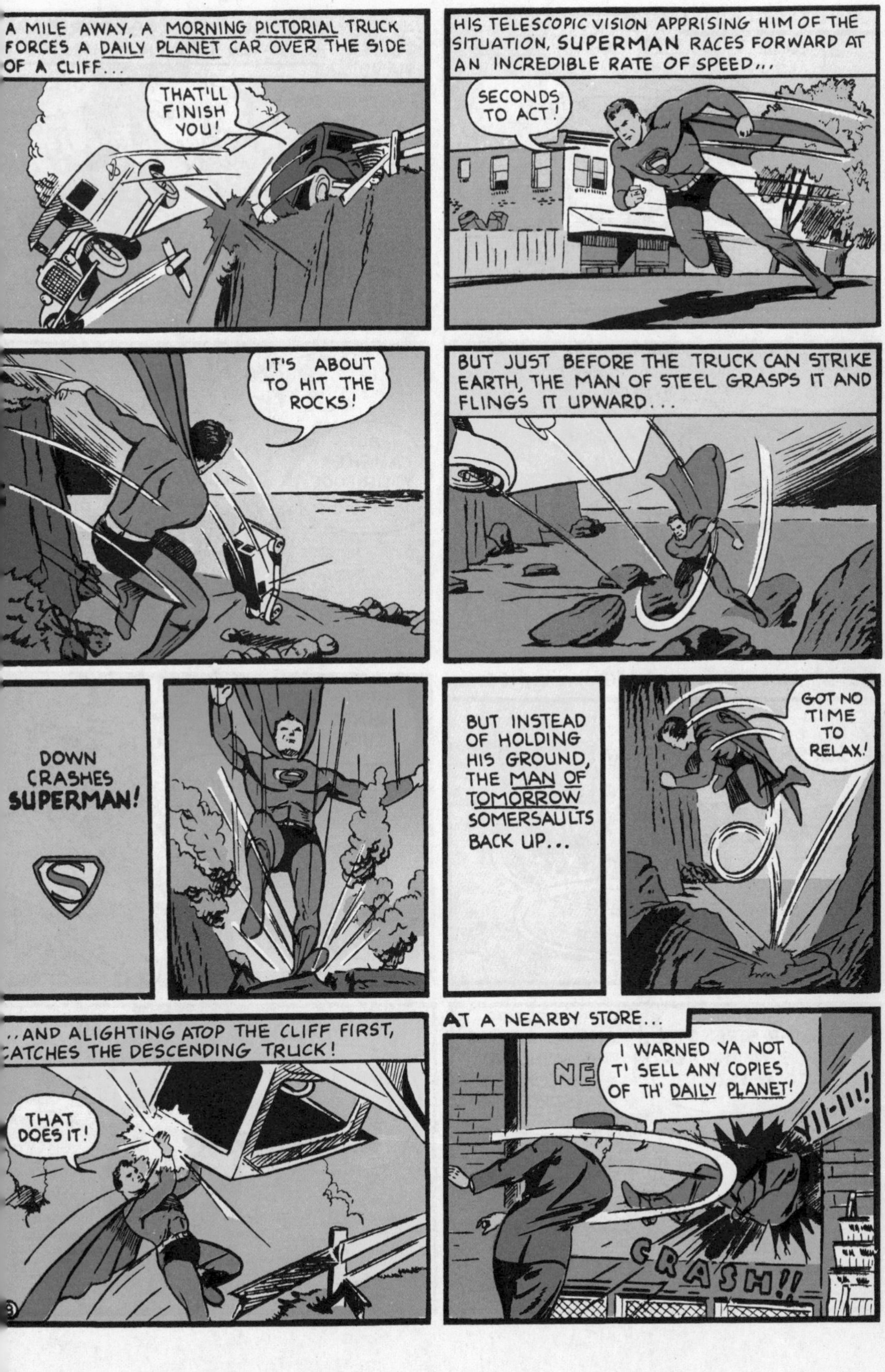
A MILE AWAY, A MORNING PICTORIAL TRUCK FORCES A DAILY PLANET CAR OVER THE SIDE OF A CLIFF...
THAT'LL FINISH YOU!
HIS TELESCOPIC VISION APPRISING HIM OF THE SITUATION, SUPERMAN RACES FORWARD AT AN INCREDIBLE RATE OF SPEED...
SECONDS TO ACT!
IT'S ABOUT TO HIT THE ROCKS!
BUT JUST BEFORE THE TRUCK CAN STRIKE EARTH, THE MAN OF STEEL GRASPS IT AND FLINGS IT UPWARD...
DOWN CRASHES SUPERMAN!
S
BUT INSTEAD OF HOLDING HIS GROUND, THE MAN OF TOMORROW SOMERSAULTS BACK UP...
GOT NO TIME TO RELAX!
..AND ALIGHTING ATOP THE CLIFF FIRST, CATCHES THE DESCENDING TRUCK!
THAT DOES IT!
AT A NEARBY STORE...
I WARNED YA NOT T' SELL ANY COPIES OF TH' DAILY PLANET!
NE
YII-III!
CRASH!!

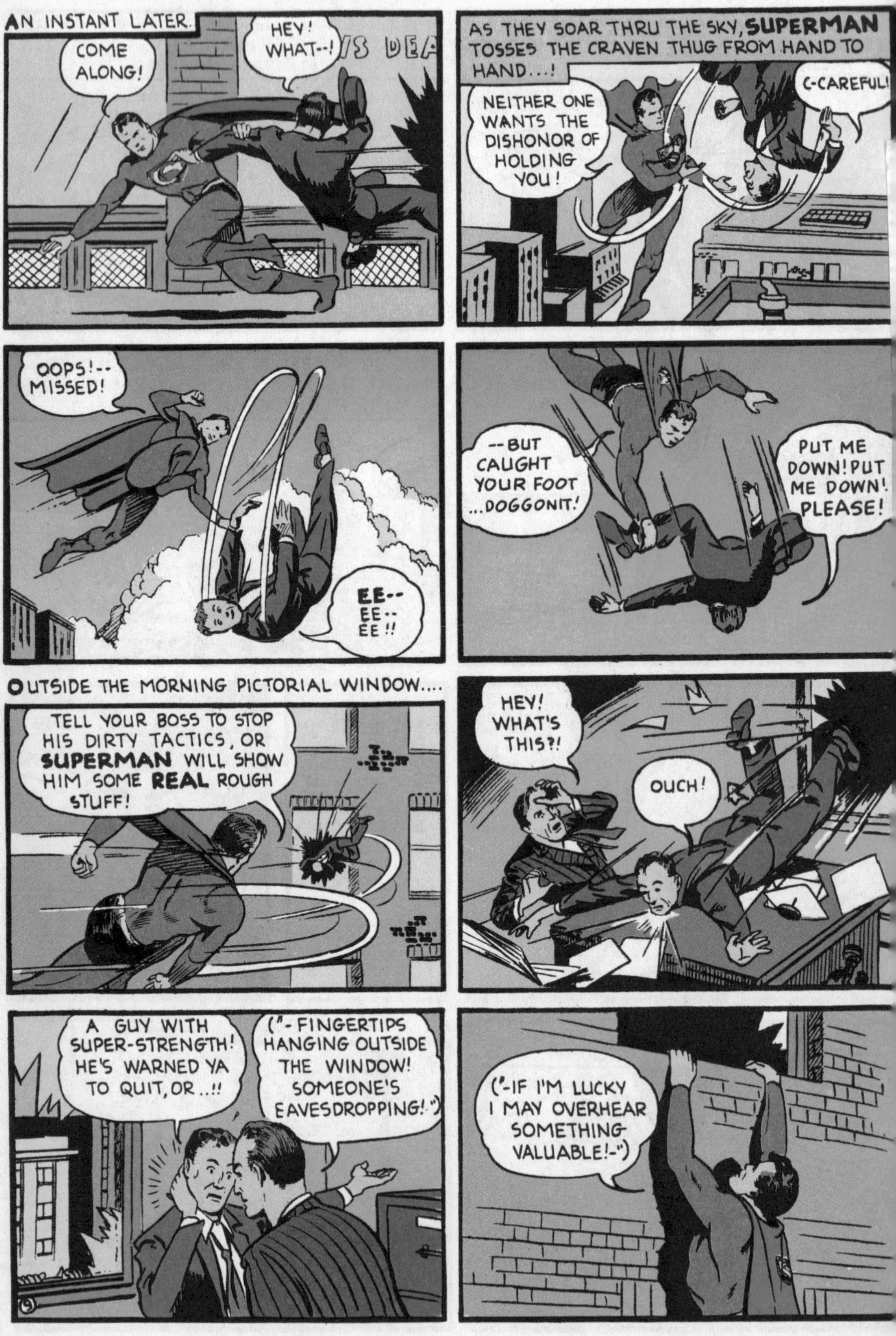
AN INSTANT LATER.
COME ALONG!
HEY! WHAT--!
AS THEY SOAR THRU THE SKY, SUPERMAN TOSSES THE CRAVEN THUG FROM HAND TO HAND...!
NEITHER ONE WANTS THE DISHONOR OF HOLDING YOU!
C-CAREFUL!
OOPS!-- MISSED!
EE-- EE-- EE!!
--BUT CAUGHT YOUR FOOT ...DOGGONIT!
PUT ME DOWN! PUT ME DOWN! PLEASE!
OUTSIDE THE MORNING PICTORIAL WINDOW....
TELL YOUR BOSS TO STOP HIS DIRTY TACTICS, OR SUPERMAN WILL SHOW HIM SOME REAL ROUGH STUFF!
HEY! WHAT'S THIS?!
OUCH!
A GUY WITH SUPER-STRENGTH! HE'S WARNED YA TO QUIT, OR..!!
("-FINGERTIPS HANGING OUTSIDE THE WINDOW! SOMEONE'S EAVESDROPPING!-")
("-IF I'M LUCKY I MAY OVERHEAR SOMETHING VALUABLE!-")

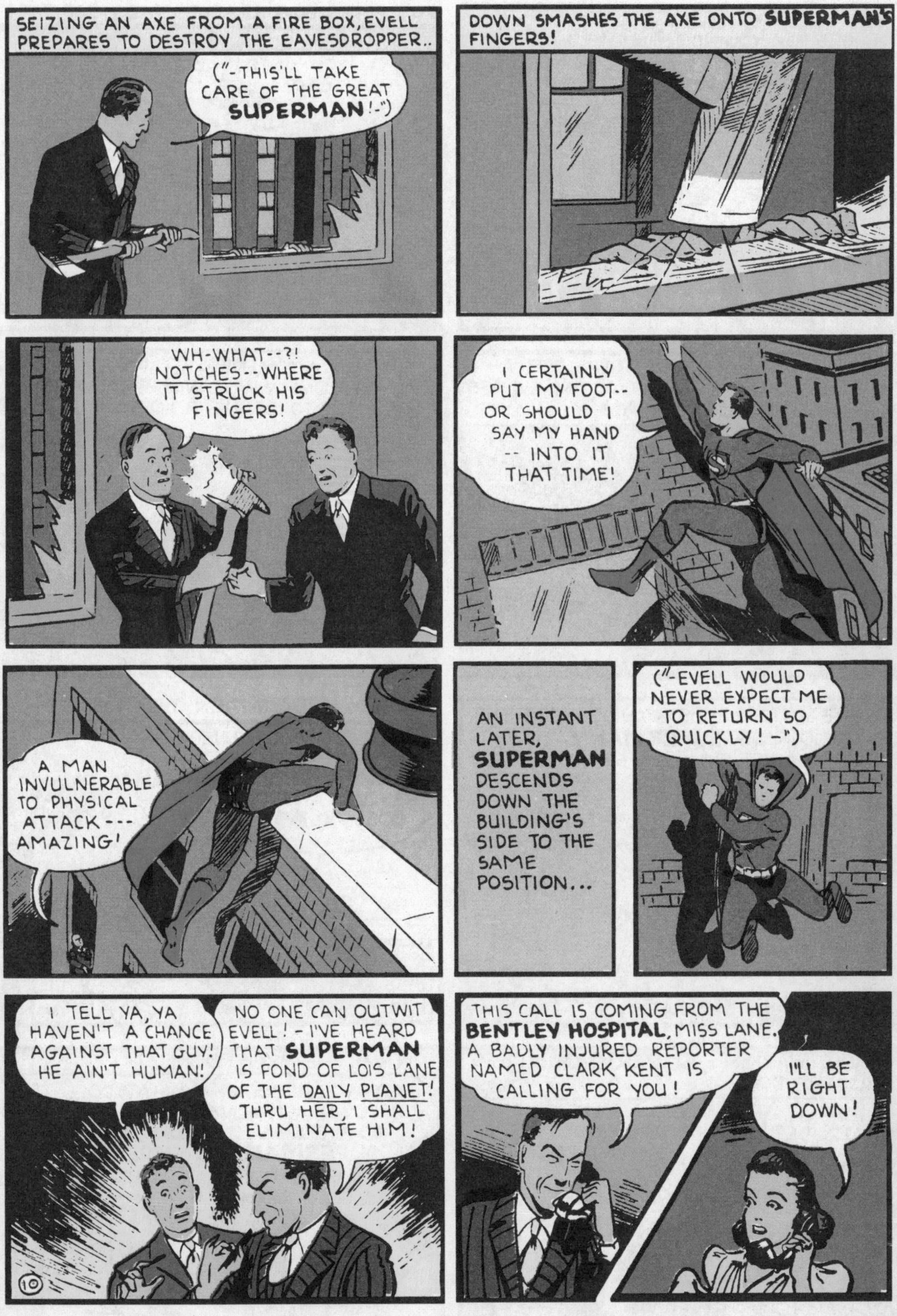
SEIZING AN AXE FROM A FIRE BOX, EVELL PREPARES TO DESTROY THE EAVESDROPPER..
("-THIS'LL TAKE CARE OF THE GREAT SUPERMAN!-")
DOWN SMASHES THE AXE ONTO SUPERMAN'S FINGERS!
WH-WHAT--?! NOTCHES--WHERE IT STRUCK HIS FINGERS!
I CERTAINLY PUT MY FOOT-- OR SHOULD I SAY MY HAND -- INTO IT THAT TIME!
A MAN INVULNERABLE TO PHYSICAL ATTACK--- AMAZING!
AN INSTANT LATER, SUPERMAN DESCENDS DOWN THE BUILDING'S SIDE TO THE SAME POSITION...
("-EVELL WOULD NEVER EXPECT ME TO RETURN SO QUICKLY! -")
I TELL YA, YA HAVEN'T A CHANCE AGAINST THAT GUY! HE AIN'T HUMAN!
NO ONE CAN OUTWIT EVELL! - I'VE HEARD THAT SUPERMAN IS FOND OF LOIS LANE OF THE DAILY PLANET! THRU HER, I SHALL ELIMINATE HIM!
10
THIS CALL IS COMING FROM THE BENTLEY HOSPITAL, MISS LANE. A BADLY INJURED REPORTER NAMED CLARK KENT IS CALLING FOR YOU!
I'LL BE RIGHT DOWN!

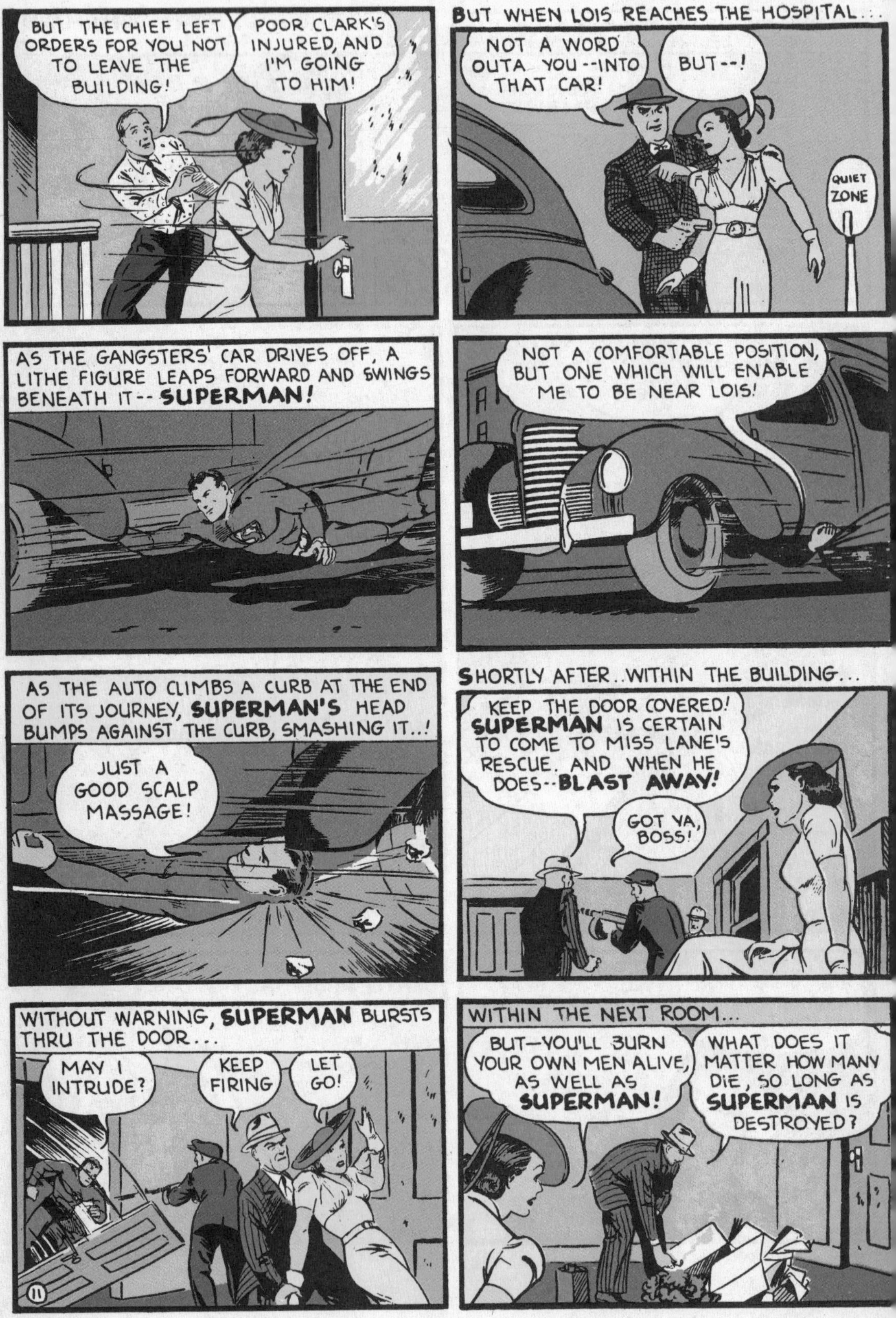
BUT THE CHIEF LEFT ORDERS FOR YOU NOT TO LEAVE THE BUILDING!
POOR CLARK'S INJURED, AND I'M GOING TO HIM!
BUT WHEN LOIS REACHES THE HOSPITAL...
NOT A WORD OUTA YOU--INTO THAT CAR!
BUT--!
QUIET ZONE
AS THE GANGSTERS' CAR DRIVES OFF, A LITHE FIGURE LEAPS FORWARD AND SWINGS BENEATH IT--SUPERMAN!
NOT A COMFORTABLE POSITION, BUT ONE WHICH WILL ENABLE ME TO BE NEAR LOIS!
AS THE AUTO CLIMBS A CURB AT THE END OF ITS JOURNEY, SUPERMAN'S HEAD BUMPS AGAINST THE CURB, SMASHING IT..!
JUST A GOOD SCALP MASSAGE!
SHORTLY AFTER..WITHIN THE BUILDING...
KEEP THE DOOR COVERED! SUPERMAN IS CERTAIN TO COME TO MISS LANE'S RESCUE. AND WHEN HE DOES--BLAST AWAY!
GOT YA, BOSS!
WITHOUT WARNING, SUPERMAN BURSTS THRU THE DOOR...
MAY I INTRUDE?
KEEP FIRING
LET GO!
11
WITHIN THE NEXT ROOM...
BUT—YOU'LL BURN YOUR OWN MEN ALIVE, AS WELL AS SUPERMAN!
WHAT DOES IT MATTER HOW MANY DIE, SO LONG AS SUPERMAN IS DESTROYED?

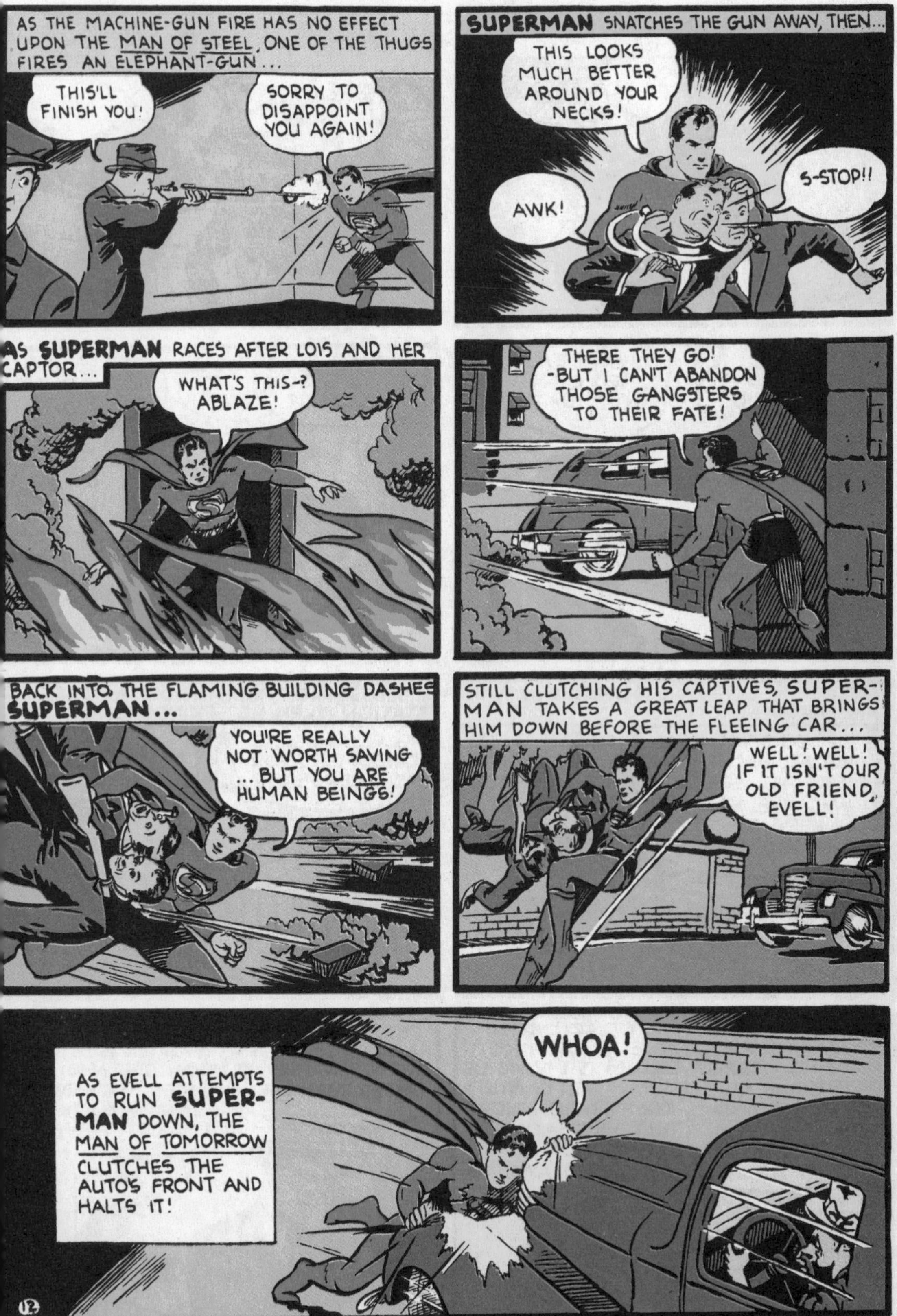
AS THE MACHINE-GUN FIRE HAS NO EFFECT UPON THE MAN OF STEEL, ONE OF THE THUGS FIRES AN ELEPHANT-GUN...
THIS'LL FINISH YOU!
SORRY TO DISAPPOINT YOU AGAIN!
SUPERMAN SNATCHES THE GUN AWAY, THEN...
THIS LOOKS MUCH BETTER AROUND YOUR NECKS!
AWK!
S-STOP!!
AS SUPERMAN RACES AFTER LOIS AND HER CAPTOR...
WHAT'S THIS-? ABLAZE!
THERE THEY GO! -BUT I CAN'T ABANDON THOSE GANGSTERS TO THEIR FATE!
BACK INTO THE FLAMING BUILDING DASHES SUPERMAN...
YOU'RE REALLY NOT WORTH SAVING ...BUT YOU ARE HUMAN BEINGS!
STILL CLUTCHING HIS CAPTIVES, SUPERMAN TAKES A GREAT LEAP THAT BRINGS HIM DOWN BEFORE THE FLEEING CAR...
WELL! WELL! IF IT ISN'T OUR OLD FRIEND, EVELL!
AS EVELL ATTEMPTS TO RUN SUPERMAN DOWN, THE MAN OF TOMORROW CLUTCHES THE AUTO'S FRONT AND HALTS IT!
WHOA!
12

SWIFTLY, **SUPERMAN** KICKS OFF THE MACHINE'S FRONT WHEELS...

YOU WON'T NEED THEM!

AND NOW TO SQUARE MATTERS WITH YOU!

DON'T HARM ME!

ARE YOU GOING TO CONFESS TO YOUR CRIMES, OR...!

I WON'T TALK! YOU CAN'T INTIMIDATE ME!

BUT WE'LL TALK! TRY TO BURN US, WILL YOU?

WE'LL GET EVEN! --YOU TRAITORS!

YOU SEE, EVELL YOUR OWN EVIL DEEDS HAVE CAUGHT UP WITH YOU!

ACROSS THE SKY LEAPS **SUPERMAN** WITH HIS CAPTIVES...

IF YOU DON'T TELL ME ALL ABOUT YOURSELF, I'LL SCREAM! WHO ARE YOU? WHERE DO YOU COME FROM? WHAT~?

SCREAM, IF YOU WANT! BUT I'M NOT AN INFORMATION BUREAU!

...DEPOSITING THEM INSIDE A POLICE STATION, THEN HE SPRINGS OFF!

HERE ARE SOME CUSTOMERS FOR YOU, SERGEANT!

SUPERMAN!

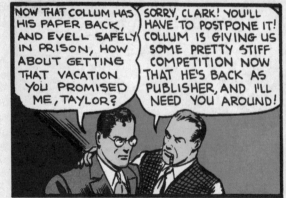

NOW THAT COLLUM HAS HIS PAPER BACK, AND EVELL SAFELY IN PRISON, HOW ABOUT GETTING THAT VACATION YOU PROMISED ME, TAYLOR?

SORRY, CLARK! YOU'LL HAVE TO POSTPONE IT! COLLUM IS GIVING US SOME PRETTY STIFF COMPETITION NOW THAT HE'S BACK AS PUBLISHER, AND I'LL NEED YOU AROUND!

ONE THING YOU'LL HAVE TO ADMIT, CHIEF-- TWO NEWSPAPERS ARE BETTER THAN ONE!

AN' ONE BUSY REPORTER IS BETTER THAN ONE WHO WASTES TIME GABBIN'! GET GOIN', CLARK! I WANT NEWS!

THE END

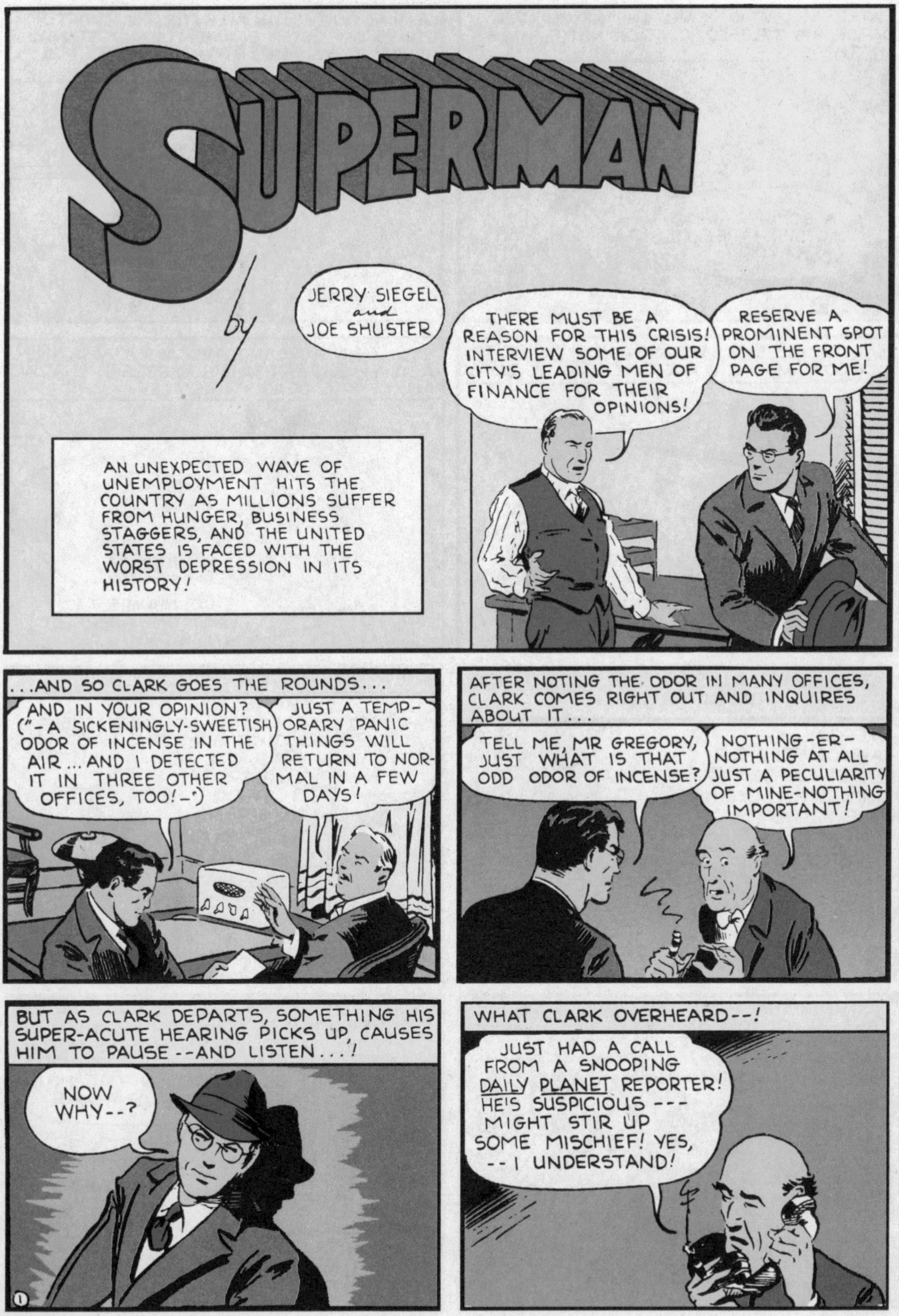
SUPERMAN
by
JERRY SIEGEL and JOE SHUSTER
THERE MUST BE A REASON FOR THIS CRISIS! INTERVIEW SOME OF OUR CITY'S LEADING MEN OF FINANCE FOR THEIR OPINIONS!
RESERVE A PROMINENT SPOT ON THE FRONT PAGE FOR ME!
AN UNEXPECTED WAVE OF UNEMPLOYMENT HITS THE COUNTRY AS MILLIONS SUFFER FROM HUNGER, BUSINESS STAGGERS, AND THE UNITED STATES IS FACED WITH THE WORST DEPRESSION IN ITS HISTORY!
...AND SO CLARK GOES THE ROUNDS...
AND IN YOUR OPINION? ("-A SICKENINGLY-SWEETISH ODOR OF INCENSE IN THE AIR ... AND I DETECTED IT IN THREE OTHER OFFICES, TOO!-")
JUST A TEMPORARY PANIC THINGS WILL RETURN TO NORMAL IN A FEW DAYS!
AFTER NOTING THE ODOR IN MANY OFFICES, CLARK COMES RIGHT OUT AND INQUIRES ABOUT IT...
TELL ME, MR GREGORY, JUST WHAT IS THAT ODD ODOR OF INCENSE?
NOTHING-ER-NOTHING AT ALL JUST A PECULIARITY OF MINE-NOTHING IMPORTANT!
BUT AS CLARK DEPARTS, SOMETHING HIS SUPER-ACUTE HEARING PICKS UP, CAUSES HIM TO PAUSE--AND LISTEN...!
NOW WHY--?
1
WHAT CLARK OVERHEARD--!
JUST HAD A CALL FROM A SNOOPING DAILY PLANET REPORTER! HE'S SUSPICIOUS --- MIGHT STIR UP SOME MISCHIEF! YES, --I UNDERSTAND!

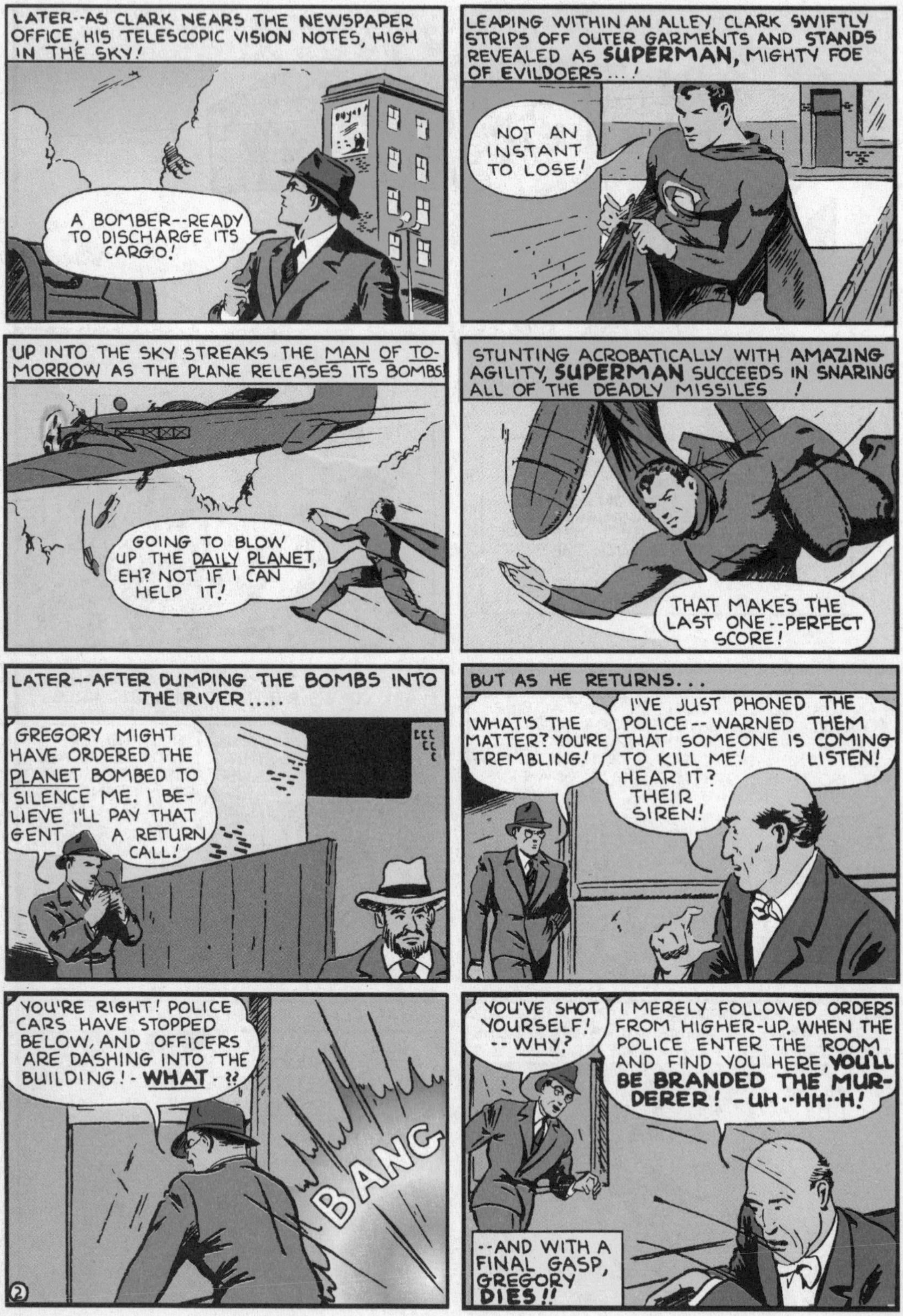

LATER--AS CLARK NEARS THE NEWSPAPER OFFICE, HIS TELESCOPIC VISION NOTES, HIGH IN THE SKY!
A BOMBER--READY TO DISCHARGE ITS CARGO!
LEAPING WITHIN AN ALLEY, CLARK SWIFTLY STRIPS OFF OUTER GARMENTS AND STANDS REVEALED AS SUPERMAN, MIGHTY FOE OF EVILDOERS...!
NOT AN INSTANT TO LOSE!
UP INTO THE SKY STREAKS THE MAN OF TO-MORROW AS THE PLANE RELEASES ITS BOMBS!
GOING TO BLOW UP THE DAILY PLANET, EH? NOT IF I CAN HELP IT!
STUNTING ACROBATICALLY WITH AMAZING AGILITY, SUPERMAN SUCCEEDS IN SNARING ALL OF THE DEADLY MISSILES !
THAT MAKES THE LAST ONE--PERFECT SCORE!
LATER--AFTER DUMPING THE BOMBS INTO THE RIVER.....
GREGORY MIGHT HAVE ORDERED THE PLANET BOMBED TO SILENCE ME. I BE-LIEVE I'LL PAY THAT GENT A RETURN CALL!
BUT AS HE RETURNS...
WHAT'S THE MATTER? YOU'RE TREMBLING!
I'VE JUST PHONED THE POLICE--WARNED THEM THAT SOMEONE IS COMING TO KILL ME! LISTEN! HEAR IT? THEIR SIREN!
YOU'RE RIGHT! POLICE CARS HAVE STOPPED BELOW, AND OFFICERS ARE DASHING INTO THE BUILDING! - WHAT - ??
BANG
2
YOU'VE SHOT YOURSELF! --WHY?
I MERELY FOLLOWED ORDERS FROM HIGHER-UP. WHEN THE POLICE ENTER THE ROOM AND FIND YOU HERE, YOU'LL BE BRANDED THE MUR-DERER! -UH--HH--H!
--AND WITH A FINAL GASP, GREGORY DIES!!

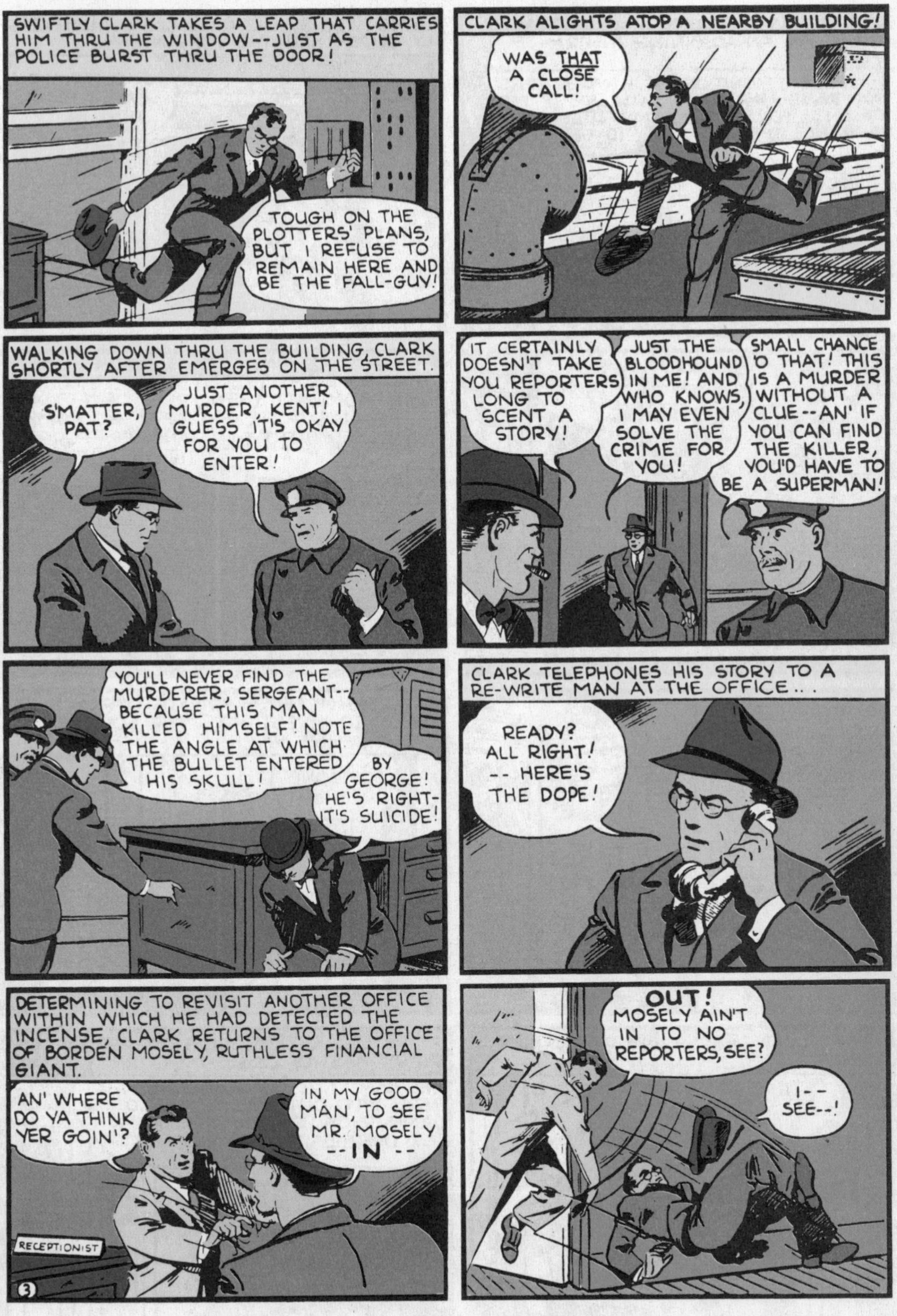
SWIFTLY CLARK TAKES A LEAP THAT CARRIES HIM THRU THE WINDOW--JUST AS THE POLICE BURST THRU THE DOOR!
TOUGH ON THE PLOTTERS' PLANS, BUT I REFUSE TO REMAIN HERE AND BE THE FALL-GUY!
CLARK ALIGHTS ATOP A NEARBY BUILDING!
WAS THAT A CLOSE CALL!
WALKING DOWN THRU THE BUILDING, CLARK SHORTLY AFTER EMERGES ON THE STREET.
S'MATTER, PAT?
JUST ANOTHER MURDER, KENT! I GUESS IT'S OKAY FOR YOU TO ENTER!
IT CERTAINLY DOESN'T TAKE YOU REPORTERS LONG TO SCENT A STORY!
JUST THE BLOODHOUND IN ME! AND WHO KNOWS, I MAY EVEN SOLVE THE CRIME FOR YOU!
SMALL CHANCE 'O THAT! THIS IS A MURDER WITHOUT A CLUE--AN' IF YOU CAN FIND THE KILLER, YOU'D HAVE TO BE A SUPERMAN!
YOU'LL NEVER FIND THE MURDERER, SERGEANT--BECAUSE THIS MAN KILLED HIMSELF! NOTE THE ANGLE AT WHICH THE BULLET ENTERED HIS SKULL!
BY GEORGE! HE'S RIGHT-IT'S SUICIDE!
CLARK TELEPHONES HIS STORY TO A RE-WRITE MAN AT THE OFFICE...
READY? ALL RIGHT! -- HERE'S THE DOPE!
DETERMINING TO REVISIT ANOTHER OFFICE WITHIN WHICH HE HAD DETECTED THE INCENSE, CLARK RETURNS TO THE OFFICE OF BORDEN MOSELY, RUTHLESS FINANCIAL GIANT.
AN' WHERE DO YA THINK YER GOIN'?
IN, MY GOOD MAN, TO SEE MR. MOSELY --IN--
RECEPTIONIST
3
OUT! MOSELY AIN'T IN TO NO REPORTERS, SEE?
I-- SEE--!

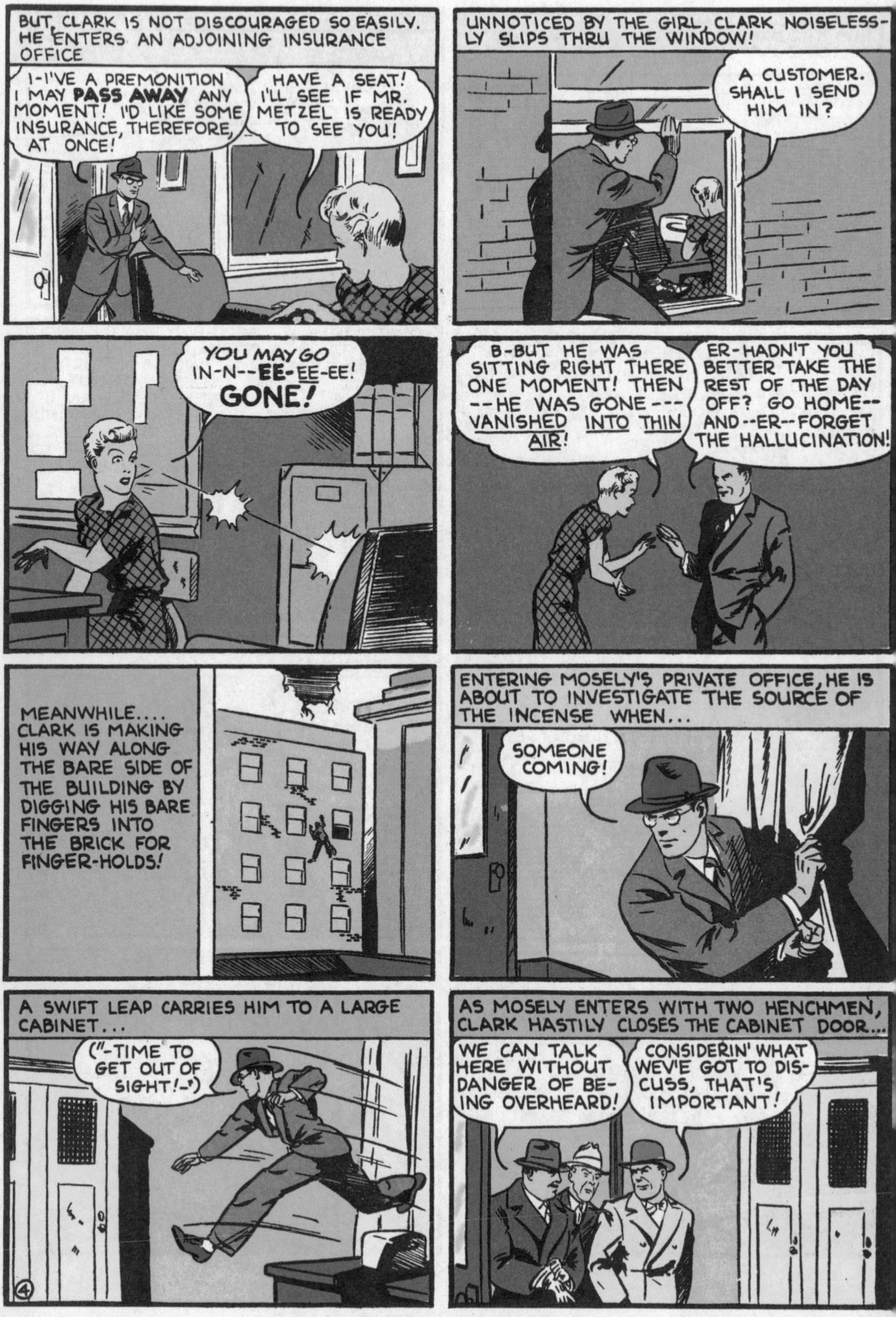
BUT, CLARK IS NOT DISCOURAGED SO EASILY. HE ENTERS AN ADJOINING INSURANCE OFFICE
I-I'VE A PREMONITION I MAY PASS AWAY ANY MOMENT! I'D LIKE SOME INSURANCE, THEREFORE, AT ONCE!
HAVE A SEAT! I'LL SEE IF MR. METZEL IS READY TO SEE YOU!
UNNOTICED BY THE GIRL, CLARK NOISELESSLY SLIPS THRU THE WINDOW!
A CUSTOMER. SHALL I SEND HIM IN?
YOU MAY GO IN-N--EE-EE-EE! GONE!
B-BUT HE WAS SITTING RIGHT THERE ONE MOMENT! THEN --HE WAS GONE--- VANISHED INTO THIN AIR!
ER-HADN'T YOU BETTER TAKE THE REST OF THE DAY OFF? GO HOME-- AND--ER--FORGET THE HALLUCINATION!
MEANWHILE.... CLARK IS MAKING HIS WAY ALONG THE BARE SIDE OF THE BUILDING BY DIGGING HIS BARE FINGERS INTO THE BRICK FOR FINGER-HOLDS!
ENTERING MOSELY'S PRIVATE OFFICE, HE IS ABOUT TO INVESTIGATE THE SOURCE OF THE INCENSE WHEN...
SOMEONE COMING!
A SWIFT LEAP CARRIES HIM TO A LARGE CABINET...
("-TIME TO GET OUT OF SIGHT!-")
4
AS MOSELY ENTERS WITH TWO HENCHMEN, CLARK HASTILY CLOSES THE CABINET DOOR...
WE CAN TALK HERE WITHOUT DANGER OF BE-ING OVERHEARD!
CONSIDERIN' WHAT WEV'E GOT TO DIS-CUSS, THAT'S IMPORTANT!

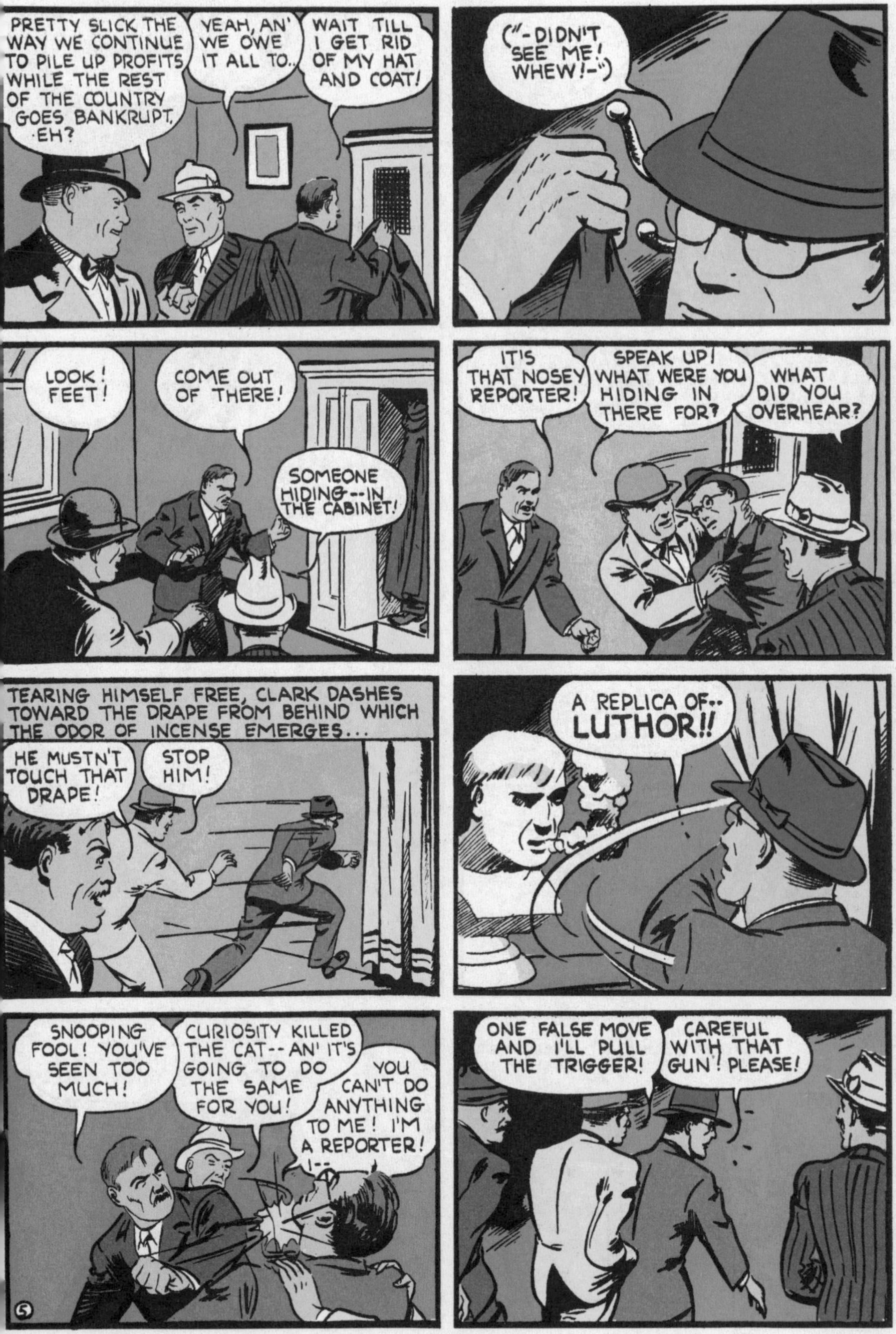
PRETTY SLICK THE WAY WE CONTINUE TO PILE UP PROFITS WHILE THE REST OF THE COUNTRY GOES BANKRUPT, EH?
YEAH, AN' WE OWE IT ALL TO..
WAIT TILL I GET RID OF MY HAT AND COAT!
("-DIDN'T SEE ME! WHEW!-")
LOOK! FEET!
COME OUT OF THERE!
SOMEONE HIDING--IN THE CABINET!
IT'S THAT NOSEY REPORTER!
SPEAK UP! WHAT WERE YOU HIDING IN THERE FOR?
WHAT DID YOU OVERHEAR?
TEARING HIMSELF FREE, CLARK DASHES TOWARD THE DRAPE FROM BEHIND WHICH THE ODOR OF INCENSE EMERGES...
HE MUSTN'T TOUCH THAT DRAPE!
STOP HIM!
A REPLICA OF.. LUTHOR!!
SNOOPING FOOL! YOU'VE SEEN TOO MUCH!
CURIOSITY KILLED THE CAT--AN' IT'S GOING TO DO THE SAME FOR YOU!
YOU CAN'T DO ANYTHING TO ME! I'M A REPORTER! I--
5
ONE FALSE MOVE AND I'LL PULL THE TRIGGER!
CAREFUL WITH THAT GUN! PLEASE!

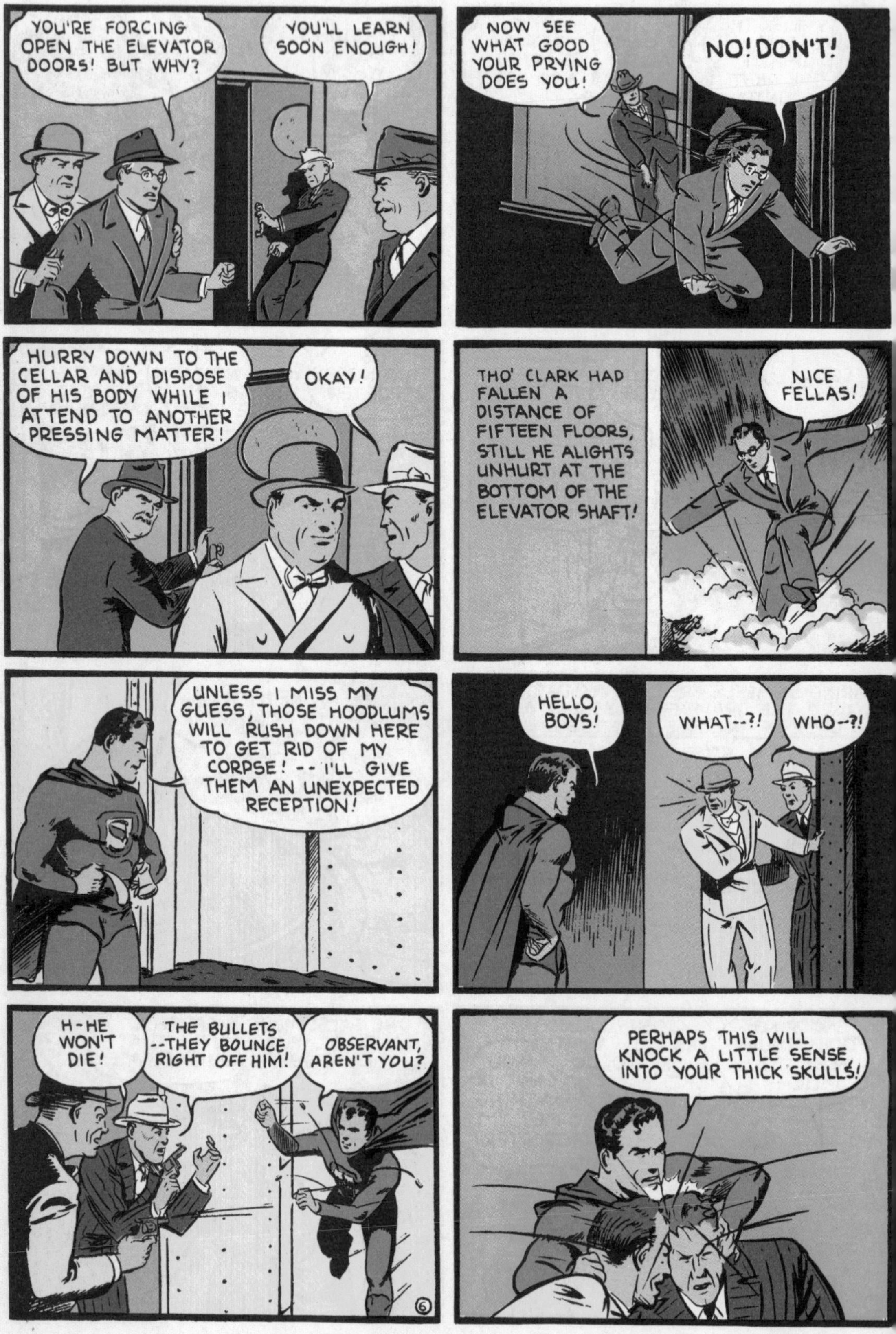
YOU'RE FORCING OPEN THE ELEVATOR DOORS! BUT WHY?
YOU'LL LEARN SOON ENOUGH!
NOW SEE WHAT GOOD YOUR PRYING DOES YOU!
NO! DON'T!
HURRY DOWN TO THE CELLAR AND DISPOSE OF HIS BODY WHILE I ATTEND TO ANOTHER PRESSING MATTER!
OKAY!
THO' CLARK HAD FALLEN A DISTANCE OF FIFTEEN FLOORS, STILL HE ALIGHTS UNHURT AT THE BOTTOM OF THE ELEVATOR SHAFT!
NICE FELLAS!
UNLESS I MISS MY GUESS, THOSE HOODLUMS WILL RUSH DOWN HERE TO GET RID OF MY CORPSE! -- I'LL GIVE THEM AN UNEXPECTED RECEPTION!
HELLO, BOYS!
WHAT--?!
WHO--?!
H-HE WON'T DIE!
THE BULLETS --THEY BOUNCE RIGHT OFF HIM!
OBSERVANT, AREN'T YOU?
6
PERHAPS THIS WILL KNOCK A LITTLE SENSE INTO YOUR THICK SKULLS!

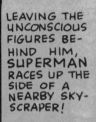

LEAVING THE UNCONSCIOUS FIGURES BEHIND HIM, SUPERMAN RACES UP THE SIDE OF A NEARBY SKYSCRAPER!

NOW TO TUNE IN ON MOSELY WITH MY TELESCOPIC X-RAY VISION, AND SEE IF HE'S BEHAVING HIMSELF!

YOU WISH ME TO COME AND MAKE A FULL REPORT? I OBEY!

SHORTLY AFTER--AS AN AUTOGYRO DESCENDS TO THE BUILDING'S ROOF, MOSELY ENTERS IT..

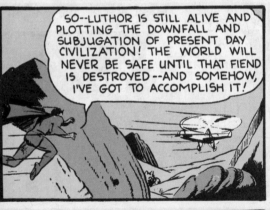

SO--LUTHOR IS STILL ALIVE AND PLOTTING THE DOWNFALL AND SUBJUGATION OF PRESENT DAY CIVILIZATION! THE WORLD WILL NEVER BE SAFE UNTIL THAT FIEND IS DESTROYED--AND SOMEHOW, I'VE GOT TO ACCOMPLISH IT!

SIGHTED ME, EH? AND ITCHING FOR A FIGHT!

STREAKING DOWN UPON THE SKY-VESSEL, SUPERMAN RIPS OFF THE WHIRLING BLADES WHICH KEEP IT ALOFT...

YOU ASKED FOR IT!

⑦

AS PLANE AND SUPERMAN PLUMMET DOWNWARD...

MOSELY!

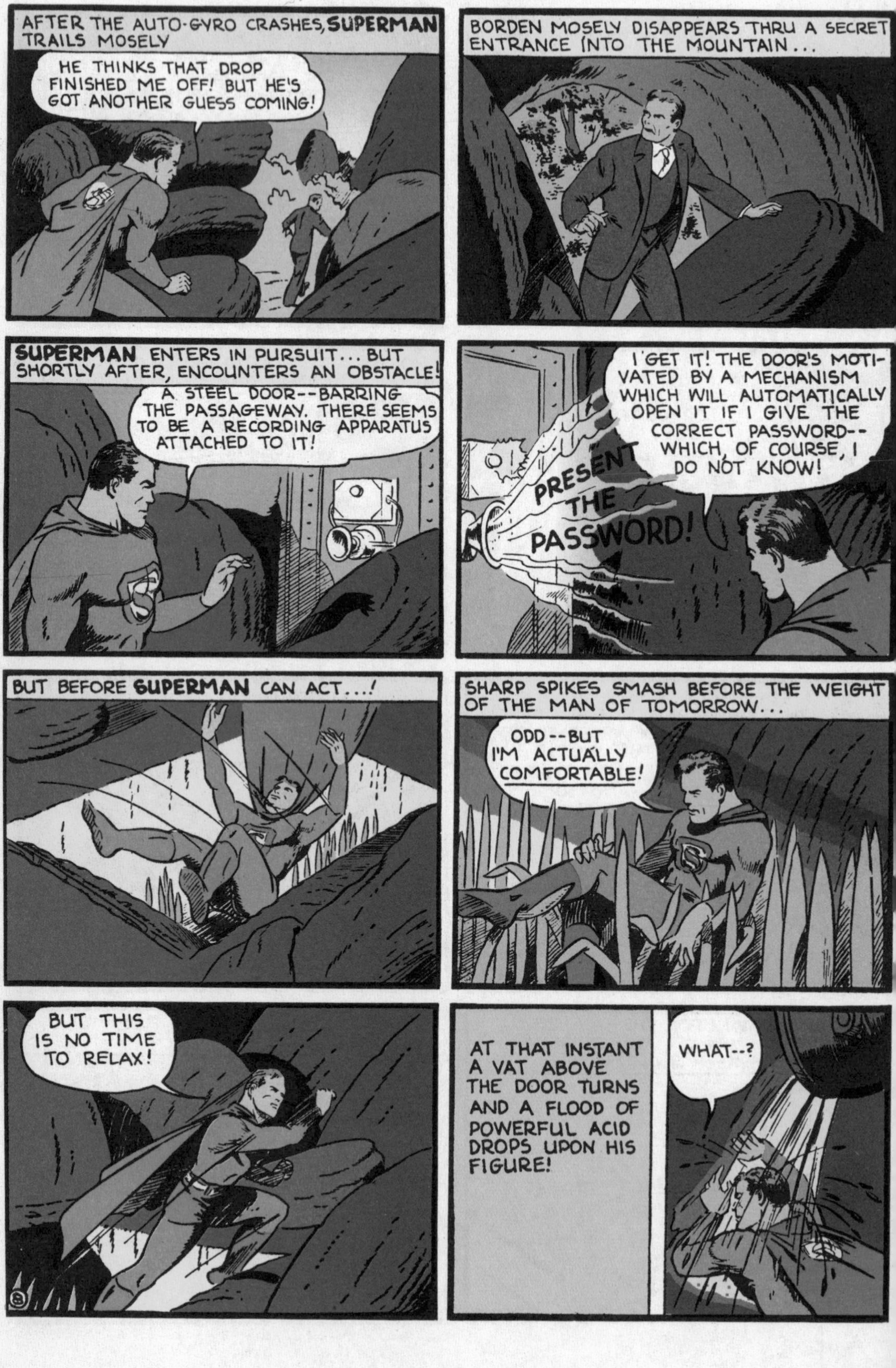

AFTER THE AUTO-GYRO CRASHES, SUPERMAN TRAILS MOSELY
HE THINKS THAT DROP FINISHED ME OFF! BUT HE'S GOT ANOTHER GUESS COMING!
BORDEN MOSELY DISAPPEARS THRU A SECRET ENTRANCE INTO THE MOUNTAIN...
SUPERMAN ENTERS IN PURSUIT... BUT SHORTLY AFTER, ENCOUNTERS AN OBSTACLE!
A STEEL DOOR--BARRING THE PASSAGEWAY. THERE SEEMS TO BE A RECORDING APPARATUS ATTACHED TO IT!
PRESENT THE PASSWORD!
I GET IT! THE DOOR'S MOTIVATED BY A MECHANISM WHICH WILL AUTOMATICALLY OPEN IT IF I GIVE THE CORRECT PASSWORD--WHICH, OF COURSE, I DO NOT KNOW!
BUT BEFORE SUPERMAN CAN ACT...!
SHARP SPIKES SMASH BEFORE THE WEIGHT OF THE MAN OF TOMORROW...
ODD--BUT I'M ACTUALLY COMFORTABLE!
BUT THIS IS NO TIME TO RELAX!
AT THAT INSTANT A VAT ABOVE THE DOOR TURNS AND A FLOOD OF POWERFUL ACID DROPS UPON HIS FIGURE!
WHAT--?

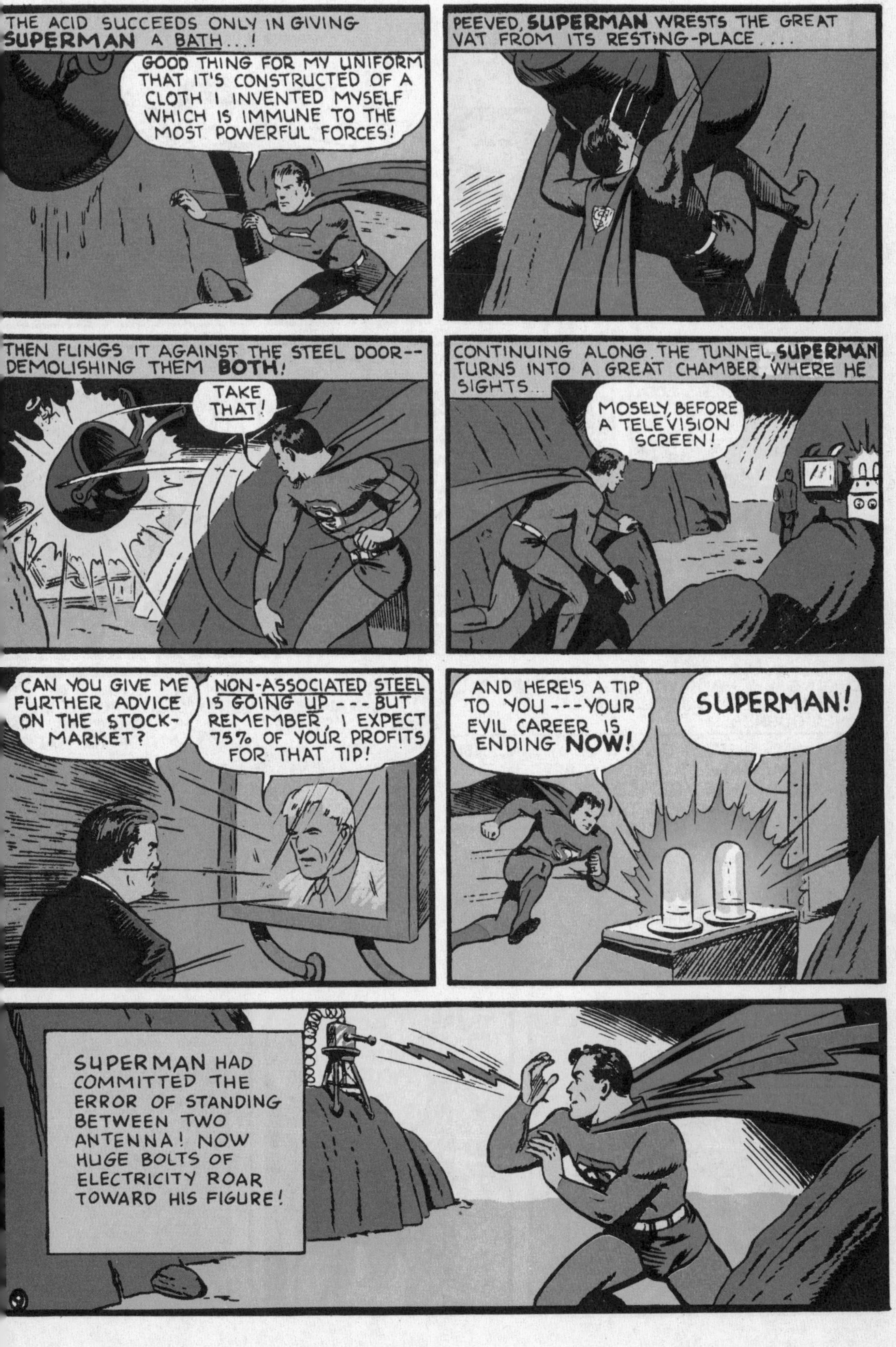
THE ACID SUCCEEDS ONLY IN GIVING SUPERMAN A BATH...!
GOOD THING FOR MY UNIFORM THAT IT'S CONSTRUCTED OF A CLOTH I INVENTED MYSELF WHICH IS IMMUNE TO THE MOST POWERFUL FORCES!
PEEVED, SUPERMAN WRESTS THE GREAT VAT FROM ITS RESTING-PLACE....
THEN FLINGS IT AGAINST THE STEEL DOOR-- DEMOLISHING THEM BOTH!
TAKE THAT!
CONTINUING ALONG THE TUNNEL, SUPERMAN TURNS INTO A GREAT CHAMBER, WHERE HE SIGHTS...
MOSELY, BEFORE A TELEVISION SCREEN!
CAN YOU GIVE ME FURTHER ADVICE ON THE STOCK-MARKET?
NON-ASSOCIATED STEEL IS GOING UP --- BUT REMEMBER, I EXPECT 75% OF YOUR PROFITS FOR THAT TIP!
AND HERE'S A TIP TO YOU --- YOUR EVIL CAREER IS ENDING NOW!
SUPERMAN!
SUPERMAN HAD COMMITTED THE ERROR OF STANDING BETWEEN TWO ANTENNA! NOW HUGE BOLTS OF ELECTRICITY ROAR TOWARD HIS FIGURE!
9

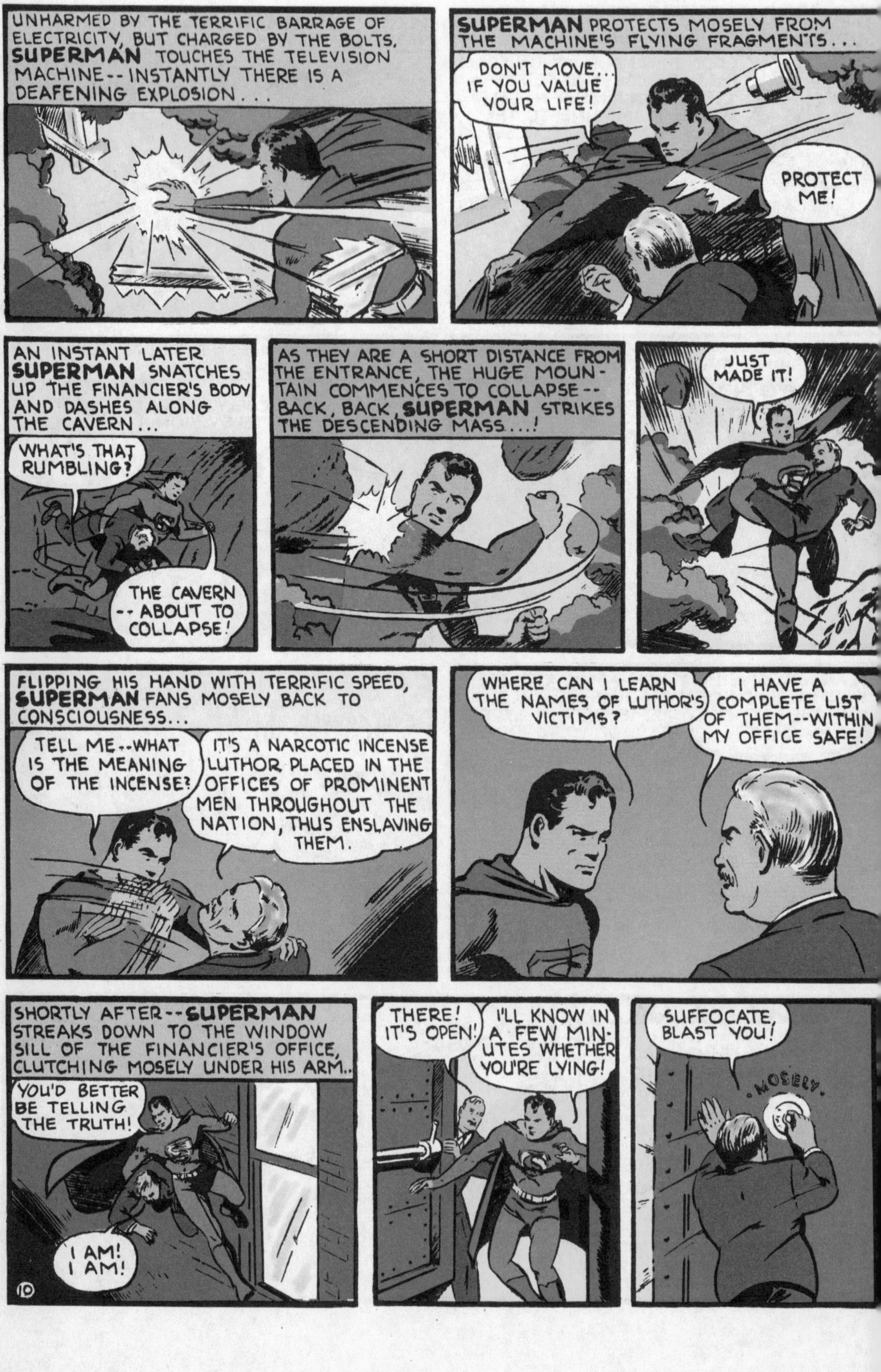
UNHARMED BY THE TERRIFIC BARRAGE OF ELECTRICITY, BUT CHARGED BY THE BOLTS, SUPERMAN TOUCHES THE TELEVISION MACHINE--INSTANTLY THERE IS A DEAFENING EXPLOSION . . .
SUPERMAN PROTECTS MOSELY FROM THE MACHINE'S FLYING FRAGMENTS . . .
DON'T MOVE... IF YOU VALUE YOUR LIFE!
PROTECT ME!
AN INSTANT LATER SUPERMAN SNATCHES UP THE FINANCIER'S BODY AND DASHES ALONG THE CAVERN...
WHAT'S THAT RUMBLING?
THE CAVERN --ABOUT TO COLLAPSE!
AS THEY ARE A SHORT DISTANCE FROM THE ENTRANCE, THE HUGE MOUN-TAIN COMMENCES TO COLLAPSE--BACK, BACK, SUPERMAN STRIKES THE DESCENDING MASS....!
JUST MADE IT!
FLIPPING HIS HAND WITH TERRIFIC SPEED, SUPERMAN FANS MOSELY BACK TO CONSCIOUSNESS...
TELL ME--WHAT IS THE MEANING OF THE INCENSE?
IT'S A NARCOTIC INCENSE LUTHOR PLACED IN THE OFFICES OF PROMINENT MEN THROUGHOUT THE NATION, THUS ENSLAVING THEM.
WHERE CAN I LEARN THE NAMES OF LUTHOR'S VICTIMS?
I HAVE A COMPLETE LIST OF THEM--WITHIN MY OFFICE SAFE!
SHORTLY AFTER--SUPERMAN STREAKS DOWN TO THE WINDOW SILL OF THE FINANCIER'S OFFICE, CLUTCHING MOSELY UNDER HIS ARM..
YOU'D BETTER BE TELLING THE TRUTH!
I AM! I AM!
10
THERE! IT'S OPEN!
I'LL KNOW IN A FEW MIN-UTES WHETHER YOU'RE LYING!
SUFFOCATE, BLAST YOU!
MOSELY

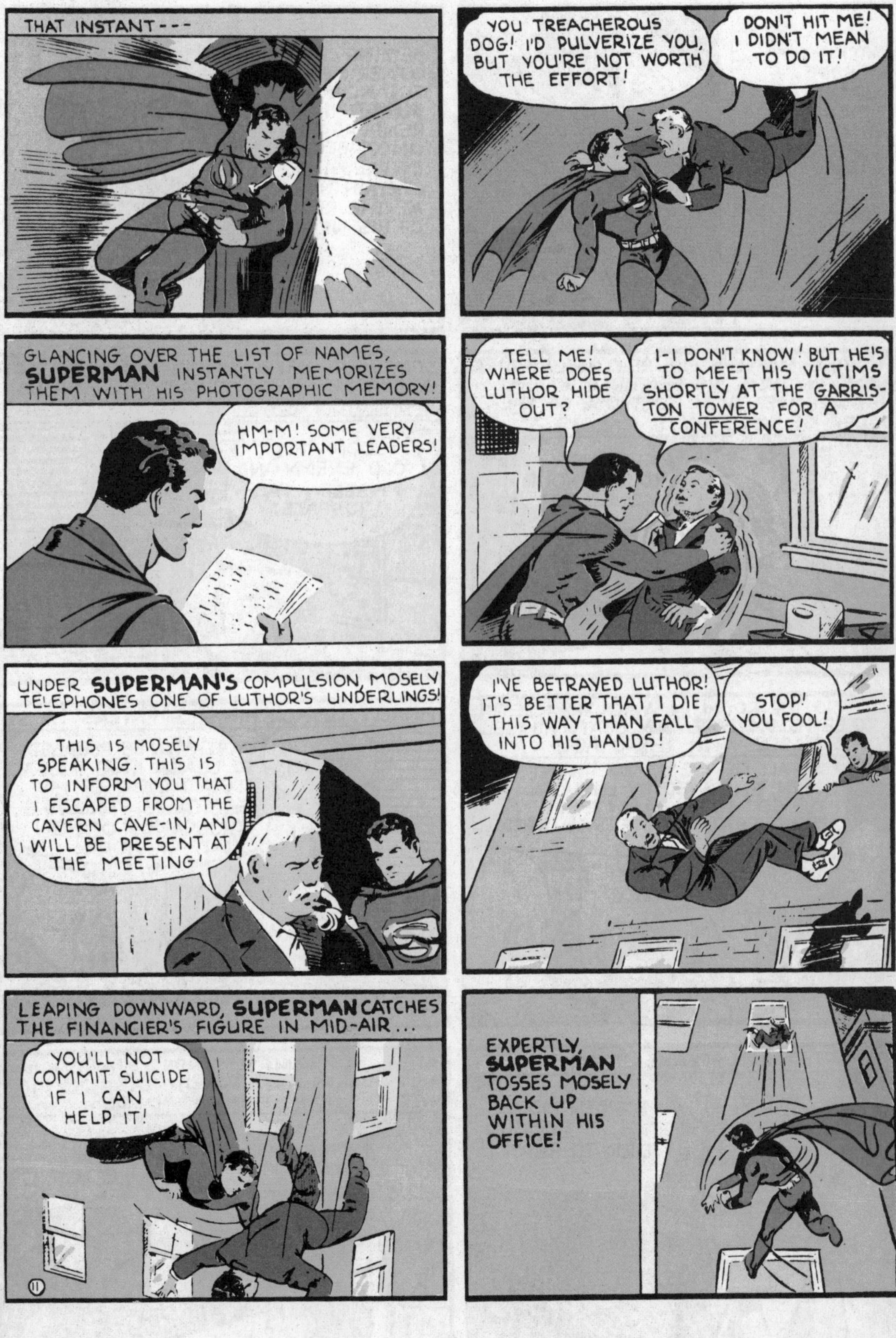
THAT INSTANT---
YOU TREACHEROUS DOG! I'D PULVERIZE YOU, BUT YOU'RE NOT WORTH THE EFFORT!
DON'T HIT ME! I DIDN'T MEAN TO DO IT!
GLANCING OVER THE LIST OF NAMES, SUPERMAN INSTANTLY MEMORIZES THEM WITH HIS PHOTOGRAPHIC MEMORY!
HM-M! SOME VERY IMPORTANT LEADERS!
TELL ME! WHERE DOES LUTHOR HIDE OUT?
I-I DON'T KNOW! BUT HE'S TO MEET HIS VICTIMS SHORTLY AT THE GARRISTON TOWER FOR A CONFERENCE!
UNDER SUPERMAN'S COMPULSION, MOSELY TELEPHONES ONE OF LUTHOR'S UNDERLINGS!
THIS IS MOSELY SPEAKING. THIS IS TO INFORM YOU THAT I ESCAPED FROM THE CAVERN CAVE-IN, AND I WILL BE PRESENT AT THE MEETING!
I'VE BETRAYED LUTHOR! IT'S BETTER THAT I DIE THIS WAY THAN FALL INTO HIS HANDS!
STOP! YOU FOOL!
LEAPING DOWNWARD, SUPERMAN CATCHES THE FINANCIER'S FIGURE IN MID-AIR...
YOU'LL NOT COMMIT SUICIDE IF I CAN HELP IT!
11
EXPERTLY, SUPERMAN TOSSES MOSELY BACK UP WITHIN HIS OFFICE!

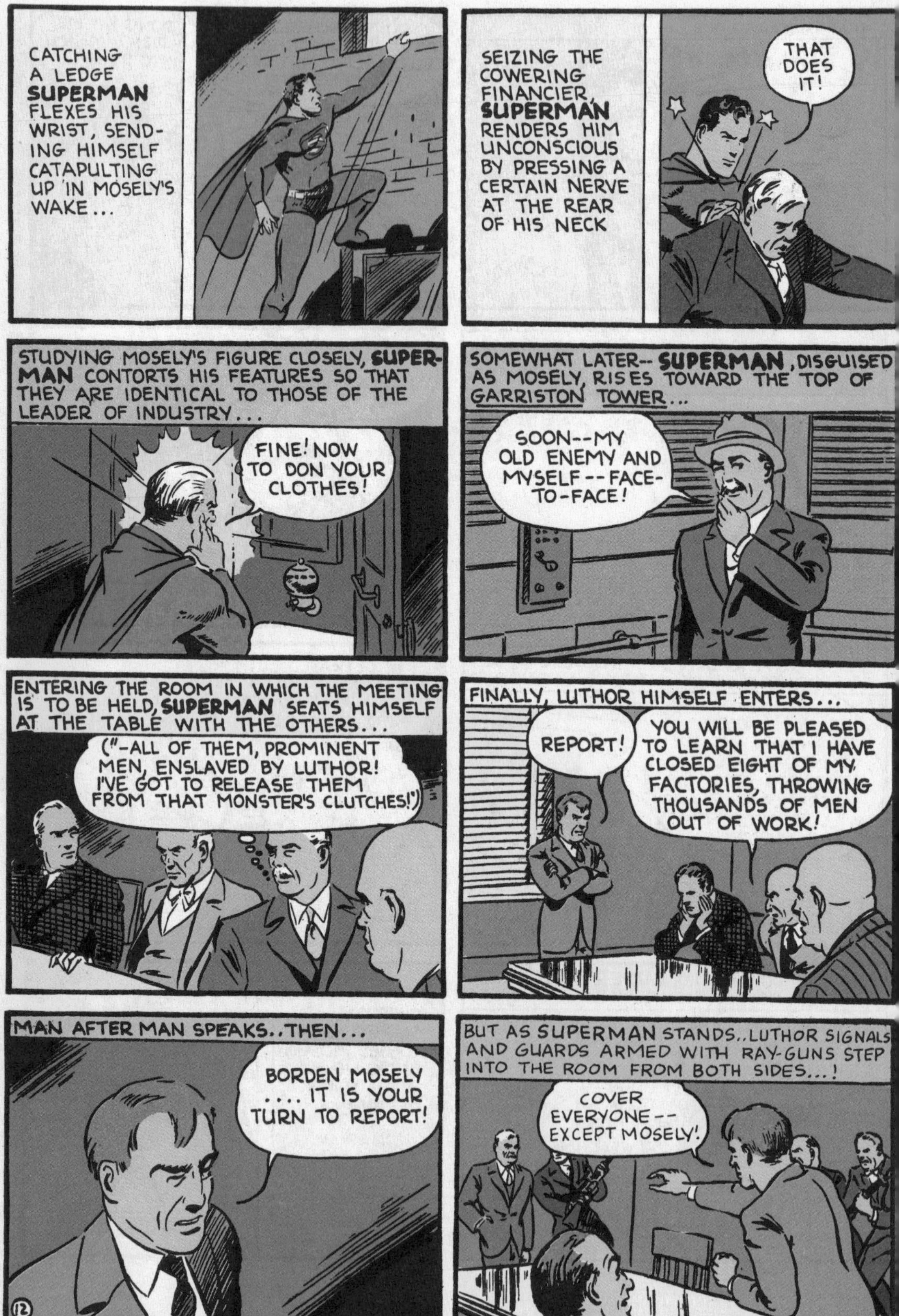
CATCHING A LEDGE SUPERMAN FLEXES HIS WRIST, SENDING HIMSELF CATAPULTING UP IN MOSELY'S WAKE...
SEIZING THE COWERING FINANCIER, SUPERMAN RENDERS HIM UNCONSCIOUS BY PRESSING A CERTAIN NERVE AT THE REAR OF HIS NECK
THAT DOES IT!
STUDYING MOSELY'S FIGURE CLOSELY, SUPERMAN CONTORTS HIS FEATURES SO THAT THEY ARE IDENTICAL TO THOSE OF THE LEADER OF INDUSTRY...
FINE! NOW TO DON YOUR CLOTHES!
SOMEWHAT LATER-- SUPERMAN, DISGUISED AS MOSELY, RISES TOWARD THE TOP OF GARRISTON TOWER...
SOON--MY OLD ENEMY AND MYSELF--FACE-TO-FACE!
ENTERING THE ROOM IN WHICH THE MEETING IS TO BE HELD, SUPERMAN SEATS HIMSELF AT THE TABLE WITH THE OTHERS...
("-ALL OF THEM, PROMINENT MEN, ENSLAVED BY LUTHOR! I'VE GOT TO RELEASE THEM FROM THAT MONSTER'S CLUTCHES!")
FINALLY, LUTHOR HIMSELF ENTERS...
REPORT!
YOU WILL BE PLEASED TO LEARN THAT I HAVE CLOSED EIGHT OF MY FACTORIES, THROWING THOUSANDS OF MEN OUT OF WORK!
MAN AFTER MAN SPEAKS..THEN...
BORDEN MOSELY .... IT IS YOUR TURN TO REPORT!
12
BUT AS SUPERMAN STANDS..LUTHOR SIGNALS AND GUARDS ARMED WITH RAY-GUNS STEP INTO THE ROOM FROM BOTH SIDES...!
COVER EVERYONE--EXCEPT MOSELY!

YOU'LL BE INTERESTED TO KNOW I AM AWARE OF YOUR TRUE IDENTITY.

IN THAT CASE, THERE'S NO NEED FOR THIS DISGUISE!

SUPERMAN PERMITS HIS FEATURES TO RETURN TO THEIR NORMAL PROPORTIONS

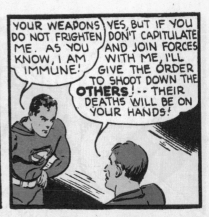

YOUR WEAPONS DO NOT FRIGHTEN ME. AS YOU KNOW, I AM IMMUNE!

YES, BUT IF YOU DON'T CAPITULATE AND JOIN FORCES WITH ME, I'LL GIVE THE ORDER TO SHOOT DOWN THE OTHERS! -- THEIR DEATHS WILL BE ON YOUR HANDS!

IN RESPONSE, SUPERMAN HURLS THE TABLE AT ONE LINE OF GUARDS --AND SPRINGS AT THE OTHER LINE --UPSETTING THEM BOTH!

BUT YOU DIDN'T COUNT ON SUPER-SPEED!

AS SUPERMAN WHIRLS TO ATTEND TO LUTHOR AN AMAZING THING OCCURS--THE ENTIRE SIDE OF THE BUILDING ON WHICH LUTHOR IS SEATED HURTLES AWAY INTO SPACE!

A PLANE-CUNNINGLY CONCEALED IN THE BUILDING'S FRAME-WORK!

THE MAN OF STEEL GIVES CHASE...!

HE WON'T ESCAPE ME THIS TIME!

CRASH! THE PLANE IS DESTROYED IN A HEAD-ON COLLISION WITH SUPERMAN!

THE END OF LUTHOR!

⑬

LATER--

CONGRATULATIONS, CLARK! BECAUSE OF THE LIST OF LUTHOR'S VICTIMS THAT YOU PUBLISHED, THE MEN WERE SUCCESSFULLY CURED!

MOST IMPORTANT OF ALL IS THAT THE MENACE IS REMOVED --AND THAT THE NATION IS RETURNING TO ITS FORMER PROSPERITY!

THE END

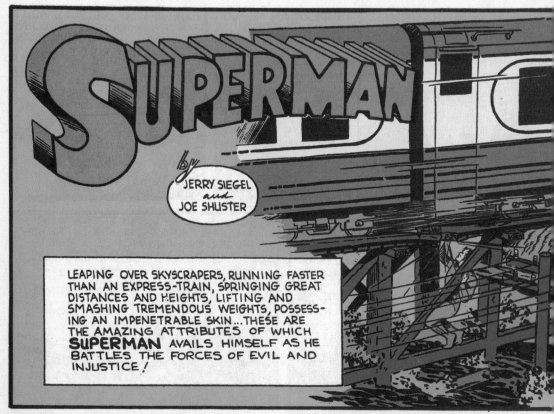

SUPERMAN

by JERRY SIEGEL and JOE SHUSTER

LEAPING OVER SKYSCRAPERS, RUNNING FASTER THAN AN EXPRESS-TRAIN, SPRINGING GREAT DISTANCES AND HEIGHTS, LIFTING AND SMASHING TREMENDOUS WEIGHTS, POSSESSING AN IMPENETRABLE SKIN...THESE ARE THE AMAZING ATTRIBUTES OF WHICH **SUPERMAN** AVAILS HIMSELF AS HE BATTLES THE FORCES OF EVIL AND INJUSTICE!

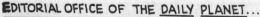

EDITORIAL OFFICE OF THE <u>DAILY</u> <u>PLANET</u>...

MORTON CRAIG HAS BEEN ARRESTED FOR GRAND LARCENY! GET A STATEMENT FROM HIM!

I COULD HAVE SWORN YOU COULDN'T FIND A MORE HONEST MAN THAN CRAIG! WONDER WHAT CAME OVER HIM?

THAT, CLARK, IS WHAT TAYLOR WANTS **YOU** TO FIND OUT!

BUT WHEN CLARK REACHES THE CITY JAIL...

BUT SURELY YOU MUST HAVE SOME JUSTIFICATION FOR YOUR ACT! WHAT DROVE YOU TO IT?

I'M NOT SAYING ANYTHING, I TELL YOU!

IF THERE'S ANYTHING I CAN DO--

YOU CAN! GET ME DR. BREN! I FEEL TERRIBLY RUN DOWN! HE'LL KNOW WHAT TO DO!

LATER...

I'LL HAVE TO ASK YOU WHAT YOU ARE GOING TO DO TO THE PRISONER, DR. BREN!

CRAIG SUFFERS FROM ANEMIA. AN INJECTION WILL HELP.- NOW, IF YOU'LL LEAVE US ALONE...

I'LL GO! IT'S PLAIN I WON'T GET ANY INFORMATION FROM CRAIG!

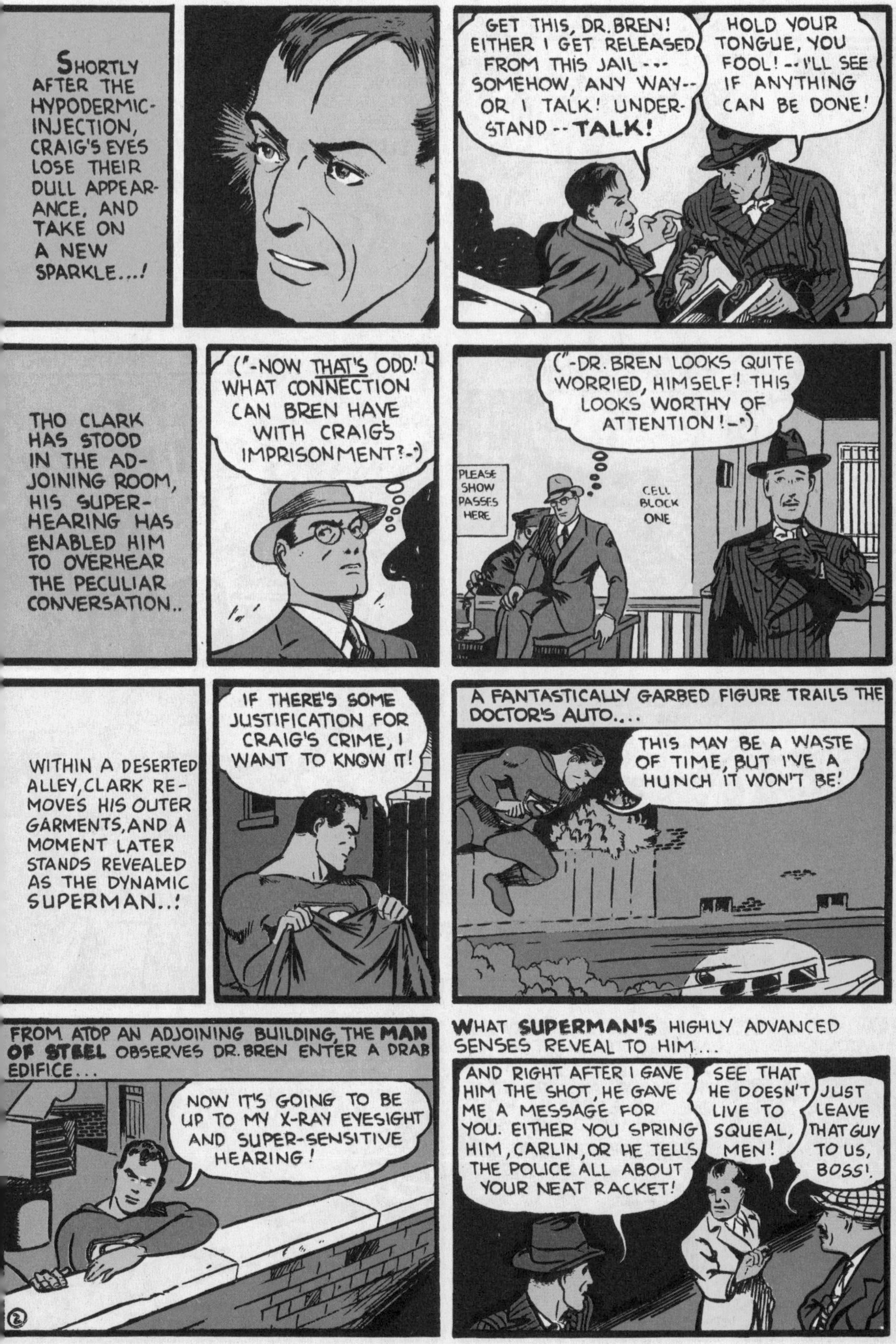
SHORTLY AFTER THE HYPODERMIC-INJECTION, CRAIG'S EYES LOSE THEIR DULL APPEARANCE, AND TAKE ON A NEW SPARKLE...!
GET THIS, DR. BREN! EITHER I GET RELEASED FROM THIS JAIL--- SOMEHOW, ANY WAY-- OR I TALK! UNDER-STAND--TALK!
HOLD YOUR TONGUE, YOU FOOL! --I'LL SEE IF ANYTHING CAN BE DONE!
THO CLARK HAS STOOD IN THE AD-JOINING ROOM, HIS SUPER-HEARING HAS ENABLED HIM TO OVERHEAR THE PECULIAR CONVERSATION..
("-NOW THAT'S ODD! WHAT CONNECTION CAN BREN HAVE WITH CRAIG'S IMPRISONMENT?-")
("-DR. BREN LOOKS QUITE WORRIED, HIMSELF! THIS LOOKS WORTHY OF ATTENTION!-")
PLEASE SHOW PASSES HERE
CELL BLOCK ONE
WITHIN A DESERTED ALLEY, CLARK RE-MOVES HIS OUTER GARMENTS, AND A MOMENT LATER STANDS REVEALED AS THE DYNAMIC SUPERMAN..!
IF THERE'S SOME JUSTIFICATION FOR CRAIG'S CRIME, I WANT TO KNOW IT!
A FANTASTICALLY GARBED FIGURE TRAILS THE DOCTOR'S AUTO....
THIS MAY BE A WASTE OF TIME, BUT I'VE A HUNCH IT WON'T BE!
FROM ATOP AN ADJOINING BUILDING, THE MAN OF STEEL OBSERVES DR. BREN ENTER A DRAB EDIFICE...
NOW IT'S GOING TO BE UP TO MY X-RAY EYESIGHT AND SUPER-SENSITIVE HEARING!
2
WHAT SUPERMAN'S HIGHLY ADVANCED SENSES REVEAL TO HIM....
AND RIGHT AFTER I GAVE HIM THE SHOT, HE GAVE ME A MESSAGE FOR YOU. EITHER YOU SPRING HIM, CARLIN, OR HE TELLS THE POLICE ALL ABOUT YOUR NEAT RACKET!
SEE THAT HE DOESN'T LIVE TO SQUEAL, MEN!
JUST LEAVE THAT GUY TO US, BOSS!

(-AND JUST LEAVE THEM TO ME !--)

AS THE GANGSTERS DRIVE AWAY FROM THE CURB, DOWN STREAKS SUPERMAN!

NOW TO THROW A HITCH INTO THEIR SMUG PLANS!

ALIGHTING BEHIND THE AUTO, THE MAN OF TOMORROW GIVES IT A TERRIFIC SHOVE...

MIND CHANGING YOUR COURSE?

...SO THAT IT HURTLES INTO A TRAFFIC LIGHT STAND!

HEY! WHO YOU TRYIN' TO KILL?

BUT--!

NONE OF YOUR LIP! DRIVE TO THE STATION! YOU'RE UNDER ARREST--ALL OF YOU!

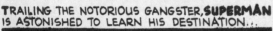

AND A FEW MOMENTS LATER

CARLIN, GOING OUT! WONDER WHAT HE'S UP TO?

TRAILING THE NOTORIOUS GANGSTER, SUPERMAN IS ASTONISHED TO LEARN HIS DESTINATION...

--THE LABORATORY OF PROFESSOR CARL GRINSTEAD ..ONE OF THE WORLD'S MOST ACCOMPLISHED CHEMISTS!

I'LL HAVE TO WAIT FOR THE GUARD TO LOOK THE OTHER WAY. PERHAPS THIS WILL HELP!

AS **SUPERMAN** HAD CALCULATED, THE SENTRY TURNS AS HE HEARS THE BRANCH FALL...

WHAT WAS THAT?

("-NOW!-")

THAT SHADOW-- LIKE A HUGE BIRD'S!

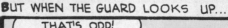

BUT WHEN THE GUARD LOOKS UP...

THAT'S ODD! NOTHING IN SIGHT! COULD I HAVE IMAGINED IT?

("-CARLIN AND PROFESSOR GRINSTEAD TOGETHER! BUT WHAT IS THE EMINENT PROFESSOR DOING IN A COMMON RACKETEER'S COMPANY?-")

CONGRATULATIONS, PROFESSOR, ON THE GREAT GOOD YOUR REMARKABLE DIS- COVERY, PARABIOLENE, IS DOING MANKIND!

A GREAT DEAL OF CREDIT BELONGS TO YOU! I AM BUT A MAN OF SCIENCE! WITHOUT YOUR FINANCIAL BACK- ING AND BUSINESS ACUMEN, I'D HAVE BEEN HELPLESS!

("-SOMEONE APPROACHING!-")

I'LL HIDE BEHIND THAT CHIMNEY -- AND AWAIT DEVELOPEMENTS!

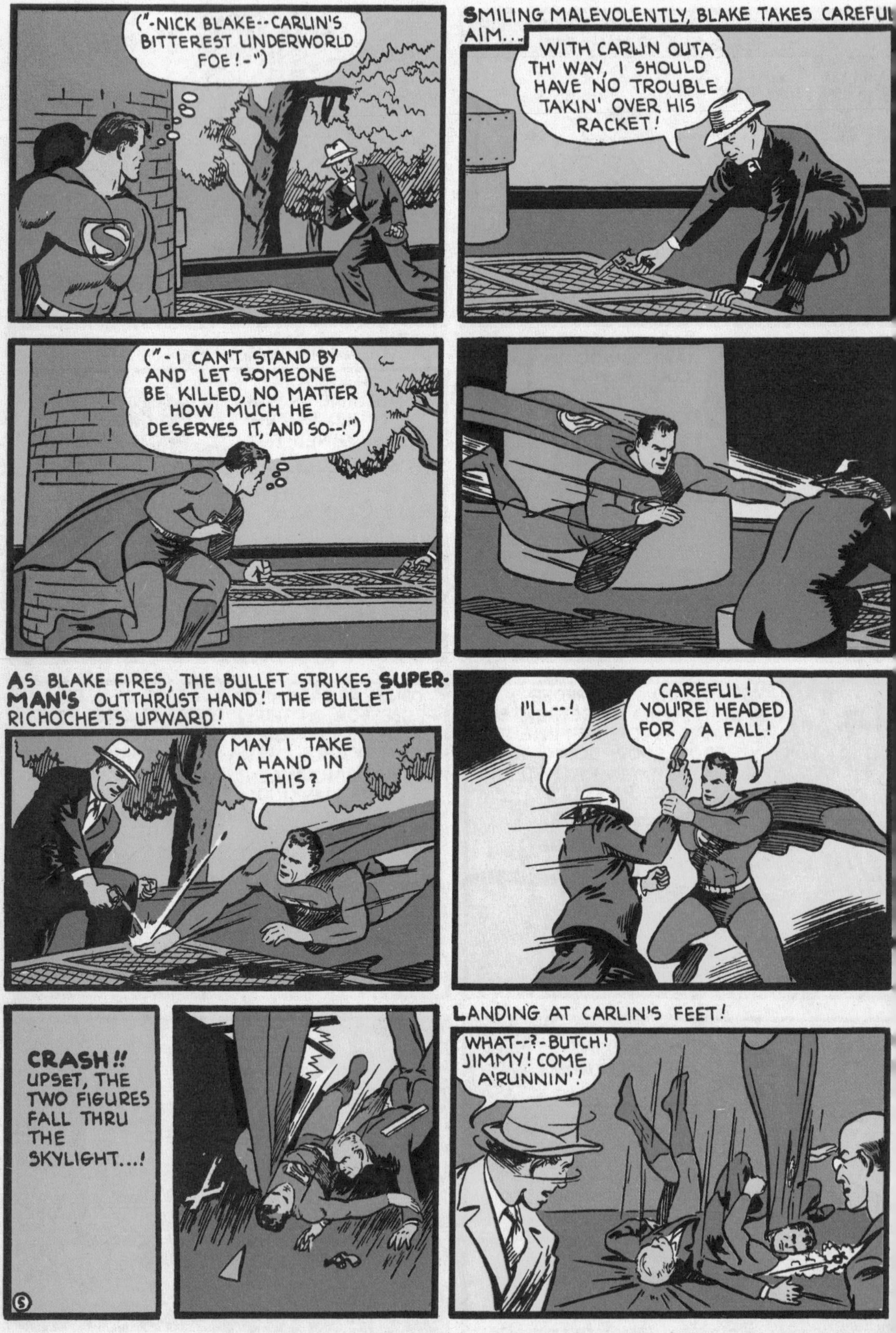
("-NICK BLAKE--CARLIN'S BITTEREST UNDERWORLD FOE!-")
SMILING MALEVOLENTLY, BLAKE TAKES CAREFUL AIM...
WITH CARLIN OUTA TH' WAY, I SHOULD HAVE NO TROUBLE TAKIN' OVER HIS RACKET!
("-I CAN'T STAND BY AND LET SOMEONE BE KILLED, NO MATTER HOW MUCH HE DESERVES IT, AND SO--!")
AS BLAKE FIRES, THE BULLET STRIKES SUPERMAN'S OUTTHRUST HAND! THE BULLET RICHOCHETS UPWARD!
MAY I TAKE A HAND IN THIS?
I'LL--!
CAREFUL! YOU'RE HEADED FOR A FALL!
CRASH!! UPSET, THE TWO FIGURES FALL THRU THE SKYLIGHT...!
LANDING AT CARLIN'S FEET!
WHAT--?-BUTCH! JIMMY! COME A'RUNNIN'!

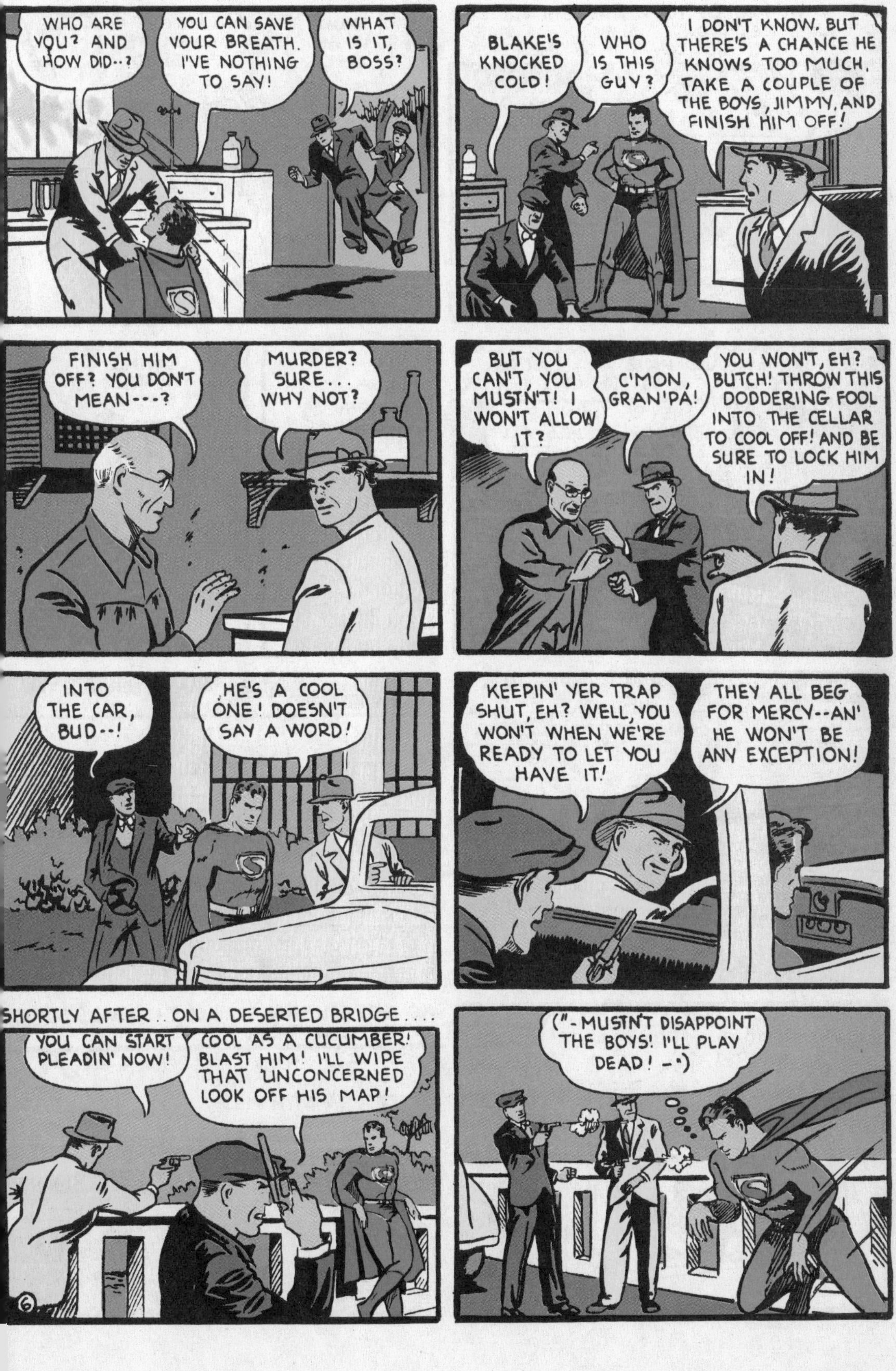
WHO ARE YOU? AND HOW DID--?
YOU CAN SAVE YOUR BREATH. I'VE NOTHING TO SAY!
WHAT IS IT, BOSS?
BLAKE'S KNOCKED COLD!
WHO IS THIS GUY?
I DON'T KNOW. BUT THERE'S A CHANCE HE KNOWS TOO MUCH. TAKE A COUPLE OF THE BOYS, JIMMY, AND FINISH HIM OFF!
FINISH HIM OFF? YOU DON'T MEAN---?
MURDER? SURE... WHY NOT?
BUT YOU CAN'T, YOU MUSTN'T! I WON'T ALLOW IT?
C'MON, GRAN'PA!
YOU WON'T, EH? BUTCH! THROW THIS DODDERING FOOL INTO THE CELLAR TO COOL OFF! AND BE SURE TO LOCK HIM IN!
INTO THE CAR, BUD--!
HE'S A COOL ONE! DOESN'T SAY A WORD!
KEEPIN' YER TRAP SHUT, EH? WELL, YOU WON'T WHEN WE'RE READY TO LET YOU HAVE IT!
THEY ALL BEG FOR MERCY--AN' HE WON'T BE ANY EXCEPTION!
SHORTLY AFTER.. ON A DESERTED BRIDGE....
YOU CAN START PLEADIN' NOW!
COOL AS A CUCUMBER! BLAST HIM! I'LL WIPE THAT UNCONCERNED LOOK OFF HIS MAP!
6
("-MUSTN'T DISAPPOINT THE BOYS! I'LL PLAY DEAD! -")

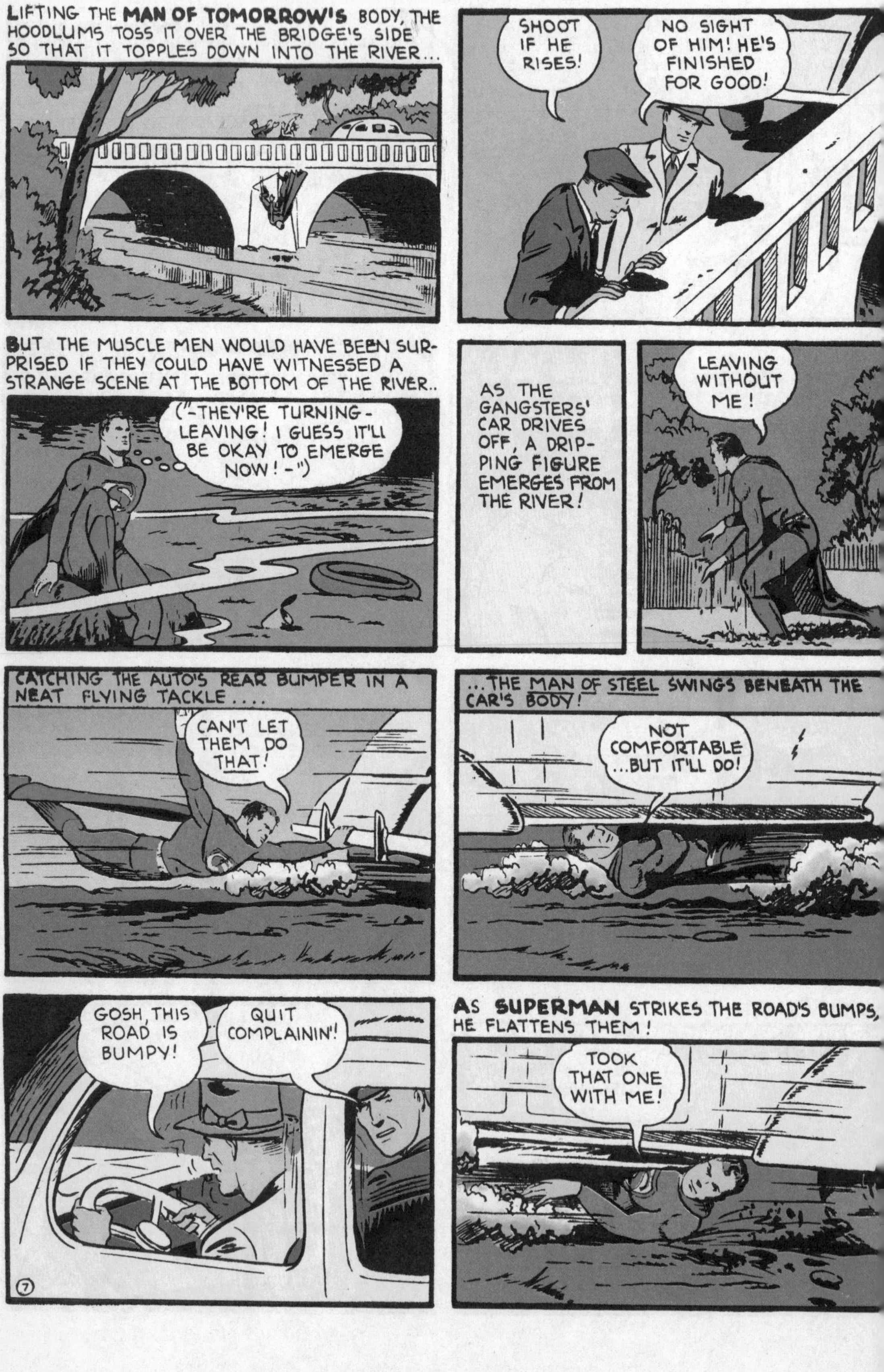
LIFTING THE MAN OF TOMORROW'S BODY, THE HOODLUMS TOSS IT OVER THE BRIDGE'S SIDE SO THAT IT TOPPLES DOWN INTO THE RIVER...
SHOOT IF HE RISES!
NO SIGHT OF HIM! HE'S FINISHED FOR GOOD!
BUT THE MUSCLE MEN WOULD HAVE BEEN SURPRISED IF THEY COULD HAVE WITNESSED A STRANGE SCENE AT THE BOTTOM OF THE RIVER..
("-THEY'RE TURNING-LEAVING! I GUESS IT'LL BE OKAY TO EMERGE NOW! -")
AS THE GANGSTERS' CAR DRIVES OFF, A DRIPPING FIGURE EMERGES FROM THE RIVER!
LEAVING WITHOUT ME!
CATCHING THE AUTO'S REAR BUMPER IN A NEAT FLYING TACKLE....
CAN'T LET THEM DO THAT!
...THE MAN OF STEEL SWINGS BENEATH THE CAR'S BODY!
NOT COMFORTABLE ...BUT IT'LL DO!
GOSH, THIS ROAD IS BUMPY!
QUIT COMPLAININ'!
7
AS SUPERMAN STRIKES THE ROAD'S BUMPS, HE FLATTENS THEM!
TOOK THAT ONE WITH ME!

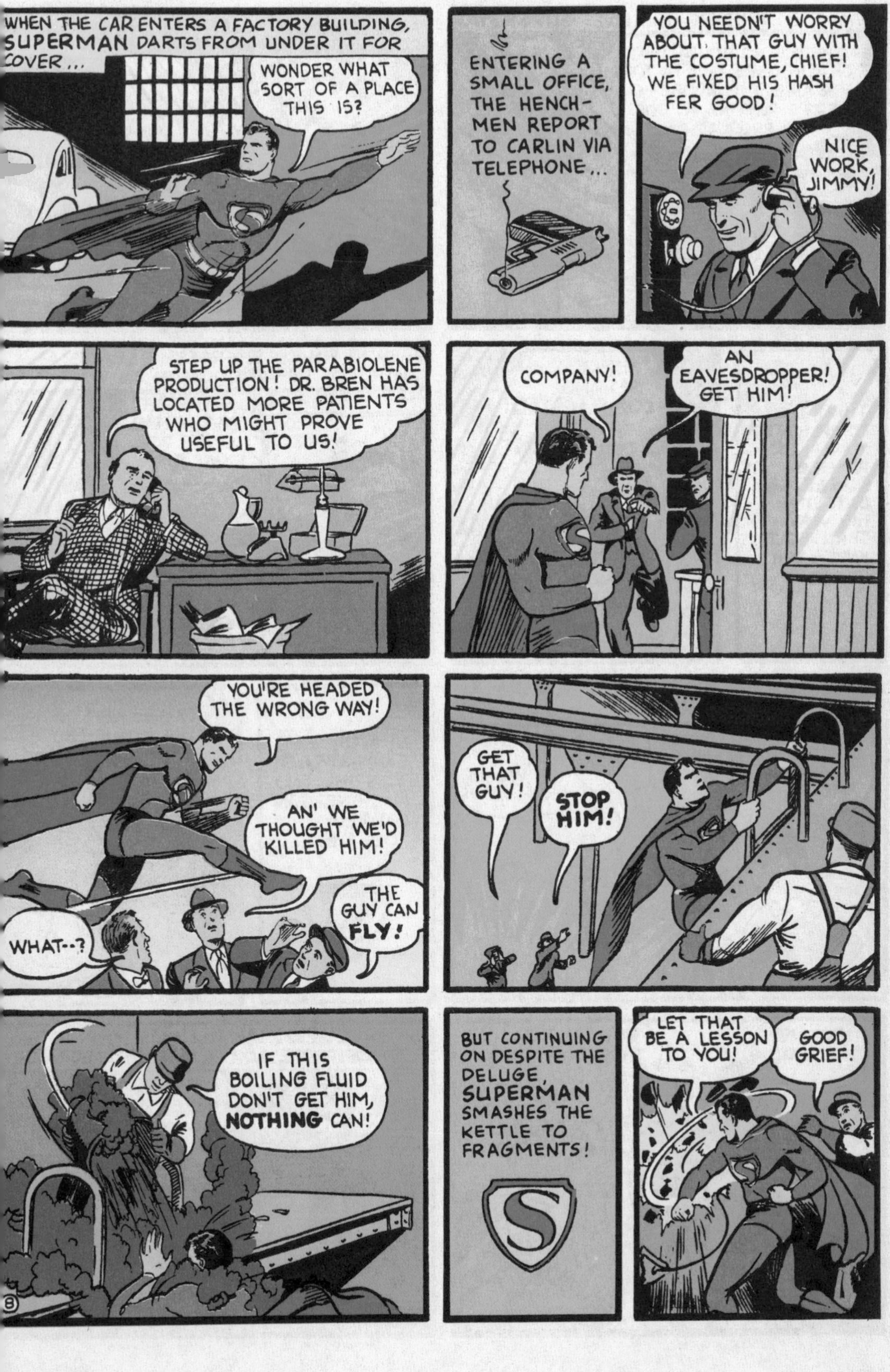
WHEN THE CAR ENTERS A FACTORY BUILDING, SUPERMAN DARTS FROM UNDER IT FOR COVER...
WONDER WHAT SORT OF A PLACE THIS IS?
ENTERING A SMALL OFFICE, THE HENCH-MEN REPORT TO CARLIN VIA TELEPHONE...
YOU NEEDN'T WORRY ABOUT THAT GUY WITH THE COSTUME, CHIEF! WE FIXED HIS HASH FER GOOD!
NICE WORK, JIMMY!
STEP UP THE PARABIOLENE PRODUCTION! DR. BREN HAS LOCATED MORE PATIENTS WHO MIGHT PROVE USEFUL TO US!
COMPANY!
AN EAVESDROPPER! GET HIM!
YOU'RE HEADED THE WRONG WAY!
AN' WE THOUGHT WE'D KILLED HIM!
WHAT--?
THE GUY CAN FLY!
GET THAT GUY!
STOP HIM!
IF THIS BOILING FLUID DON'T GET HIM, NOTHING CAN!
BUT CONTINUING ON DESPITE THE DELUGE, SUPERMAN SMASHES THE KETTLE TO FRAGMENTS!
LET THAT BE A LESSON TO YOU!
GOOD GRIEF!

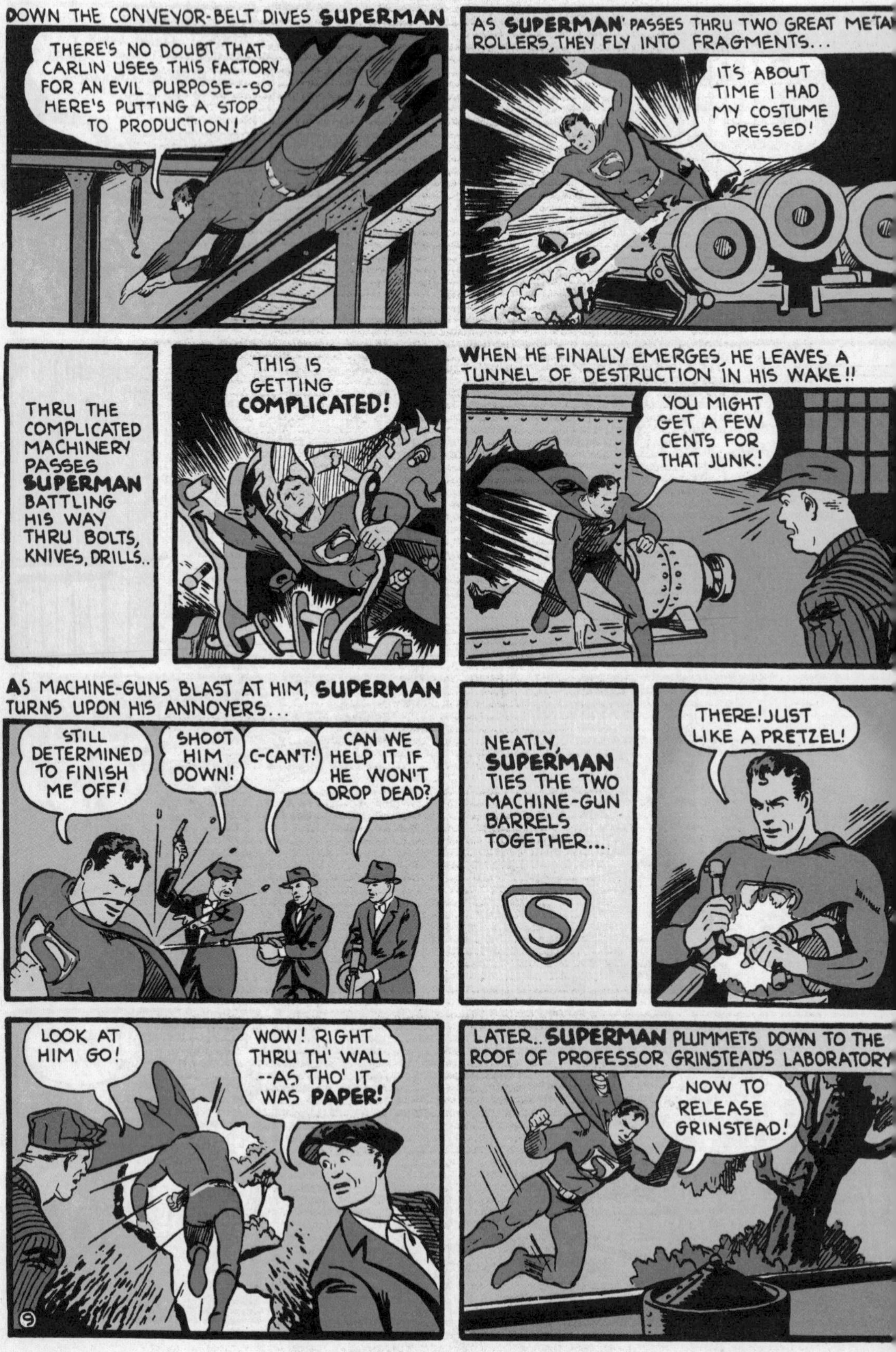
DOWN THE CONVEYOR-BELT DIVES SUPERMAN
THERE'S NO DOUBT THAT CARLIN USES THIS FACTORY FOR AN EVIL PURPOSE--SO HERE'S PUTTING A STOP TO PRODUCTION!
AS SUPERMAN PASSES THRU TWO GREAT METAL ROLLERS, THEY FLY INTO FRAGMENTS...
IT'S ABOUT TIME I HAD MY COSTUME PRESSED!
THRU THE COMPLICATED MACHINERY PASSES SUPERMAN BATTLING HIS WAY THRU BOLTS, KNIVES, DRILLS..
THIS IS GETTING COMPLICATED!
WHEN HE FINALLY EMERGES, HE LEAVES A TUNNEL OF DESTRUCTION IN HIS WAKE!!
YOU MIGHT GET A FEW CENTS FOR THAT JUNK!
AS MACHINE-GUNS BLAST AT HIM, SUPERMAN TURNS UPON HIS ANNOYERS...
STILL DETERMINED TO FINISH ME OFF!
SHOOT HIM DOWN!
C-CAN'T!
CAN WE HELP IT IF HE WON'T DROP DEAD?
NEATLY, SUPERMAN TIES THE TWO MACHINE-GUN BARRELS TOGETHER...
THERE! JUST LIKE A PRETZEL!
LOOK AT HIM GO!
WOW! RIGHT THRU TH' WALL --AS THO' IT WAS PAPER!
9
LATER.. SUPERMAN PLUMMETS DOWN TO THE ROOF OF PROFESSOR GRINSTEAD'S LABORATORY
NOW TO RELEASE GRINSTEAD!

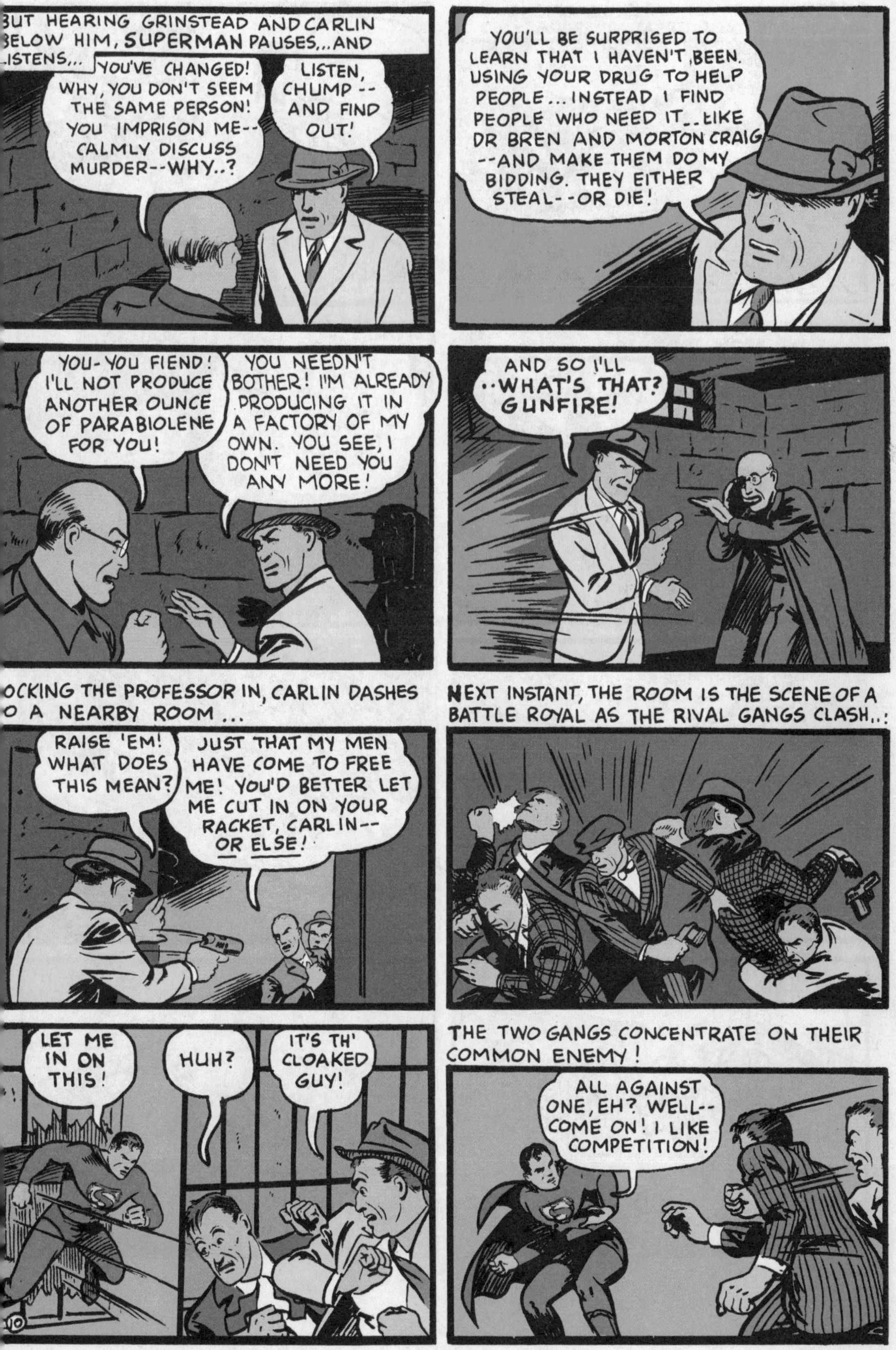

BUT HEARING GRINSTEAD AND CARLIN BELOW HIM, SUPERMAN PAUSES... AND LISTENS...
YOU'VE CHANGED! WHY, YOU DON'T SEEM THE SAME PERSON! YOU IMPRISON ME-- CALMLY DISCUSS MURDER--WHY..?
LISTEN, CHUMP -- AND FIND OUT!
YOU'LL BE SURPRISED TO LEARN THAT I HAVEN'T BEEN USING YOUR DRUG TO HELP PEOPLE... INSTEAD I FIND PEOPLE WHO NEED IT..LIKE DR BREN AND MORTON CRAIG --AND MAKE THEM DO MY BIDDING. THEY EITHER STEAL--OR DIE!
YOU-YOU FIEND! I'LL NOT PRODUCE ANOTHER OUNCE OF PARABIOLENE FOR YOU!
YOU NEEDN'T BOTHER! I'M ALREADY PRODUCING IT IN A FACTORY OF MY OWN. YOU SEE, I DON'T NEED YOU ANY MORE!
AND SO I'LL ..WHAT'S THAT? GUNFIRE!
LOCKING THE PROFESSOR IN, CARLIN DASHES TO A NEARBY ROOM...
RAISE 'EM! WHAT DOES THIS MEAN?
JUST THAT MY MEN HAVE COME TO FREE ME! YOU'D BETTER LET ME CUT IN ON YOUR RACKET, CARLIN-- OR ELSE!
NEXT INSTANT, THE ROOM IS THE SCENE OF A BATTLE ROYAL AS THE RIVAL GANGS CLASH..:
LET ME IN ON THIS!
HUH?
IT'S TH' CLOAKED GUY!
10
THE TWO GANGS CONCENTRATE ON THEIR COMMON ENEMY!
ALL AGAINST ONE, EH? WELL-- COME ON! I LIKE COMPETITION!

SUPERMAN EASILY HURLS HIS OPPONENTS BACK DESPITE THEIR GREAT NUMBERS ...

PLEASE!--THIS IS TOO SIMPLE!

UPSYDAISY!

WITHIN MOMENTS THE GANGSTERS ARE ALL DANGLING FROM TROPHIES...

WHAT AN INSPIRING PICTURE THIS WOULD MAKE! IF I ONLY HAD MY CANDID CAMERA HERE!

WITHIN GRINSTEAD'S LABORATORY...

I TRIED TO CREATE A BLESSING FOR MANKIND --- BUT SUCCEEDED ONLY IN CREATING A CURSE!

THERE-IS-ONLY-ONE-HONORABLE-WAY-TO-PAY-FOR-MY-CRIME!

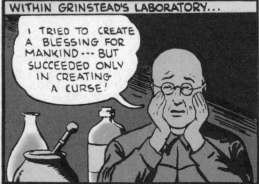

GRINSTEAD --DYING!

I'VE GOT TO GET HIM TO A HOSPITAL IN A HURRY!

WHEN **SUPERMAN** REACHES THE WAYSIDE HOSPITAL...

BUT WE CAN'T DO ANYTHING FOR GRINSTEAD! HE'S ALREADY DEAD!

PLEASE DO AS I SAY! PUT HIM IN AN ARTIFICIAL FEVER MACHINE AND KEEP THE TEMPERATURE HIGH UNTIL I RETURN!

MINUTES LATER, **SUPERMAN** SPRINGS INTO DR. BREN'S OFFICE

WHO..?

NEVER MIND THE FORMALITIES! PROFESSOR GRINSTEAD IS DYING! I NEED SOME PARABIOLENE!

GRINSTEAD DYING!? WAIT! TAKE ME WITH YOU!

SWELL!

THIS-- THIS IS FANTASTIC!

YOU'VE GOT TO SAVE HIS LIFE, DR. BREN! THE WORLD NEEDS HIM!

LATER--AT THE HOSPITAL, DR. BREN ADMINISTERS THE DRUG TO GRINSTEAD...

SHORTLY AFTER THE PROFESSOR'S EYES FLUTTER..

IT'S A MIRACLE! HE'S ALIVE!

A MIRACLE OF HIS OWN MAKING--HE DISCOVERED THIS MARVELOUS DRUG!

ONE LAST TASK! I STILL HAVE TO MAKE CARLIN RELEASE HIS VICTIMS!

WITHIN THE LABORATORY, CARLIN SUCCEEDS IN FREEING HIMSELF

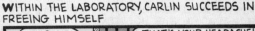

HELP US DOWN!

THAT'S YOUR HEADACHE! I'M CLEARIN' OUTA HERE WHILE TH' GETTIN'S GOOD!

12

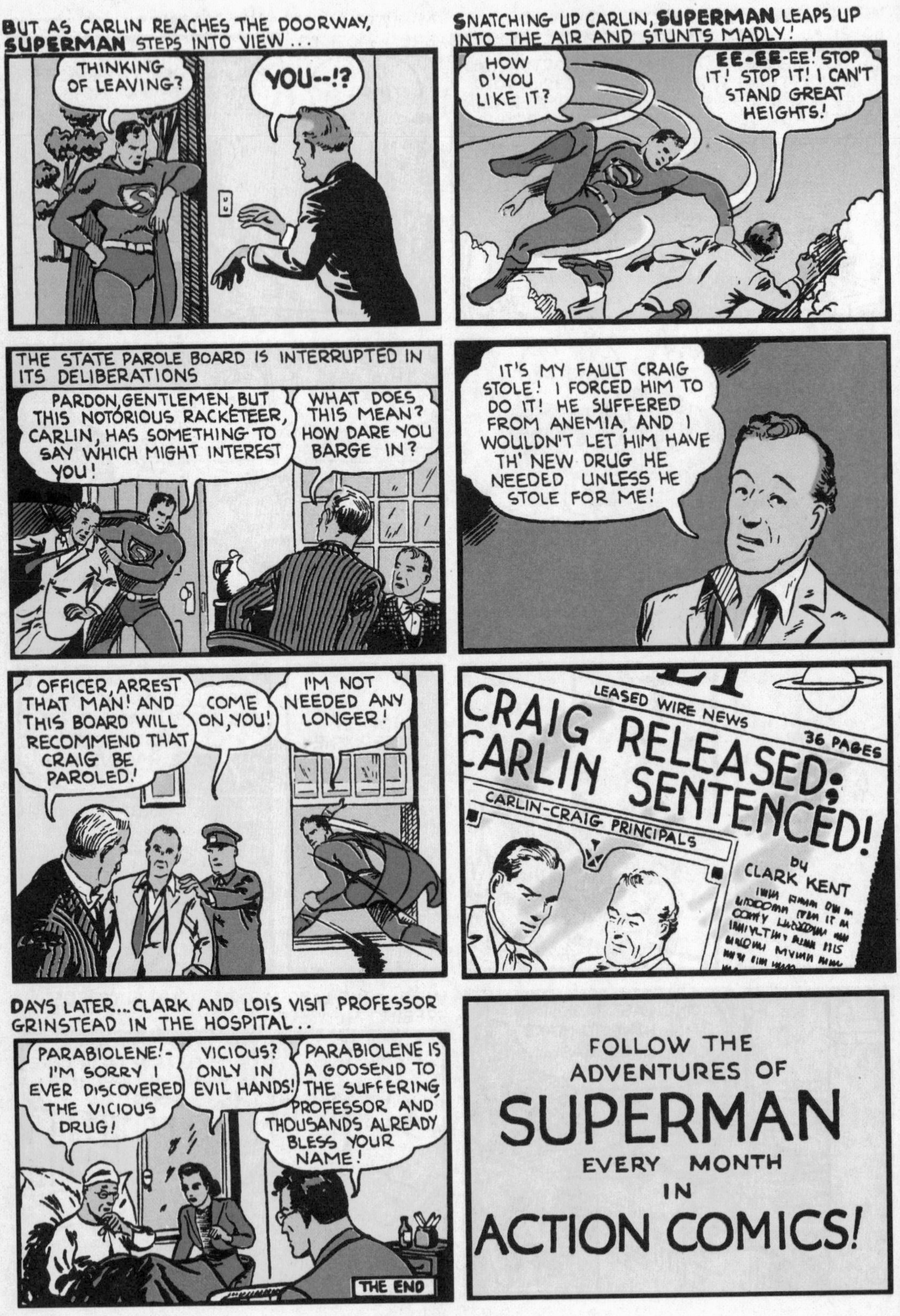
BUT AS CARLIN REACHES THE DOORWAY, SUPERMAN STEPS INTO VIEW...
THINKING OF LEAVING?
YOU--!?
SNATCHING UP CARLIN, SUPERMAN LEAPS UP INTO THE AIR AND STUNTS MADLY!
HOW D'YOU LIKE IT?
EE-EE-EE! STOP IT! STOP IT! I CAN'T STAND GREAT HEIGHTS!
THE STATE PAROLE BOARD IS INTERRUPTED IN ITS DELIBERATIONS
PARDON, GENTLEMEN, BUT THIS NOTORIOUS RACKETEER, CARLIN, HAS SOMETHING TO SAY WHICH MIGHT INTEREST YOU!
WHAT DOES THIS MEAN? HOW DARE YOU BARGE IN?
IT'S MY FAULT CRAIG STOLE! I FORCED HIM TO DO IT! HE SUFFERED FROM ANEMIA, AND I WOULDN'T LET HIM HAVE TH' NEW DRUG HE NEEDED UNLESS HE STOLE FOR ME!
OFFICER, ARREST THAT MAN! AND THIS BOARD WILL RECOMMEND THAT CRAIG BE PAROLED!
COME ON, YOU!
I'M NOT NEEDED ANY LONGER!
LEASED WIRE NEWS
36 PAGES
CRAIG RELEASED; CARLIN SENTENCED!
CARLIN-CRAIG PRINCIPALS
by CLARK KENT
DAYS LATER... CLARK AND LOIS VISIT PROFESSOR GRINSTEAD IN THE HOSPITAL..
PARABIOLENE!- I'M SORRY I EVER DISCOVERED THE VICIOUS DRUG!
VICIOUS? ONLY IN EVIL HANDS!
PARABIOLENE IS A GODSEND TO THE SUFFERING PROFESSOR AND THOUSANDS ALREADY BLESS YOUR NAME!
THE END
FOLLOW THE ADVENTURES OF SUPERMAN EVERY MONTH IN ACTION COMICS!

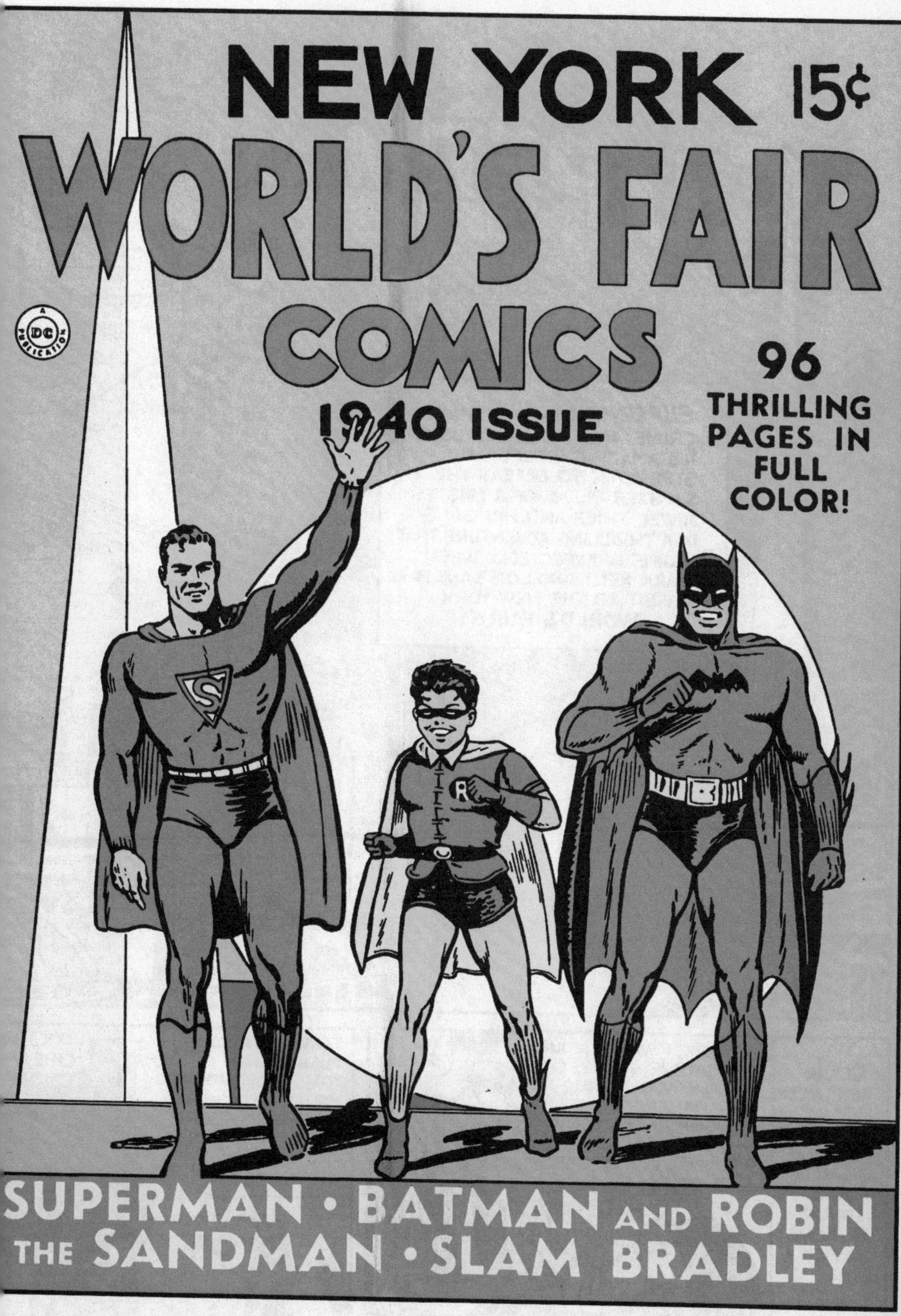

NEW YORK
15¢
WORLD'S FAIR
COMICS
A DC PUBLICATION
1940 ISSUE
96 THRILLING PAGES IN FULL COLOR!
SUPERMAN • BATMAN AND ROBIN
THE SANDMAN • SLAM BRADLEY

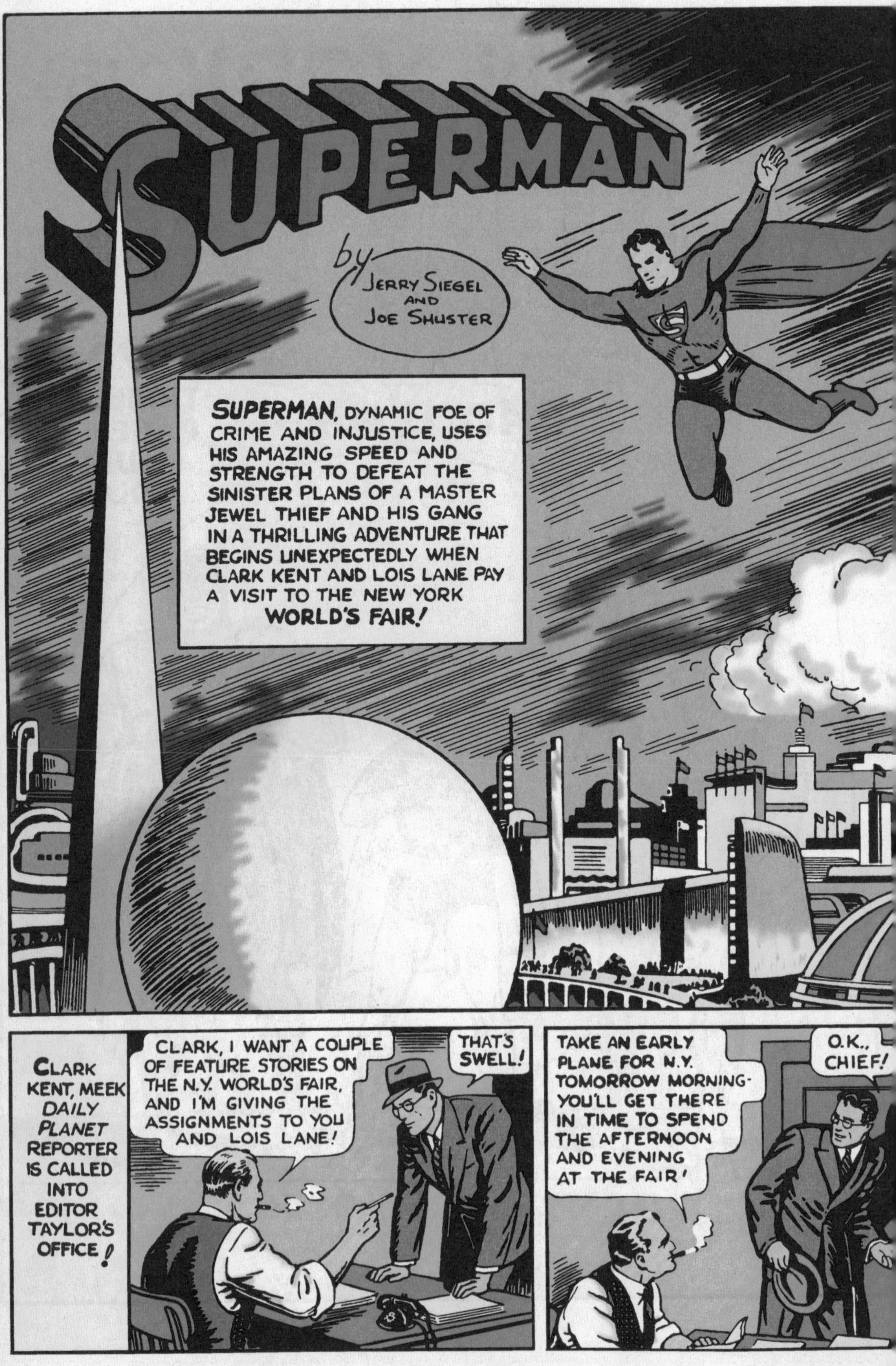
SUPERMAN
by JERRY SIEGEL AND JOE SHUSTER
SUPERMAN, DYNAMIC FOE OF CRIME AND INJUSTICE, USES HIS AMAZING SPEED AND STRENGTH TO DEFEAT THE SINISTER PLANS OF A MASTER JEWEL THIEF AND HIS GANG IN A THRILLING ADVENTURE THAT BEGINS UNEXPECTEDLY WHEN CLARK KENT AND LOIS LANE PAY A VISIT TO THE NEW YORK WORLD'S FAIR!
CLARK KENT, MEEK DAILY PLANET REPORTER IS CALLED INTO EDITOR TAYLOR'S OFFICE!
CLARK, I WANT A COUPLE OF FEATURE STORIES ON THE N.Y. WORLD'S FAIR, AND I'M GIVING THE ASSIGNMENTS TO YOU AND LOIS LANE!
THAT'S SWELL!
TAKE AN EARLY PLANE FOR N.Y. TOMORROW MORNING-YOU'LL GET THERE IN TIME TO SPEND THE AFTERNOON AND EVENING AT THE FAIR!
O.K., CHIEF!

CLARK, DELIGHTED AT THE PROSPECT OF GOING TO THE FAIR WITH LOIS, RUSHES OUT TO TELL HER THE NEWS!

ISN'T THAT GREAT, LOIS? WE'LL COVER THIS ASSIGNMENT TOGETHER! TAYLOR WANTS YOU TO GIVE THE FEMININE SLANT ON THE FAIR!

I DON'T SEE WHY TAYLOR HAD TO SEND CLARK ALONG--I COULD HANDLE THE STORY WITHOUT HIS HELP! ANYWAY, THIS WILL GIVE ME A CHANCE TO SHOW HIM UP!

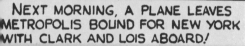

NEXT MORNING, A PLANE LEAVES METROPOLIS BOUND FOR NEW YORK WITH CLARK AND LOIS ABOARD!

THIS SEEMS MORE LIKE A HOLIDAY TRIP THAN AN ACTUAL WORKING ASSIGNMENT, LOIS!

HERE WE ARE AT LA GUARDIA FIELD!

A CAB WILL GET US TO THE FAIR IN A JIFFY!

A FEW MINUTES LATER, THEY ARRIVE AT THE FAIR!

ISN'T IT MARVELOUS?

THE FAIR IS BETTER THAN EVER, THIS YEAR!

CLARK AND LOIS ENJOY EVERY MINUTE OF THEIR VISIT, AS THEY GO THROUGH MANY OF THE FAIR'S COLORFUL BUILDINGS--

THERE CERTAINLY ARE A LOT OF FASCINATING SIGHTS AND EXHIBITS FOR US TO WRITE ABOUT

YES-- AND I READ THAT ONE OF THE WORLD'S LARGEST PRECIOUS JEWELS, THE FAMOUS MADRAS EMERALD, HAS JUST ARRIVED FROM INDIA AND WILL BE PRESENTED FOR EXHIBITION HERE AT THE HOUSE OF JEWELS, TONIGHT AT 8 O'CLOCK!

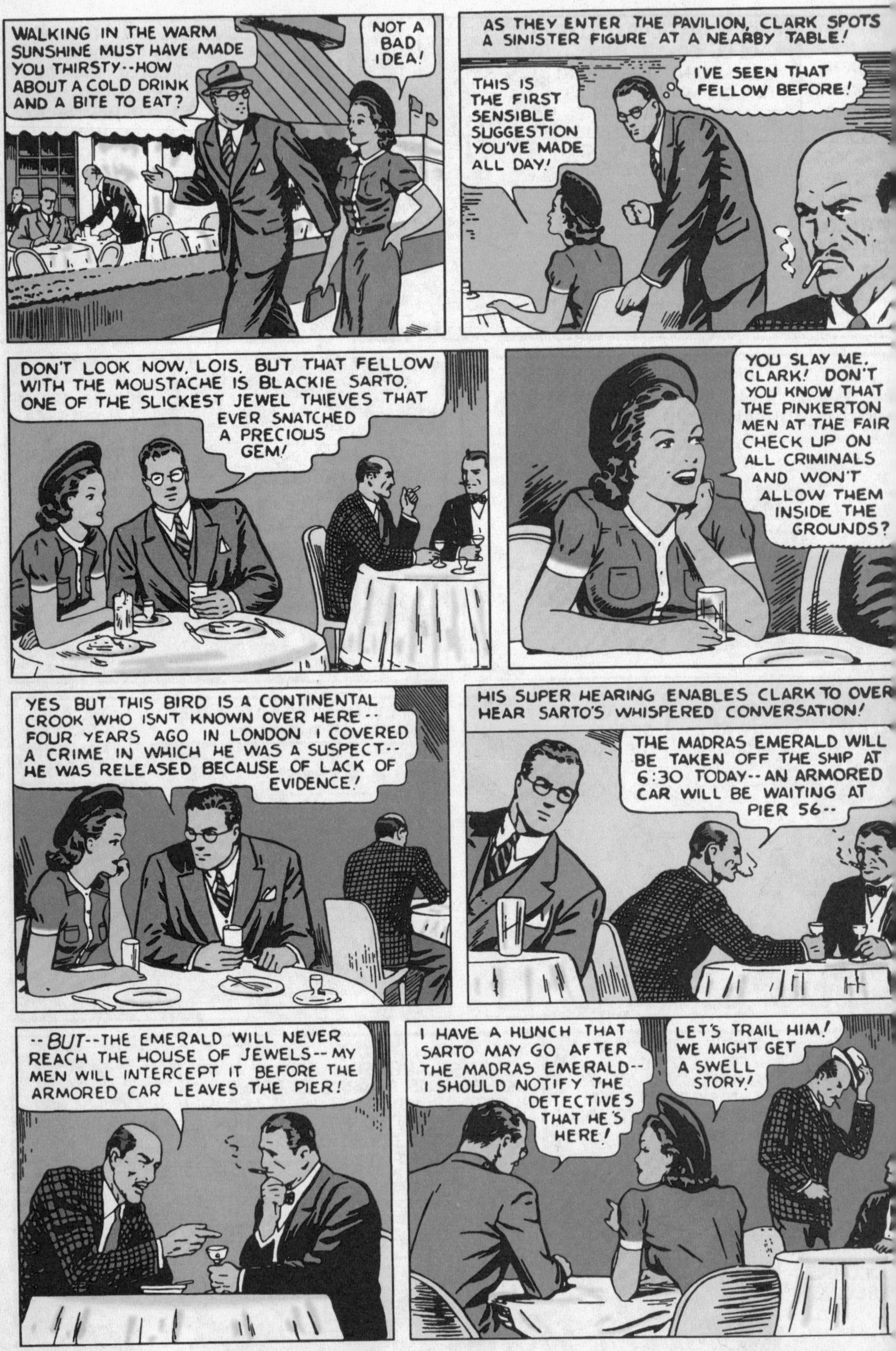
WALKING IN THE WARM SUNSHINE MUST HAVE MADE YOU THIRSTY--HOW ABOUT A COLD DRINK AND A BITE TO EAT?
NOT A BAD IDEA!
AS THEY ENTER THE PAVILION, CLARK SPOTS A SINISTER FIGURE AT A NEARBY TABLE!
THIS IS THE FIRST SENSIBLE SUGGESTION YOU'VE MADE ALL DAY!
I'VE SEEN THAT FELLOW BEFORE!
DON'T LOOK NOW, LOIS, BUT THAT FELLOW WITH THE MOUSTACHE IS BLACKIE SARTO, ONE OF THE SLICKEST JEWEL THIEVES THAT EVER SNATCHED A PRECIOUS GEM!
YOU SLAY ME, CLARK! DON'T YOU KNOW THAT THE PINKERTON MEN AT THE FAIR CHECK UP ON ALL CRIMINALS AND WON'T ALLOW THEM INSIDE THE GROUNDS?
YES BUT THIS BIRD IS A CONTINENTAL CROOK WHO ISN'T KNOWN OVER HERE--FOUR YEARS AGO IN LONDON I COVERED A CRIME IN WHICH HE WAS A SUSPECT--HE WAS RELEASED BECAUSE OF LACK OF EVIDENCE!
HIS SUPER HEARING ENABLES CLARK TO OVERHEAR SARTO'S WHISPERED CONVERSATION!
THE MADRAS EMERALD WILL BE TAKEN OFF THE SHIP AT 6:30 TODAY--AN ARMORED CAR WILL BE WAITING AT PIER 56--
--*BUT*--THE EMERALD WILL NEVER REACH THE HOUSE OF JEWELS--MY MEN WILL INTERCEPT IT BEFORE THE ARMORED CAR LEAVES THE PIER!
I HAVE A HUNCH THAT SARTO MAY GO AFTER THE MADRAS EMERALD--I SHOULD NOTIFY THE DETECTIVES THAT HE'S HERE!
LET'S TRAIL HIM! WE MIGHT GET A SWELL STORY!

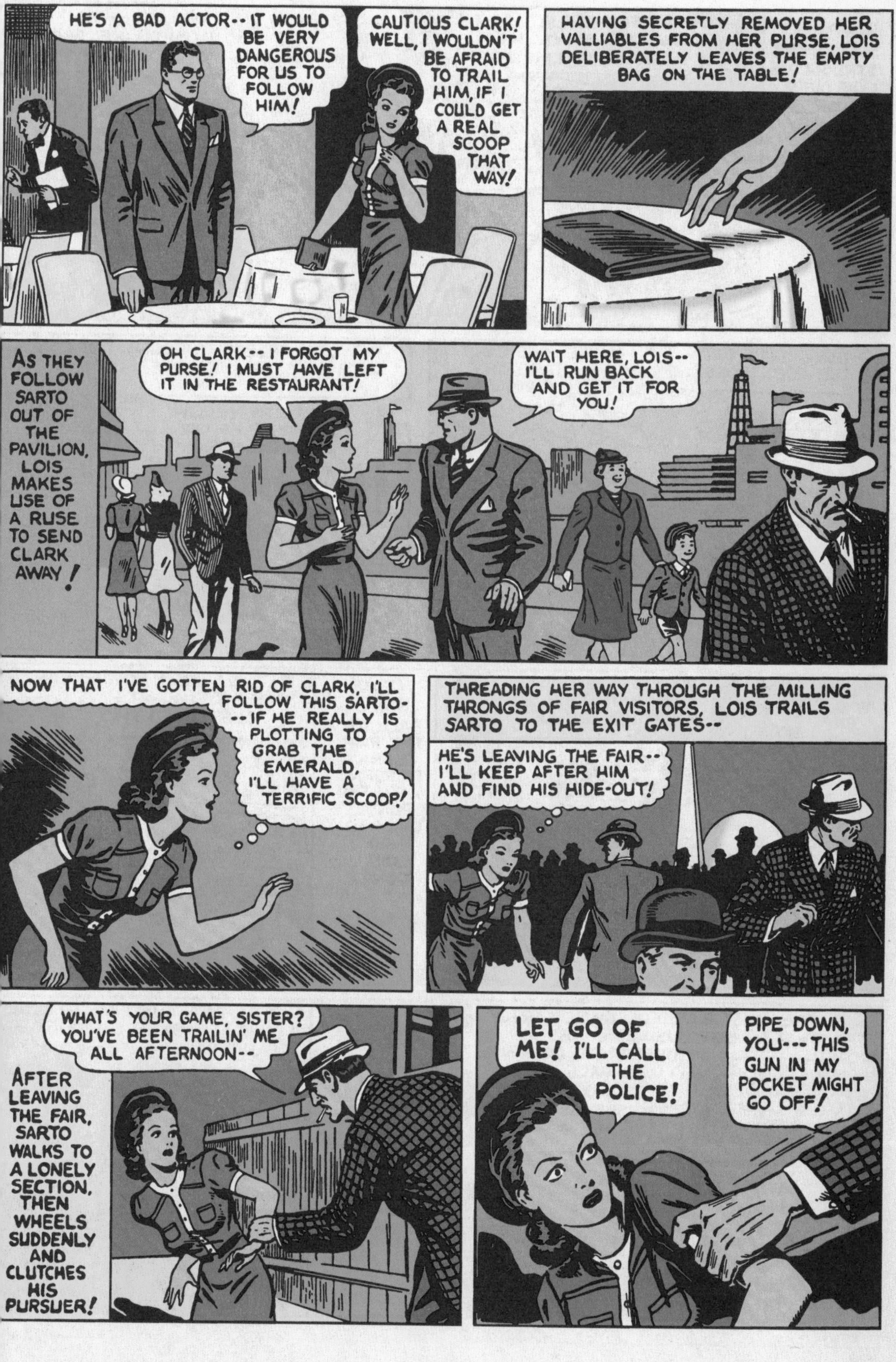

HE'S A BAD ACTOR-- IT WOULD BE VERY DANGEROUS FOR US TO FOLLOW HIM!
CAUTIOUS CLARK! WELL, I WOULDN'T BE AFRAID TO TRAIL HIM, IF I COULD GET A REAL SCOOP THAT WAY!
HAVING SECRETLY REMOVED HER VALLIABLES FROM HER PURSE, LOIS DELIBERATELY LEAVES THE EMPTY BAG ON THE TABLE!
AS THEY FOLLOW SARTO OUT OF THE PAVILION, LOIS MAKES USE OF A RUSE TO SEND CLARK AWAY!
OH CLARK-- I FORGOT MY PURSE! I MUST HAVE LEFT IT IN THE RESTAURANT!
WAIT HERE, LOIS-- I'LL RUN BACK AND GET IT FOR YOU!
NOW THAT I'VE GOTTEN RID OF CLARK, I'LL FOLLOW THIS SARTO- --IF HE REALLY IS PLOTTING TO GRAB THE EMERALD, I'LL HAVE A TERRIFIC SCOOP!
THREADING HER WAY THROUGH THE MILLING THRONGS OF FAIR VISITORS, LOIS TRAILS SARTO TO THE EXIT GATES--
HE'S LEAVING THE FAIR-- I'LL KEEP AFTER HIM AND FIND HIS HIDE-OUT!
AFTER LEAVING THE FAIR, SARTO WALKS TO A LONELY SECTION, THEN WHEELS SUDDENLY AND CLUTCHES HIS PURSUER!
WHAT'S YOUR GAME, SISTER? YOU'VE BEEN TRAILIN' ME ALL AFTERNOON--
LET GO OF ME! I'LL CALL THE POLICE!
PIPE DOWN, YOU--- THIS GUN IN MY POCKET MIGHT GO OFF!

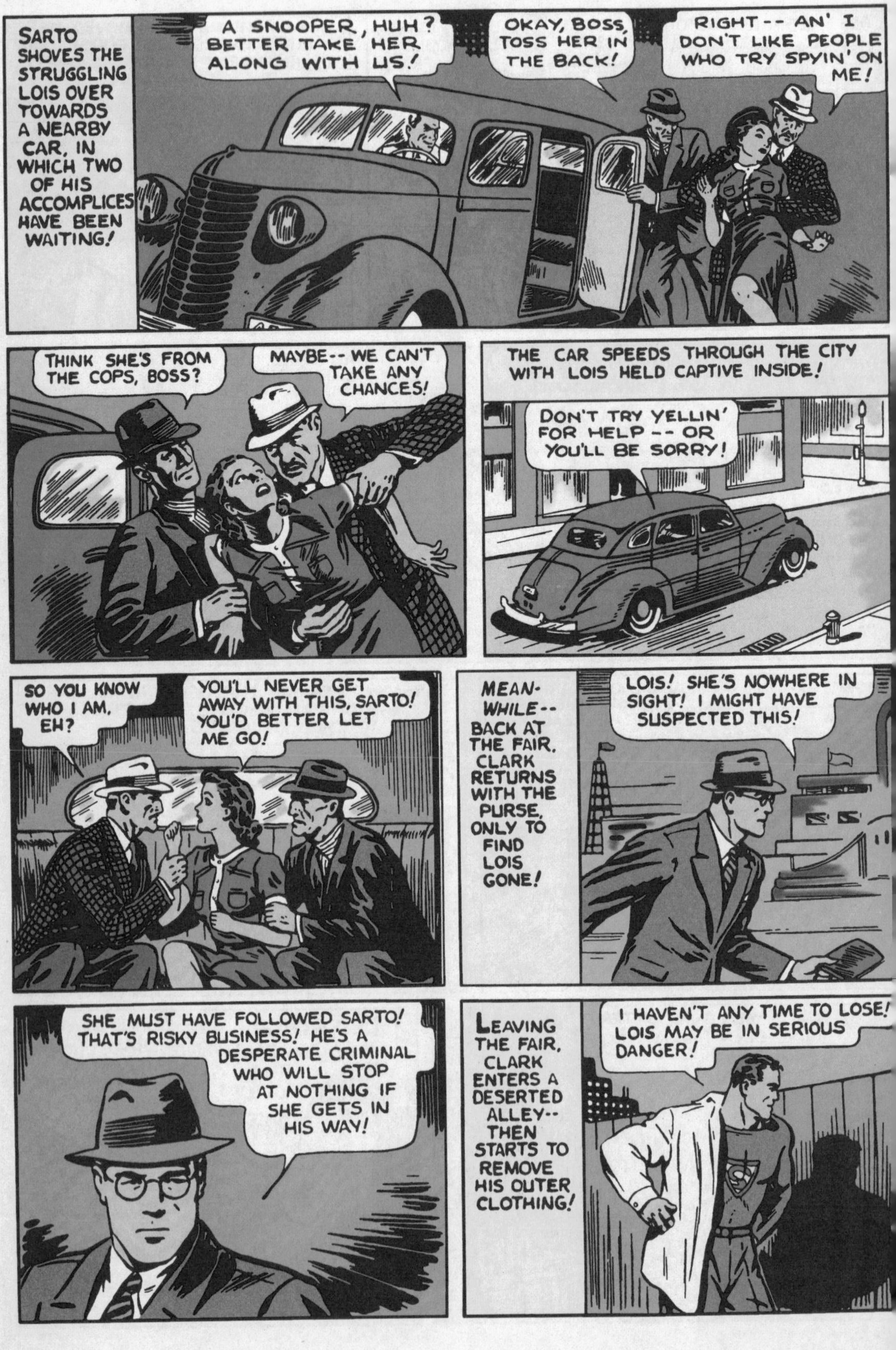
SARTO SHOVES THE STRUGGLING LOIS OVER TOWARDS A NEARBY CAR, IN WHICH TWO OF HIS ACCOMPLICES HAVE BEEN WAITING!
A SNOOPER, HUH? BETTER TAKE HER ALONG WITH US!
OKAY, BOSS, TOSS HER IN THE BACK!
RIGHT -- AN' I DON'T LIKE PEOPLE WHO TRY SPYIN' ON ME!
THINK SHE'S FROM THE COPS, BOSS?
MAYBE -- WE CAN'T TAKE ANY CHANCES!
THE CAR SPEEDS THROUGH THE CITY WITH LOIS HELD CAPTIVE INSIDE!
DON'T TRY YELLIN' FOR HELP -- OR YOU'LL BE SORRY!
SO YOU KNOW WHO I AM, EH?
YOU'LL NEVER GET AWAY WITH THIS, SARTO! YOU'D BETTER LET ME GO!
MEAN-WHILE -- BACK AT THE FAIR, CLARK RETURNS WITH THE PURSE, ONLY TO FIND LOIS GONE!
LOIS! SHE'S NOWHERE IN SIGHT! I MIGHT HAVE SUSPECTED THIS!
SHE MUST HAVE FOLLOWED SARTO! THAT'S RISKY BUSINESS! HE'S A DESPERATE CRIMINAL WHO WILL STOP AT NOTHING IF SHE GETS IN HIS WAY!
LEAVING THE FAIR, CLARK ENTERS A DESERTED ALLEY -- THEN STARTS TO REMOVE HIS OUTER CLOTHING!
I HAVEN'T ANY TIME TO LOSE! LOIS MAY BE IN SERIOUS DANGER!

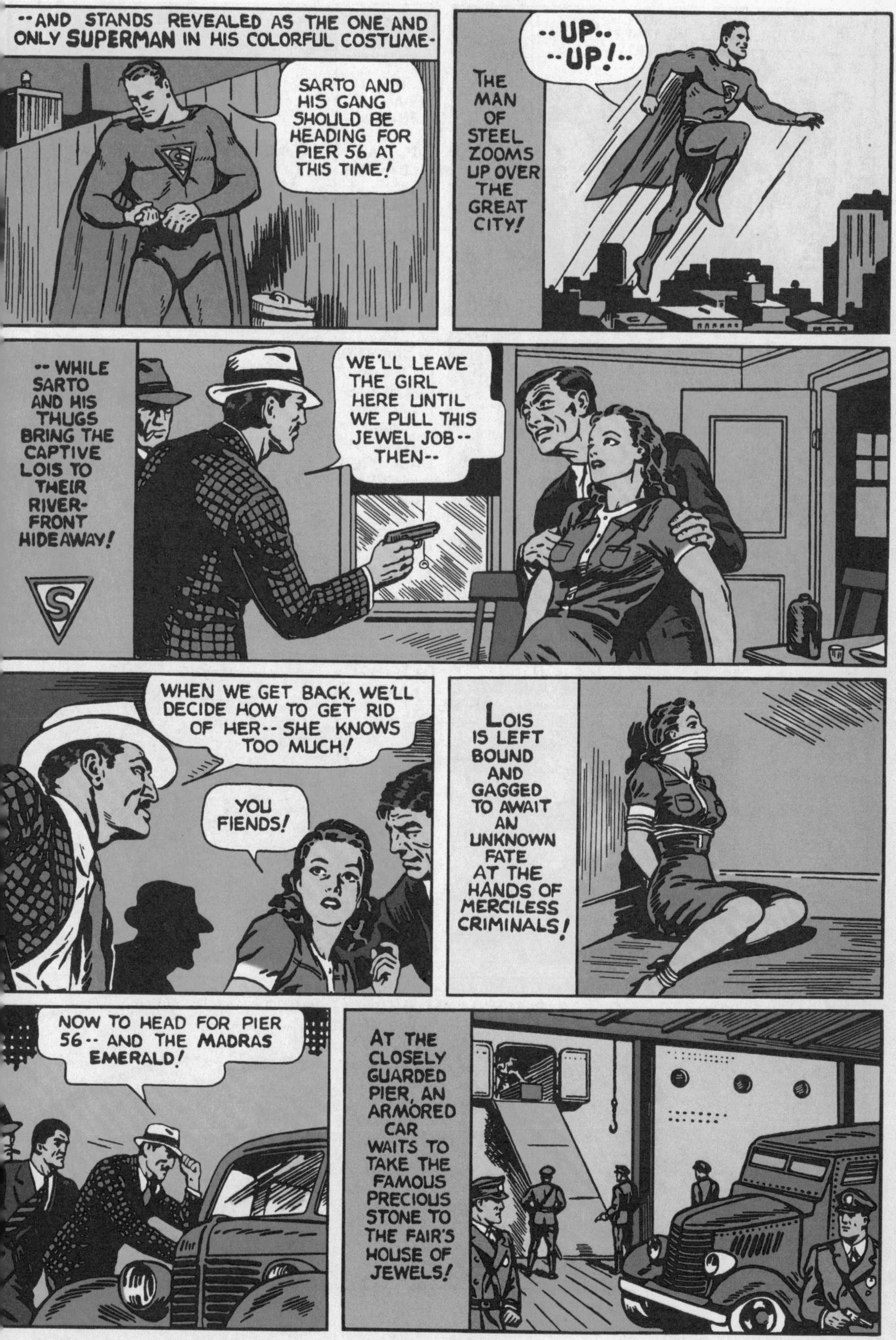
--AND STANDS REVEALED AS THE ONE AND ONLY SUPERMAN IN HIS COLORFUL COSTUME-
SARTO AND HIS GANG SHOULD BE HEADING FOR PIER 56 AT THIS TIME!
--UP.. --UP!--
THE MAN OF STEEL ZOOMS UP OVER THE GREAT CITY!
--WHILE SARTO AND HIS THUGS BRING THE CAPTIVE LOIS TO THEIR RIVER-FRONT HIDEAWAY!
WE'LL LEAVE THE GIRL HERE UNTIL WE PULL THIS JEWEL JOB-- THEN--
WHEN WE GET BACK, WE'LL DECIDE HOW TO GET RID OF HER-- SHE KNOWS TOO MUCH!
YOU FIENDS!
LOIS IS LEFT BOUND AND GAGGED TO AWAIT AN UNKNOWN FATE AT THE HANDS OF MERCILESS CRIMINALS!
NOW TO HEAD FOR PIER 56-- AND THE MADRAS EMERALD!
AT THE CLOSELY GUARDED PIER, AN ARMORED CAR WAITS TO TAKE THE FAMOUS PRECIOUS STONE TO THE FAIR'S HOUSE OF JEWELS!

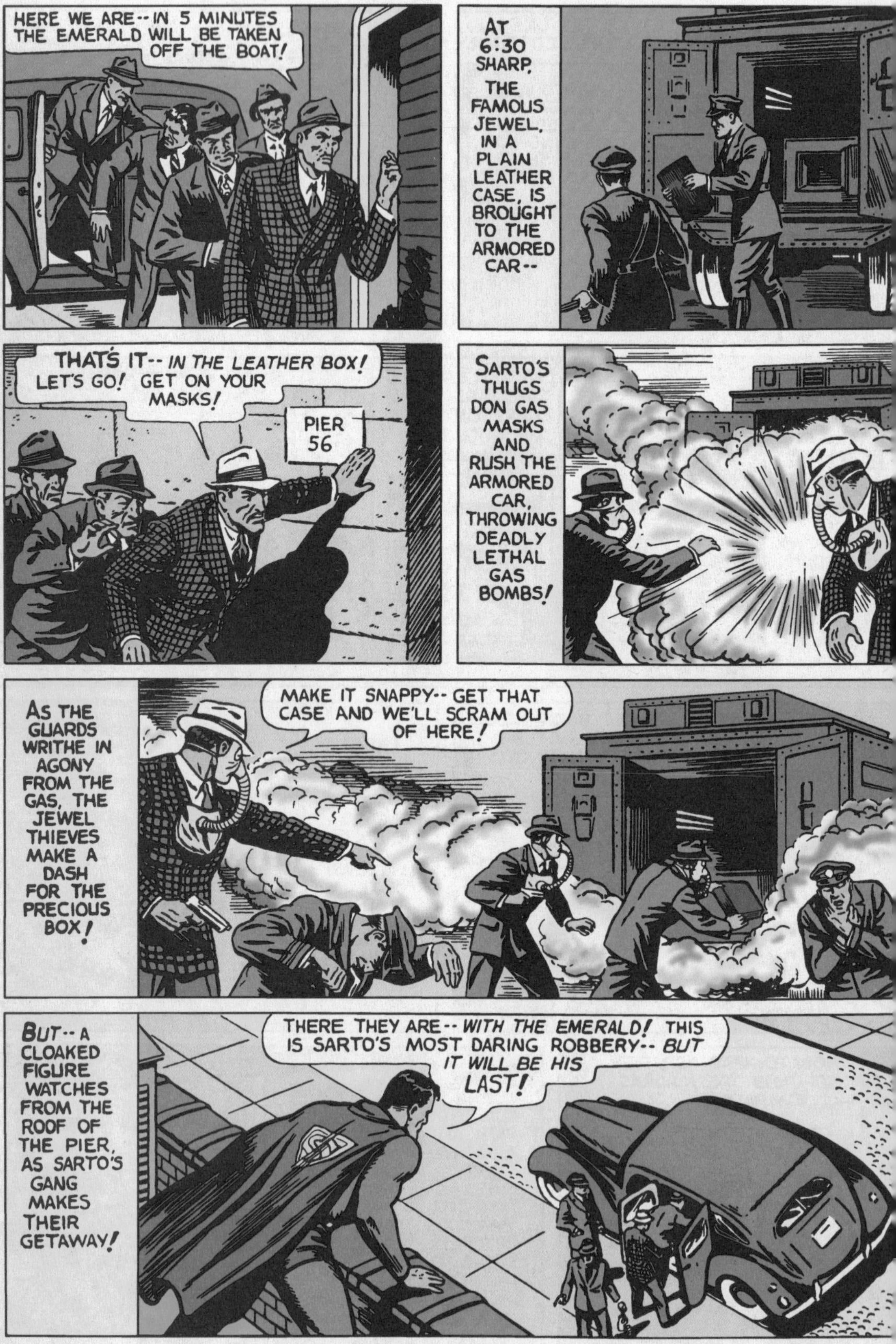
HERE WE ARE--IN 5 MINUTES THE EMERALD WILL BE TAKEN OFF THE BOAT!
AT 6:30 SHARP, THE FAMOUS JEWEL, IN A PLAIN LEATHER CASE, IS BROUGHT TO THE ARMORED CAR--
THAT'S IT-- IN THE LEATHER BOX! LET'S GO! GET ON YOUR MASKS!
PIER 56
SARTO'S THUGS DON GAS MASKS AND RUSH THE ARMORED CAR, THROWING DEADLY LETHAL GAS BOMBS!
AS THE GUARDS WRITHE IN AGONY FROM THE GAS, THE JEWEL THIEVES MAKE A DASH FOR THE PRECIOUS BOX!
MAKE IT SNAPPY-- GET THAT CASE AND WE'LL SCRAM OUT OF HERE!
BUT-- A CLOAKED FIGURE WATCHES FROM THE ROOF OF THE PIER, AS SARTO'S GANG MAKES THEIR GETAWAY!
THERE THEY ARE-- WITH THE EMERALD! THIS IS SARTO'S MOST DARING ROBBERY-- BUT IT WILL BE HIS LAST!

THE MAN OF TOMORROW LEAPS EASILY FROM THE ROOF TO THE STREET BELOW!

TO MAKE THINGS A LITTLE MORE EVEN, I'LL LET THEM HAVE A HEAD-START!

A GUY RUNNING AFTER US? --YOU'RE NUTS--WE'RE DOING EIGHTY!

I KNOW, BOSS-- BUT HE'S CATCHIN' UP TO US!

SUPERMAN SWIFTLY OVERTAKES THE SPEEDING LIMOUSINE!

IT AIN'T POSSIBLE FOR A MAN TO RUN THAT FAST!

THE AMAZED THUGS ARE PANIC-STRICKEN AS THE MAN OF STEEL DRAWS ALONGSIDE THEIR CAR, STILL GOING AT TOP SPEED!

STOP YOUR CAR-- OR I'LL STOP IT MYSELF!

WHAT'LL WE DO, BOSS?

MY GOSH! HE'S GRABBIN' AT THE CAR!

--Z·Z·Z---

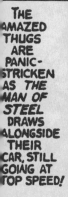

HE'S PULLIN' THE CAR TO A STANDSTILL!

WE'RE SUNK!

NO, WE'RE NOT! GIMME THAT MACHINE GUN!

AFTER SUPERMAN STOPS THE CAR, SARTO STEPS OUT, BLAZING AWAY WITH THE GUN!

WANT TO SEE US, WISE GUY?

HE AIN'T HUMAN! THE BULLETS BOUNCE OFF HIS BODY!

WELL--ARE YOU THROUGH PLAYING WITH THOSE TOYS?

Tossing the machine-gun aside, Superman collars the cowering crook!

YOUR CRIMINAL CAREER IS FINISHED, SARTO! I'M TURNING YOU OVER TO THE POLICE-- THEY'LL TAKE GOOD CARE OF YOU!

As Superman's back is turned, Sarto's thugs leap on him from behind-- the man of steel scatters them with a cuff!

L-LET GO OF ME!

WHY DON'T YOU BOYS BEHAVE?

SOCK!

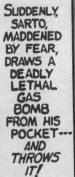

Suddenly, Sarto, maddened by fear, draws a deadly lethal gas bomb from his pocket--- and throws it!

YOU'LL NEVER TAKE ME TO JAIL! I'LL TAKE YOU ALL TO ETERNITY WITH ME!

THE GAS DOESN'T AFFECT ME--BUT I'LL HAVE TO ACT QUICKLY TO SAVE THEM!

THEY DON'T DESERVE SAVING-- BUT IT'S BETTER THAT THEY PAY THE LAW'S PENALTY FOR THEIR CRIMES!

The man of steel piles the unconscious crooks into the car--then carries the car with him, as he leaps up into the sky!

THE POLICE WILL BE GLAD TO SEE THESE GENTLEMEN!

SUPERMAN TURNS THE THUGS OVER TO THE POLICE!

WHAT!?

HERE ARE YOUR JEWEL THIEVES!--I'LL TAKE THE EMERALD TO THE FAIR MYSELF!

THE MAN OF STEEL SPEEDS TO THE OLD HOUSE WHERE LOIS STILL REMAINS A PRISONER--

--ENTERING A WINDOW, HE QUICKLY FREES THE FRIGHTENED CAPTIVE, AND THEN--

HAVEN'T I WARNED YOU BEFORE ABOUT YOUR HABIT OF ALWAYS GETTING INTO DANGEROUS SCRAPES?

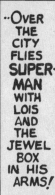

..OVER THE CITY FLIES SUPERMAN WITH LOIS AND THE JEWEL BOX IN HIS ARMS!

THIS IS A WONDERFUL THRILL!

--AND NOW TO HEAD FOR THE WORLD'S FAIR TO PRESENT THE EMERALD!

AT THE FAIR, OFFICIALS ARE NOTIFIED OF THE THIEVES' CAPTURE!

WHAT! YOU SAY SUPERMAN IS BRINGING THE JEWEL TO THE FAIR?

A FEW MINUTES LATER, THE MADRAS EMERALD IS PRESENTED TO THE GRATEFUL OFFICIALS, BEFORE A CHEERING THRONG!

WHAT A MAGNIFICENT STONE!

HERE IS THE EMERALD, GENTLEMEN!

ON BEHALF OF THE WORLD'S FAIR, WE THANK YOU!

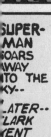

SUPERMAN SOARS AWAY INTO THE SKY--

LATER-- CLARK KENT RETURNS AND FINDS LOIS AT THE FAIR--

LOIS! GEE, I'M GLAD TO FIND YOU!--WHY DID YOU DELIBERATELY TRICK ME LIKE THAT?

YOU WERE TOO MUCH OF A COWARD TO FOLLOW SARTO-- I TRAILED HIM AND GOT A TERRIFIC STORY ON THE JEWEL ROBBERY--YOU WERE ASLEEP AT THE SWITCH!

PERHAPS -- BUT I WOKE UP IN TIME TO GET AN INTERVIEW WITH SUPERMAN BEFORE HE LEFT THE FAIR--AND I'VE ALREADY WIRED HIS EXCLUSIVE STORY OF THE GEM'S RECOVERY TO THE EDITOR!

THE END!

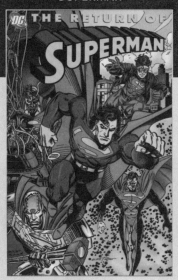

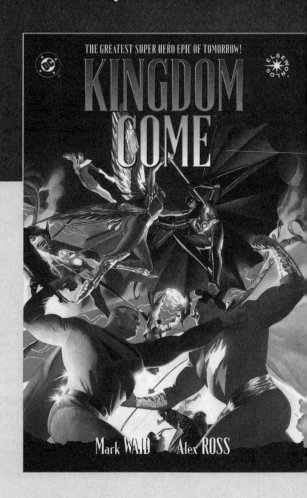
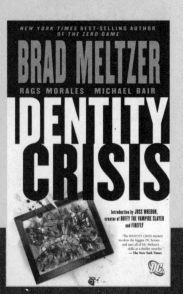